Japan Business and Economics Series

This series provides a forum for empirical and theoretical work on Japanese business enterprise, Japanese management practices, and the Japanese economy. Japan continues to grow as a major economic world power, and Japanese companies create products and deliver services that compete successfully with those of the best firms around the world. Much can be learned from an understanding of how this has been accomplished and how it is being sustained.

The series aims to balance empirical and theoretical work, always in search of a deeper understanding of the Japanese phenomenon. It also implicitly takes for granted that there are significant differences between Japan and other countries and that these differences are worth knowing about. The series editors expect books published in the series to present a broad range of work on social, cultural, economic, and political institutions. If, as some have predicted, the 21st century sees the rise of Asia as the largest economic region in the world, the rest of the world needs to understand the country that is, and will continue to be, one of the major players in this region.

Editorial Board

Japan Business and Economics Series

Japanese Multinationals in Asia

Regional Operations
in Comparative Perspective

Edited by Dennis J. Encarnation

New York   Oxford

Oxford University Press

1999

Oxford University Press

Oxford   New York
Athens   Auckland   Bangkok   Bogotá   Buenos Aires   Calcutta
Cape Town   Chennai   Dar es Salaam   Delhi   Florence   Hong Kong   Istanbul
Karachi   Kuala Lumpur   Madrid   Melbourne   Mexico City   Mumbai
Nairobi   Paris   São Paulo   Singapore   Taipei   Tokyo   Toronto   Warsaw

and associated companies in
Berlin   Ibadan

Copyright © 1999 by Oxford University Press, Inc.

Published by Oxford University Press, Inc.
198 Madison Avenue, New York, New York 10016

Oxford is a registered trademark of Oxford University Press

Library of Congress Cataloging-in-Publication Data
Japanese multinationals in Asia : regional operations in
comparative perspective / edited by Dennis J. Encarnation.
p.   cm. — (Japan business and economics series)
Includes bibliographical references and index.
ISBN 0-19-512065-5
1. Investments, Japanese—Asia.   2. Corporations, Japanese—Asia.
3. International business enterprises—Asia.
I. Encarnation, Dennis J.   II. Series.
HG5702.I576   1998
338.8'895205—DC21   98-23711

9 8 7 6 5 4 3 2 1

Printed in the United States of America
on acid-free paper

Acknowledgments

The editor and contributors thank the MIT Japan Program—especially Professor Richard Samuels and Ms. Patricia Gercik—for their steady encouragement and financial support of this long project.

Contents

Contributors

Michael Borrus, Co-director, Berkeley Roundtable on the International Economy (BRIE), University of California

Dennis J. Encarnation, Director, Asia-Pacific Policy Program, Center for Business and Government, Kennedy School, Harvard University

Edward M. Graham, Senior Fellow, Institute for International Economics

Yoshihide Ishiyama, Chief Economist, IBM-Japan

Mark Mason, Research Professor, Landegger Program in International Business Diplomacy, School of Foreign Service, Georgetown University

Subramanian Rangan, Assistant Professor, European Institute of Business Administration (INSEAD)

John Ravenhill, Professor, Research School of Pacific and Asian Studies, Australia National University

Mitchell W. Sedgwick, PhD Candidate, Department of Social Anthropology, University of Cambridge

Dennis S. Tachiki, Visiting Senior Fellow, Fujitsu Research Institute

Shujiro Urata, Professor, Department of Economics, Waseda University

Japanese Multinationals in Asia

1

Introduction

Japanese Multinationals in Asia

Dennis J. Encarnation

During the mid to late 1980s, Japanese corporations rushed headlong into Asia, pushed in part by the sharply rising value of the Japanese yen and pulled by the alluring prospect of lower labor and other factor costs, plus very large and rapidly growing markets. Today, a decade later, multinational corporations (MNCs) based in Japan remain the largest national source of foreign direct investment (FDI) in Asia, a driving force behind much of that region's rapidly growing trade in goods and services and a principal source there of technology transfer. By weaving these FDI, trade, and technology flows into cross-border networks, Japanese multinationals have fundamentally reorganized production across Asia. Thus, they have been linked both to the "hollowing out" back home of the Japanese economy, and to the "economic miracle" visible in those Asian economies hosting Japanese FDI.

The dramatic spread of Japanese multinationals across much of Asia has stimulated enormous interest among academic scholars, government policy makers, and business managers eager to understand the real significance of recent trends. Several of them were invited to the Massachusetts Institute of Technology (MIT), beginning in 1995, to participate in an interrelated series of workshops and conferences generously financed by the MIT Japan Program. Here, an interdisciplinary and multinational gathering of anthropologists, economists, historians, management specialists, political scientists, policy analysts, and sociologists—drawn from the United States, Japan, and elsewhere in the Asia-Pacific region—presented successive drafts of the research papers subsequently collected in this volume.

The resulting 10 chapters are paired in five separate sections organized sequentially: moving from FDI to related merchandise trade, to the specific case of technology transfer, to the cross-border formation of production networks, to the relative effects of such operations on home and host economies. Each chapter seeks answers to several interrelated questions. How do Japanese multinationals actually operate in Asia? How do their regional operations vary over time? And how do they compare to the regional operations of multinationals based in the United States and elsewhere? What are the economic impacts of these operations in Japan, as well as in host economies across Asia? Finally, what are the implications of our various findings for prevailing theory, as well as public policy and corporate strategy?

While specifically directed toward the Asian operations of Japanese multinationals, these questions explicitly complement a related set of empirical questions addressed in an earlier study of the European operations of Japanese multinationals. That earlier study, *Does Ownership Matter? Japanese Multinationals in Europe* (1994), was also edited by me (in collaboration with coeditor Mark Mason) and, like this volume, was published by Oxford University Press. Together, these two volumes offer a comprehensive comparison of the regional operations of Japanese multinationals investing in both Asia and Europe.

Foreign Direct Investment Flows

In Asia, as elsewhere, FDI has become integral to the regional operations of Japanese multinationals. As typically measured, FDI is a cross-border movement of financial capital by multinationals seeking some degree of managerial control (usually at least 5–10 percent) through equity ownership. But this traditional measure only captures a small portion of the total cross-border flows associated with FDI. For example, later chapters in this volume will demonstrate that FDI can actually alter the value, direction, and composition of merchandise trade as well as technology transfers. In turn, these flows can combine to form cross-border production networks across Asia, with a corresponding impact on both home and host economies. From this perspective, then, any discussion of the regional operations of Japanese multinationals in Asia must begin with a better understanding of FDI patterns and trends—first viewed historically, over the past century of turbulence in Asia, then viewed comparatively, in relation to multinationals based in the United States and elsewhere.

The Asian operations of Japanese corporations can actually be traced back to the late nineteenth century. In "The Origins and Evolution of Japanese Direct Investment in East Asia," Mark Mason charts the historical development of Japanese corporations across the region and then analyzes the successive patterns of continuity and change that have characterized their regional investments. After documenting the early origins of Japanese FDI in Asia, Mason subsequently identifies four distinct periods: the first began hesitantly and culminated with World War l; the second period witnessed the rapid expansion of Japanese FDI in Asia across the interwar years; the third period followed the Pacific War and saw the slow resumption of Japanese FDI until the early 1970s; the subsequent, fourth period brought an acceleration and diversification of Japanese FDI and continues today. For the first three of these periods, Mason concludes that the relative value, sectoral composition, geographical location, and economic motivation of Japanese FDI—as well as the relative impact of Japanese government policy—all remained remarkably constant.

But since the early 1970s, in the most recent period of development, many of these same characteristics have dramatically altered. Specifically, over the last two decades, Japanese FDI in Asia has skyrocketed to unprecedented levels, thanks in large part to the rapid appreciation in the value of the Japanese yen (beginning in 1973 and sharply accelerating in 1985) and the gradual liberalization of Japanese controls on FDI outflows. With this growth has come a dramatic shift in the sectoral and geographic distribution of Japanese FDI in Asia, which is now far more geographically dispersed, especially across Southeast Asia, where Japanese multinationals have located many of their overseas manufacturing sites, notably in electronics and automobiles. These recent changes, Mason concludes from his earlier research (see his opening chapter in the first Oxford volume, *Does Ownership Matter? Japanese Multinationals in Europe*), are not limited to Asia but largely replicate the historical evolution of Japanese FDI in Europe. Yet the recent surge of Japanese FDI in Asia has propelled that region beyond Europe to rank behind the United States as the second largest regional destination for Japanese FDI.

This recent surge also pushed Japanese FDI in Asia well past comparable investments from the United States (now ranked as the second largest national source of that region's FDI) and the several member-states of the European Union. But during the 1990s, these more industrialized economies were easily surpassed by FDI from Asia's newly industrialized economies—Korea, Taiwan, Hong Kong, Singapore, and other Association of Southeast Asian Nations (ASEAN) countries. Such diversity among FDI sources allows me, as the MIT conference chairman, to compare the regional operations of American, Japanese, and (to a lesser extent, given available data) other Asian multinationals. In "Asia and the Global Operations of Multinational Corporations," I examine many of the same regional operations that I examined in earlier research on multinationals in Europe (see chapter 6 in *Does Ownership Matter?*). These include the geographic and industrial concentration of FDI, as well as a multinational's equity shareholdings (majority vs. minority), source of foreign sales (FDI vs. trade), value-added activities (pro-duction vs. distribution), markets for outputs (local host vs. export), sources of inputs (imported vs. local content), and organization of trade (intrafirm vs. arm's-length).

For each of these operations, I document both emerging similarities and persistent differences among multinationals investing in Asia and elsewhere. These similarities provide evidence that the regional operations of American, Japanese, and other multinationals have begun to converge over time, despite obvious differences in their geographic and historical origins. Indeed, convergence is sometimes more pronounced in Asia than elsewhere in the world, as demonstrated by the common geographic and industrial concentration of FDI emanating from a variety of national sources. More often, however, multinationals operating in Asia more closely mimic patterns of convergence apparent elsewhere, as in the growing pursuit of majority (not minority) shareholdings and FDI-generated (not trade-generated) sales. Yet important differences in MNC operations persist, even in the same geographic location and industrial sector. With regard to home-country sourcing and intrafirm trade, for example, multinationals operating in Asia differ as they do elsewhere in the world, with Japanese multinationals evidencing the strongest preferences for these internal transactions. Such differences may be even more pronounced in Asia than elsewhere, as demonstrated by wide variation in host-market and export sales. Here, for example, Japanese MNCs emphasize the former; American MNCs, the latter. Taken together, then, the regional operations of MNCs in Asia confirm the persistence of important operational differences yet also reaffirm that these same multinationals are moving along an otherwise common evolutionary path.

Foreign Direct Investment and Trade Flows

As chapter 3 documents, FDI and international trade are complexly interrelated. The second section of this volume seeks to untangle this complex set of relationships, paying special attention to how FDI can work to alter the value, direction, and composition of merchandise trade. First, the authors address two contradictory results that seem theoretically plausible and have both received empirical support. Either the foreign sales generated by FDI substitute for comparable sales otherwise generated by trade, so that an increase in FDI is associated with a decline in trade, or FDI and trade simultaneously generate complementary sales, so that an increase in one is positively associated with an increase in the other. Second, the section examines the trade-off between foreign sourcing and local content to understand how multinationals manufacturing offshore respond to rapid and sharp changes in foreign-exchange rates. Once again, two contradictory results seem theoretically plausible, but in this case neither has been subjected to much empirical analysis until now. Either multinationals manufacturing abroad adjust their imported and local content in predictable responses to foreign-exchange movements, or these multinationals delay their responses to changing foreign exchange rates to preserve existing ratios of local and imported content. To discern which of these theoretical propositions receives empirical support, both chapters in this section employ advanced econometric techniques on large data sets to isolate individual effects from multiple determinants of FDI and trade.

Using these techniques, Edward Graham reports statistical results consistent with the argument that FDI and trade are most often complementary. In "Foreign Direct Investment Outflows and Manufacturing Trade: A Comparison of Japan and the United States," Graham demonstrates that a strong, positive relationship between FDI and trade exists even after controlling for other plausible determinants of these two flows. These other determinants include the physical distance (from the United States or Japan) to the foreign market, as well as that market's per capita income and absolute (population) size. But Graham's results vary depending upon the direction of trade. They are weaker for merchandise imports into both Japan and the United States. By contrast, Graham's results are much stronger (measured both in terms of the size of the coefficient and its significance) for FDI outflows and merchandise exports from both Japan and the United States. And his results hold for the world as a whole and for most geographic regions: Europe and East Asia for U.S. data, Europe and North America for Japanese data.

However, Graham's results are reversed when he examines FDI and trade for regions near either Japan or the United States. For Japan, this means East Asia; for the United States, the Americas. Indeed, for the Americas, where import-substitution policies have long attracted local production by American multinationals, Graham reports statistical results consistent with the argument that U.S. FDI outflows substitute for U.S. merchandise exports, again after controlling for other plausible determinants. By contrast, for East Asia, Graham finds that Japanese FDI outflows and Japanese merchandise trade (both exports and imports) are statistically unrelated. But in this case, the regional results are confounded by a single country—Indonesia, which historically has hosted the largest share of Japanese FDI outflows, thanks not only to abundant natural resources but also to a large market long protected by import-substituting policies (akin to those shaping U.S. FDI and export to Latin America). So when Graham removes Indonesia from his East Asia sample, he again finds ample evidence to conclude that Japanese FDI outflows and Japanese merchandise trade (both imports and exports) strongly complement one another.

Among the principal determinants of the relative complementarity or substitutability of FDI and trade are sharp changes in foreign-exchange rates. Especially for multinationals manufacturing abroad, such changes may force their foreign subsidiaries to alter the relative mix of local and imported content, employing one to substitute for the other. So, even if aggregate imports actually rise with FDI (as Graham generally concludes), that same FDI could nonetheless work to reduce the relative level of imported content in a foreign subsidiary's production—depending, in part, on prevailing exchange rates. But do the manufacturing subsidiaries of multinationals actually increase (to decrease) their local content—and thus reduce (or raise) their imported content—when host-country exchange rates sharply rise (or fall)? Or put differently, in the words of Subramanian Rangan, "Do Multinationals Shift Production in Response to Exchange Rate Changes?" To answer this question, Rangan chooses to look at a multinational's responses on the margin, where the last unit sold is either imported or produced locally. Based on this methodology, Rangan's answer is an unambiguous yes, both for American multinationals manufacturing abroad between 1973 and 1993 and, during that same period, for Canadian, European, and Japanese multinationals manufacturing in the United States.

At least three of Rangan's findings are especially noteworthy. First, American, European, and Japanese multinationals manufacturing abroad all exhibit systematically predictable and statistically significant responses to exchange-rate changes. On the margin, local content increases (and, correspondingly, imported content declines) when host-country exchange rates rise, whereas the reverse consistently holds when these same exchange rates fall. Second, such responses vary widely across different industries (e.g., greater in chemicals than in autos) depending on a variety of factors, including capacity utilization and scale economies, the availability of substitutes and local suppliers, switching costs, and entry barriers. Third, by contrast, a multinational's responses within a given industry to exchange-rate changes do not vary widely across multinationals of different national origins; that is, American, Canadian, Japanese, and European multinationals operating in the same industry generally respond similarly, at least on the margin. Of course, statistically speaking, it may take a while for even large changes on the margin to narrow what are still—according to other chapters in this volume—significant differences among these same multinationals in the average share of foreign sales generated either by imports or local production. So, on average, persistent differences between American, Japanese, and other multinationals may still be observed, but on the margin, such differences based on national origin need not matter if markets—such as those for foreign exchange—are operating efficiently and effectively.

Foreign Direct Investment and Technology Flows

Just as FDI can work to alter the value, direction, and composition of international trade, it can similarly shape cross-border transfers of technology. Although such transfers may be separately recorded as international trade of either goods (e.g., production machinery) or services (e.g., licensing royalties), technology transfers also include intangible managerial skills, as well as a broad range of tangible and intangible product and process technologies. For most of these technologies, reliable data on cross-border transfers are hard to obtain, since few such transfers are conducted at arm's length. Rather, most technology is bundled with FDI and transferred inside the multinational, among MNC parents to their subsidiaries. To assess these intrafirm transfers, the two chapters in this section analyze previously untapped sources of information. The first provides regional breadth, by tapping company-level surveys of a large sample of Japanese multinationals operating across Asia; the second provides greater depth, by relying on personal interviews and participant observations over an extended period at Japanese manufacturing subsidiaries operating in one Asian country—Thailand.

In "Intrafirm Technology Transfer by Japanese Multinationals in East Asia," Shujiro Urata reports the results of a unique survey of internal transactions involving the parent and subsidiaries of the same multinational. In particular, Urata analyzes what technologies have been transferred, how they were transferred, and with what relative success. Here, he is especially interested in examining cross-national (principally comparing ASEAN and the Asian newly industrialized economies [NIEs]) and interindustry (four manufacturing sectors, including electronics and autos) variation in the cross-border transference of different product and process technologies. These technologies range from the simple to the complex, from the application of existing operational methods to the development of new products and processes. For Urata, relative success in technology transfer is measured in two ways: in terms of the perceived distance from some subjective target, and in terms of who is actually responsible for carrying out a specific operation. From this latter perspective, technology transfer is deemed completed if the local staff, and not Japanese expatriates, are responsible for implementing a given technology.

Urata's analysis yields several noteworthy findings. First, the intrafirm rate of technology transfer is inversely correlated with technological complexity: the simpler the technology, the higher the transfer rate. Second, that intrafirm rate is generally higher in the Asian NIEs than in ASEAN, and this differential grows as technology transfer moves from the simple to the complex. Third, while moving from the simple to the complex, the intrafirm transfer rate is generally comparable across industries—except automobiles, where that rate is consistently higher. Fourth, across these industries, when low-cost labor is the principal factor of production, the intrafirm rate of technology transfer declines, especially for more complex products and processes. Fifth, the rate of technology transfer from the parent of a Japanese multinational to its manufacturing subsidiary in Asia increases with that subsidiary's operating age—at least for simpler processes and controls but not for more complex design and development. Sixth, for more complex technologies, however, that intrafirm transfer rate actually increases with higher levels of local ownership and with a greater use of locally translated manuals. In short, then, the rate and level of technology transfer between a Japanese MNC parent and its Asian subsidiaries vary systematically. And, according to Urata, that rate and level are likely to grow as Japanese FDI in Asia expands and matures.

Adding depth to Urata's breadth, Mitchell Sedgwick examines the internal processes of technology transfer within Japanese multinationals in Asia, but with an exclusive focus on Japanese subsidiaries manufacturing in Thailand. Sedgwick further narrows his focus to what is presumably one of the most important intangible technologies to be transferred abroad by Japanese multinationals—their management skills. Sedgwick is especially interested in well-known Japanese shop-floor techniques. The successful transfer of these techniques allows Japanese manufacturers investing abroad to produce standardized output (e.g., electronic products) in unfamiliar local environments (e.g., Thailand). Among possible determinants of a successful transfer, Sedgwick discovers that the interactions between expatriate Japanese and local Thai engineers prove to be the most critical—and the most difficult.

In "Do Japanese Business Practices Travel Well? Managerial Technology Transfer to Thailand," the simple answer Sedgwick gives to his own question is no—albeit a qualified no. The reasons are many and varied and often depend on the particular perspective of the interviewee. For example, to account for the difficulties they encounter transferring Japanese practices to Thailand, Japanese managers frequently cite high production pressure, low wages and education levels, high local turnover rates, and the absence of a local industrial tradition. But Thais employed in the same Japanese subsidiaries typically cite a different set of explanations, all focused on the internal structures and processes of Japanese multinationals: individual and organizational rigidities, centralized decision making in Japan, the high incidence of expatriate Japanese managers, and correspondingly reduced career prospects for upward mobility. On each of these dimensions, Sedgwick concludes that Japanese multinationals differ markedly from American and European multinationals—and as a result, these Westerners are more likely to transfer managerial skills and other technologies with greater success than Japanese multinationals.

Production Networks: Foreign Direct Investment, Trade, and Technology Flows Combined

By coordinating international transfers of FDI, trade, and technology, MNCs have managed to reorganize the geographic location of production and other value-added activities into cross-border networks that span the Asia-Pacific region. These so-called production networks incorporate the full range of intrafirm transactions analyzed in earlier chapters. And they incorporate a broad range of more arm's-length, but nonetheless highly interdependent interfirm transactions up, down, and across the value-added chain. One early example of a production network is the vertical Japanese *keiretsu* linking Japanese buyers with Japanese suppliers; so this section begins with an empirical examination of the regional extension of Japanese production networks into the rest of Asia. There, Japanese multinationals encounter a growing number of production networks established by American multinationals, as well as by emerging Asian multinationals based in Korea, Taiwan, and elsewhere in the region. Such an encounter, especially common in the electronics industry, provides rich data for a comparative study (the second chapter in this section) of the internal operations of American, Japanese, and other Asian networks.

The internal operations of Japanese production networks are guided, according to Dennis Tachiki, by their business plans, which reveal the strategic and structural choices made by Japanese corporations in their effort to manage the wide-ranging uncertainties associated with global competition. In "The Business Strategies of Japanese Production Networks in Asia," Tachiki presents a detailed evaluation of the business plans for a large number of Japanese multinationals, from which he draws several conclusions. Initially, to reduce uncertainties, Japanese multinationals try to internalize large segments of their business environments. So, for example, they close their labor markets above the entry level, or they significantly narrow the range of buyers and suppliers available to them by establishing vertical keiretsu. Most remaining uncertainties lie outside the corporation or its corporate group, in the larger economy, polity, and society. Here, to help reduce such uncertainties, Japanese corporations have long relied on the Japanese government. Even so, inevitable structural changes in the larger economy, polity, and society often make adjustment necessary. To adjust, Japanese corporations often choose some combination of rationalization (reducing costs, improving quality, and speeding delivery) and diversification (increasing the value-added to existing products or moving into new products).

While rationalization and diversification may be preferred, FDI is not, according to Tachiki. Instead, Japanese corporations prefer to supply foreign markets through increased exports from Japan. By contrast, FDI is seldom the first choice because it adds a whole new set of business uncertainties: unfamiliar business and government practices, unreliable supplier networks and labor markets. To begin reducing these uncertainties, Japanese multinationals again try to internalize their now-foreign operations. For example, they consistently rely on a large number of Japanese expatriates to fill key managerial and technological positions, and they expectantly rely on their keiretsu suppliers in Japan to move with them to Asia. To address most other remaining uncertainties, Japanese multinationals try to enlist the political support of the Japanese government, especially through its application of economic assistance and trade policies. And they actively support various attempts by Asian governments to liberalize their policies and to expand economic cooperation across the region. Although the results of these government actions are today uneven, they have produced what Tachiki calls trade and investment corridors. Through these subregional corridors, Japanese multinationals channel goods and services, money and people, technology and information—all tied closely together by their ever-expanding Asian business plans.

As Japanese multinationals try to reduce uncertainties abroad by progressively internalizing their foreign operations, they establish "closed, cautious, centralized, long-term and stable" production networks, according to Michael Borrus. These characteristics strengthen Japanese networks, but they are the source of great weakness. Nowhere is this more apparent to Borrus than in the electronics industry. Here, American, Taiwanese, and other Asian multinationals—seeking in part to mimic the Japanese—have adopted a common form of industrial organization (the production network) and have located these networks in the same region (East Asia) to exploit a common set of location-specific advantages (initially relative wages, but increasingly other competencies). But unlike the Japanese, Borrus says, American multinationals have established more "open, fast, flexible, formal and disposable" production networks. By comparison, Taiwanese and other Chinese-owned businesses are in the process of establishing production networks that are a hybrid of the American and Japanese variants—"insular, fast, flexible, *guanxi*-mediated, and fluid." So, despite the documented convergence in industrial organization toward production networks, American, Japanese, and other Asian multinationals manage their networks differently.

Such variation in the internal management of different production networks has helped to reverse earlier competitive outcomes, as Borrus suggests in the title of his chapter—"Exploiting Asia to Beat Japan: Production Networks and the Comeback of U.S. Electronics." But it is not the only reason for the rebirth of that industry. In addition, the electronics case demonstrates that a multinational's home country can also confer enormous location-specific advantages (and disadvantages) on global competitors, favoring one set of competitors over another (thus, again, the title of his chapter). In this case, the U.S. market has come to confer both technological (e.g., the microprocessor) and marketing (e.g., the "PC revolution") advantages on electronics firms based here, reversing earlier disadvantages (e.g., a strong currency). But as Borrus suggests, such home-country differences may have begun to give way to more important variation at a regional or (more likely) subregional level, as production networks move across national borders and become more significant determinants of global competition.

Home-Economy and Host-Economy Effects

The recent emergence of American, Japanese, and other Asian production networks across the Asia-Pacific region can have important implications for both home and host economies, implications examined in the concluding chapters. The section begins with an empirical analysis of the home economy in Japan, where current debate extrapolates from the earlier American experience to conclude that the recent confluence of a wide variety of economic factors (FDI outflows, currency appreciation, increased imports, reduced exports) has again connived to "hollow out" a country's manufacturing sector. This popular Japanese perception becomes a working hypothesis and is subsequently tested empirically in the chapter that follows. Next, the section moves from Japan to elsewhere in the region, to analyze the corresponding effects of these same economic factors on Asian economies that host Japanese multinationals manufacturing abroad. Because these host economies also attract large numbers of American multinationals, as well as emerging Asian multinationals, they facilitate a comparative study of the regional operations of multinationals based in the United States, Japan, and elsewhere in Asia. The concluding chapter summarizes much of what has been documented throughout the book.

According to those who hypothesize that Japan is hollowing out, recent increases in FDI outflows should lead to a corresponding decline in manufacturing's contribution to economic activity (e.g., output or employment) back home. In relation, an appreciation of the Japanese yen and, subsequently, an increase in Japanese imports and a decline in Japanese exports should also precipitate a decline in manufacturing activity. Seeking to test these several hypothesized relationships, Yoshihide Ishiyama asks "Is Japan Hollowing Out?" His answer, in a word, is no. To support this conclusion, Ishiyama first concentrates on the period following the yen's rapid appreciation in 1985. Subsequently, as expected, Japanese FDI outflows and real Japanese imports (the latter as a proportion of real gross domestic product [GDP] increased. But so too did manufacturing's contribution to both real and nominal GDP back in Japan—contrary to the hollowing out hypothesis. Also contrary to that hypothesis, real Japanese exports during the late 1980s remained a constant proportion of real GDP. To help explain these potentially contradictory findings, Ishiyama reports over this same period no obvious change in manufacturing's contribution to Japanese employment, leaving a measured rise in labor productivity to explain manufacturing's growing contribution to Japan's GDP. In addition, he turns to plausible complementarities between FDI and exports, arguing that these complementarities could also have bolstered Japanese manufacturing during the late 1980s.

During the early 1990s, by contrast, manufacturing's contribution both to Japanese (nominal and real) GDP and to Japanese employment began to decline as the yen appreciated in value, supporting those who hypothesized that Japan had finally begun to hollow out. But contrary to their predictions, Japanese FDI outflows during this same period also began to decline. Not until 1993 did Japanese FDI outflows begin to grow again, along with real imports into Japan, as the yen continued to strengthen in value. By then, moreover, manufacturing's share in Japan's real GDP had also begun to decline, finally confirming the fears of those who had long anticipated that Japan was hollowing out. But Ishiyama dismisses this decline as merely cyclical, noting that a downturn in Japan's labor productivity is at least as important as a strong yen, import growth, and FDI outflows in explaining the relative decline in Japanese manufacturing. Ishiyama also dismisses the argument that Japan after 1992 looks much like the United States in 1982. Except for an increase in real imports, he argues that the manufacturing sectors in these two countries responded differently to a rapid appreciation in the comparative value of their respective currencies.

Finally, John Ravenhill moves us from the home economies of American and Japanese multinationals to the Asian economies hosting their FDI. In "Japanese and U.S. Subsidiaries in East Asia: Host-Economy Effects," Ravenhill concludes this volume with a question that runs through the preceding chapters (as well as through the first Oxford volume, on Japanese multinationals in Europe). Does ownership matter? Ravenhill's answer to this question is yes—but with important qualifications. He begins his analysis with a simple reminder, that there is no obvious relationship between a country's policies toward FDI inflows and its rate of economic growth. Indeed, the East Asia "miracle" occurred alongside restrictive controls over FDI (e.g., in Japan and Korea) and the aggressive promotion of FDI (e.g., in Singapore). From this perspective, then, ownership should not matter, for each of these economies has enjoyed high growth rates with very different levels of foreign and domestic ownership over its productive assets. Yet for those Asian economies that do promote FDI, Ravenhill finds that ownership can and does matter in meaningful ways: namely, that American and Japanese multinationals operating in East Asia behave differently, and these differences have important consequences for their Asian host economies.

Specifically, after conducting an exhaustive review of existing research (including the research reported here), Ravenhill concludes that Japanese multinationals were less likely than their American counterparts to generate positive benefits for host economies. He begins by documenting that the Japanese are much less likely than the Americans to facilitate the transfer of technology to the local economy. Compared to U.S.-owned subsidiaries also operating in Asia, expatriates dominate far more key management and technical positions in Japanese subsidiaries; these subsidiaries enjoy far less autonomy to source inputs locally since they are more deeply embedded in cross-border production networks; these production networks are dominated by Japanese buyers who erect higher entry barriers to locally owned suppliers by granting preferential access to Japanese suppliers who either export from home or invest abroad. All of this, Ravenhill argues, means that Japanese multinationals have a far less positive impact on the balance of trade of the host economy than do American multinationals also investing in Asia. Japanese subsidiaries import a greater share of their inputs, especially from their parents back home in Japan, and they export a much smaller proportion of their foreign production, either back home (where they may displace exports from other Asian suppliers) or to third-country markets. But these differences, while still large, have actually begun to diminish, according to Ravenhill—who ends his chapter and the book by questioning whether the nationality of ownership will be of decreasing importance to both multinational corporations and national economies.

We thus return to the questions that guide our inquiry into the regional operations of Japanese multinationals in Asia. How do Japanese multinationals actually operate in Asia? How do their regional operations vary over time? And how do they compare to the regional operations of multinationals based in the United States and elsewhere? What are the economic impacts of these operations in Japan, as well as in host economies across Asia? Finally, what are the implications of our various findings for prevailing theory, as well as public policy and corporate strategy?

PART I

FOREIGN DIRECT INVESTMENT FLOWS

2

The Origins and Evolution of Japanese Direct Investment in East Asia

Mark Mason

Introduction

Japanese foreign direct investment (FDI) in East Asia has increased substantially in recent years.[1] Japan's FDI outflows to the region have exceeded $5 billion annually since 1987, for example, and totaled almost $10 billion during the 1994 fiscal year.[2] (See fig. 2.1.) Indeed, official Japanese figures suggest that in 1994 Japan's FDI flows to Asia as a whole exceeded such flows to Europe for the first time in more than a decade. As a result, after North America, Asia has once again become the second largest recipient of Japanese direct investment flows.

This rise of Japanese FDI in East Asia has led to considerable speculation about its character and ultimate consequences. When Japanese FDI beginning in the late 1980s surged into North American and European markets—regions never before recipients of substantial Japanese direct investment inflows—a number of observers voiced concerns about the implications of a future increasingly influenced by companies headquartered in Japan. As Japanese FDI has increased in East Asia, in partial contrast, some have focused rather on a past in which Japan gained significant control over a number of East Asian economies through FDI and other means.[3] Other observers have asked related questions about whether the development of Japanese FDI in East Asia is distinctive or even unique in comparison to its development in other recipient regions.

Expanding Japanese FDI in East Asia also has raised concerns about its impact on American economic interests in that region. In recent years, of course, there has been widespread debate about the nature and consequences for extra-regional economies of integration in East Asia through trade and technology as well as investment flows. One critical aspect of this larger debate centers on the effects of growing Japanese and other intraregional FDI for external economies such as that of the United States. A number of observers have wondered in particular whether rising Japanese FDI in the region is correspondingly diminishing foreign investment and other economic opportunities for American firms.[4]

Although numerous scholars have examined the nature of Japanese FDI in East Asia to explore these and related questions, few have systematically done so

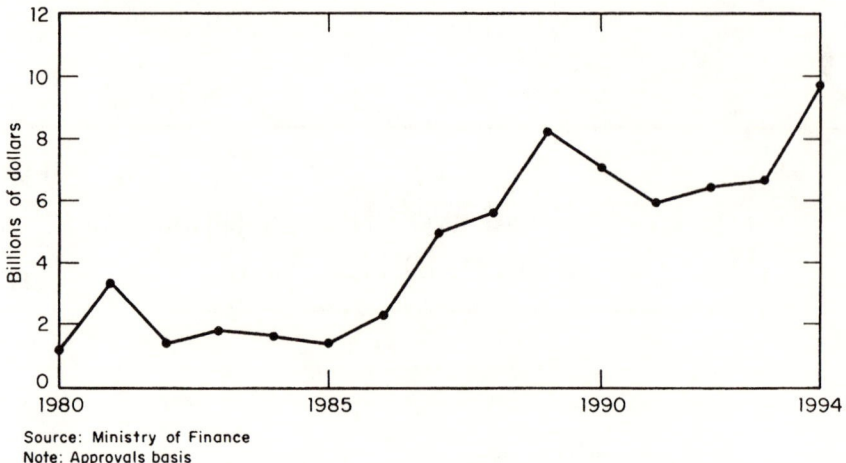

Source: Ministry of Finance
Note: Approvals basis

Figure 2.1 Japanese FDI Outflows to Asia, 1980–1994 (fiscal years).

through comparative historical perspectives.[5] How, indeed, does Japanese FDI in East Asia today compare with such investment in the past? What, specifically, are the chief characteristics of such investment in each period, and how have they changed over time? How does this investment record compare with the development of Japanese FDI in the West? In what ways does the development of Japanese FDI in East Asia contrast with the development of U.S. FDI in the region?

To address these issues, this chapter will explore the origins and evolution of Japanese FDI in East Asia in comparative perspective. First, it will trace the historical development of such investment in the region in terms of amount, sector, location, motivation, and the role of the Japanese government. Second, I will compare these various features of Japanese FDI in East Asia over time to identify major continuities and discontinuities in their respective evolutions. Third, the chapter concludes with a comparison of this record through a broader international perspective.

The Development of Japanese Direct Investment in East Asia

Origins

Japanese FDI first entered East Asia well over a century ago. As a late developer eager to industrialize yet lacking requisite technologies and endowed with only limited natural resources, Japan beginning in the late 1800s strove to develop export markets for its goods to purchase needed imports of capital equipment, raw materials, and other items.[6] In pursuit of this national strategy, a substantial proportion of Japanese FDI in East Asia (and elsewhere) concentrated in service sectors that could directly facilitate such trade.[7]

Japanese trading firms (nascent *sogo shosha*) were among the very first enterprises to establish operations in East Asia during the late nineteenth and early twentieth centuries to achieve this critical goal.[8] Most of this investment was concentrated in China. Just one year after its founding, for example, Mitsui & Co. in 1877 set up its first overseas office in Shanghai to exploit the government-granted export monopoly on coal from the state-run Miike mines. Before the turn of the century, however, a burgeoning export business in cotton textiles had assumed a far greater position in Mitsui & Co.'s Chinese export business, together with growing imports from China of raw cotton, soybeans, and other basic items. This rising trade led to the establishment of a whole network of Mitsui & Co. branch offices in China in the late 1890s and early 1900s. (See table 2.1.) Indeed, between 1877 and 1914 the trading company had set up some 46 branches in Asia—mostly in China—but just five in Europe, two in the United States and one in Australia. Nor was Mitsui & Co. the only Japanese trading firm that operated in East Asia during these early years. Mitsubishi Ltd., Nihon Menka, and Takashimaya Iida, for example, also directly invested in Chinese trading operations well before World War I, exporting such commodities as glass, paper, beer, and matches in addition to cotton textiles and importing agricultural products and natural resources. C. Itoh and Kanematsu Shoten opened branches in Korea, and others set up offices in Taiwan, Indonesia, the Philippines, and elsewhere in the region.

Major proportions of Japanese FDI initially entered the transportation sector in East Asia also largely to support the physical movement of goods between Japan and elsewhere in the region. By far the largest Japanese direct investments in this sector were in railways, and by far the largest such investment was in the South Manchuria Railway Company (SMRC). This firm, founded in 1906 and partially owned by the Japanese government, stood at the heart of the transporta-

Table 2.1 The Opening of Mitsui & Co. Branch Offices Abroad, 1893–1910

Year	Asia	Europe, the United States, and others
1893	Bombay	
1896	Yingkou (Niuzhuang), Taipei	New York (reopened)
1898		San Francisco
1899	Jinsen, Xiamen (Amoy), Zhifu	Hamburg
1900	Hankow, Seoul, Guandongzhou, Manila	
1901	Java	Sydney
1902	Beijing, Guangdong	
1903	Tainan	
1904	Dalny (Dairen)	
1905	Fuzhou	
1906	Shantou, Dagou (Gaoxiong), Andong Xian, Tieling, Calcutta, Shenyang, Bangkok, Qingdao	Oklahoma City
1907	Rangoon, Jilin, Kuanchengzi (Changchun), Saigon, Harbin	Portland, Vladivostok
1908	Pusan, Zhanghua (Taizhong)	Lyons (reopened)
1910	Akou	

Source: Kawabe Nobuo, "Development of Overseas Trading Operations by General Trading Companies, 1868–1945," in Yonekawa Shinichi and Yoshihara Hideki, eds., Business History of General Trading Companies (Tokyo: University of Tokyo Press, 1987), p. 76.

tion system linking the then Japanese-controlled port of Dalien with outlying Manchurian markets. According to one estimate, more than *half* of all Japanese FDI in China in 1914 was invested in this one firm alone.[9] Japanese direct investments likewise financed the establishment of railroad lines in Korea both to facilitate Japanese export penetration of Korean markets and to boost imports of Korean rice and other agricultural products back into Japan.[10]

A significant share of Japanese FDI in regional transportation networks also was concentrated in the shipping industry. As early as 1875, for example, Mitsubishi Goshi set up a Shanghai branch to operate its newly established shipping business between Japan and China.[11] Other Japanese firms, such as Nippon Yusen Kaisha (NYK), Osaka Shosen Kaisha (OSK), and even the SMRC also directly invested in facilities located at many of the principal shipping ports of China and elsewhere in East Asia to foster the flow of goods via this critical mode of transportation.[12] These investments helped pay for the establishment of branch offices, port facilities, warehouses, and other items.

In addition to FDI in the overseas operations of trading companies and in the regional transportation infrastructure, to facilitate trade substantial shares of Japanese direct investment also entered the financial services sector in East Asia during these years. Japanese banks, for example, set up branches or subsidiaries in Chinese and other East Asian economic centers to provide foreign exchange and other banking services to Japanese traders in the area. For example, the government-controlled Yokohama Specie Bank (YSB)—"the bank of banks in the sphere of foreign trade financing," as one scholar has characterized it—provided such services through a network of offices in China and elsewhere, including branches established in Shanghai (1893) and Hong Kong (1896).[13] Indeed, according to one account, "every time Mitsui & Co. opened a new branch overseas a new [YSB] branch opened in the same city."[14] No fewer than 10 new YSB Asian branches were opened—all in East Asia—between 1898 and 1907.[15]

Other Japanese-controlled banks in East Asia that directly or indirectly supported Japan's trade with the region included the colonial First National Bank of Korea and Bank of Taiwan.[16] Among private firms, Yasuda Bank apparently operated its own offices in China more than a decade before the start of World War I.[17] Insurance companies also set up offices in a number of the main capitals of East Asia in part to protect against losses from the movement of goods between Japan and elsewhere in East Asia via the maritime trade.[18]

Very little Japanese FDI, however, entered East Asia's manufacturing sector during these years.[19] It is true that a few Japanese firms directly invested in cotton spinning factories in China shortly after the turn of the century. Japanese trading firms such as Mitsui & Co. and Nihon Menka operated spinning factories in Shanghai in the early 1900s, for example, as did the Japanese-based manufacturer Naigaiwata.[20] Yet these investments were the exception rather than the rule. In 1914, for example, it is estimated that just 5.5 percent of Japanese FDI in the critically important Chinese economy was in the manufacturing sector, and, more generally, Japanese FDI in East Asian manufacturing prior to 1914 was very limited.[21]

Through various means the Japanese government played a critical role in shaping the flow of FDI from Japan to East Asia during these years. First, the authorities often encouraged selected investments through subsidized loans and guarantees for specified FDI projects, as well as through export financing and other trade assistance that helped shape the overseas investment strategies of many leading sogo shosha. Second, through commitments of its own capital in the SMRC and other major projects in East Asia, the government itself directly participated in a number of key investments in this period.[22]

And third, the authorities supported and otherwise influenced the outflow of Japanese FDI through broader political activities in a number of key East Asian markets. During the years preceding World War I, of course, a number of neighboring East Asian economies came under direct or indirect political control by Japan. Following its military success during the Sino-Japanese War of 1894–1895, Japan gained control of Taiwan, expanded its already considerable influence in Korea, and acquired greater commercial privileges in China. After winning the Russo-Japanese War 10 years later, Japan took over the Russian lease on the Kwantung Peninsula, the southern half of Sakhalin, and other assets. And in 1910, Japan annexed Korea.[23] These events motivated large numbers of Japanese entrepreneurs to channel investment funds into these overseas markets in particular. Indeed, "Japan probably would not have exported capital in any considerable amounts" to East Asia (or elsewhere) prior to World War I, one leading analyst therefore declared, "had it not been for State protection and encouragement in areas under heavy Japanese influence or control."[24]

Nonetheless, absolute quantities of Japanese FDI flows to East Asia were quite limited prior to World War I. China, by far the largest host to Japanese direct investment during this period in East Asia or any other region, had received only negligible amounts of such investment by 1897, a mere $1 million by 1900 and a larger but still very modest $190 million by 1914.[25] (See table 2.2.) Indeed, despite the rapid economic gains Japan had achieved by 1914, the best estimates suggest that total Japanese portfolio as well as direct investment in foreign countries totaled just $260 million by that year. These data do not, however, include the substantial Japanese direct investments in its Taiwanese and Korean colonial possessions.[26]

Expansion

A number of major international political events largely shaped the contours of Japanese FDI in East Asia during the ensuing three decades. The advent of World War I in 1914 marked the beginning of rapidly intensifying Japanese economic involvement with neighboring countries and regions, which came to an abrupt halt at the end of World War II. In the interim, Japan expanded its influence in China in particular following the Manchurian Incident (1931) and the onset (1937) of the Sino-Japanese War. Japan projected its power still further afield in East Asia following the outbreak of the Pacific War in 1941. This growing regional influence coincided with Japan's efforts to construct a so-called Greater East Asia Co-Prosperity Sphere designed to more tightly integrate the economies at the periphery with markets in Japan proper.

Levels of Japanese FDI grew considerably in East Asia during the three decades following the start of World War I. For example, the data set out in table 2.2 suggest that such investment in the critically important Chinese market alone more than doubled from $190 million to $377 million between 1914 and 1919, and roughly doubled again, to $763 million, by 1930.[27] A similar estimate of Japan's "direct business investments" in China reported a roughly fourfold increase

Table 2.2 Japan's Foreign Investment Before World War II (millions of dollars)

	1914	1919	1930	1936
China	216.2	588.8	1,283.1[a]	463.2
Loans to government	9.4	105.3		
Loans to local governments		30.4		
Loans to private enterprises	17.2	75.9		
Direct investment	189.6	377.2	150.6	
General loans			405.8	
Manchuria			726.7	868.5
Loans			114.5	
Direct investment			612.2	
The Philippines and South Sea Islands	19.7			
South Sea Islands and other regions		40.5	64.2	86.9
Hawaii				
And the United States	24.6			
And North and South America		25.3	24.9	29.0
Loans to Allied power countries		312.9		
Miscellaneous investment (especially expatriates)				86.9
Total	260.5 (¥100 = $49.25)	967.5 (¥100 = $50.625)	1,372 (¥100 = $49.367)	1,534.5 (¥100 = $28.951)

Source: Yasumuro Kenichi, "The Contribution of Sogo Shosha to the Multinationalization of Japanese Industrial Enterprises in Historical Perspective," in Okochi Akio and Inoue Tadakatsu, eds., *Overseas Business Activities* (Tokyo: University of Tokyo Press, 1984), p. 84.

Figures exclude Japanese direct investments in colonial possessions.
[a]Figure includes 556.4 to mainland China, 726.7 to Manchuria.

between 1914 and 1930, rising from $192.5 million at the start of World War I to $874.1 million some 16 years later.[28] And anecdotal evidence suggests that this FDI expanded still further as Japan worked to solidify its regional sphere of influence prior to surrender in August 1945.[29]

Despite this rapid increase, however, as compared to more recent years, levels of Japanese FDI in East Asia generally remained modest throughout the period. Although Japan had concentrated the vast majority of its FDI in China by 1930, for example, its stock of FDI in that country still ranked second to that of the United Kingdom—yet only a tiny fraction of total U.K. FDI was located in China at that time.[30] And, according to Lockwood, at least through the late 1930s Japan's "overseas business enterprise," though "significant in relation to Japanese trade and imperialism," was not terribly significant in comparison to overall national rates of savings and investment.[31] On the other hand, Japanese direct investment in its colonial possessions grew considerably during this period.[32] Indeed, one scholar, apparently including Japanese direct investments in its colonial possessions as well as in foreign countries, calculated that the ratio of Japanese FDI to gross national income was greater in 1930 than in 1986.[33]

Building on earlier trends, that investment remained highly concentrated in those East Asian economies in which Japan wielded major political influence. As suggested in table 2.2, for example, between 1914 and 1936 Japanese FDI was overwhelmingly located in the East Asian region in general and in China in particular.[34] Anecdotal evidence suggests that this concentration bias continued (and may well have become still more pronounced) as Japan worked to further solidify its regional base and simultaneously became increasingly cut off from many Western markets. Moreover, a comprehensive Allied occupation survey of Japanese "external assets"—of which reportedly 76 percent were in the form of business investments owned by Japanese corporations—points to a similarly high concentration of Japanese foreign direct (and other) investments in its regional sphere of influence at the end of World War II (see fig. 2.2). Indeed, according to

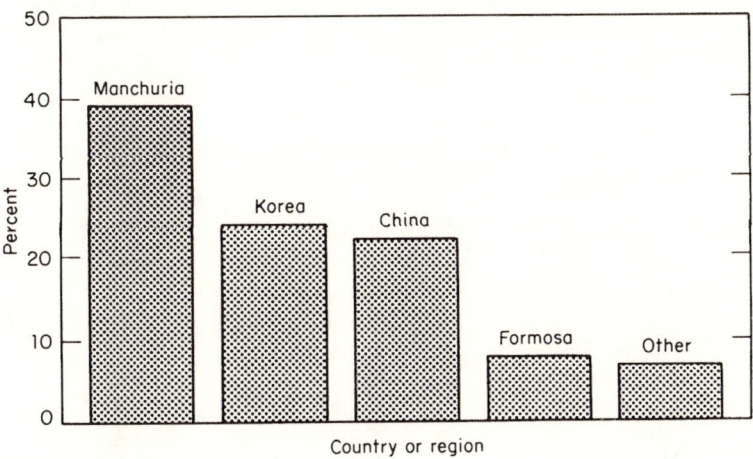

Source: Supreme commander for the allied powers
Note: Excludes military and naval material

Figure 2.2 Location of Japanese External Assets as of August 1945.

this survey, no less than 93.69 percent of Japan's total external assets were located in Manchuria, Korea, China, and Formosa in August 1945![35]

In sectoral terms, nonmanufacturing industries continued to predominate. As suggested in table 2.3, for example, in the key Chinese market Japanese FDI in the transportation, import and export, and banking and finance sectors alone constituted a majority of all such investment in that market in 1932. Still more pronounced was the Japanese preference for nonmanufacturing FDI in Manchuria in particular.[36] Other studies point to the same general sectoral pattern of Japanese FDI in East Asia during this period.[37] Indeed, at least in terms of paid-in capital, this pattern apparently held in the Dutch East Indies as well. (See table 2.4.)

As in the years prior to World War I, Japanese general trading companies accounted for a major share of this nonmanufacturing investment. As intra-Asian trade grew (see figs. 2.3 and 2.4 on the growth of such trade in comparison to other key regions), virtually all of Japan's major trading companies expanded their direct presence in China and elsewhere in the region. Among key Japanese imports were not only agricultural goods but also raw materials needed to satisfy the demands of a rapidly industrializing (yet resource-poor) nation, together with growing exports of manufactured goods. It is reported that Mitsubishi Corp. alone made some hundred separate investments in Asia during the three decades after World War I.[38] As the period progressed, a considerable number of these and other Japanese trading firms invested in key Southeast Asian markets as well, although not nearly as greatly as in their investments in Northeast Asia. Ataka opened some 25 offices in the Southeast Asian subregion after 1941, for example, following closely the progressive conquests of the Japanese Imperial Army.[39] Many other trading firms pursued similar strategies. (Table 2.4 lists the extensive 1937 investments of Japanese trading firms in the Dutch East Indies.)

In addition to the direct investments of the trading companies and again building on earlier trends, large shares of fresh Japanese FDI inflows to East Asia entered the trade-facilitating transportation sector. Remer reports, for example, that Japanese FDI in the Manchurian transportation sector more than tripled between

Table 2.3 Japanese Direct Business Investments in China by Sector (as of 1932)

	¥ thousands	% of total
Transportation	408,649	23.4
Public Utilities	31,300	1.8
Mining	174,930	10.0
Manufacturing	331,299	18.9
Banking and finance	147,614	8.4
Real estate	145,990	8.4
Import and export	365,927	20.9
Miscellaneous	142,550	8.2
Total	1,748,259	100.0

Source: C. F. Remer, *Foreign Investments in China* (New York, 1933), p. 505.

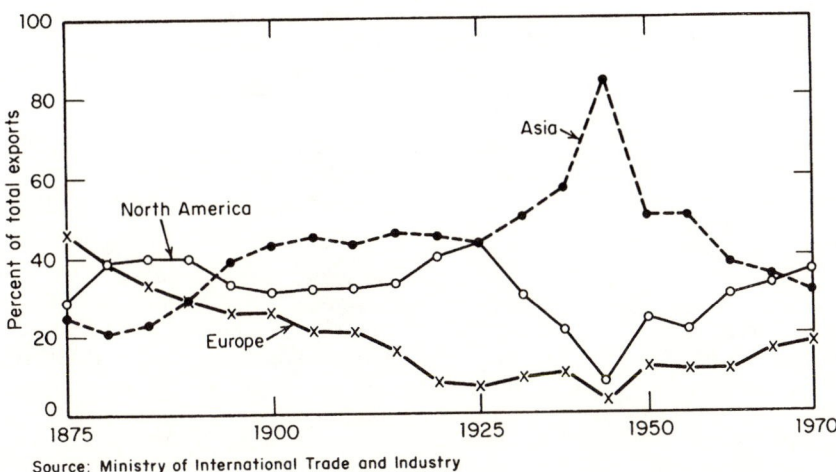

Source: Ministry of International Trade and Industry

Figure 2.3 Japanese Export Shares to Three Principal Regional Destinations, 1875–1970.

1914 and 1930. Much of this increase, of course, was accounted for by the government's growing investment in the SMRC, together with that company's own extensive direct investments in regional transportation projects.[40] Greater amounts of Japanese FDI also entered the railroad and other transportation sectors in other parts of China and in Korea, Formosa, and elsewhere.[41]

Finally, FDI in the trade-related financial services sector continued to expand greatly during these years. The Yokohama Specie Bank, for example, progressively shifted a greater share of its resources away from other regions and toward East Asia as the period progressed. Indeed, between 1932 and 1945 the bank set up

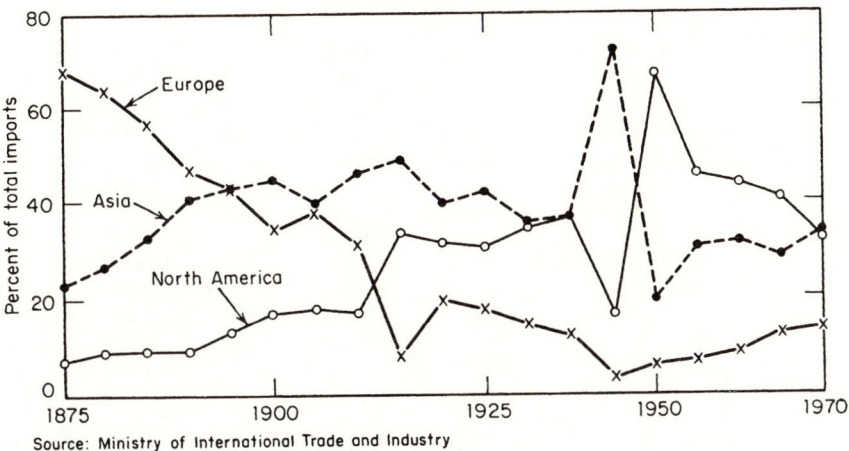

Source: Ministry of International Trade and Industry

Figure 2.4 Japanese Import Shares from Three Principal Regional Sources, 1875–1970.

Table 2.4 Leading Japanese Enterprises in the Dutch East Indies (1937)

Company name	Paid-in capital (¥ millions)	Location	Industry
Agriculture			
Borneo Rubber	20	Sumatra	Rubber
Nanyo Rubber	20	Sumatra, Johore	Rubber
Sumatra Industries Development	19	Sumatra	Rubber, cocoa
Sumatra Products	35	Sumatra	Rubber
Nangoku Rubber	7	Sumatra	Rubber
Nanwa Company	15	Sumatra	Rubber
Nanwa Rubber Plant	7	Borneo	Rubber
Nomura East Indies	50	Borneo, Sumatra	Rubber, coffee, etc.
Okura Sumatra Agriculture	15	Sumatra	Rubber
Indonesia Development	10	Borneo	Rubber, cocoa
Nangoku Industries	20	Java	Tea, coffee, etc.
Nangoku Plantation	10	Java	Rubber, etc.
Dai Nippon Sugar	19	Java	Vegetables
Indonesia Forest Industry	15	Java	Fruit
Furukawa Gomei Development	NA	Sumatra	Oil
Higashiyama Plantation	20	Sumatra	Oil
Nanyo Trading	15	Celebes	Cocoa
Nanyo Development	11	New Guinea	Cotton, etc.
Commerce			
Mitsu & Co.	1,000	Surabaya	Trading
Mitsubishi Corp.	225	Surabaya	Trading
Toyo Cotton	200	Surabaya	Trading
Daido Trading	20	Surabaya	Trading
Chida Trading	15	Surabaya	Trading
KO Trading	155	Sumaran	Trading
Japan Cotton	68	Surabaya	Trading
Dai Shin Trading	NA	Surabaya, etc.	Trading, department stores
Nanyo Warehouse	80	Surabaya, etc.	Storage
Finance			
Yokahama Specie Bank	1,000	Surabaya, etc.	Foreign exchange
Mitsui Bank	600	Surabaya	Foreign exchange
Bank of Taiwan	131	Surabaya, etc.	Foreign exchange, investment
Bank of South China	18	Sumaran	Foreign exchange, investment
Other			
Nanyo Shipping	85	Surabaya	Shipping
Nichi Ran Petroleum	20	Borneo	Oil exploration
Nanyo Forestry	1	Borneo	Forestry
Hōton Pearls	1	Bhutan Island	Cultured pearls
Ishizu Fishery	3	Borneo, etc.	Fisheries
Taisho Company	2	Batavia	Fisheries
Nichi Ran Fishery	0.7	Menado	Fisheries

Source: Numaguchi Gen, "Nihon no kaigai jigyo toshi: sono rekishiteki kado to keieiteki yoran" (The Overseas Investments of Japanese Enterprise: The Historical Process and Key Managerial Aspects), in *Chiba Shodai Ronso*, no. 14–18 (December 1970), p. 256.

some 32 offices in China alone, together with many other such facilities in the Straits countries.[42] Tokyo Marine and other insurance companies likewise expanded their earlier direct investments in the region.[43]

Japanese FDI in East Asian manufacturing also grew considerably as compared to earlier years, although in relative terms this growth remained fairly modest. Much of this new investment entered the Chinese cotton spinning industry. At first enjoying huge increases in cotton textile exports to China following the outbreak of World War I and the consequent rupture of British and other Western sources of textile supplies to that large Asian market, Japanese firms rushed to invest in Chinese manufacturing in that sector following the imposition in 1919 of higher Chinese textile import tariffs. As a result, no less than 7 of Japan's 10 leading cotton spinning companies had established factories in China by the early 1920s to defend their local market shares.[44] Yet cotton spinners were not the only Japanese enterprises to establish direct manufacturing investments in East Asia during these years. In the motor vehicle industry, for example, Nissan moved its headquarters to Manchuria in 1937 and Toyota set up plants in Tientsin and Shanghai shortly thereafter.[45] Manufacturing investments in China entered a number of other fields as well. (See table 2.5.)

Complex motives beyond the purely economic became increasingly important determinants of Japanese FDI in the region. In addition to trade facilitation

Table 2.5 Number of Direct Investments and Military-Controlled Plants in China in 1938

Industry	Direct control (wholly or majority-owned)	Joint venture with China (50%)	Government-controlled	Military-controlled and management entrusted
Mining	11	10	3	26
Coal	(6)	(7)	(1)	(21)
Iron	(1)	(1)	(1)	(5)
Gold and others	(4)	(2)	(1)	(0)
Textile	22	2	0	33
Cotton spinning	(18)	(1)	(0)	(33)
Other textiles	(4)	(1)	(0)	(0)
Foodstuffs	8	4	0	39
Brewing	2	0	0	0
Tobacco	6	0	0	2
Metals and machinery	12	5	0	8
Matches	5	3	0	9
Rubber products	7	1	0	2
Chemicals	20	2	0	15
Stone, clay, and glass	7	4	0	9
Miscellaneous products	22	3	0	12
Unknown	400[a]	2	0	4
Total	522	35	3	159[b]

Source: Yasumuro Kenichi, "The Contribution of Sogo Shosha," p. 72.

[a]Small-scale, personally managed concerns.
[b]Chinese plants occupied by the Japanese Army whose management was entrusted to Japanese industrial enterprises.

across a variety of sectors and efforts to defend overseas market shares in limited cases, increasing numbers of direct investments were undertaken to support wider Japanese political and military goals in the region. These goals included the growing transportation needs of Japan's colonial army and closer economic integration of the expanding Japanese Empire. (Table 2.6, for example, illustrates the enormous trade dependence of colonies such as Taiwan on the markets of Japan proper.)

To support these goals, the government played a leading role in the development of Japanese direct investment in the region through World War II. As in earlier years, the authorities influenced such investment in multifarious ways. Colonial officials enticed Japanese firms to invest in their locales through a host of tax, infrastructural, and other incentives.[46] The home government, as in previous years, offered protection and encouragement through its influence and control over many regional economies. And as in the pre-1914 period, the public sector itself participated in a number of key direct investments in the region. (In addition to the SMRC see, for example, table 2.5.) Finally, during this period some leading Japanese enterprises may have been simply *ordered* by the authorities to directly invest in a particular project.[47]

Resumption

As in the period of expansion, major political events also ushered in the ensuing era of Japanese FDI resumption in East Asia. The end of World War II, of course, brought about a temporary hiatus in the development of such investment in the region. Surrender brought not only the termination of hostilities but also the ter-

Table 2.6 External Trade of Taiwan, 1929

Source or Destination	Imports		Exports	
	¥ thousands	% of total	¥ thousands	% of total
Japan proper[a]	140,369	68.5	238,705	87.8
China	29,573	14.4	17,690	6.5
British India	9,422	4.6	24	—
Germany	6,643	3.2	11	—
Great Britain	3,938	1.9	1,026	0.4
United States	3,901	1.9	4,067	1.5
French Indo-China	2,861	1.4	—	—
Kwantung Province	2,240	1.1	1,116	0.4
Dutch East Indies	1,541	0.8	4,296	1.6
Siam	1,000	0.5	24	—
Hong Kong	74	0.1	4,116	1.5
Other areas	3,348	1.6	818	0.3
Total	204,910	100.0	271,893	100.0

Source: Harold Moulton, *Japan: An Economic and Financial Appraisal* (Washington, DC: Brookings Institution, 1931), p. 599.

[a]Includes trade of negligible importance with other colonies.

mination of Japanese control over virtually all its external assets. As Japan regained its independence and the occupation drew to a close, however, the government embarked on new economic policies that once again decisively determined the development of Japan's FDI in East Asia.

The Allied occupation's supreme commander for the Allied powers (SCAP) froze and then systematically inventoried Japanese FDIs and virtually all other external assets shortly after taking power in 1945.[48] That September SCAP explicitly prohibited persons in Japan from engaging in transactions involving these overseas assets in order to maintain them intact until a definitive policy could be adopted. In the interim, the Allied authorities compiled an exhaustive, three-volume inventory of all such assets, intangible as well as tangible, owned by both public and private interests. In that inventory, SCAP found that, although these assets were located in some 80 different geographical areas and denominated in 90 different national currencies, the vast majority, as noted before, were concentrated in Northeast Asia.[49]

Toward the close of the occupation, a new policy was adopted to dispose of these external assets. After a period of almost five years, during which SCAP allowed the authorities of the territory in which they had been found to control them, it was decided to handle these possessions in one of two ways. Countries that had been at war with Japan and who signed the peace treaty were given authority to confiscate and liquidate these assets and dispose of the proceeds as they saw fit. On the other hand, assets located in former Axis and wartime neutral countries were transferred to and later sold by the International Committee of the Red Cross, which distributed the proceeds as indemnification to former Allied prisoners of war. By the time the occupation ended in 1952, the entire stock of Japanese FDI in East Asia had therefore been completely eliminated.

The Japanese government fashioned a new policy toward outward FDI as the nation moved to regain its independence. This new policy, which operated throughout the 1950s and 1960s, severely restricted fresh outflows of virtually all Japanese direct investments. Behind this policy lay the government's fierce determination to conserve scarce quantities of foreign exchange and to prevent "reverse imports" of manufactured and other goods produced by Japanese companies abroad, which might then be shipped back to home markets. Reflecting this latter motivation, in general the government authorized only those direct investments in East Asia that facilitated exports of Japanese goods and imports of critical natural resources.

To control the movement of Japanese direct investment abroad, the government scrutinized each individual investment application through a rigorous, interagency screening process. A company whose request was denied simply could not gain access to requisite foreign exchange. On the other hand, the small number of firms whose applications were approved found that the government not only granted them the necessary foreign exchange permits but also generally supported their overseas investments with generous tax breaks and other financial incentives. Yet even in many of these cases the government obliged the investing firm to pledge that it would not engage in so-called reverse importing.[50]

Responding to this new government policy, a modest number of Japanese firms—many of which had invested in the region during the prewar and wartime periods—managed to gain requisite permissions and directly invest in postwar

East Asia. Trading companies and limited numbers of banks were permitted to directly invest in the region to help re-create in the postwar period aspects of the trade-facilitating infrastructure they had once owned and operated before and during World War II. Mitsui & Co., Mitsubishi Corp., and other major Japanese trading firms, for example, systematically reestablished import-export operations in a number of leading East Asian markets beginning in the 1950s. A small number of private banks likewise were permitted to set up facilities largely to provide trade financing in support of these trading operations.

Some trading and other Japanese firms also directly invested in East Asian natural resource projects to help satisfy the nation's growing appetite for such resources as the postwar economic miracle developed. In the 1960s, for example, increasing quantities of Japanese FDI participated in projects such as iron ore and copper mining in Malaysia and the Philippines and in natural gas extraction in Brunei.[51] Also during that decade the government participated in at least one major "national project" to directly invest in the Indonesian oil sector.[52] Other Japanese FDI during the 1950s and 1960s entered regional projects in the agricultural, forestry, and fisheries industries.[53]

A limited number of Japanese direct manufacturing investments also entered East Asia during this period. Before 1960, for example, Yoshihara reports that the Japanese government approved a total of nine such investment projects in East Asia, of which four were bound for Thailand.[54] A far greater number of Japanese overseas manufacturing investments received approval beginning in the 1960s, however, and most of them apparently entered this same region.[55] Motivated by rising import restrictions in Southeast Asia and other factors, increasing numbers of Japanese manufacturers opted to establish small-scale local production facilities in the region. Japanese FDI in Southeast Asian synthetic fiber and consumer electronics (the latter principally to assemble intermediate goods shipped from Japan) are two major cases in point.[56] As in previous periods, many of these investments were carried out in concert with leading trading firms.[57]

Despite the early resumption of Japanese FDI in postwar East Asia, however, overall investment remained extremely limited. Between 1951 and 1960, for example, approved FDI outflows to all regions combined averaged a minuscule $28 million annually between 1951 and 1960 and only $329 million annually between 1961 and 1970.[58] Of these totals, an annual average of just $13 million was approved for FDI in manufacturing to all external destinations during the 1950s and a mere $81 million during the following decade. Asia attracted roughly one fifth of cumulative Japanese FDI outflows during the 1950s and 1960s, according to the Ministry of Finance (MOF), placing the region second behind North America among global recipients.[59]

As in earlier periods, this investment was concentrated in a small number of regional markets. The specific markets Japanese FDI entered, however, changed. The postwar communist rulers of China and North Korea blocked virtually all FDI inflows after they assumed power, for example, and anti-Japanese feeling contributed to the continuation of an effective South Korean ban on Japanese FDI until formal diplomatic relations were reestablished in 1965.[60] Rather than reentering contiguous markets of the old Greater East Asia Co-Prosperity Sphere, in the postwar period the Japanese instead focused their regional direct investments in Indonesia, the Philippines, Malaysia, and elsewhere in Southeast Asia.[61] In short,

Japanese FDI remained geographically concentrated in a limited number of East Asian markets, though the specific markets they entered differed after war (and occupation).

Growth and Diversification

Again punctuated by important political events, Japanese FDI in East Asia entered a new era beginning in the early 1970s. In concert with its larger initiatives to deregulate the nation's international economic controls, in 1969 the government embarked on a five-stage process to liberalize FDI outflows.[62] Although the entire deregulation process took some nine years to complete, following the mid-1971 implementation of phase three, the MOF, with few exceptions, automatically validated greenfield direct investments abroad by Japanese companies without financial limit. Rising domestic business pressure, as well as increasing balance of payments surpluses, motivated the government to take this critical policy initiative.

Changed Japanese government policies, together with many other political and economic developments, encouraged Japan's multinationals to directly invest in East Asia far more aggressively beginning in the 1970s. Following the collapse of the Bretton Woods regime, the value of the yen appreciated sharply and thereby escalated production costs in Japan as compared to other regional economies. A coincident increase in real wage rates in Japan encouraged the migration of labor-intensive manufacturing industries in particular to neighboring markets such as South Korea, Taiwan, Hong Kong, and the countries of the Association of Southeast Asian Nations (ASEAN).[63] In addition, rising trade protectionism in the key U.S. market encouraged still greater Japanese manufacturing FDI in numerous East Asian countries as a means to circumvent the threat of further American import restrictions on goods produced in and directly exported from Japan.[64] More recent motivations include the desire to supply through local production the rapidly expanding domestic markets of East Asia together with new and far more liberal foreign investment laws in countries such as China, Indonesia, and Vietnam.[65]

These factors contributed to a dramatic rise in Japanese manufacturing FDI in East Asia during this period.[66] In the early 1970s much of that investment entered the region's textile industry, in which Japanese firms such as Toray and Teijin (often with sogo shosha partners) directly invested considerable sums to produce a variety of synthetic fibers.[67] Joined in this early, postliberalization "investment rush" were a host of Japanese electronics firms such as Matsushita and Sanyo, which set up regional plants to assemble home appliances such as radios, televisions, refrigerators, fans, and so forth.[68] Japan's automobile firms likewise directly invested in local assembly operations. (See table 2.7.) Yet in later years still greater sums would be invested in these and many other Asian manufacturing industries. As a result, by 1995 approved Japanese manufacturing FDI in the region amounted to more than $33.5 billion, or roughly 43% of all approved Japanese FDI in Asia. The electrical machinery, chemical, and metal industries had by then attracted the largest shares of such investment in the manufacturing sector. (See fig. 2.5.)

In addition, Japanese firms operating in a whole host of service sectors greatly increased their direct presence in East Asia during these years. By 1995, for ex-

Table 2.7 Japanese Automobile Assembly Plants in East Asia as of 1976

Country or territory	Nissan	Toyota	Toyo Kogyo	Mitsubishi	Isuzu	Honda	Hino	Fuji Heavy Industries
Hong Kong	X		X	X	X			
Taiwan	X	X		X	X	X	X	
Philippines	X	X	X	X	X			
Indonesia	X	X	X	X	X	X	X	X
Malaysia	X	X	X	X				
Thailand	X	X	X	X	X		X	X
Singapore	X							

Source: Fujii, M., et al., eds., *Nihon takokuseki kigyo no shiteki tenkai* (The Historical Development of Japanese Multinational Enterprises), vol. 2, p. 166.

X represents plant placement.

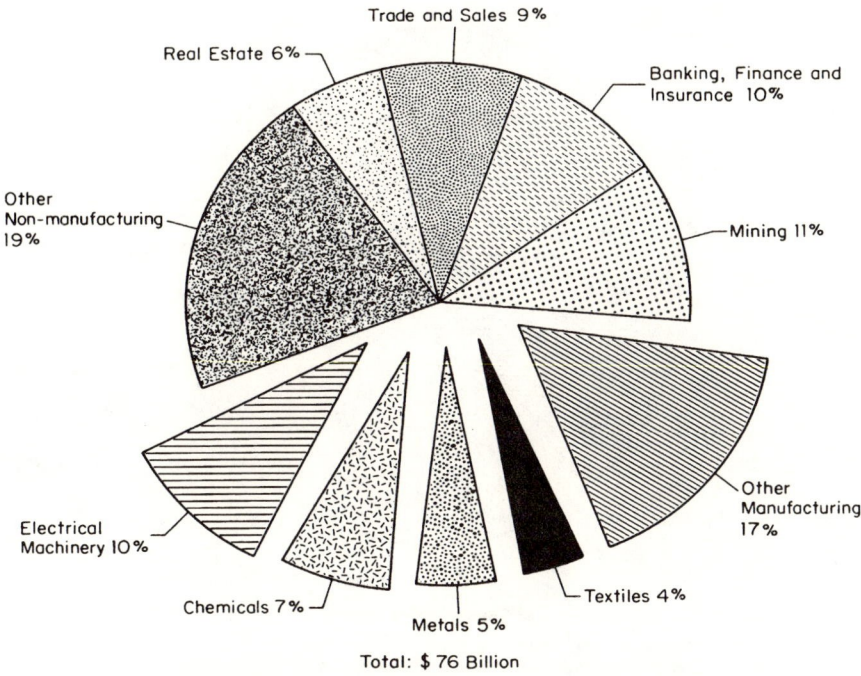

Figure 2.5 Japanese FDI Position in Asia by Sector as of March 31, 1995 (percent).

ample, approved stocks of Japanese FDI in regional banking, insurance, and other financial services amounted to more than $7.5 billion, or roughly 10 percent of all approved Japanese FDI in the region. Trading and sales exceeded $6.5 billion, or about 9 percent of the overall regional total that same year. And, as calculated by the Ministry of Finance, the service sector as a whole accounted for roughly 30 percent of all approved Japanese FDI stocks in Asia by early 1995. In addition to manufacturing and services, roughly 27 percent of accumulated Japanese FDI approvals in Asia entered other nonmanufacturing sectors such as mining, real estate, and transportation.

Absolute amounts of Japanese FDI in East Asia expanded prodigiously beginning in the 1970s as compared to earlier decades. Between 1971 and 1980, for example, approved outflows of Japanese FDI to Asia (of which the great majority went to East Asia) exceeded $9 billion, whereas total approved outflows of such investment to that region amounted to less than $800 million throughout the previous two decades.[69] Moreover, between 1981 and 1990 stocks of approved Japanese direct investment in Asia increased to more than $37 billion, and by 1995 such stocks in Asia amounted to roughly $76 billion. (See fig. 2.6.) This rapid in-

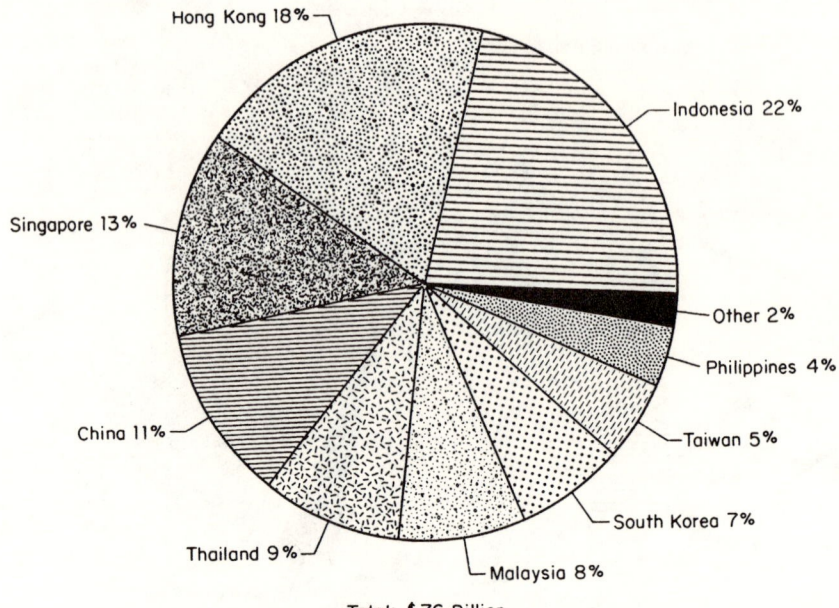

Total: $76 Billion

Source: Ministry of Finance (Japan)
Notes: Percentages do not equal 100 due to rounding. Approvals basis.

Figure 2.6 Japanese FDI Position in Asia by Country as of March 31, 1995 (percent).

crease was fueled in particular by large, sustained Japanese outflows beginning in the mid-1980s. (See fig. 2.1.)

Also in contrast to earlier periods, within East Asia Japanese FDI in geographical terms had become far more dispersed. Prior to 1950, as we have seen, the great majority of Japanese FDI entered the economies of Northeast Asia. During the early decades of the postwar period, that investment in the region was mainly situated in Southeast Asia. Yet during the quarter century beginning in 1970, fresh outflows of Japanese FDI to the region created a pattern of much wider geographical dispersion of these investment stocks. As suggested in figure 2.6, for example, by 1995 substantial proportions of regional stocks were located not only in Southeast Asia but also in China, South Korea, Taiwan, and elsewhere in the region.

Finally, and again largely in contrast to earlier periods, since the 1970s the government has played a less significant role in influencing Japanese FDI in the region. There are, to be sure, a number of notable exceptions. These include low-interest loans provided by the Export-Import Bank of Japan and other public agencies, investment guarantees backed by the Ministry of International Trade and Industry (MITI), the use of overseas development assistance to support the external activities of Japanese firms, and periodic MITI "vision" statements, which can have important signaling effects for Japanese management decision making.[70] These and other instances of Japanese public-sector activity affecting the overseas direct investments of its private-sector firms suggest that the role of government in this domain remains more important in Japan than in most other major industrialized countries. At the same time, however, these and other examples of official Japanese involvement do not compare to either the depth or the range of government actions in previous periods of Japan's modern history to encourage, discourage, or otherwise shape the nation's direct investments in East Asia.

Continuities and Discontinuities

How does Japanese FDI in East Asia in recent years compare with such investment in earlier times? An examination of the past versus current character of five key features of this investment suggests at least one broad generalization.

Investment Levels

Quantities of Japanese FDI in East Asia across time stands as an important case in point. Historically, of course, overall levels of such investment in general were quite modest. Although there are recorded instances of Japanese FDI entering the region at least as early as 1875, for example, total amounts of such investment remained very limited throughout the nineteenth and early twentieth centuries. Rising Japanese FDI in China and elsewhere in Northeast Asia beginning in the 1930s constitutes the only important exception to this larger historical pattern. Yet even these investments were eliminated after World War II, and during the first two postwar decades following the occupation total amounts of Japanese FDI again were extremely limited. By contrast, of course, beginning in the 1970s, and particularly from the mid-1980s, quantities of such investment have increased enormously.

Sectoral Composition

The sectoral composition of Japanese FDI in the region likewise points to a more general pattern. Beginning in the late nineteenth century and for many decades thereafter, the vast majority of Japanese direct investment in East Asia entered the service and other nonmanufacturing sectors. Although the proportion of such investments that entered manufacturing increased as World War II approached, available evidence suggests that this proportion reached only moderate levels as compared to those of the most recent period. It is also true that this proportion was probably even more substantial during the first two postwar decades, yet the absolute quantities of such investment remained extremely small throughout the 1950s and 1960s. Far greater sums entered East Asian manufacturing beginning in the 1970s, however, and by 1995 well over 40 percent of the estimated $76 billion in approved Japanese FDI in the region was located in this sector.

Location

In addition to level and sector, the location of Japanese FDI in East Asia points to a similar historical trajectory. Although there are scattered cases of such investment entering diverse regional economies from the late 1800s, at least as early as the turn of the century this investment was highly concentrated in China and elsewhere in Northeast Asia. Such geographical concentration became still more pronounced as Japan both developed its Greater East Asia Co-Prosperity Sphere and was increasingly cut off from most Western markets. A similar pattern of geographic concentration occurred during the early postwar period, although in those years the emphasis was on Southeast rather than Northeast Asia. Yet here again the most recent period contrasts with this century-old historical pattern, for Japanese FDI in East Asia has become far more geographically diffuse throughout the region.

Motivation

The more recent economic factors motivating Japanese FDI contrast with those of earlier periods. As noted earlier, for decades the primary economic motivation for such investment was to facilitate the flow of goods between Japan and various East Asian markets. The rapidly growing but resource-poor prewar economy required large supplies of natural resources and other primary products scarce in Japan but often plentiful in neighboring economies. To pay for the import of these goods and consume the output of its own increasingly industrialized economy, Japan sought growing regional markets for its own products. A very substantial proportion of all Japanese FDI in East Asia then and during much of the postwar period therefore was used to create a trade-facilitating infrastructure of trading companies, transportation firms, and financial services organizations.[71] (Added to this critical economic motive were a series of political and military factors important principally during the 1930s and early 1940s.) In recent years, however, the economic motives for such investment have become far more complex. Although trade facilitation remains an important factor, additional motives such as sourcing cheaper labor, defending regional markets, and deflecting trade tension with the United States also have become increasingly important.

The Role of the Japanese Government

Finally, the role of the Japanese government has changed in recent periods. Throughout the first century of Japanese FDI in East Asia, the government played an enormously influential role in shaping its development. Specific government actions until the end of World War II included major financial incentives and creation of politically secure investment environments as well as direct public participation in selected overseas investment projects. And during the postwar period, the government heavily influenced the development and character of Japanese FDI in East Asia through application of both strict controls over all outward investment flows and provision of financial inducements in many approved cases.

Yet here again the period of growth and diversification contrasts with the established pattern. Clearly the government has continued to play an important role in the overseas development of Japanese firms—particularly in comparison with the analogous roles of the governments of the United States and most other advanced economies. At the same time, however, the Japanese government became far less influential in shaping the development of Japanese FDI in the region after capital liberalization.

In sum, as compared to earlier historical periods, the recent development of Japanese FDI in East Asia along a number of important dimensions generally is characterized by discontinuity. There are, to be sure, certain limited exceptions. As in recent years, during the prewar and wartime period, levels of such investment rose substantially as Japan solidified its control over neighboring territories, and, again similar to current trends, during the postwar period as well, a relatively high proportion (but in absolute terms small quantity) of this investment entered the region's manufacturing sector.

More striking, however, are the many and highly significant discontinuities. First, the geographical distribution of Japanese FDI in East Asia has become far more diffuse in recent times. Second, economic motivations other than trade facilitation have become far more important factors in encouraging the spread of Japanese investment to the region. Third, the role of the Japanese government is less significant today. Fourth, absolute levels of Japanese FDI in East Asia today far surpass levels registered in earlier years. And fifth, with the limited exception noted above, a far greater proportion of such investment has entered the region's manufacturing industries in recent years.

This investment record hardly suggests that Japanese FDI in East Asia today is re-creating a modern version of the Greater East Asia Co-Prosperity Sphere. Although current levels of such investment exceed those of the 1930s and early 1940s, the government, as noted, does not today shape Japan's direct investments in the region with either the same degree of influence or with similar regional designs as in the late 1930s and early 1940s. In addition, that investment is now far less concentrated in neighboring Northeast Asia than it was during this previous era, and the overriding motivations are economic rather than political or military.[72]

International Perspectives

In contrast to the many discontinuities between contemporary and earlier Japanese FDI in East Asia, the historical record points to a number of striking similarities between the historical development of Japanese FDI in Europe and the United States versus East Asia.[73] Indeed, a cross-regional comparison of such investment along the five dimensions analyzed here points to a remarkable resemblance in the nature of Japanese FDI in East and West during earlier years. Consider, for example, investment levels. With the partial exception of the latter expansionary phase in Northeast Asia, quantities of Japanese FDI in East and West remained exceptionally small throughout (the roughly parallel) first century of its development in both regions. Yet in East and West those levels have expanded enormously since the 1970s and, in particular, beginning in the late 1980s.

This same general pattern holds for each of the other four characteristics of Japanese FDI across these regions. With respect to sectoral composition, for instance, such investment in East Asia, as well as the United States and Europe, largely focused in services and other nonmanufacturing sectors throughout its first century of development, but the proportion entering manufacturing has increased greatly in both areas during the last 25 years. In locational terms, a similar pattern holds. Historically, Japanese FDI in the United States and Europe, as in East Asia, was geographically concentrated in a small number of locales. Beginning in the 1970s, however, Japanese firms have dispersed their direct investments far more widely in the West and East.

In addition, throughout most of its first century of development Japanese FDI in the United States and Europe, as well as in East Asia, was based largely on the economic motive of facilitating trade flows between Japan and economies receiving such investment, yet in both areas those economic motives have become far more complex in recent times. And, finally, the government was enormously influential in shaping the development of Japanese FDI in East and West from the origins of such investment through the 1960s, yet in the last 25 years that influence has declined substantially. In short, when comparing current versus past Japanese FDI in East Asia, as opposed to the development of Japanese FDI in East versus West, the major similarities or continuities are apparently spatial (i.e., geographic) rather than temporal.[74]

A second broad comparison, juxtaposing the historical development of U.S. and Japanese FDI in East Asia, provides some insight into current debates over America's evolving economic presence in the region. With respect to the prewar era, the U.S. Department of Commerce estimates that total U.S. FDI in all of Asia amounted to a meager $175 million in 1919 and just $446 million 10 years later.[75] (See table 2.8.) By contrast, estimates place Japanese FDI at $377 million in China alone in 1919, and at roughly $763 million just in China and Manchuria in 1930. (See table 2.2.) Moreover, in 1929 and 1930 the vast majority of Japanese FDI was located in the East Asian region, whereas the proportion of U.S. FDI in this region as a share of total U.S. FDI abroad then reached barely 6 percent. Commerce Department data for 1929 also point to a far greater geographical dispersion of U.S. FDI in Asia—to key Southeast Asian recipients such as the Philippines and the Dutch East Indies as well as Northeast Asian recipients such as China—than is the case for Japanese FDI in the region at this time.[76]

The relative position and location of U.S. and Japanese FDI in East Asia alternated twice in later years. Following some two decades of rapid postwar U.S. FDI growth abroad, together with simultaneously strict enforcement of Japanese controls on capital outflows, by 1970 stocks of U.S. direct investment in East Asia far exceeded those of Japan—even though just 3 percent of all U.S. FDI stocks (versus 21 percent for Japan) were located in the region at that time.[77] In fact, by 1970 the United States had directly invested almost as much in the Philippines ($640 million) as Japan had directly invested in the entire region.

By 1995, however, the Japanese FDI presence in East Asia once again exceeded that of the United States. In stock terms, for example, in 1995 Japanese FDI in East Asia amounted to roughly $76 billion, whereas the corresponding U.S. total stood at roughly $46 billion (see figs. 2.6 and 2.7). On the other hand, the share of U.S. FDI stocks in the region as a proportion of its global direct investment levels had risen substantially—from roughly 3 percent to about 7.5 percent—during the latest quarter century. (Indeed, as suggested in fig. 2.8, at the end of 1994 U.S. FDI in the Asia/Pacific region as a whole accounted for roughly 18 percent of total U.S. FDI stocks abroad.) By contrast, the corresponding Japanese share in East Asia had somewhat declined, from 21 percent to 16 percent, during this same period (see fig. 2.9 for the global breakdown of Japanese FDI at the end of the 1994 fiscal year). Therefore, throughout most of the twentieth century both in absolute terms and as a percentage of its worldwide stocks during the last quarter century, U.S.

Table 2.8 U.S. FDI—Estimates for 1919 and 1929 ($ millions)

Country or region	Total		Manufacturing		Sales		Petroleum		Mining		Agriculture		Utilities		Railroads	
	1919	1929	1919	1929	1919	1929	1919	1929	1919	1929	1919	1929	1919	1929	1919	1929
Europe	694	1,340	280	637	95	133	158	239	—	37	—	—	5	138	—	—
Canada and Newfoundland	814	1,657	400	820	30	38	30	55	200	318	50	30	15	245	76	73
Mexico	644	709	8	6	5	9	200	206	222	248	48	58	32	90	123	82
Cuba and other West Indies	567	1,026	26	47	10	15	15	62	21	18	382	652	59	105	41	84
Central America	112	251	—	7	1	1	3	4	14	8	44	130	6	33	43	64
South America	665	1,720	50	170	55	94	113	512	404	528	29	44	4	348	4	6
Asia	175	446	15	77	25	34	50	151	4	10	32	63	17	65	10	—
Africa	31	117	—	7	10	16	10	32	11	54	—	8	—	2	—	—
Oceania	53	162	16	50	12	22	25	81	—	6	—	—	—	—	—	—
Banking	125	125	—	—	—	—	—	—	—	—	—	—	—	—	—	—
Total	3,880	7,553	795	1,821	243	362	604	1,341	876	1,227	587	986	138	1,025	297	309

Source: Adapted from Mira Wilkins, The Maturing of Multinational Enterprise: American Business Abroad from 1914 to 1970 (Cambridge: Harvard University Press, 1974).

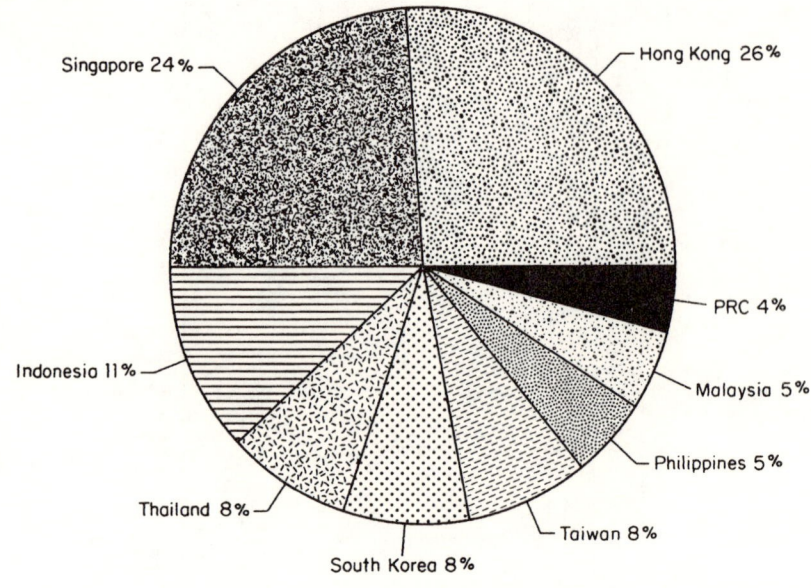

Total: $46 Billion

Source: U.S. Department of Commerce
Notes: Percentages do not equal 100 due to rounding. Historical cost basis.

Figure 2.7 U.S. FDI Position in East Asia Excluding Japan as of December 31, 1994 (percent).

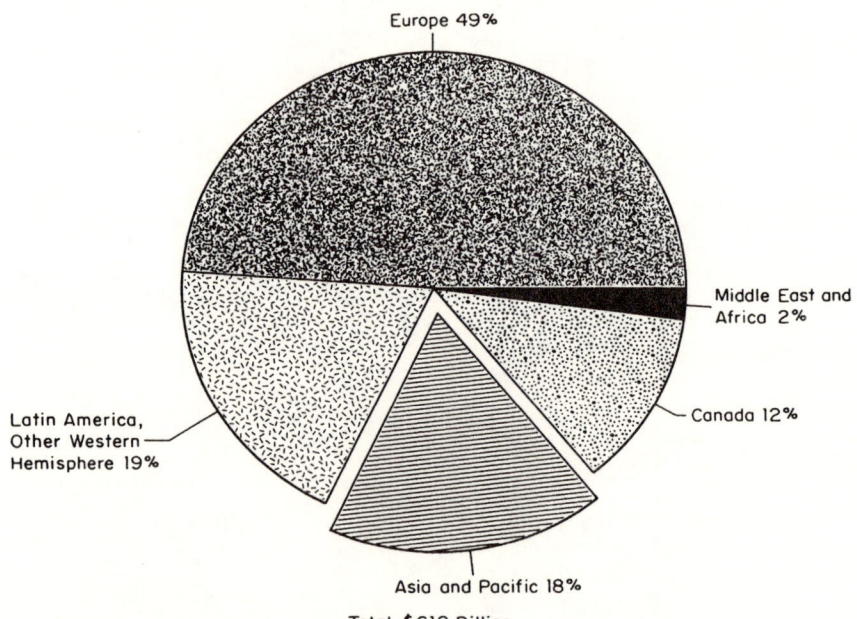

Total: $612 Billion

Source: U.S. Department of Commerce
Notes: Historical cost basis; percentage for East Asia, excluding Japan, is roughly 7.5%

Figure 2.8 U.S. FDI Position by Region as of December 31, 1994 (percent).

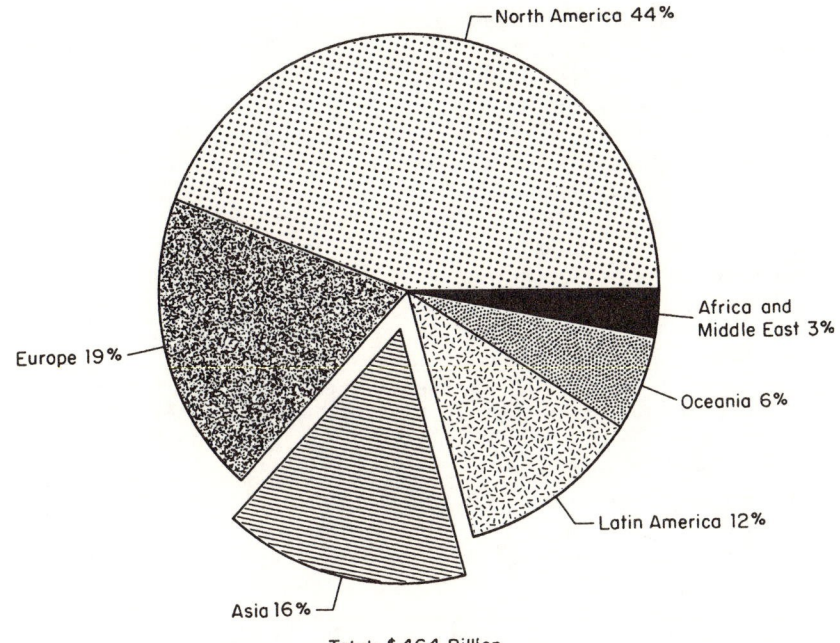

Total: $464 Billion

Source: Ministry of Finance (Japan)
Notes: Percentages do not equal 100 due to rounding. Approvals basis.

Figure 2.9 Japanese FDI Position by Region as of March 31, 1995 (percent).

FDI in East Asia has expanded prodigiously, yet in absolute terms the rapid growth of Japanese FDI in the region in recent years has been still more dramatic.

Notes

I gratefully acknowledge the comments of Dennis Encarnation, Geoffrey Jones, Hugh Patrick, and Mira Wilkins on an earlier draft of this chapter.

1. Unless otherwise noted, in this chapter East Asia excludes South Asia, Australia, and New Zealand but includes Southeast Asia and Japan's colonial territories through World War II.

2. Data from Ministry of Finance; approvals basis.

3. See, for example, "The New East Asia Co-Prosperity Sphere," *Fortune*, July 1, 1991, p. 12, and "Sphere Fears," *Far Eastern Economic Review*, October 17, 1991, p. 55.

4. See, for example, "Japan Builds a New Power Base: Its Emerging Clout in East Asia Could Come at America's Expense," *Business Week*, April 10, 1989, p. 42ff.

5. Among many other studies focusing on recent trends, see Richard Doner, "Japanese Foreign Investment and the Creation of a Pacific Asian Region," in Jeffrey Frankel and Miles Kahler, eds., *Regionalism and Rivalry: Japan and the United States in Pacific Asia* (Chicago: University of Chicago Press, 1993), chapter 5; and Edward Graham and Naoko Anzai, "Is Japanese Direct Investment Creating an Asian Economic Bloc?" *Columbia Journal of World Business*, Autumn 1994. Important exceptions to this contemporary focus are the historical accounts in Den-

nis Encarnation, *Rivals Beyond Trade: America versus Japan in Global Competition* (Ithaca: Cornell University Press, 1992), chapter 4, and Peter Petri, "The East Asian Trading Bloc: An Analytic History" in Frankel and Kahler, eds., *Regionalism and Rivalry*, chapter 1.

6. Also important were technology imports, which came primarily from the West.

7. In the case of then underdeveloped East Asia, of course, Japanese trade-facilitating FDI mostly sought to boost imports of raw materials rather than capital goods.

8. The following account is based on Kawabe Nobuo, "Development of Overseas Operations of General Trading Companies, 1868–1945," in Yonekawa Shinichi and Yoshihara Hideki, eds. *Business History of General Trading Companies* (Tokyo: University of Tokyo Press, 1987), pp. 74–79; Mira Wilkins, "Japanese Multinational Enterprise before 1914," *Business History Review* (Summer 1986), pp. 199–231; Nagasawa Yasuaki, "The Overseas Branches of Mitsubishi Limited during the First World War," *Japanese Yearbook on Business History* (1989), p. 117; Mitsui & Co., *The 100-Year History of Mitsui & Co., Ltd.* (Tokyo: Mitsui & Co., Ltd., 1977), chapters 1 and 2; and Yasumuro Kenichi, "The Contribution of Sogo Shosha to the Multinationalization of Japanese Industrial Enterprises in Historical Perspective," in Okochi Akio and Inoue Tadakatsu, eds., *Overseas Business Activities* (Tokyo: University of Tokyo Press, 1984), pp. 67–68.

9. C. F. Remer, *Foreign Investments in China* (New York: Howard Fertig, 1968), pp. 427–428.

10. See Peter Duus, "Economic Dimensions of Meiji Imperialism: The Case of Korea, 1895–1910," in Ramon Myers and Mark Peattie, eds., *The Japanese Colonial Empire, 1895–1945* (Princeton: Princeton University Press, 1984), pp. 155–158.

11. Yasumuro, "The Contribution of Sogo Shosha," p. 66.

12. William Wray, *Mitsubishi and the N.Y.K., 1879–1914: Business Strategy in the Japanese Shipping Industry* (Cambridge: Harvard University Press, 1984), pp. 61, 97, 349, 414. After NYK's 1885 founding, it replaced the Mitsubishi operation. Wilkins, "Japanese Multinational Enterprise before 1914," p. 216.

13. Tamaki Norio, "The Yokohama Specie Bank: A Multinational in the Japanese Interest 1879–1931," in Geoffrey Jones, ed., *Banks as Multinationals* (London: Routledge, 1990), pp. 197, 199. See, also, Ishii Kanji, "Japan," in Rondo Cameron and V. I. Bovykin, eds., *International Banking, 1870–1914* (New York: Oxford University Press, 1991), p. 219.

14. Mitsui & Co., *The 100-Year History*, p. 55.

15. Norio, "The Yokohama Specie Bank," p. 202.

16. Kanji, "Japan," pp. 227–228, and Harold Moulton, *Japan: An Economic and Financial Appraisal* (Washington, DC: Brookings Institute, 1931), chapter 9.

17. Wilkins, "Japanese Multinational Enterprise before 1914," p. 216.

18. See, for example, *The 100-Year History of Nippon Life* (Tokyo: Nippon Life Insurance Company, 1991), pp. 33 and 66; and Nihon keieishi kenkyujo, ed., *Tokyo Kaijo no Hyakunen* (The 100–year history of Tokyo Marine), tables section.

19. In addition, during this period little Japanese FDI entered the natural resource sector. Political as well as economic factors apparently explain this pattern. Exceptional, therefore, was the entry of such FDI into the rubber industries of, for example, the Dutch East Indies. (See table 2.4). Comments of Hugh Patrick.

20. Kawabe, "Development of Overseas Operations," p. 77; Kuwahara Tetsuya, "The Business Strategy of Japanese Cotton Spinners: Overseas Operations, 1890 to 1931," in Okochi Akio and Yonekawa Shinichi, eds., *The Textile Industry and Its Business Climate* (Tokyo: University of Tokyo Press, 1982), p. 141.

21. Remer, *Foreign Investments in China*, p. 429; "Numaguchi gen nihon no

kaigai jigyo katsudo: sono rekishiteki katei to keieiteki sho yoin" (The overseas activities of Japanese enterprise: The historical process and various managerial factors), *Chiba Shodai Ronso*, 13-B (June 1970), p. 245; Inoue Tadakatsu, "A Comparison of the Emergence of Multinational Manufacturing by U.S., European and Japanese Firms," in Okochi Akio et al., eds., *Overseas Business Activities*, p. 12.

22. For example, the Japanese government owned half of the capital stock in the SMRC. Remer, *Foreign Investments in China*, p. 427. Moreover, during these years the government helped finance the nation's FDI in Northeast Asia by applying funds obtained through the Industrial Bank of Japan's foreign portfolio borrowings. See Hugh Patrick, "Japan, 1868–1914," in Rondo Cameron, ed., *Banking in the Early Stages of Industrialization: A Study in Comparative Economic History* (New York: Oxford University Press, 1967), pp. 270–271.

23. See Petri, "The East Asian Trading Bloc," pp. 30–31, and Edwin Reischauer and Albert Craig, *Japan: Tradition and Transformation* (Tokyo: Charles Tuttle, 1978), pp. 184–186.

24. William Lockwood, *The Economic Development of Japan: Growth and Structural Change, 1868–1945* (Princeton: Princeton University Press, 1954), p. 531.

25. Remer, *Foreign Investments in China*, p. 426.

26. On Japanese direct investments in those prewar colonies, see, for example, Mizoguchi Toshiyuki and Yamamoto Yuzo, "Capital Formation in Taiwan and Korea," in Ramon Myers and Mark Peattie, eds., *The Japanese Colonial Empire, 1895–1945*, chapter 10.

27. The data in table 2.2, however, do not provide a breakdown of direct versus portfolio investment for the year 1936.

28. Remer, *Foreign Investments in China*, p. 549.

29. Although I was unable to locate reliable estimates of Japanese FDI in East Asia during the wartime years, the literature on Japanese business history suggests that such investment continued to increase substantially throughout the late 1930s and early 1940s. See, for example, Akio et al., eds., *Overseas Business Activities* and Mitsui & Co., *The 100-Year History of Mitsui & Co.*

30. Remer, *Foreign Investments in China*, p. 75ff.

31. Lockwood, *The Economic Development of Japan*, p. 262.

32. See, for example, Mizoguchi and Yamamoto, "Capital Formation in Taiwan and Korea."

33. Kuwahara Tetsuya, "Trends in Research on Overseas Expansion by Japanese Enterprises Prior to World War II," *Japanese Yearbook on Business History* (7) 1990, p. 61.

34. As Wilkins has rightly pointed out, Western spheres of influence in pre-World War II Asia—for example, French Indochina, the Dutch East Indies, and British Southeast Asia—further shaped the geographical distribution of Japanese FDI in the East Asian region during this period.

35. Supreme Commander for the Allied Powers (SCAP), *History of the Non-Military Activities of the Occupation of Japan, ii: Reparations and Property Administration*, part C (unpublished).

36. Remer, *Foreign Investments in China*, p. 506. On Japanese FDI in Manchurian manufacturing and other sectors during this period, see Ann R. Kinney, *Japanese Investment in Manchurian Manufacturing, Mining, Transportation and Communications, 1931–1945* (New York: Garland Publishing, 1982).

37. See, for example, the Hou Chi-ming data cited in W. G. Beasley, *Japanese Imperialism 1894–1945* (Oxford: Clarendon Press, 1991), p. 140.

38. Kawabe, "Development of Overseas Operations," p. 86.

39. Kawabe, "Development of Overseas Operations," p. 93.

40. Remer, *Foreign Investments in China.*

41. See, for example, the several contributions in Myers and Peattie, eds., *The Japanese Colonial Empire.*

42. Tamaki, "The Yokohama Specie Bank," p. 212.

43. Nihon keieishi kenkyujo, ed., *Tokyo Kaijo no Hyakunen*, p. 354ff.

44. See Kuwahara Tetsuya, "The Business Strategy of Japanese Cotton Spinners" and "The Japanese Cotton Spinners' Direct Investments into China before the Second World War," in Alice Teichova, et al., eds., *Historical Studies in International Corporate Business* (New York: Cambridge University Press, 1989), chapter 14.

45. Toyota Motor Corporation, *Toyota: A History of the First 50 Years* (Toyota City: Toyota Motor Corporation, 1988), p. 75. See, also, Michael Cusumano, *The Japanese Automobile Industry: Technology and Management at Nissan and Toyota* (Cambridge: Harvard University Press, 1985), p. 32.

46. Samuel Pao-San Ho, "Colonialism and Development: Korea, Taiwan and Kwantung," in Myers and Peattie, eds., *The Japanese Colonial Empire*, p. 356.

47. See, for instance, the account in Toyota Motor Corporation, *Toyota*, p. 75.

48. The following account is drawn from SCAP, *History of the Non-Military Activities.*

49. These SCAP calculations include all assets outside the four main Japanese islands.

50. Michael Yoshino, "The Multinational Spread of Japanese Manufacturing Investment since World War II," *Business History Review* (Autumn 1974).

51. Encarnation, *Rivals Beyond Trade*, p. 168.

52. Komiya Ryutaro, *The Japanese Economy: Trade, Industry and Government* (Tokyo: University of Tokyo Press, 1990), p. 118.

53. Sekiguchi, *Japanese Direct Foreign Investment*, pp. 26–27.

54. Yoshihara Hideki, *Japanese Investment in Southeast Asia* (Honolulu: University Press of Hawaii, 1978), pp. 18, 65. The remaining investments were approved to enter Taiwan (3 projects), Hong Kong (1) and Singapore (1).

55. See Yoshino, "The Multinational Spread," p. 358 (for the MITI survey) and *Japan's Multinational Enterprises* (Cambridge: Harvard University Press, 1976), p. 91; Yoshihara Hideki, "Multinational Growth of Japanese Manufacturing Enterprises," in Okochi Akio, et al., eds., *Overseas Business Activities*, p. 103 (for Yoshihara's own survey data); and Hamada Koichi, "Japanese Investment Abroad" in Peter Drysdale, ed., *Direct Foreign Investment in Asia and the Pacific* (Canberra: Australian National University Press, 1972), chapter 7 (for MOF data).

56. Yoshino, "The Multinational Spread."

57. Indeed, between 1950 and 1970 Mitsui & Co. alone had directly invested in roughly 50 manufacturing operations just in Southeast Asia. Mitsui & Co., *The 100-Year History*, Appendix. On the spread of "sogo shosha-participated joint ventures" in the postwar period, see Yasumuro in Okochi and Inoue, p. 77ff.

58. The MOF data as cited in Komiya, *The Japanese Economy*, p. 114.

59. The MOF data as cited in Hamada, "Japanese Investment Abroad," p. 176.

60. Encarnation, *Rivals Beyond Trade*, p. 168. In addition, Mira Wilkins reports that fears of antagonizing the United States discouraged Japanese companies even from considering major direct investments in China during this period.

61. Encarnation, *Rivals Beyond Trade*, p. 168.

62. See Mark Mason, "The Origins and Evolution of Japanese Direct Investment in Europe," *Business History Review* 66 (Summer 1992), pp. 435–474.

63. Komiya, *The Japanese Economy*, p. 120.

64. Encarnation, *Rivals Beyond Trade*, p. 172.

65. Although the years beginning in the early 1970s are treated here as a single period, the sharply increased levels of Japanese FDI abroad following the (1985) Plaza Accord and other events provide the basis for a division of the past quarter-century into the early 1970s through 1985, and 1986 to the present.

66. Although the following sectoral FDI data pertain to the entire Asian region, the vast majority of such investment was located in East Asia. For further discussion on rising Japanese FDI in the region's manufacturing industries during this period, see Ozawa Terutomo, *Multinationalism, Japanese Style: The Political Economy of Outward Dependency* (Princeton: Princeton University Press, 1979), especially chapter 3.

67. Yoshihara, "Multinational Growth," p. 105.

68. Yoshihara, "Multinational Growth," p. 105.

69. The MOF data as cited by Ryutaro, *The Japanese Economy*, p. 123.

70. See, for example, Richard F. Doner, "Japan in East Asia: Institutions and Regional Leadership," in Peter J. Katzenstein and Takashi Shiraishi, eds., *Network Power: Japan and Asia* (Ithaca: Cornell University Press, 1997), pp. 197–233.

71. Exceptions include the prewar cotton spinning investments noted before.

72. In addition, as pointed out by Graham and Anzai, "Is Japanese Direct Investment Creating an Asian Economic Bloc?" Japanese FDI in East Asia as a percentage of total FDI in the region has remained limited in recent years due to the rapid influx of large amounts of FDI from numerous sources to that rapidly growing region.

73. Mason, "The Origins and Evolution," and Mira Wilkins, "Japanese Multinationals in the United States: Continuity and Change, 1879–1990," *Business History Review* 64 (Winter 1990), pp. 585–629.

74. In addition, there are equally striking contrasts between the development of Japanese FDI in East Asia and the reciprocal development of East Asian FDI in Japan: there has been an almost complete absence of East Asian FDI in Japan throughout the years analyzed in this study.

75. Prewar (and subsequent postwar) Department of Commerce FDI data cited here are calculated on an historical basis and cover estimates for the entire Asia/Pacific region excluding Japan. Prewar Japanese data are calculated using a variety of different measurement techniques, whereas postwar data are based on official approvals. For both pre- and postwar periods, the Japanese FDI statistics cover all of Asia.

76. In 1929, for example, the Commerce Department reports that, of a total of $446 million of U.S. FDI in Asia, just $114 million was located in China, but $80 million was in the Philippines, $66 million was in the Dutch East Indies, and much of the rest was scattered throughout the region.

77. In 1970, U.S. FDI stocks in Asia and the Pacific (excluding Japan) totaled $2.3 billion on an historical cost basis, whereas approved Japanese FDI flows to the rest of Asia that year amounted to just $750 million. Commerce and MOF data. Measurement techniques differ, of course, so figures are not strictly comparable.

3

Asia and the Global Operations of Multinational Corporations

Dennis J. Encarnation

Today, Asia (outside of Japan) is the principal host to foreign direct investment (FDI) destined for newly industrializing economies.[1] Asia now ranks behind North America and Western Europe, which continue to account for the lion's share of both existing stocks and new flows of FDI. But Asia's leading status, even among newly industrializing economies (NIEs), is quite new. Just a decade ago, in 1985, FDI flows to Latin America still outpaced comparable flows to Asia, leaving accumulated stocks in that region well below FDI found elsewhere. But subsequently, FDI flows to Asia accelerated rapidly, especially during the 1990s, when they jumped well beyond levels recorded in any other developing region.

Within Asia, as we shall see here, most of this FDI is concentrated in a very few economies and comes from a very few sources. Today, just three hosts—Hong Kong, Indonesia, and Singapore—account for over one half of all accumulated stocks originating in either the United States or Japan, still the two largest national sources of FDI in Asia. Shifting from stocks to flows, just one host—China—accounts today for over one half of all new FDI in Asia. Even as recently as 1990, Singapore received more FDI inflows than did China. Subsequently, however, FDI to China skyrocketed, accounting for nearly half of all Asian inflows. Leading this recent surge are Asian investors, from Korea and especially the Chinese communities located in Hong Kong, Taiwan, and across ASEAN. During the 1990s, these regional investors surpassed both the Americans and the Japanese as Asia's leading sources of FDI flows.

Much of that FDI is now integral to the Asian operations of multinational corporations (MNCs) based in the United States, Japan, Korea, and elsewhere in Asia. Over time, as documented in great detail in this chapter, these operations have begun to converge despite obvious differences among MNCs in their geographic and historical origins. Such convergence has at times been even more pronounced in Asia than elsewhere in the world, as demonstrated by the common geographic and industrial concentration of FDI from various sources. More often, MNCs in Asia more closely mimic patterns of convergence apparent elsewhere, as they do in the pursuit of majority shareholdings and FDI-generated sales. Yet important differences in MNC operations persist, even in the same location and industry. In home-country sourcing and intrafirm trade, for example, MNCs in Asia differ as they do elsewhere in the world. Such differences may be even more pronounced in Asia than elsewhere, as demonstrated by wide variation in host-market and export sales. Taken together, then, the regional operations of multinational corporations in Asia confirm the persistence of important operational differences, while also reaffirming that these same multinationals are moving along a common evolutionary path.

These emerging similarities and persistent differences have important implications for both corporate strategy and government policy, implications explored in my concluding section. As we shall see, sharp differences can still be discerned between multinationals in their determination of markets for outputs, sources for inputs, and the organization of that trade between markets (arm's-length transactions) and hierarchies (intrafirm transactions). The relationship between FDI and trade varies significantly among multinational corporations, as well as among national economies. Bounded in absolute value by more macro-economic determinants, FDI can contribute proportionately to trade, while also altering its composition and direction—not only for individual multinationals, but also for host (and home) economies. Simultaneously, such trade can have a significant impact on the value, direction, and composition of FDI, again at both the microlevel of multinationals and the macrolevel of national economies. These complementarities between FDI and trade have important policy consequences: cross-national differences in trade and FDI regimes can explain much of the wide variation in the relative contribution of multinationals to host-country exports and imports across Asia.

Beginning with a broad survey of FDI sources and destinations, I will examine in greater detail the regional operations of multinationals making that investment and conclude with an assessment of the broad implications of these findings for both corporate strategy and government policy.

FDI Sources and Destinations

The two largest national sources of FDI in Asia are Japan and the United States. By 1993 (the most recent year for which comparable data are available, reported in table 3.1), American and Japanese multinationals each contributed roughly one sixth (between 15 and 17 percent) of all FDI flows into newly industrializing Asia—a share that rises to one quarter of all FDI flowing into Asia outside of China. By contrast, according to the best available estimates, European multinationals probably contributed no more than 10 percent of Asia's FDI inflows[2]—less than half the relative contribution of either American or Japanese multinationals. The remainder, contributing well over two thirds of all FDI flows into Asia (and over four fifths of all FDI flows into China), came from other, principally Asian investors largely based in the newly industrializing economies of Hong Kong, Korea, and Taiwan.

U.S. and Japanese FDI

Historically, American multinationals have long concentrated most of their foreign direct investment outside of Asia, in North and South America, as well as in Western Europe—in marked contrast to the Japanese, who have long emphasized

Table 3.1   Foreign Direct Investment (FDI) Flows into
Asia, by Destination and Source, 1993

	$ billions
Asia including China	
"Greater China"	
China	27.5
Less "round-tripping"[a]	−10.0
Estimated FDI in China	17.5
Hong Kong[b]	1.7
Taiwan	0.9
Other East Asia[c]	17.2
Singapore	6.8
South Asia	1.1
Total FDI flows into Asia[d]	38.4
U.S. FDI	5.8
Japanese FDI	6.6
Korean, Chinese, other	26.0
Asia excluding China	
"Three Dragons"	
Singapore	6.8
Hong Kong[b]	1.7
Taiwan	0.9
Other East Asia[c]	10.4
South Asia	1.1
Total FDI flows into Asia[d]	20.9
U.S. FDI	5.2
Japanese FDI	4.9
Korean, Chinese, other	10.8

Sources: IMF Balance of Payments Statistics and World Bank estimates,
May 1995, UNCTAD estimates, July 1995.

[a]Domestic Chinese investment temporarily recycled principally through
Hong Kong in order to receive foreign-investment incentives upon reentry into China.
[b]Includes only FDI from OECD member countries.
[c]Excludes Japan.
[d]Excludes Western Asia and former Soviet Central Asian Republics.

their Asian neighbors. Prior to World War II, Asia attracted the lion's share (over
three quarters, by one estimate)[3] of all Japanese direct investments abroad; while
for the Americans, the comparable Asian share was minuscule (probably under
5 percent),[4] less than any other region of the world except Africa. After the war,
that Asian share actually declined for the Americans, leveling out to roughly
3 percent, where it stayed well into the 1970s. Meanwhile, most Japanese investments in Asia were nationalized by their host countries after the war, and new
FDI outflows were reduced to a trickle, as capital controls at home and lingering
animosities abroad nearly eradicated the prewar investments of Japanese corporations in Asia.

But during the 1970s and (especially) the 1980s, both Japanese and American
multinationals greatly accelerated their new investments in Asia. At least for the
Americans, that growth greatly outpaced increases elsewhere, leading Asia to nearly

double its share of U.S. FDI, from less than 4 percent as recently as 1977, to nearly 8 percent by 1994 (calculated from table 3.2). That growth actually catapulted Asia past South America as the leading site for U.S. FDI among emerging markets. For the Japanese, however, Asia consistently ranked much higher, among the top two or three destinations for their FDI. By 1994, Asia had come to account for 16 percent of all approved Japanese FDI worldwide—comparable to Western Europe (see table 3.2) but well behind North America and comparable figures before the war.

Although American and Japanese multinationals continue to differ in terms of the relative importance they assign Asia as a desirable destination for their FDI, they both have long concentrated their different Asian investments in a very few host countries. Before the war, for example, China, the Philippines, and the Neth-

Table 3.2   Accumulated Stocks of Foreign Direct Investment (FDI) by American and Japanese Multinationals (MNCs), 1994

Location of FDI	American MNCs abroad[a] $ (billions) or %	Japanese MNCs abroad[b] $ (billions) or %
Worldwide	$612.1	$463.6
North America	$89.2	$202.7
Western Europe	$300.2	$89.9
Japan	$37.0	
Other East Asia, of which:	$47.3	$76.2
% by country		
Four NIEs		
Korea	7.6%	7.0%
Taiwan	8.2%	5.2%
Hong Kong	25.3%	18.2%
Singapore	23.2%	12.5%
ASEAN Four		
Thailand	8.0%	9.4%
Malaysia	5.0%	8.4%
Indonesia	10.6%	22.3%
Philippines	5.0%	3.7%
Big Two		
India	1.7%	0.6%
China	3.6%	11.4%
% by industry		
Manufacturing	34.8%	43.2%[c]
Chemicals	5.9%	3.8%
Electronics	11.8%	10.1%
All Other	65.2%	56.8%
Petroleum	20.7%	12.2%
Wholesaling	16.3%	9.1%
Finance	20.9%	10.2%

Sources: U.S. Commerce Department, Bureau of Economic Analysis, "U.S. Direct Investment Abroad: Detail for Position and Balance of Payments Flows," *Survey of Current Business* (August, 1995), pp. 88–124; Japan, Ministry of Finance, *Statistics for the Approval/Notification of Overseas Direct Investment* [*Taigai chyokusetsu-toshi no kyoka todokede zisseki*] (Tokyo: Ministry of Finance Printing Bureau, 1995), n.p.

[a]Historical-costs basis.
[b]Approval basis.
[c]1993 data.

erlands East Indies (later, Indonesia) each hosted more U.S. FDI than did Japan.[5] Among these, the United States long harbored colonial ambitions in China's large domestic market, while the Philippines had become a U.S. territory, one blessed with plentiful natural resources, many of which also became available in greater abundance in the Netherlands East Indies. Colonization had an even stronger impact on the Japanese: on the eve of the war, China (especially Manchuria) hosted the lion's share of all Japanese FDI worldwide, followed by Korea and Taiwan. After the war, however, the Japanese were excluded from most of their former colonial possessions, while the Americans remained concentrated in the Philippines, which, along with India, accounted for over half of all U.S. FDI in Asia as late as 1966.[6] Through the 1960s, host governments in the Philippines, India, and elsewhere across the region had erected steep trade barriers, which (as we shall see) induced a few prospective U.S. exporters to invest in foreign manufacturing in order to supply protected local markets.

Subsequently, however, the principal incentives for FDI in Asia shifted dramatically, as did the geographic concentration of that investment. As a result, by 1994, three economies—Hong Kong, Indonesia, and Singapore—accounted for well over one half of all the FDI located in Asia by either American or Japanese multinationals. Of course, they differed in their rank-ordering of these three hosts. Hong Kong and Singapore accounted for roughly one half of all U.S. FDI in Asia outside of Japan, with Indonesia leading a third tier of host countries. For the Japanese, Indonesia retained its historical lead, but its relative share had nearly been cut in half during the 1980s, leaving it by 1994 with less than one quarter of all Japanese FDI in Asia (see table 3.2). Growing during the 1980s at twice the rate recorded in Asia as a whole, Hong Kong and Singapore raced past Korea on the way to ranking second and third (respectively) among Asian hosts to Japanese FDI.

By concentrating FDI in these three countries, American and Japanese multinationals followed comparable strategies. For both, Hong Kong bolstered its position as the regional center for distribution, finance, and other trade-related service (all increasingly directed at China); Indonesia remained the Asian center for petroleum, mining, and other extractive industries; Singapore emerged as a regional center for manufacturing, especially of electronics. Thus, across these three countries, a similar pattern of national specialization has attracted both American and Japanese multinationals.

The Americans, at least, have contributed to such national specialization by concentrating their Asian operations in few countries, where they have invested in few economic sectors (see table 3.2). Simply put, American multinationals in Asia engage in a narrower range of extractive, manufacturing, and service industries than they do elsewhere in the world. Petroleum, for example, contributes twice the proportion of U.S. FDI in Asia than it does elsewhere in the world, even though its share has recently begun to decline.[7] Moreover, the ever-growing share of U.S. FDI invested in Asian wholesaling is also much higher than in other regions. Only manufacturing attracts shares of U.S. FDI comparable to those elsewhere, yet, even here, those shares have been growing in Asia while declining worldwide. And within manufacturing, U.S. FDI in the electronics industry stands out for its greater concentration in Asia (12 percent of all U.S. FDI in Asia versus 3 percent of all U.S. FDI worldwide).[8] By comparison, U.S. FDI in chemicals stands out for its limited presence in Asia, especially since it is the largest source of U.S.

FDI in manufacturing worldwide. But this is a recent pattern. As recently as 1977, what little U.S. FDI entered Asian manufacturing was more likely to produce chemicals and not electronics. In short, the surge of U.S. FDI into Asian electronics is quite recent, having principally occurred during the 1980s, reflecting that region's growing specialization in electronics.

Compared to the Americans, Japanese multinationals are more widely dispersed both sectorally and geographically. In Asian manufacturing, for example, Japanese multinationals have become even more diversified than their American counterparts, with far more investment spread across numerous sectors and several countries. To illustrate, while electronics attracts much FDI in Asia, that industry nevertheless accounts for a smaller proportion of Japanese investment across the region than it does for the Americans (see table 3.2). Alternatively, textiles attracts a much higher proportion of Japanese FDI in the region—not just because U.S. FDI in that sector is virtually nonexistent, but also because textiles was the leading recipient of Japanese FDI in Asian manufacturing up until the 1980s, when American and then Japanese FDI in Asian electronics took off. Such growth in Japanese FDI has actually increased the geographic spread of Japanese investments in Asian manufacturing. Indeed, the second tier of Asian hosts (especially China and Thailand) is rapidly approaching the first tier as principal destinations for Japanese FDI. And with that growth, the Asian investments of Japanese multinationals are becoming more diffuse across countries and industries—moving in a direction opposite that of the Americans.

While both American and Japanese multinationals have come to concentrate a sizable—at least in recent years, growing—share of their FDI in Asia, European multinationals have not. Indeed, according to the best estimates available, Asia actually accounts for a small and declining share of the worldwide FDI of multinationals based in the European Union.[9] As a result, European multinationals probably contributed no more than 10 percent of Asia's FDI inflows—less than half the relative contribution of either American or Japanese multinationals. And this European contribution was minuscule compared to large and growing levels of intraregional FDI from Asia's newly industrializing economies. For in addition to Japan, the principal sources of intraregional FDI in Asia are either Korea or the largely ethnic Chinese sources of Hong Kong, Singapore, and Taiwan.

Korean and Ethnic Chinese FDI

By 1993, Korean multinationals had concentrated their modest FDI (stocks) in the Pacific Basin, roughly balanced between North America (mainly the United States) and Asia, with each region accounting for nearly 40 percent of all Korean FDI.[10] Of the remaining 20 percent, half was located in Western Europe. By sector, manufacturing accounted for over two fifths of all Korean FDI worldwide, with much of this engaged in the production of basic and fabricated metals. Much of the remaining Korean FDI was engaged in wholesale (and retail) trade, followed by the processing of petroleum and other natural resources. But the geographic location of these sectoral investments varies widely across critical markets and sources of supply. Of these, three—the United States, Indonesia, and China—accounted for well over half of all Korean FDI worldwide. And they illustrated the broad range of investment strategies adopted by Korean multinationals.

The United States has long been the single largest host for Korean direct investments, accounting in 1993 for nearly a third of total stocks. Existing trade patterns help explain this concentration of Korean FDI: the United States is also the single largest market for Korean exports, accounting for over a quarter of that trade, and Korea's second largest supplier of imports, accounting for over a fifth of the total.[11] To assist in this two-way flow of trade, in ways discussed later, FDI engaged principally in retail and especially wholesale trade accounted for nearly half of all Korean stocks in the United States. So large are Korean investments in this U.S. sector that they represented approximately two thirds of all Korean FDI engaged in wholesale and retail trade around the world. Beyond wholesaling, the United States was also the single largest host to Korean FDI engaged in manufacturing, which accounts for more than a fifth of all Korean stocks in the United States. There, the largest share of Korean manufacturing FDI produces basic metals, which, as we shall see, are destined for sale principally in the domestic U.S. market—the sales destination for most multinationals operating in the United States.

Indonesia has long been the second largest destination for Korean FDI, accounting for less than half the stocks invested in the United States during 1993—but well above any other Asian destination. In marked contrast to the United States, Indonesia hosts negligible Korean FDI engaged in either wholesale or retail trade. Of course, for Korea, Indonesia is neither a leading export market (ranked eighth in 1992) nor a leading import source (ranked seventh).[12] What is imported from Indonesia, however, consists principally of petroleum and other natural resources. In these sectors, Indonesia is the largest single destination worldwide for Korean FDI, accounting for nearly two fifths of all Korean FDI stocks. As a result, Korean FDI in petroleum and other natural resources, presumably for export back home, accounted for well over half of all Korean FDI in Indonesia during 1993. What remained of Korean FDI in Indonesia was engaged principally in manufacturing a wide range of products, of which textiles and leather products contributed the largest share. Since textiles and leather products figure prominently among Korean exports to the United States and elsewhere,[13] it seems safe to assume that Korean multinationals in these sectors are also exporting their Indonesian products to these critical markets—a common strategy, as we shall see, for all multinationals operating in Asia.

China only recently emerged as the third largest destination for Korean FDI, accounting for nearly 9 percent of all stocks in 1993, up from less than 1 percent as recently as 1990.[14] Although Korean multinationals have focused more on wholesale trade in the United States and on natural resources in Indonesia, they have concentrated nearly all of their FDI in China in the manufacturing sector. There, Korean manufacturers produced a broad range of products, of which textiles and leather products again contributed the largest share. While the domestic Chinese market undoubtedly consumes a sizable proportion of this manufactured output, much of that output—especially textiles and leather products—is again presumably exported either back home for additional processing or directly to the United States and other third-country markets. Thus, China is emerging as the largest single Asian repository of Korean manufacturing outside of Korea itself.

For newly emergent Asian multinationals, especially those based in Hong Kong and Taiwan, China has emerged as the largest single destination for their FDI. But the actual size of their FDI in China is difficult to calculate. For example, the World

Bank estimated that roughly $4 out of ever $11 directly invested in China during 1992 was actually domestic Chinese investment temporarily recycled through Hong Kong in order to receive foreign-investment incentives upon reentry into China (so-called "round-tripping"). Applying this estimate to 1993 means that $27.5 billion of recorded FDI inflows should actually be reduced to $17.5 billion of actual FDI inflows (see table 3.1).

Of this sum, between three quarters[15] and four fifths[16] originate in either Hong Kong or Taiwan. Among these two sources, the precise division remains unclear for at least two reasons. First, until recently, capital controls in Taiwan limited (if not proscribed) direct flows of capital from Taiwan to China; to circumvent such controls, Taiwanese investors reportedly channeled their FDI through Hong Kong as an intermediary stop on their way to China. Second, the Taiwanese are not the only foreign investors who have routed their FDI first through their subsidiaries in Hong Kong before entering China, even in the absence of capital controls back home. Even though both routings inflate Hong Kong's contribution to FDI in China, that contribution probably still exceeds $13 billion. This sum certainly represented roughly a third of all FDI flows to Asia during 1993 and probably represented well over half of all FDI flows across Asia recorded by ethnic Chinese multinationals.

Of course, China is not the only host of intraregional FDI inflows from either Hong Kong or Taiwan, as the case of Thailand illustrates.[17] Nor are Hong Kong and Taiwan the only home bases for ethnic Chinese multinationals, many of which also arise from the Chinese communities located either in Singapore or scattered across the rest of ASEAN (mainly Indonesia, Malaysia, the Philippines, and Thailand). Indeed, a Sino-Thai conglomerate, CP, is reportedly the largest single foreign investor in China. Meanwhile in Thailand, largely ethnic Chinese investors based in Hong Kong, Singapore, and Taiwan contributed nearly two fifths of all FDI inflows between 1990 and 1993, finally surpassing Japan (the largest source of FDI inflows during the second half of the 1980s), and double the relative contribution of U.S. FDI inflows. In short, ethnic Chinese multinationals have emerged as a major source of intraregional FDI flows, especially in East and Southeast Asia.

Not only is the Asian FDI of ethnic Chinese corporations more widely dispersed geographically, but also sectorally. In Asian manufacturing, if there is a bias, it is toward agribusiness, electronics, and textiles. Among services, FDI ranges broadly from construction and real estate, to financial services, to wholesale and retail trade. Perhaps only in extractive industries is the range of Asian investments smaller in mining and petroleum than that recorded by American and Japanese multinationals. In short, the Asian investments of ethnic Chinese multinationals are diffusing across countries and industries—moving in a direction opposite that of the Americans, but consistent with that of Asia's other intraregional investors, the Japanese and Koreans.

Operational Characteristics of Multinationals

This study extends earlier comparisons of American and Japanese multinationals to identify and explain emerging similarities and persistent differences in the strategies and structures these MNCs have adopted across Asia and elsewhere in the world. Of particular concern, in light of prior research, is the multinational management of an interrelated series of strategic trade-offs concerning both the strategy and structure of foreign operations.[18] These trade-offs are stylized below as six sets of binary choices affecting a multinational's shareholdings, sales, value-added, markets, sourcing, and trade. Such choices are common to all multinational corporations, and thus permit a comparative analysis of American and Japanese multinationals not only in Asia but also in North America and Western Europe.

Shareholdings: Majority Subsidiaries versus Minority Affiliates

Choices regarding equity ownership and managerial control are among the first to be confronted by all multinationals investing abroad. The logic for majority ownership and undisputed control is often compelling: MNCs create and sustain a competitive advantage through the skillful management of tangible and intangible assets in technology, marketing, and organization. Such assets, specific to each individual firm, are often best exploited when that firm owns a majority (including all) of the equity shareholdings in its foreign subsidiaries. Compared to minority shareholdings, a majority position can grant the multinational parent a higher degree of managerial control over the foreign use of assets. Such managerial control, in turn, often helps to reduce the high costs that can plague more arm's-length transactions between foreign suppliers of firm-specific assets and unaffiliated buyers overseas. Instead of using such arm's-length transactions, these foreign suppliers transfer their tangible and intangible assets internally—directly to their majority-owned subsidiaries abroad. Later, reverse transfers also take place, as foreign subsidiaries begin to ship goods and services back to their multinational parent, as well as to other related affiliates overseas. In the end, this circular flow enhances the total pool of technological, marketing, and organizational assets available to both the multinational parent and its majority subsidiaries.

At least since World War II, American multinationals have consistently invested in majority-owned subsidiaries, rather than in minority-owned affiliates. Indeed, as early as 1957, U.S. MNCs reported to the U.S. Commerce Department (in its first postwar census of the foreign operations of U.S. companies) that they owned more than three quarters of the equity invested in their subsidiaries abroad.[19] For the Americans, relative shareholdings continued to grow slowly over the next decade,[20] so that by 1992 majority U.S. subsidiaries accounted for over four fifths of the assets owned by American multinationals abroad (see table 3.3). As a result of these investments, U.S. MNCs reported that their majority-owned subsidiaries contributed an ever-larger share of their total foreign sales, reaching three quarters by 1966 (in the Commerce Department's first benchmark survey of U.S. FDI),[21] and climbing to over four fifths by 1992 (in the department's most recent annual survey, summarized in table 3.3). What little remained was dispersed across equal-partnership joint ventures and minority U.S.-owned affiliates. Thus, today, for American multinationals, majority ownership of foreign subsidiaries remains a prominent characteristic of their foreign-investment strategies.

Similarly, majority ownership has become central to the investment strategies of Japanese multinationals. Indeed, for 1992 (again, the most recent year for which

Table 3.3   Overseas Sales and Assets by Level of Foreign Shareholdings, Across Regions, 1992–1993

	Sales			Assets[c]		
	$ billions	Majority[a]	Minority[b]	$ billions	Majority[a]	Minority[b]
American multinationals abroad, 1992						
Worldwide	1,578.7	82.3%	17.7%	1,746.8	82.3%	17.7%
North America	232.1	88.4%	11.6%	240.0	84.9%	15.1%
Western Europe	858.8	89.1%	10.9%	947.7	89.9%	10.1%
Japan	161.7	44.6%	55.5%	163.9	54.4%	45.6%
Other Asian countries	120.0	83.8%	16.2%	108.8	77.1%	22.9%
Korea	11.8	33.9%	66.1%	11.5	33.9%	66.1%
Foreign multinationals in the United States, 1992						
All foreign MNCs	1222.7	85.3%	14.7%	1,809.9	79.8%	20.2%
European MNCs	534.5	88.9%	11.1%	752.7	80.6%	19.4%
Japanese MNCs	334.8	90.9%	9.1%	458.5	87.1%	12.9%
Other Asian MNCs	22.4	88.4%	11.6%	34.8	99.7%	0.3%
Korean MNCs	9.5	89.5%	10.5%	8.0	88.7%	11.3%
Japanese multinationals abroad, 1992						
Worldwide	633.2	80.1%	19.9%	88.1	69.9%	30.1%
North America	268.8	86.9%	13.1%	43.3	83.6%	16.4%
Western Europe	178.7	77.4%	22.6%	16.6	74.7%	25.3%
Asia	124.7	69.2%	30.8%	15.5	53.6%	46.4%
Korean multinationals abroad, 1993						
Worldwide				5.6	79.9%	20.1%
North America				2.2	93.4%	6.6%
Western Europe				0.6	79.6%	20.4%
Asia				2.2	71.6%	28.4%

Sources: U.S. Commerce Department, Bureau of Economic Analysis, *U.S. Direct Investment Abroad: Operations of U.S. Parent Companies and their Foreign Affiliates, Preliminary 1992 Estimates* (Washington, DC: USGPO, June 1994), tables II.A.1 and III.A.1, n.p.; *U.S. Direct Investment Abroad: 1992 Benchmark Survey, Preliminary Results* (Washington, DC: USGPO, August 1994), tables A-2 and N-4, n.p.; Japan, Ministry of International Trade and Industry, Industrial Policy Bureau, International Business Affairs Division, *The Fifth Comprehensive Survey of Foreign Investment Statistics [Dai go-kai wagakuni kigyo no kaigai jigyo katsudo]* (Tokyo: MITI, 1994), tables 2-9 and 4-2, pp. 134, 481; Bank of Korea, Foreign Exchange Department, *Overseas Direct Investment Statistics Yearbook: 1994* (Seoul: BOK, 1994), table 11.4, pp. 70–71.

[a]Majority foreign-owned subsidiaries.
[b]Minority foreign-owned subsidiaries and equal partnership (50:50) joint ventures.
[c]Capital for Japanese multinationals abroad; investment for Korean multinationals abroad.

comprehensive data are available), Japanese multinationals reported to Japan's Ministry of International Trade and Industry (MITI) that majority-owned subsidiaries accounted for over two thirds of the capital invested in their subsidiaries abroad (see table 3.3). As a result of that investment, Japanese multinationals reported that their majority subsidiaries contributed four fifths of their foreign sales—a share roughly comparable to sales reported by the majority subsidiaries of American multinationals.[22]

Korean and other Asian multinationals report a similar preference for majority ownership. For example, in the United States (the one country where comparable data are available, reported in table 3.3), they all report that majority-owned subsidiaries contributed nearly nine tenths of their sales and accounted for nearly all of their assets. Moreover, this preference for majority ownership seems to have strengthened over time. Majority Korean-owned subsidiaries, for example, accounted for just over half (56 percent) of all Korean investments abroad as recently as 1987.[23] But by 1993 (the most recent year for which data are available) Korean multinationals reported to the Bank of Korea that majority Korean-owned subsidiaries accounted for nearly four fifths of their net investments abroad—a share comparable to that reported by American and Japanese multinationals. As a result, Korean and other Asian (principally ethnic Chinese) multinationals have become indistinguishable from their American and Japanese counterparts in the shared pursuit of majority ownership in foreign subsidiaries.

For all of these multinationals, however, the incidence of majority ownership varies across industries, and especially across the value-added chain. On the extremes of that chain, subsidiaries engaged principally in overseas distribution generally evidence a larger proportion of foreign shareholdings than do those subsidiaries engaged principally in natural-resource extraction abroad. As a result, American and Japanese multinationals report that their majority mining or petroleum subsidiaries account for below-average investments and sales, while their majority-owned manufacturers and especially wholesalers are above average.[24] Such variation within and across industries reflects, in part, differences in financial (and other operational) risks, especially since average investments are typically lower in downstream wholesaling than, say, in upstream mining or refining, where greater risks may be shared with joint-venture partners. Moreover, variations in ownership patterns also reflect differences in a multinational's need for managerial control, for (as we shall see) downstream wholesaling is often tightly linked to intrafirm trade between multinational parents and their foreign subsidiaries.

Moreover, within any one of these sectors (say, manufacturing), additional variation can be found, reflecting important differences in firm-specific assets and industrial structures. In textiles, for example, Japanese manufacturers often teamed up with Japanese trading companies (*sogo shosha*), which could claim extensive trading experience across Asia. By 1974, at least three such sogo shosha—C. Itoh, Marubeni, and Mitsui—had invested aggressively in Asian textiles, typically through multiparty joint ventures with Japanese manufacturers.[25] Moreover, while establishing these subsidiaries, Japanese trading companies showed particular biases reflecting longer-term structural relationships between traders and manufacturers. C. Itoh and Marubeni spread their investments among Japan's three largest textile manufacturers (Toray, Teijin, and Toyobo); Mitsui concentrated its investments in Toray alone. By concentrating their investments in this way, and by teaming manufacturers with traders in a single joint venture, Japanese multinationals could ensure majority Japanese shareholdings.

Yet, while sogo shosha often proved crucial to Japanese investments in Asian textiles, they remained notably absent from electronics and most other industries—where joint ventures with local partners also proved of less value.[26] For example, during the 1970s, the median Japanese equity holding in Asian textiles was 51 percent; meanwhile, in electronics, Japanese shareholdings reached figures as high as 66 percent, the industrywide average at that time. As we shall see, electronics and other differentiated products, especially those requiring after-sales service, often require producers to integrate vertically from production to distribution, prompting little demand for the commodity-trading expertise of Japanese trading companies or the host-market expertise of local partners.

In addition, variations in shareholding patterns also reflect wide differences in the government policies prevailing across host countries. For example, the incidence of capital controls is generally lower in industrialized North America than in the European Union (EU), and lower in these two regions than in Asia. As a result, American and Japanese multinationals report that the incidence of majority foreign ownership is generally higher in North America than in Western Europe, and higher in the EU than in Asia (see table 3.3). Moreover, within these regions, the incidence of majority shareholdings varies widely across countries.[27] In Asia, for example, Hong Kong and Singapore have the highest incidence of majority foreign ownership. Given a multinational's strong preference for majority ownership, plus the several locational advantages of Hong Kong and Singapore, both economies (as we saw earlier) ranked among the top three investment destinations for American and Japanese multinationals in Asia (see table 3.1).

By contrast, India lost its early postwar ranking among the top Asian destinations for American multinationals in part because domestic capital controls severely limited both the inflow of FDI and the subsequent level of foreign ownership.[28] As a result, as recently as 1992, majority U.S.–owned subsidiaries accounted for less than one quarter of either the sales or the assets of all U.S.–affiliated companies operating in India,[29] up only slightly from one fifth of total sales and assets nearly two decades earlier, in 1977.[30] Similarly, in Korea, limited investments in majority U.S.–owned subsidiaries generated barely a third of the sales recorded by all American multinationals operating there, up from one fifth back in 1977. As a result, both countries have come to attract very little new FDI from either American or Japanese multinationals; to reverse this trend, both countries have begun to relax their capital controls as part of a larger liberalization of their national economies.

Yet, long after capital liberalization, Japan illustrates the extreme impact of a long legacy of capital controls on foreign ownership patterns.[31] Specifically, in Japan, limited investments in majority U.S.–owned subsidiaries still generated less than half of the sales recorded by all American multinationals as recently as 1992 (see table 3.3), more than a decade after formal liberalization. The remainder, accounting for most multinational sales in Japan, still came from minority U.S. affiliates, even though the relative position of these minority affiliates had actually declined over the previous decade, thanks in large part to the liberalization of capital controls. Indeed, with such a great preponderance of minority affiliates, Japan actually has more in common with newly industrializing Korea and developing India than with most other Asian countries, which on this measure have more in common with the several countries of North America and Western Europe.

Sales: Foreign Investment versus International Trade

After securing majority ownership and managerial control, multinationals often employ their foreign subsidiaries to sell in overseas markets far more than they and other exporters at home ship to these same markets. As a practical matter, pressures to increase foreign sales through direct investment abroad, and not just through international trade alone, increase when any of several conditions arise: when foreign governments severely constrain or credibly threaten to limit imports, when global competitors derive significant cost and other country-specific advantages from their overseas location, when indigenous buyers in large markets demand closer relations with their foreign suppliers, and when foreign exporters seek to hedge against exchange-rate risks by matching both revenues and costs in the same currency. Otherwise, multinationals will continue to supply offshore markets through international trade. Thus, the strategic choice is often viewed simply (and, as we shall see, somewhat incorrectly) as one between foreign investment and international trade.

For the Americans, the predominance of foreign sales derived from FDI rather than from international trade is not new.[32] As early as 1957, the foreign (largely majority U.S.–owned) subsidiaries of American multinationals reported total overseas sales at twice the value of total U.S. exports.[33] A decade later, by 1966, the combined foreign sales of these majority U.S. subsidiaries had risen to represent three times the value of all U.S. exports.[34] Subsequently, that 3:1 ratio of foreign sales to U.S. exports has remained largely unaltered. In fact, during 1992, American multinationals continued to sell nearly three times as much overseas through their majority subsidiaries than the United States exported to the world (see table 3.4)—further testimony to the fact that U.S. FDI continues to carry international competition well beyond cross-border trade.

Similarly, Japanese corporations have also come to generate more of their overseas sales through foreign investment rather than through international trade. But for the Japanese, this evolution is of very recent origin, reflecting their prolonged status as traders rather than investors. In fact, as late as 1977, Japanese subsidiaries reported total foreign sales to be roughly equivalent to Japanese exports worldwide.[35] But by 1992, following a decade of rapid growth in Japanese FDI abroad, Japanese subsidiaries (most of which were majority Japanese-owned) reported foreign sales nearly two times larger than all Japanese exports worldwide (see table 3.4). Thus, beginning in the 1980s and continuing into the 1990s, Japanese multinationals have begun to follow the lead of their American counterparts by generating more overseas sales through foreign investment than through international trade.

For both the Americans and the Japanese, the relative mix of overseas sales generated either by foreign investment or international trade again varies widely across regions and industries. On one extreme is Western Europe, where both the majority subsidiaries of American and Japanese multinationals record above-average sales. In fact, during 1992, the majority U.S.–owned subsidiaries sold in Europe over six times more than did all U.S.–based exporters (see table 3.4). Leading the way here during 1992 were U.S. automakers and component suppliers, who sold over 20 times more through majority subsidiaries operating in the European Community (EC) than they did through U.S. exports to the EC.[36] By comparison, Japanese automakers lagged behind their U.S. counterparts, as did most of Japanese industry. Consequently, Japanese subsidiaries in Europe sold three times more than did all Japan-based exporters—well above their worldwide average, but half the comparable ratio reported by the Americans (see table 3.4).

Table 3.4 The Ratio of Foreign Sales by Multinational Subsidiaries to U.S. and Japanese Trade, 1992 ($ billions)

	All countries	North America	EC	Japan	Other Asia	Korea
Ratio of U.S. subsidiaries' sales abroad to U.S. exports, 1992[a]						
Foreign sales by majority U.S. subsidiaries (A)	1,298.5	205.2	678.7	72.1	100.6	4.0
U.S. exports (B)	448.2	131.2	103.0	47.8	79.1	14.6
Ratio of sales to exports (A/B)	2.9	1.6	6.6	1.5	1.3	0.3
Ratio of foreign affiliates' sales in the United States to U.S. imports[b]						
U.S. sales by majority foreign subsidiaries (A)	1,043.1		475.2	304.4	19.7	8.5
U.S. imports (B)	532.7		94.0	97.4	135.7	16.1
Ratio of sales to imports (A/B)	2.0		5.1	3.1	0.1	0.5
Ratio of Japanese affiliates' sales abroad to Japanese exports[c]						
Foreign sales by Japanese affiliates (A)	633.2	268.8	178.7		124.7	
Japanese exports (B)	340.0	107.6	62.9		117.6	
Ratio of sales to exports (A/B)	1.9	2.5	3.0		1.1	

Sources: U.S. Commerce Department, Bureau of Economic Analysis, *U.S. Direct Investment Abroad: Operations of U.S. Parent Companies and Their Foreign Affiliates, Preliminary 1992 Estimates* (Washington, DC: USGPO, June 1994), table III.E.3, n.p.; *Foreign Direct Investment in the United States: 1992 Benchmark Survey, Preliminary Results* (Washington, DC: USGPO, August 1994), table E-4, n.p.; International Trade Administration, Office of Trade and Investment Analysis, *U.S. Foreign Trade Highlights: 1993* (Washington, DC: USGPO, July 1994), tables 14 and 15, pp. 34–41; Japan, Ministry of International Trade and Industry, Industrial Policy Bureau, International Business Affairs Division, *The Fifth Comprehensive Survey of Foreign Investment Statistics [Dai go-kai wagakuni kigyo no kaigai jigyo katsudo]* (Tokyo: MITI, 1994), table 2-25, pp. 188–199; International Monetary Fund, *Direction of Trade Statistics Yearbook: 1993* (Washington, DC: IMF, 1993), pp. 240-242.

[a]Location of subsidiaries/destination of exports.
[b]National origin of subsidiaries/source of imports.
[c]Location of sales/destination of exports.

Moreover, for the Japanese, this 3:1 ratio was somewhat new, in marked contrast to the Americans, who can trace their quite stable 6:1 ratio back at least to the mid-1960s.[37] By then, several factors combined to attract the foreign investments of American and, later, Japanese multinationals to Europe: the growth in European demand for sophisticated products already available in the United States and Japan, the erection of common EC barriers to U.S. and Japanese exports of these products, the reduction of comparable barriers to internal EC trade of these products, the emergence of scale economies in the production and distribution of these products, and the exertion of formidable pressures by both strong European buyers and powerful European competitors.

These same pressures have also pulled European and, more recently, Japanese multinationals to the United States. Among the first to respond, European subsidiaries in the United States during 1992 sold over five times more than did European exporters (see table 3.4)—thus approaching the ratio of foreign sales to exports recorded by the Americans in Europe for over 30 years. But for the Europeans, that 5:1 ratio has lagged behind that of the Americans by at least a couple of decades. By 1974, for example, European subsidiaries sold three times more in the United States than did European-based exporters.[38] Like the Europeans then, so too the Japanese by 1992, reported that their majority subsidiaries in the United States sold over three times more than did Japanese exporters (see table 3.4). For the Japanese, this ratio of U.S. sales to exports was nearly double their worldwide average and was of very recent origin: just five years earlier, in 1987, the ratio of foreign sales to international trade was barely over 2:1.[39] By increasing the ratio of foreign sales to national exports, Japanese corporations are following a similar evolutionary path to that charted earlier by European multinationals in America and by American multinationals in Europe.

Ranked well behind both the Japanese and (especially) the Europeans are Korean and other Asian multinationals. For example, in 1992, majority Korean subsidiaries operating in the United States reported U.S. sales with half the value recorded then by all U.S. imports from Korea (see table 3.4)—up from less than 40 percent of the value just five years earlier, in 1987.[40] During those five years, the nominal value of U.S. imports from Korea remained roughly constant, while the corresponding value of Korean FDI in the United States nearly tripled.[41] As a result, the recent growth of U.S. sales generated by majority Korean subsidiaries in the United States outpaced comparable sales generated by Korean exports. In comparison with the Koreans, however, other Asian multinationals still remain far more dependent on international trade to generate their U.S. sales. By this measure, then, Korean multinationals are much further advanced than other Asian multinationals in their evolution along the same path charted earlier by European and Japanese multinationals in the United States.

Extending that same evolutionary path back to Asia, however, has been difficult. To understand why, consider the fate of foreign subsidiaries in Japan. There, by 1992, majority U.S. subsidiaries fared only slightly better than did U.S.–based exporters (see table 3.4); similarly, European multinationals also reported low levels of foreign sales to match an equally low level of exports.[42] Nevertheless, these figures represented a modest improvement over the previous decade. In 1982, Japanese sales by majority U.S. subsidiaries were nearly identical to those of U.S.–based exporters.[43] Specifically, in Japan, several factors help to account for such limited market access.[44] Early on, import protection combined with capital controls both to limit overall FDI inflows and to concentrate those inflows in minority foreign-owned affiliates. This legacy, however, has begun to change with trade and capital liberalization—but only slowly, since liberalization came well after fresh outflows of U.S. FDI reached their postwar high (during the late 1960s and early 1970s). Subsequently, fresh outflows of U.S. FDI actually fell off, to be replaced by reinvested earnings in existing subsidiaries.[45] But without investment earnings to reinvest, American multinationals soon realized that Japanese industrial organization had come to replace Japanese government policies as the principal barrier to market access in Japan. As a result, American and European multinationals have moved at a slower pace in Japan as they progress along an evolutionary path charted earlier by them—and later followed by Japanese multinationals—in other industrialized countries.

Meanwhile, elsewhere in Asia, progress on that same evolutionary path has also proved difficult not only for American multinationals but also for the Japanese. Specifically, both reported in 1992 that foreign sales generated through foreign investment were slightly larger those generated through international trade (see table 3.4). Moreover, the ratio of subsidiaries' sales to international trade has actually *declined* over the past decade, at least for the Americans. In 1982, foreign sales by majority U.S. subsidiaries in Asia were actually twice the value of all U.S. exports to that region,[46] not near the parity reported in 1992 (see table 3.4). It seems that trade and capital liberalization over the past decade in Asia had a differential impact on the Americans, favoring U.S. exports more immediately than U.S. FDI. Between 1982 and 1992, the value of U.S. exports to Asia actually tripled, while the value of foreign sales by majority U.S. subsidiaries in Asia only doubled. By contrast, for the Japanese, subsidiaries' sales and exports both grew fourfold in Asia between 1980 and 1992,[47] leaving the ratio of subsidiaries' sales to exports roughly comparable. As a result of these different changes, Asia has little in common with the more advanced market—not just in North America and Western Europe, but also Japan—where the historical evolution of both American and Japanese multinationals favors foreign investment over international trade as the preferred means for generating foreign sales.

However, the relative mix of overseas sales generated either by foreign investment or international trade varies widely across the region. In Korea, for example, 1992 sales by majority U.S. subsidiaries still fail to equal U.S. exports there, given the limited value of U.S. FDI in that country. By contrast, in Singapore, the second largest Asian host to U.S. FDI, the sales of majority U.S. subsidiaries are three times larger than U.S. exports there[48]—roughly the same ratio recorded by the Japanese in both North America and Western Europe (see table 3.4). Between the extremes represented by Singapore and Korea, however, the rest of Asia looks more like Japan, at least when measured by the near parity in foreign sales generated by both U.S. investors and U.S. exporters operating across the region.

Compared to either the Americans or the Japanese in Asia, Korean multinationals seem much less reliant on foreign investment, and far more reliant on international trade, to generate their Asian sales. In this region, Japan, Hong Kong, and Singapore are Korea's three largest export markets. Of these, neither Hong Kong nor Singapore ranked among the top 10 hosts for Korean FDI in 1993. Only Japan ranked among the top five hosts, but over two thirds of all Korean FDI there was concentrated in real estate,[49] with little obvious impact on trade. Most of the remaining Korean FDI in Japan was concentrated in the wholesale sector, where it presumably did provide limited sales support for Korean exports. Elsewhere in Asia, however, Korean FDI was concentrated not in downstream exports markets but rather in geographic locations—notably Indonesia and China—where FDI in offshore manufacturing and natural-resource extraction serve as potential sources of upstream supply for markets back home and in third countries.

Value-Added: Offshore Production versus Overseas Distribution

To generate their foreign sales, multinational corporations often invest in majority-owned subsidiaries that produce offshore goods and services that are then supplied to markets both abroad and at home. In addition to the more general pressures promoting FDI already outlined, that investment is more likely to establish offshore production when national governments not only limit imports but also promote exports; when factor costs, relative productivity, and other location-specific advantages figure prominently in global competition; and when erstwhile exporters can significantly reduce their exchange rate risks by matching more of their costs in the same currency as their revenues. Otherwise, multinationals will continue to supply offshore markets through international trade, often supplemented by direct investments in overseas distribution. Such distribution is especially important in industries wherein multinationals derive distinct competitive advantages by establishing dedicated sales channels and by offering more after-sales service.

The Americans have been quick to respond to the pressures for offshore production. At least as early as 1957, and continuing for more than three decades,[50] the value of offshore production by American multinationals was nearly twice the value of U.S. manufactured exports (see table 3.4). The Americans concentrated most of their foreign manufacturing in advanced markets, especially in the EC, where during 1992 majority U.S.–owned manufacturing subsidiaries generated sales over four times larger than U.S.–based manufacturers exported to the EC (see table 3.4). To illustrate an extreme case, consider how American automakers and parts suppliers generate their European sales. During 1990, for example, U.S. auto exports (including parts and components) to the EC totaled roughly $3 billion; compare this sum to the sales generated both in local host markets ($37 billion) and in nearby regional markets ($34 billion) by the EC plants of U.S. automakers.[51] For American corporations, then, direct investment in offshore production has become their principal strategy for gaining and maintaining market access in the EC.

Like the Americans in the EC, the Europeans in the United States have come to employ direct investment in offshore production as their principal strategy for gaining and maintaining market access. But their movement is of more recent origin. As late as 1974, the value of U.S. production by European multinationals roughly equaled U.S. imports of European manufactured goods.[52] (Even when we add to this figure the estimated value of additional assembly operations by European subsidiaries engaged principally in U.S. wholesaling, the total value of local production probably does exceed all U.S. imports from Europe.) Still, such offshore manufacturing remained well below comparable production by American multinationals in Europe. However, over the next two decades, the Europeans moved to cut this difference in half, so that by 1992 their manufacturing subsidiaries in the United States actually reported U.S. sales nearly 2.5 times larger than U.S. imports of European manufactured goods (see table 3.5). As a result, both American and European multinationals have generally managed to produce and sell many more manufactured goods in each other's home market than they and other national exporters shipped across the Atlantic.

In contrast to both the Americans and the Europeans, Japanese multinationals have continued to pursue a very different offshore-manufacturing strategy, one that still lags behind Japanese exports of manufactured goods. As recently as 1992, for example, foreign sales resulting from offshore production by Japanese subsidiaries in North America and the EC were less than three quarters the total value of Japanese manufactured exports to these markets (see table 3.5). Even when we add to these local sales the assembly operations of Japanese subsidiaries engaged principally in overseas distribution, the total value of Japanese production in America and Europe still barely equals U.S. or European imports of manufactured goods from Japan. For the Japanese, however, this low ratio of foreign production to international trade actually represented a significant *increase* in offshore manufacturing. Indeed, less than two decades earlier (in 1977), Japanese manufacturers and (to a much lesser extent) Japanese trading companies had reported exports from home four times larger than the worldwide production recorded by Japanese subsidiaries abroad.[53] Yet, despite such growth, these Japanese subsidiaries had little in common either with American multinationals in Europe or with EC multinationals in the United States.

Instead, the Japanese in America and Europe share more in common with the Americans and Europeans in Japan. There, as recently as 1992, majority U.S.–owned manufacturing subsidiaries recorded foreign sales roughly equal in value to U.S. manufactured exports there (see table 3.5). The Americans, of course, are not alone in their failure to implement the same offshore production strategy that served them so well in other industrialized countries. To the contrary, European multinationals also evidence the same low level of Japanese production to match their limited exports to Japan.[54] Nevertheless, for foreign multinationals in Japan, these 1992 ratios represented a significant improvement from just a decade earlier. In 1982, for example, majority U.S.–owned manufacturing subsidiaries recorded foreign sales roughly half the value of U.S. manufactured exports there.[55] Subsequently, even as U.S. manufactured exports to Japan grew, the Japanese sales of U.S. manufacturers operating majority subsidiaries in Japan grew even faster. This is the most obvious impact in Japan of increased U.S. FDI in majority subsidiaries, an increase made easier by the liberalization of Japanese capital controls. With such growth in local production, American (and European) multinationals have only recently begun to follow in Japan an evolutionary path they charted much earlier in North America and Western Europe.

Progress along that evolutionary path has advanced less quickly elsewhere in Asia, the one region where both American and Japanese multinationals do have much in common. Specifically, both rely more on international trade than offshore production to generate sales in that region. In fact, majority U.S. subsidiaries manufacturing in Asia reported 1992 sales roughly three fifths the value of all U.S. manufactured exports to that region (see table 3.5), just slightly more than

Table 3.5 Offshore Production, Manufactured Exports, and Overseas Distribution by American, European, and Asian Multinationals, 1992 ($ billions)

	All countries	All MNCs	North America	EC	Japan	Other Asia	Korea
American multinationals abroad[a]							
Sales by majority U.S. subsidiaries engaged principally in manufacturing	629.5		120.6	369.8	28.4	36.6	
U.S. exports of manufactured goods	368.5		115.4	87.1	30.3	59.9	
Sales by majority U.S. subsidiaries engaged principally in wholesaling	242.2		22.8	124.1	19.5	21.7	
Foreign multinationals in the United States[b]							
Sales by foreign affiliates engaged principally in U.S. manufacturing		427.0		217.6	68.3	6.4	1.2
U.S. imports of manufactured goods		434.3		84.1	95.8	112.4	16.3
Sales by foreign affiliates engaged principally in U.S. wholesaling		374.0		112.0	214.2	12.4	8.1
Japanese multinationals abroad[c]							
Sales by Japanese affiliates principally engaged in foreign manufacturing	201.3		80.7	42.1		63.7	
Japanese exports of manufactured goods	340.0		107.6	62.9		117.6	
Sales by Japanese affiliates principally engaged in foreign wholesaling	391.0		173.4	125.7		54.8	

Sources: U.S. Commerce Department, Bureau of Economic Analysis, *U.S. Direct Investment Abroad: Operations of U.S. Parent Companies and Their Foreign Affiliates, Preliminary 1992 Estimates* (Washington, DC: USGPO, June 1994), table III.E.3, n.p.; *Foreign Direct Investment in the United States: 1992 Benchmark Survey, Preliminary Results* (Washington, DC: USGPO, August 1994), table E-4, n.p.; International Trade Administration, Office of Trade and Investment Analysis, *U.S. Foreign Trade Highlights: 1993* (Washington, DC: USGPO, July 1994), tables 14 and 15, pp. 34–41; Japan, Ministry of International Trade and Industry, Industrial Policy Bureau, International Business Affairs Division, *The Fifth Comprehensive Survey of Foreign Investment Statistics [Dai go-kai wagakuni kigyo no kaigai jigyo katsudo]* (Tokyo: MITI, 1994), table 2–25, pp. 188–199; International Monetary Fund, *Direction of Trade Statistics Yearbook: 1993* (Washington, DC: IMF, 1993), pp. 240–242.

[a]Location of subsidiaries/destination of exports.
[b]National origin of subsidiaries/source of imports.
[c]Location of sales/destination of exports.

the comparable ratio for the Japanese. Moreover, these ratios had improved only marginally over the last decade, at least for the Americans. Between 1982 and 1992, both U.S. manufactured exports to Asia and sales by majority U.S. manufacturing subsidiaries had both more than tripled.[56] However, for the Japanese, the rapid rise of Japanese FDI in Asian manufacturing had significantly altered the ratio of offshore production to manufactured trade. Between 1980 and 1992, even as Japanese exports to Asia grew fourfold, the offshore production of Japanese subsidiaries in the region grew sixfold.[57] Yet, even though American and Japanese multinationals had both increased their FDI in Asian manufacturing during the 1980s, the resulting production from that investment had still not overtaken manufactured exports as the principal source of supply.

Moreover, wide variation in the ratio of local production to manufactured trade can be also discerned across countries. On one extreme is Singapore where, as recently as 1982, U.S. exports were much larger than total sales by U.S. subsidiaries manufacturing there. But a decade of ever increasing FDI by American manufacturers in Singapore dramatically reversed that ratio, so that by 1992 the majority subsidiaries of these U.S. manufacturers reported sales from local production with a total value greater than all U.S. manufactured exports to Singapore.[58] By contrast, on the other extreme is India. There, the value of local production by majority U.S. subsidiaries remained well below the value of otherwise small U.S. exports to India—and the value of that local production had actually *declined* over the prior decade, despite a modest increase in U.S. trade. In short, while Singapore has emerged as a major offshore production site for American (and Japanese) multinationals, India has not—and most of the rest of Asia falls between these two extremes.

In addition to offshore production, Asia has also emerged as an important depot for overseas distribution—the upstream buying and downstream selling of both goods and services. Here, again, both American and Japanese multinationals have much in common. For both, offshore production exceeds overseas distribution in Asia. But for the Americans, Asia represents the one region where overseas distribution is not dwarfed by offshore production—while for the Japanese, Asia is the one region where offshore production actually exceeds overseas distribution. And for both, Hong Kong is a major distribution center, given the concentration there of FDI in wholesaling and other trade-related services. As a result of that U.S. FDI, for example, U.S. wholesalers in Hong Kong report foreign sales over twice as large as those U.S. manufacturers report there.[59] A decade earlier, in 1982, Singapore could also claim to be a distribution center for American multinationals, given the rough parity in sales there between overseas distribution and offshore production,[60] but by 1992 sales by U.S. distributors were barely one third the size of sales by U.S. manufacturers.[61] In both Hong and Singapore, then, we see the recent effects of economic specialization, emphasizing in these two cases either offshore manufacturing or overseas distribution.

Such specialization, of course, is not limited to countries but is also visible at the company level, where dedicated trading companies may differentiate themselves from more traditional manufacturers. Among the Japanese, for example, we have already seen that sogo shosha have often teamed up with textile manufacturers to form joint ventures in Asia. In all of these joint ventures, Japanese trading companies considered their Asian investments as growing markets for trade arbitrage, principally serving as purchasing agents authorized to buy commodities upstream but also serving as marketing agents authorized to sell commodities downstream.[62] However, the same relationship did not hold in electronics, automobiles, and several other industries where, as I have also noted, sogo shosha did not prove crucial to Japanese FDI in Asia.[63] Outside of textiles, then, Japanese manufacturers often established dedicated sales channels and after-sales service networks to aid their overseas distribution of goods produced at home and abroad.

By investing aggressively in overseas distribution, Japanese multinationals are following a strategy they have long pursued in Japan, where they tightly control their own proprietary distribution systems.[64] Such control over distribution channels has severely constrained foreigners' access to the Japanese market.[65] Seeking to overcome such entry barriers in Japan, American (and European) multinationals have aggressively invested in majority subsidiaries engaged principally in Japanese distribution; in this way, they have pursued an unusual strategy, one without parallel for Americans operating in other industrialized countries (see table 3.5).

By contrast, in these more advanced markets, overseas distribution has been far more central than offshore production to the foreign-investment strategies of Japanese multinationals, certainly when compared to their American counterparts (see table 3.5). In both North America and Western Europe—but not in Asia—foreign sales by Japanese-owned wholesalers are between two and three times larger than the foreign sales of Japanese-owned manufacturers. By contrast, in all three of these regions, majority U.S.–owned manufacturers report foreign sales larger than those generated by majority U.S.–owned distributors. Indeed, in North America and Western Europe, these U.S. manufacturers sell three to five times more than do U.S. distributors also operating there. So, in marked contrast to the Americans, Japanese multinationals have invested far more aggressively in wholesaling subsidiaries in order to lower the transaction and information costs associated with upstream purchasing and downstream marketing.

Far more like the Japanese were the Koreans, who generated eight times more U.S. sales during 1992 through their direct investments in U.S. wholesaling than through their FDI in U.S. manufacturing—far in excess of other Asian multinationals (see table 3.5). To generate these sales, nearly half of all Korean FDI in the United States is invested in U.S. retail and wholesale trade, far more than the one fifth invested in manufacturing. Similarly, in Japan, retail and wholesale trade is the second largest category (falling well behind real estate) of otherwise limited Korean investments there, well ahead of minuscule investments in Japanese manufacturing.[66] By contrast, elsewhere in Asia, Korean manufacturing investments dwarf those in retail and wholesale trade, in a sharp departure from Japanese strategy across that region. In short, the striking similarities evidenced by both Japanese and Korean multinationals operating in the United States do not carry over to Asia.

Markets: Local versus Export Markets

In general, foreign sales come from three sources: the host-country market of the foreign subsidiary, the home-country market of that subsidiary's parent, and third-country markets typically in close geographic proximity to the host country.

Choices among these three are determined by a wide range of variables, including the following: market size and growth prospects, market access resulting from government policies, and competitor behavior. Given these relative weightings, as a practical matter, multinational corporations typically generate most of their foreign sales in the local market or one of two export markets (either at home or in third countries) but seldom spread equally between two or among all three. Indeed, until quite recently, multinationals have long focused almost exclusively on the local market hosting their foreign direct investments.

For the Americans, at least during the 1950s and 1960s, these local markets accounted for three quarters of all foreign sales generated abroad by majority U.S. subsidiaries.[67] Subsequently, beginning in the late 1970s and continuing through the 1980s, that share gradually declined,[68] so that it reached two thirds of total foreign sales worldwide by 1992 (see table 3.6). That same year, Japanese multinationals worldwide also reported a comparable sales contribution by local host-country markets (see table 3.6). For the Americans as well as the Japanese, such a contribution had also declined over the last two decades; in the early 1970s, for example, local markets also contributed three quarters of total foreign sales by Japanese subsidiaries abroad.[69] Thus, for both the Americans and the Japanese, local markets hosting their FDI remain the principal sources of multinational sales globally. And they have reached this comparable outcome by again evolving in a common direction, marked this time by a general decline in the relative importance of local markets to generate foreign sales.

Of course, the relative importance of the host-country market in generating a multinational's foreign sales varies widely across countries and regions. On one extreme are the examples of the United States and Japan. For example, European and Japanese multinationals both reported in 1992 that the local U.S. market consumed well over 85 percent of their subsidiaries' total U.S. sales.[70] Consequently, exports back home and to third countries have remained quite small. Similarly, in Japan, American subsidiaries sold nearly 90 percent of their goods and services in the local market (see table 3.6)—a figure comparable to the local sales also generated there by European multinationals.[71] In short, the sheer size of the world's two largest markets continues to exert a powerful and common influence on the investment strategies of American, European, and Japanese multinationals.

In contrast to the United States and Japan, Western Europe offers both American and Japanese multinationals greater opportunities to generate sales not only in the local market hosting their investments but also in so-called third-country markets, typically located in close geographic proximity to the host country. Thanks in large part to the EU, exports to third countries contributed roughly a third of the total Western European sales recorded by both American and Japanese multinationals operating there (see table 3.6). Those shares were higher still in manufacturing, where third-country exports mostly to other EC members contributed nearly comparable shares—40 percent—of the total European sales recorded by American and Japanese multinationals engaged in production there. Such a percentage is well above both their global averages. U.S. manufacturing subsidiaries sold just over a quarter of their total foreign sales in third-country markets, compared to one sixth or so for their Japanese counterparts. Thus, the common pressures of regional integration are having a similar impact on both American and Japanese multinationals, and that impact varies across regions as well as across industrial sectors.

Table 3.6 The Destination of Foreign Sales, 1992

		Sales destination		
	$ billions	Local	Back to United States	Third markets
American multinationals abroad[a]				
All industries[a]				
Worldwide	1,298.5	65.9%	10.1%	24.0%
North America	205.2	71.3%	25.9%	2.8%
Western Europe	765.0	64.0%	3.8%	32.2%
Japan	72.1	89.0%	4.7%	6.3%
Other Asia	100.6	51.7%	19.5%	28.8%
Manufacturing only[a]				
Worldwide	629.6	58.7%	12.3%	29.0%
North America	120.5	59.5%	37.1%	3.4%
Western Europe	387.4	55.5%	3.7%	40.8%
Japan	28.4	84.2%	7.4%	8.4%
Other Asia				
Manufacturing total	36.6	37.4%	35.0%	27.6%
Electronics only	13.0	23.8%	47.7%	28.5%
Wholesaling only[a]				
Worldwide	242.2	71.1%	4.3%	24.6%
North America	22.8	88.2%	7.0%	4.8%
Western Europe	160.6	69.2%	2.1%	28.7%
Japan	19.5	88.2%	4.6%	7.2%
Other Asia	21.8	49.5%	17.9%	32.6%
Japanese multinationals abroad				
All industries				
Worldwide	633.2	66.3%	14.5%	19.2%
North America	268.8	78.4%	12.6%	9.0%
Western Europe	178.7	54.8%	8.4%	36.8%
East Asia	124.7	59.4%	21.8%	18.8%
Manufacturing only				
Worldwide	201.3	76.7%	6.3%	17.0%
North America	80.7	91.9%	2.8%	5.3%
Western Europe	42.1	55.7%	1.2%	43.1%
Other Asia				
Manufacturing total	63.7	66.1%	15.8%	18.1%
Electronics only	23.0	45.7%	27.2%	27.1%
Wholesaling only				
Worldwide	391.0	60.3%	19.4%	20.3%
North America	173.4	70.8%	18.0%	11.2%
Western Europe	129.7	54.4%	11.6%	33.0%
Asia	54.8	47.9%	31.2%	20.9%

Source: U.S. Commerce Department, Bureau of Economic Analysis, *U.S. Direct Investment Abroad: Operations of U.S. Parent Companies and Their Foreign Affiliates, Preliminary 1992 Estimates* (Washington, DC: USGPO, September 1992), table III.F.2, n.p.; *Foreign Direct Investment in the United States: 1992 Benchmark Survey, Preliminary Results* (Washington, DC: USGPO, August 1994), tables G-2 and G-24, n.p.; Japan, Ministry of International Trade and Industry, Industrial Policy Bureau, International Business Affairs Division, *The Fifth Comprehensive Survey of Foreign Investment Statistics* [*Dai go-kai wagakuni kigyo no kaigai jigyo katsudo*] (Tokyo: MITI, 1994), table 2-25, pp. 188–199.

[a]Data for majority U.S.–owned subsidiaries only.

But these same pressures are having a different impact in both North America and Asia. In North America, third-country sales by both American and Japanese multinationals remain small, especially in manufacturing. But in Asia, American multinationals lead the way in promoting intraregional trade. In both manufacturing and wholesaling, these third-country sales contributed nearly 30 percent of the total revenues generated across Asia by U.S. subsidiaries, well above comparable shares (less than 20 percent) generated by all Japanese subsidiaries operating in that region (see table 3.6). So, American and Japanese multinationals are following comparable export strategies regarding third-country markets in Western Europe and North America but not in Asia.

In addition to third-country exports, Asia also provides these multinationals with sizable—yet different—opportunities to export to their home markets (see table 3.6). Indeed, when combined across industries, both American and Japanese multinationals during 1992 generated roughly one fifth of their total Asian sales through exports back home. For the Japanese, this share is well above comparable sales generated by home-bound exports from their subsidiaries elsewhere in the world, whereas for the Americans, this share is just below comparable sales for their subsidiaries operating closer to home, in Canada and Mexico. As this comparison suggests, geography matters, with distance from the home country an important determinant of FDI-related trade.

But in Asia, the importance of the home country as an export market varies widely across industries and between multinationals (see table 3.6). For the Japanese, most of these home-bound shipments come from Asian subsidiaries engaged in the wholesale trade of local purchases exported to Japan; these Japanese-owned wholesalers accounted for twice as many exports to Japan as did Japanese manufacturing subsidiaries in Asia. For the Americans, by contrast, most home-bound shipments come from majority subsidiaries engaged in Asian manufacturing. These U.S. manufacturing subsidiaries generated 35 percent of their total Asian sales from exports to the U.S. market. This share is roughly comparable to that generated by U.S. manufacturing subsidiaries in both Canada and Mexico and is well over twice the share generated through exports back home by Japanese manufacturers operating in Asia. Once again, we see that American and Japanese manufacturers in Asia are following different export strategies, this time concerning their home markets.

Nowhere is the difference in market orientation between American and Japanese multinationals more apparent than in the manufacture of electronics (see table 3.6). In this industry, an American preoccupation with export markets at home has been matched by a Japanese preoccupation with the local host-country market. In fact, shipments back home to the United States accounted for nearly half of the total sales reported in 1992 by U.S. electronics subsidiaries in Asia, while their Japanese counterparts generated a roughly comparable share of their total sales in the local host-country market. In a similar juxtaposition, these same Japanese electronics subsidiaries in Asia generated roughly a quarter of their 1992 sales from exports to Japan—nearly the same share generated by their U.S. counterparts from sales in the local host-country market. Only in shipments to third-country markets, principally located elsewhere in Asia, did American and Japanese electronics manufacturers in Asia follow a common trade strategy, and thus generate comparable shares of their total sales.

More generally, then, Japanese multinationals in Asia are far more interested in the local market hosting their FDI than in exporting either to their home or to third-country markets. For example, Japanese manufacturing subsidiaries in Asia generated fully two thirds of their 1992 sales in the host-country market—nearly twice the comparable share recorded by American manufacturers. Indeed, the last time local markets generated such a sizable share of American MNCs' Asia sales was nearly three decades earlier when, in 1966, their majority subsidiaries reported that host-country markets contributed fully three quarters of their Asian sales. For the Americans at least, that earlier attention to local markets was a response to the import-substituting policies operating then across Asia.

But with the subsequent liberalization of these policies, and the movement toward more outward-oriented policies, Asia illustrates some of the most rapid decline in the relative importance of host-country markets in generating sales, especially for American multinationals. In fact, by 1977, the sales contribution of the local market in Asia had declined significantly, reaching two fifths of total Asian sales; nearly as much was now being exported to the United States, with the remainder shipped to third-country markets. By comparison, that same year, Japanese multinationals sold much less outside of the local market hosting their Asian investments. In fact, during 1977, that local host-country market accounted for fully three fifths of total foreign sales generated by all Japanese multinationals in Asia. Thus, for both the Americans and the Japanese, sharp differences in export strategies visible as early as 1977 were only accentuated by 1992.

The conclusion that American multinationals generate a greater proportion of their subsidiaries' sales in Asia from export markets strongly contradicts a popular argument advanced by at least one important school of Japanese scholars. These scholars have long argued that Japanese multinationals pursue investment strategies that are far more trade-enhancing than those favored by American multinationals.[72] For relevant data, these scholars focus on the 1970s and 1980s, and especially on Asia, the only region where both American and Japanese multinationals can claim long histories of direct investment. Yet, when we combine exports back home with exports to third countries, we reach a very different conclusion: for the last two decades, Japanese multinationals have been less reliant on international trade to generate their foreign subsidiaries' sales in Asia than have American multinationals.

Trade: Intracompany Shipments versus Arm's-Length

Much of the trade conducted by multinational corporations is shipped intracompany, among and between parents and their subsidiaries—a fact that has recently attracted the renewed attention of academic scholars.[73] For multinationals, such hierarchical trade ensures greater control over both upstream supplies and downstream markets than do more arm's-length transactions among unaffiliated buyers and suppliers. Intracompany trade also substantially lowers the high costs these arm's-length transactions normally impose on cross-border exchanges of the technological, marketing, and organizational assets necessary to compete successfully through foreign production and overseas distribution. As I argued already, only with majority ownership do multinationals exercise sufficient managerial control to dictate their subsidiaries' decisions about these exchanges; such control is far more circumscribed in minority affiliates. Empirically, intracompany trade seems especially prominent in auto and other industries wherein significant economies can be achieved through the integration and coordination of multiplant operations, or where additional advantages can be gained through after-sales service.

On one extreme, U.S. and Japan trade illustrate the growing predominance of intracompany shipments. Here, Japanese multinationals exercise unrivaled control over the two-way flow (see table 3.7). By 1992, in fact, over two thirds of all U.S. imports from Japan *and* over half of all U.S. exports to Japan were shipped intracompany, largely between the parents of Japanese multinationals and their (principally majority) subsidiaries in the United States. Among imports, for ex-

Table 3.7   U.S. Trade, by Intracompany and Arm's-Length Shipments, Across Regions and Countries, 1992

U.S. trade	Direction of trade	
	U.S. exports	U.S. imports
With the world		
Total value ($ billions) (A)	448.7	532.7
% by U.S. parents to/from majority U.S. subsidiaries worldwide (B)	22.1	16.0
% by all foreign affiliates in U.S. to/from their parents (C)	10.5	25.2
% intracompany (D) = (B) + (C)	32.6	41.2
% by all other, arm's length (E) = 100% – (D)	67.4	58.8
With the EC		
Total value ($ billions) (A)	122.6	110.7
% by U.S. parents to/from majority U.S. subsidiaries in the EC (B)	26.3	11.8
% by EC affiliates in U.S. to/from their parents (C)	8.4	34.2
% intracompany (D) = (B) + (C)	34.7	46.0
% by all other, arm's length (E) = 100% – (D)	65.3	54.0
With Japan		
Total value ($ billions) (A)	47.8	97.4
% by U.S. parents to/from majority U.S. subsidiaries in Japan (B)	15.5	2.1
% by Japanese affiliates in U.S. to/from their parents (C)	52.7	67.7
% intracompany (D) = (B) + (C)	68.2	69.7
% by all other, arm's length (E) = 100% – (D)	31.8	30.3
With Asia (outside Japan)		
Total value ($ billions) (A)	90.5	135.7
% by U.S. parents to/from majority U.S. subsidiaries in Asia (B)	9.3	11.1
% by Asian affiliates in U.S. to/from their parents (C)	5.6	6.8
% intracompany (D) = (B) + (C)	14.9	17.3
% by all other, arm's length (E) = 100% – (D)	85.1	82.2

Sources: U.S. Commerce Department, Bureau of Economic Analysis, *U.S. Direct Investment Abroad: Operations of U.S. Parent Companies and Their Foreign Affiliates, Preliminary 1992 Estimates* (Washington, DC: USGPO, June 1994), table III.H.1, n.p.; *Foreign Direct Investment in the United States: 1992 Benchmark Survey, Preliminary Results* (Washington, DC: USGPO, August 1994), table G-2, n.p.; International Trade Administration, Office of Trade and Investment Analysis, *US Foreign Trade Highlights: 1993* (Washington, DC: USGPO, July 1994), tables 6 and 7, pp. 17–24.

ample, the auto industry—cars, parts, and components—accounted for over a quarter of all Japanese shipments to the United States, most of which (over 80 percent) were shipped by Japanese automakers and parts suppliers directly to their U.S. subsidiaries.[74] Similarly, for U.S. exports to Japan, intracompany trade again predominates: shipments from Japanese subsidiaries in the United States back to their Japanese parents account for more than two thirds of all U.S. exports to Japan. Largely raw materials and agricultural products, these U.S. exports are then channeled by Japanese multinationals into their proprietary distribution channels at home. There, Japanese trading companies and manufacturers often enjoy lower information and transaction costs, as well as related advantages, than do more arm's-length U.S. exporters. For the Japanese, then, foreign direct investment has created the *principal* channels for two-way trade flows with the United States.

By contrast, American multinationals exercise no appreciable influence over U.S. bilateral trade with Japan. Here, limited U.S. FDI, and the concentration of that FDI in minority foreign-owned affiliates, serves as an especially high barrier in Japan to U.S. exports. Indeed, minority affiliates typically represent poor markets for national exports, even in those host countries where affiliates' sales are relatively large. For example, during 1992, U.S. exports to minority U.S. affiliates worldwide remained negligible—accounting for only 6 percent of all U.S. exports to U.S. multinationals abroad—even though minority affiliates contributed just under 20 percent of all U.S. multinational sales.[75] More specifically, in Japan, U.S. exports to minority U.S. affiliates during 1992 barely totaled $2.5 billion, much less than the $7 billion of U.S. exports shipped that same year to majority U.S. subsidiaries in Japan.[76] Yet these majority subsidiaries accounted for barely $72 billion of sales in Japan, well below the $90 billion in Japanese sales recorded by minority U.S. affiliates (calculated from table 3.7).

In short, because Japan has long hosted a disproportionately large share of minority U.S. affiliates, and because these affiliates generally refrain from purchasing U.S. exports, American multinationals in Japan have contributed a relatively small share of this bilateral trade. By contrast, for the Japanese, the higher incidence of majority subsidiaries in the United States actually has granted Japanese exports far greater access to the U.S. market than the Americans, through their limited investments concentrated in minority affiliates, have been able to secure in Japan.

In marked contrast to U.S.–Japan trade, U.S.–EC trade remains far more symmetrical—as do U.S.–EC investment flows—permitting neither American nor European multinationals to dominate these bilateral flows. As a result of these multinationals, in fact, intracompany trade contributed over two fifths of all U.S. imports from the EC (see table 3.7). Here again, autos figure prominently: they constitute the largest class of traded goods (accounting for 16 percent of U.S. imports from the EC), of which nearly 90 percent are shipped intracompany, by BMW and other EC automakers to their majority subsidiaries in the United States.[77] Indeed, as a general rule, the parents of EC multinationals are the largest suppliers of U.S. imports from Europe, with their (largely majority) subsidiaries in the United States the largest buyers.

Conversely, in U.S. exports to the EC, the parents of U.S. multinationals are the largest contributors, often through intracompany shipments to their majority subsidiaries in the EC. In such trade, U.S. auto exports remain small because U.S.

automakers manufacture in the EC most of what they sell there. In the absence of much auto trade, then, intracompany shipments to the EC accounted for just over a third of all U.S. exports to the EC (see table 3.7). Finally, what remains of U.S.– EC trade is shipped at arm's length, between unaffiliated exporters and importers. Such trade accounted for well over two thirds of all U.S. exports to Europe and over half of all U.S. imports from Europe (see table 3.7). Here again, MNCs play a prominent role; for example, the U.S. parents of American multinationals are major exporters to unaffiliated EC buyers, accounting for a full third of all U.S. exports to Europe.[78] In each of these ways, then, U.S.–EC trade more closely mimics U.S. trade with the world as a whole, in its relative mix of intracompany and arm's-length trade (see table 3.7).

If U.S.–EC trade more closely approximates average U.S. trade, with U.S.– Japan trade on one extreme dominated by intracompany shipments, then U.S. trade with the rest of Asia is on an opposite extreme, dominated by more arm's-length transactions. Such transactions, in fact, accounted during 1992 for well over four fifths of all U.S. exports to, and all U.S. imports from, Asia (outside Japan). Of course, American multinationals did play a role in that trade; for example, through shipments to unaffiliated buyers, their U.S. parents shipped roughly one quarter of all U.S. exports to Asia.[79] In addition, intracompany shipments between these U.S. parents and their Asian subsidiaries contributed another 10 percent to bilateral trade flows (see table 3.7). That limited contribution reflects the fact that during 1992 Asia outside Japan continued to account for a smaller proportion of all U.S. FDI (stocks) abroad than did, say, Western Europe.

Moreover, even within Asia, only a very few countries attracted U.S. FDI, especially investments in majority U.S. subsidiaries. Singapore ranks among the two largest hosts to U.S. FDI in Asia (outside Japan). And, as a result, in U.S. trade with Singapore, intracompany trade within American multinationals accounted for well over a quarter of all U.S. exports and nearly three fifths of all U.S. imports. By contrast, Korea has long restricted FDI inflows, especially in majority foreign-owned subsidiaries. And, as a result, in U.S trade with Korea, shipments between the parents and subsidiaries of American multinationals accounted for less than 2 percent of all U.S. exports and barely 4 percent of all U.S. imports. What remaining impact American multinationals had on U.S.–Korea trade was principally through shipments between U.S. parents and unaffiliated Korean buyers; for example, these arm's-length shipments accounted for nearly two fifths of all U.S. exports to Korea.[80] This paucity of U.S. intracompany trade, and the greater reliance by American multinationals on more arm's-length transactions, is reminiscent of U.S. trade with Japan. In Korea, as in Japan, limited U.S. FDI concentrated in minority U.S.–owned affiliates helps to account for this absence of U.S. intracompany trade.

Similarly, limited Asian FDI in the United States has also constrained intracompany trade between the parents and subsidiaries of Asian multinationals (see table 3.7). Only Korean multinationals have employed their limited FDI to exercise a disproportionate influence over their country's trade with the United States. For example, intracompany shipments between the parents and (largely majority-owned) subsidiaries of Korean multinationals during 1992 exceeded one quarter for all U.S. imports from Korea. This share was nearly equal to the average contribution of intracompany trade by foreign multinationals to all U.S. imports, and it was three times larger than what Asian multinationals generally contributed to U.S. imports from the region (see table 3.7). Even for U.S. exports to Korea, the relative contribution of intracompany shipments by Korean multinationals again exceeds that recorded by other Asian multinationals. During 1992, Korean subsidiaries in the United States shipped nearly one tenth of all U.S. exports back to their Korean parents. This share was twice the relative contribution recorded by shipments between American multinational parents and their majority subsidiaries in Korea, and it equaled the average contribution of intracompany trade by European multinationals to U.S. exports to Europe. Outside of Korea, however, the absence of significant two-way FDI flows between the United States and Asia (outside Japan) limits most intracompany transactions, leaving arm's-length trade to predominate.

Similarly, Japan's trade with the rest of Asia is dominated by arm's-length shipments. Nevertheless, during 1992, intracompany trade between the parents and subsidiaries of Japanese multinationals contributed over 15 percent of all Japanese exports to the region and nearly 23 percent of all Japanese imports—roughly twice comparable levels of intracompany trade recorded by American multinationals. Thus, in Asia, as in the rest of the world, Japanese multinationals continue to exercise a greater influence over Japan's bilateral trade than do American multinationals.

Implications for Corporate Strategy and Government Policy

Just as FDI has become integral to the Asian operations of MNCs, so it has also become critical to economic performance and, consequently, government policy across Asia. Of particular concern here is the complementarity between FDI and trade visible at both the microlevel of multinational corporations and the macrolevel of host economies. For both multinationals and their hosts, wide variation persists in this FDI-trade nexus, and that variation can be explained in part by persistent differences in government policy across Asia, and in part by persistent differences among multinationals operating from different home bases.

Corporate Strategy

What emerges from our comparative analysis of multinational corporations are two models of foreign investment and related trade: a trans-Atlantic model evidenced in the strategies and structures pursued by both American and European multinationals and a trans-Pacific model evidenced in the strategies and structures pursued by Japanese, Korean, and other Asian MNCs. Distinguishing these two models are persistent differences in the relationship between foreign investment and international trade (much of which is summarized in table 3.8). Namely, compared to American and European multinationals, Japanese and other Asian multinationals still sell more of their output in the host-country market than they do through exports to markets at home or in third countries; they continue to source more of their inputs from back home than from local or other third-country suppliers; and they more aggressively control this two-way trade of outputs and

Table 3.8   Home-Country Exports to Multinational Subsidiaries, as a Share of Subsidiaries' Sales, 1992 ($ billions)

	All countries	North America	EC	Japan	Other Asia
Ratio of U.S. subsidiaries' sales abroad to U.S. exports[a]					
Foreign sales by majority U.S. subsidiaries abroad (A)	1,298.5	205.2	678.7	72.1	100.6
U.S. exports to U.S. subsidiaries abroad (B)	114.1	52.5	32.1	7.8	9.5
U.S. exports to U.S. subsidiaries as a % of subsidiaries' sales (B/A)	8.8	25.6	4.7	10.8	9.4
Ratio of U.S. imports to foreign affiliates' sales in the U.S.[b]					
U.S. sales by foreign subsidiaries in the U.S. (A)	1,222.6		649.8	334.8	22.5
Home-country exports to foreign subsidiaries in the U.S. (B)	182.2		41.0	73.5	12.2
Home-country exports to foreign subsidiaries as a % of subsidiaries' sales (B/A)	14.9		6.3	22.0	54.2
Ratio of Japanese exports to Japanese affiliates' sales abroad[c]					
Foreign sales by Japanese affiliates abroad (A)	633.2	268.8	178.7		124.7
Japanese exports to Japanese affiliates abroad (B)	118.3	52.9	33.8		21.7
Japanese exports to Japanese affiliates as a % of affiliates' sales (B/A)	18.6	19.7	18.9		17.4

Sources: U.S. Commerce Department, Bureau of Economic Analysis, *U.S. Direct Investment Abroad: Operations of U.S. Parent Companies and Their Foreign Affiliates, Preliminary 1992 Estimates* (Washington, DC: USGPO, June 1994), table III.E.3, n.p.; *Foreign Direct Investment in the United States: 1992 Benchmark Survey, Preliminary Results* (Washington, DC: USGPO, August 1994), tables E-4 and G-30, n.p.; Japan, Ministry of International Trade and Industry, Industrial Policy Bureau, International Business Affairs Division, *The Fifth Comprehensive Survey of Foreign Investment Statistics [Dai go-kai wagakuni kigyo no kaigai jigyo katsudo]* (Tokyo: MITI, 1994), table 2-25, pp. 188–199.

[a]Location of subsidiaries/destination of exports.
[b]National origin of affiliates/source of imports.
[c]Location of affiliates/destination of exports.

inputs through intracompany shipments linking multinational parents and their foreign subsidiaries. These persistent differences cannot be dismissed easily as mere "vintage effects," vestigial remnants reflecting various stages in a multinational's evolution, for they persist over time. Nor can they be dismissed as the result of wide variation in the sectoral distribution or geographic location of these multinationals, for these differences persist in the same industrial sector and host economy. Rather, the persistence of these differences reflects important variation in the strategies and structures pursued by MNCs based in different countries.

Although sharp variation in the complex relationship between FDI and trade confirms the persistence of important differences among multinationals, other operational characteristics suggest a greater convergence in regional operations—as American, European, Japanese, and other Asian multinationals continue to move along an otherwise common evolutionary path. First, they all increasingly invest overseas in majority subsidiaries, all the more so when their investments are unimpeded by capital controls in the host country, and when their investments move down the value-added chain from extraction to manufacturing to wholesaling. Second, through these majority subsidiaries, they increasingly generate a greater proportion of their foreign sales through direct investments in markets overseas, and not just through international trade unassisted by any such investments. Third, both to assist trade and to generate additional foreign sales, they all invest offshore in majority subsidiaries engaged in some combination of wholesaling and production, with the latter becoming an increasingly important source of supply.

Fourth, with these new sources of supply, American, European, Japanese, and other Asian MNCs all employ foreign subsidiaries to supply local markets hosting their direct investments, as well as to supply export markets either at home or in third countries. Fifth, and finally, they all employ their foreign subsidiaries both as internal markets for exported products and as internal sources of imported supplies, linked to their parents back home (and to related subsidiaries elsewhere abroad) through intracompany trade. While American multinationals pioneered many of these investment and trade strategies immediately after World War II, they were later followed to varying degrees by the Europeans (especially during the 1970s), then the Japanese (especially during the 1980s), and now the Koreans, Chinese, and other Asians (during the 1990s). In short, several of the foreign operations of multinationals originating in different geographic locations have begun to converge, as they all move along an otherwise common evolutionary path.

At times, that convergence has been even more pronounced in Asia than elsewhere in the world, as demonstrated by the common geographic and industrial concentration of FDI from various sources. More often, MNCs in Asia more closely mimic patterns of convergence apparent elsewhere, as they do in the pursuit of majority shareholdings and FDI-generated sales. Yet important differences in MNC operations persist, even in the same host economy and industrial sector. In home-country sourcing and intrafirm trade, for example, MNCs in Asia differ much as they do elsewhere in the world. Such differences may be even more pronounced in Asia than elsewhere, as demonstrated by wide variation in host-market and export sales. When totaled, then, those operational differences that remain are largely limited to the relationship between FDI and trade: on export markets for outputs, on imported sources of inputs, and on the organization of this two-way trade either through markets (arm's-length transactions) or hierarchies (intrafirm transactions).

Government Policy

The relationship between FDI and trade varies significantly among multinational corporations as well as across host economies. With the total value of an economy's exports and imports bounded by savings rates and other macrolevel determinants, FDI can nevertheless contribute proportionately to that trade, while also altering its composition and direction—not only for individual multinationals, but also for host (and home) economies. Simultaneously, such trade can have a significant impact on the value, direction, and composition of FDI, again at both the microlevel of multinationals and the macrolevel of national economies. These complementarities between FDI and trade have recently attracted much attention.[81] And they have important policy implications: trade and FDI regimes shape a multinational subsidiary's contribution to a host country's exports and imports.

Consider the relative contribution of multinational subsidiaries to Asian exports. Among the region's 10 largest economies, that export contribution ranges from a high that approaches 90 percent in Singapore to a low that remains under 10 percent in India (see table 3.9). These two extremes cannot be explained simply in terms of obvious differences in domestic market size. To the contrary, in marked contrast to India, China reports that foreign-affiliated firms have come to contribute well over a third of total national exports in 1994, up from practically zero a decade earlier. That third, moreover, was comparable to relative shares reported in quite different economies, such as Indonesia and Thailand. Indeed, across Southeast Asia, multinationals have emerged as major exporters, contributing over half of national exports not only in Singapore, but also in Malaysia. (So large is the value both of these exports and of domestic value-added that, in Malaysia at least, multinationals export far more than they import.) In North Asia, by contrast, the export contribution of multinationals is much smaller, as we can see in both Taiwan and Korea. What distinguishes these two Asian NIEs from Singapore is a combination of government policies that simultaneously limit FDI (especially in Korea) and encourage domestic producers.

Table 3.9   The Relative Contribution of Multinationals to Asian Exports, Late 1980s to Early 1990s

	All industries (% of total exports)	Electronics only (% of total exports)
Four NIEs		
Korea (1986)	26.1	NA
Taiwan (1986)	17.8	30.8
Hong Kong	NA	NA
Singapore (1989)	86.1	NA
ASEAN Four		
Thailand (1990)	33.0[a,b]	82.0[b]
Malaysia (1991)	57.1	82.5[a]
Indonesia (1992)	32.0[a]	76.0
Philippines	NA	NA
Big Two		
India (1991)	9.1	NA
China (1994)	36.1	NA

Source: Dennis J. Encarnation, *Integrating Asia: Multinationals and the Political Economy of Regionalization* (forthcoming, 1999)

[a]Manufacturing only.
[b]Government-promoted firms only.
NA = Not available.

As FDI can contribute proportionately to the value of trade, it can also shape its composition. Nowhere is this more apparent than in the electronics industry, which (as I noted before) has attracted considerable FDI from American, Japanese, Korean, Taiwanese, and other regional electronics producers. Much of that FDI is concentrated in Southeast Asia, where (as I also noted before) it is primarily export-oriented. In the near absence of corresponding exports by domestically owned electronics manufacturers, we find that multinationals contribute more than three quarters of all electronics exports from Thailand, Malaysia, Singapore, and Indonesia (see table 3.9). Thus, across these ASEAN economies, FDI by multinationals has helped to change the composition of manufactured exports to include electronics. By contrast, in Taiwan, a thriving electronics industry populated largely by domestically owned producers results in a much lower contribution by multinationals to electronics exports. Yet, even in Taiwan, that foreign contribution to the economy's exports is higher in the electronics industry than in most other industrial sectors, further testimony to the continuing importance of FDI in helping to determine the composition of an economy's trade.

Finally, FDI can also influence the direction of trade by facilitating access to output markets and supply sources, especially those in industrialized countries. This seems especially true in Japan, where market access has long been limited for foreign exporters unaffiliated with Japanese manufacturers and distributors. Nowhere is this more apparent than in bilateral U.S.–Japan trade. Here, Japanese-owned subsidiaries contribute well over half of all U.S. exports to Japan and account for well over two thirds of all U.S. imports from Japan—nearly all shipped intracompany, between these subsidiaries and their Japanese parents. By comparison, Japanese subsidiaries in Asia still exercise less hierarchical control over bilateral trade between their Asian hosts and Japan. While the reasons for this are multiple, one stands out: Japanese multinationals in Asia have been far more reluctant than their American counterparts to export large proportions of their Asian output back home (or to third countries), preferring instead to sell in the local host-country market. By contrast, Japanese multinationals in Asia have been much less reluctant than the Americans to rely on their home-based suppliers as principal sources of their Asian inputs. In this way, multinationals reinforce the prevailing structure of Asian trade, in which the United States remains the principal export market and Japan remains the principal source of imported supplies.

These persistent differences in corporate strategy continue to pose challenges for government policy makers across Asia. To illustrate one such challenge, with export revenues denominated principally in U.S. dollars and import costs (not to mention the foreign debt often incurred to finance these imports) denominated in large part by Japanese yen, government policy makers must manage exchange-rate risks quite similar to those faced by global managers of multinational corporations. One response, for policy maker and manager alike, is to try to match revenues and costs in the same currency. This could be accomplished, for example, through the diversification of markets, suppliers, and products (both outputs and inputs), with a corresponding redirection of two-way trade and resultant shifts in the relative value of bilateral flows. But as this chapter documents, such a structural adjustment in Asian trade will be difficult to accomplish without a corresponding impact on FDI. For, as we have seen, sharp differences can still be discerned between multinationals in their determination of markets for outputs, sources for inputs, and the organization of that trade between markets (arm's-length transactions) and hierarchies (intrafirm transactions). These institutional factors, bounded by more macroeconomic determinants, shape the relative complementarities between trade and FDI.

Notes

1. World Bank, unpublished estimates, May 1995, summarized in table 3.2.

2. Asia-Pacific Economic Cooperation (APEC) Economic Committee, "Foreign Direct Investment and APEC Economic Integration" (Ottawa: Investment Canada, unpublished manuscript, June 1995).

3. Mira Wilkins, "Japanese Multinational Enterprise before 1914," *Business History Review* (Summer 1986), tables 1–2, p. 209, and note 41, p. 217.

4. U.S. Commerce Department, Office of Business Economics, *U.S. Business Investments in Foreign Countries: A Supplement to the Survey of Current Business* (Washington, DC: USGPO, 1960), table 3, p. 92; hereafter cited as Commerce Department, *U.S. FDI, 1957 Survey*.

5. U.S. Commerce Department, *U.S. FDI, 1957 Survey*, table 3, p. 92.

6. U.S. Commerce Department, *U.S. Direct Investment Abroad, 1994* (Washington, DC: USGPO, 1996), table 3, p. 63; 1986, table 1, pp. 1–5; 1982, table 1, pp. 1–27; hereafter cited as *U.S. FDI, 1994*.

7. U.S. Commerce Department, *U.S. FDI, 1994*, table 3, p. 63; 1986, table 1, pp. 1–5; 1982, table 1, pp. 1–27.

8. For citations, see table 3.1.

9. United Nations Conference on Trade and Development (UNCTAD), Division of Transnational Corporations and Investment, "Foreign Direct Investment in Asia and the Pacific," Document number TD/B/ITNC/3, 24 April 1995, esp. pp. 7–11.

10. Bank of Korea, Foreign Exchange Department, *Overseas Direct Investment Statistics Yearbook: 1994* (Seoul: BOK, 1994).

11. International Monetary Fund (IMF), *Direction of Trade Statistics Yearbook: 1993* (Washington, DC: IMF, 1993), pp. 247–249.

12. IMF, *Direction of Trade Statistics Yearbook: 1993*, pp. 247–249.

13. For the United States, see U.S. Commerce Department, International Trade Administration, Office of Trade and Investment Analysis, *U.S. Foreign Trade Highlights: 1993* (Washington, DC: USGPO, July 1994), pp. 168–169. Various years of *U.S. Foreign Trade Highlights* are cited hereafter.

14. Bank of Korea, Foreign Exchange Department, *Overseas Direct Investment Statistics Yearbook: 1994* (Seoul: BOK, 1994), table 4, p. 26.

15. The Hong Kong Trade Development Corporation estimates that Hong Kong accounted for 63 percent—and Taiwan, another 9 percent—of the cumulative FDI flows into China during 1979–1993, the period of liberalization.

16. The U.S. Commerce Department estimates that U.S. FDI flows into China during 1993 barely exceeded $500 million, while Japan's Ministry of Finance reports that it approved roughly $1.7 billion of Japanese FDI in China that same year. These flows account for 3 percent and 10 percent, respectively, of all FDI flows into China. This leaves some 87 percent from other sources, which presumably means Hong Kong and (to a lesser extent) Taiwan.

17. According to the Bank of Thailand, for example.

18. For sources, see note 3.

19. Commerce Department, *U.S. FDI, 1957 Survey*, table 20, p. 108.

20. For example, during 1977, American multinationals reported to the Commerce Department that over 80 percent of their "owners' equity" resided in majority U.S.–owned subsidiaries; see U.S. Commerce Department, Bureau of Economic Analysis, *U.S. Direct Investment Abroad, 1977* (Washington, DC: USGPO, 1981), table II.A.18, p. 123, and table III.A.18, p. 242; hereafter cited as Commerce Department, *U.S. FDI, 1977 Benchmark.*

21. U.S. Commerce Department, Bureau of Economic Analysis, *U.S. Direct Investment Abroad, 1966: Final Data* (Washington, DC: USGPO, 1975), esp. table J-4, p. 167, and table L-1, p. 197; hereafter cited as Commerce Department, *U.S. FDI, 1966 Benchmark.*

22. This finding contradicts a long-standing consensus among Japanese scholars, who have argued (incorrectly) that Japanese investors are more likely than their American counterparts to establish abroad minority-owned and equal-partnership joint ventures, occasionally with multiple Japanese partners. For sources, see note 2.

These earlier findings, however, may well represent a simple artifact of the specific indicator that scholars examined: the actual number of joint ventures and majority subsidiaries established by Japanese multinationals. Such a measure may overestimate the relative importance of small investments in a large number of minority-owned and equal-partnership joint ventures. Indeed, by this measure, American multinationals during 1977 (the same year examined in many of the earlier Japanese studies) proved as likely to establish minority U.S.–owned affiliates as they did to invest in majority subsidiaries. Specifically, that year, American multinationals reported direct investments in 11,900 majority U.S.–owned subsidiaries and 11,800 minority U.S.–owned affiliates; see Commerce Department, *U.S. FDI, 1977 Benchmark,* table D, p. 20. Moreover, even by this peculiar measure, what limited data exist for the 1970s (when this consensus among Japanese scholars began to emerge) suggest that majority subsidiaries accounted for roughly two thirds of all projects established by Japanese multinationals, at least in East Asia, the one region most often cited by these scholars (for data, see Yoshihara, 1978, tables 4.8 and 5.1, pp. 118, 166). And by the early 1990s, majority Japanese-owned subsidiaries accounted for three out of every four Japanese affiliates established worldwide. Japan, Ministry of International Trade and Industry, Industrial Policy Bureau, International Business Affairs Division, *The Fifth Comprehensive Survey of Foreign Investment Statistics [Dai go-kai wagakuni kigyo no kaigai jigyo katsudo]* (Tokyo: MITI, 1994), table 2-12-12, p. 147. It therefore seems accurate to claim that by the late 1970s, and continuing into the 1990s, any earlier differences in patterns of ownership that distinguished American from Japanese subsidiaries abroad had surely withered away.

23. Bank of Korea, *Overseas Direct Investment Statistics, 1994,* table 7, p. 65.

24. For sources, see table 3.2.

25. Yoshihara Hideki, *Japanese Investment in Southeast Asia* (Honolulu: University Press of Hawaii, 1978), tables 4.9, 4.10, and 4.11, pp. 122–125; Wilkins, 1986, esp. pp. 208–218, 229–231.

26. Yoshihara, *Japanese Investment,* tables 4.8 and 5.1, pp. 118, 166, 169–170.

27. For citations, see table 3.2.

28. Dennis J. Encarnation, *Dislodging Multinationals: India's Strategy in Comparative Perspective* (Ithaca, NY: Cornell University Press, Cornell Series in Political Economy, 1989).

29. For citations, see table 3.2.

30. Commerce Department, *U.S. FDI, 1977,* tables II.F.5 and III.F.5, pp. 138, 282–283.

31. For Japan, see Dennis J. Encarnation, *Rivals beyond Trade: America vs. Japan in Global Competition* (Ithaca, NY: Cornell University Press, 1992), esp. pp. 209–212; also see Dennis J. Encarnation and Mark Mason, "Neither MITI nor America: The Political Economy of Capital Liberalization in Japan," *International Organization* (Winter 1990): 25–54. For Korea, see Encarnation, *Dislodging Multinationals*, esp. pp. 204–215.

32. Yet some analysts have only recently discovered this relationship. See, for example, Susan Strange, "The Name of the Game," in Nicholas X. Rizopoulos, ed., *Sea-Changes: American Foreign Policy in a World Transformed* (New York: Council on Foreign Relations Press, 1991), p. 242: in the "evolution of international business . . . the mid-1980s were a milestone as the volume of international production for the *first time* exceeded the volume of international trade" (emphasis added).

33. For sales data, see Commerce Department, *U.S. FDI, 1957 Survey*, table 22, p. 110; for trade data, see U.S. Commerce Department, Bureau of International Commerce, "United States Trade with Major World Areas, 1955 and 1956," *Overseas Business Reports* (May 1957): 2, 8.

34. For sales data, see Commerce Department, *U.S. FDI, 1966 Benchmark*, table L-2, p. 198; for trade data, see U.S. Commerce Department, Bureau of International Commerce, "United States Trade with Major World Areas, 1965 and 1966," *Overseas Business Reports* (May 1967): 3, 12.

35. During 1977, when Japanese exports to the world totaled $85 billion, Japanese affiliates abroad reported foreign sales of roughly $85 billion (or ¥22.8 trillion). For sales data, see Japan, Ministry of International Trade and Industry, Industrial Policy Bureau, *The 8th Survey of the Overseas Business Activities of Japanese Enterprises [Dai hachi-kai wagakuni kigyo no kaigai jigyo katsudo]* (Tokyo: MITI, 1979), table 51, p. 54; hereafter cited as MITI, *Japanese FDI, 8th Survey*. For trade data, see International Monetary Fund, *International Trade Statistics Yearbook: 1980* (Washington, DC: IMF, 1981), p. 243.

36. Commerce Department, *U.S. Direct Investment Abroad: Preliminary 1992 Estimates* (Washington, DC: USGPO, 1993), table III.E.3; hereafter cited as *U.S. FDI, 1992 Survey*; Commerce Department, *U.S. Foreign Trade Highlights: 1992*, p. 88.

37. For sources, see note 19.

38. For sales data, U.S. Commerce Department, Bureau of Economic Analysis, *Foreign Direct Investment in the United States, Volume 2, Report of the Secretary of Commerce, Benchmark Survey, 1974* (Washington, DC: USGPO, April 1976), table K-5, p. 139; for trade data, see U.S. Commerce Department, *U.S. Foreign Trade Highlights* (various years).

39. U.S. Commerce Department, Bureau of Economic Analysis, *Foreign Direct Investment in the United States: 1987 Benchmark Survey, Final Results* (Washington, DC: USGPO, August 1990), table E-2, p. 76; Commerce Department, *U.S. Foreign Trade Highlights, 1991*, p. 89.

40. For sources, see note 24.

41. Commerce Department, *U.S. Foreign Trade Highlights: 1993*, table 7, p. 22; Bank of Korea, *Overseas Direct Investment Statistics: 1994*, table 4.

42. Japan, Ministry of International Trade and Industry, Industrial Policy Bureau, International Business Affairs Division, *The 25th Survey of Business Activities of Foreign Enterprises in Japan [Dai nijyugo-kai gaishikei kigyo no doko]* (Tokyo: Ministry of Finance Printing Bureau, 1992), table 24-4, p. 80; hereafter cited as MITI, *FDI in Japan, 25th Survey*.

43. U.S. Commerce Department, Bureau of Economic Analysis, *U.S. Direct Investment Abroad: 1982 Benchmark Survey Data* (Washington, DC: USGPO, 1985),

table III.D.3, p. 215, hereafter cited as Commerce Department, *U.S. FDI, 1982 Survey*; U.S. Commerce Department, *U.S. Foreign Trade Highlights: 1988*, table V.1, pp. 82–86.

44. Encarnation and Mason, "Neither MITI nor America," pp. 29–54.

45. Robert E. Lipsey, "Changing Patterns of International Investment in and by the United States," in Martin Feldstein, ed., *The United States in the World Economy* (Chicago: University of Chicago Press for the National Bureau of Economic Research, 1988), pp. 488–492; David J. Goldsbrough, "Investment Trends and Prospects: The Link with Bank Lending," in Theodore H. Moran, ed., *Investing in Development: New Roles for Private Capital?* (Washington, DC: Overseas Development Council, 1986).

46. U.S. Commerce Department, *U.S. FDI, 1982 Survey*, table III.D.3, p. 215; Commerce Department, *U.S. Foreign Trade Highlights: 1988*, table V.1, pp. 82–86.

47. For 1980 data, see MITI, *The First Comprehensive Survey of Foreign Investment Statistics*, 1983, table II.53.3, p. 330; IMF, *Direction of Trade Statistics*, various years.

48. For sources, see table 3.3.

49. Bank of Korea, *Overseas Direct Investment Statistics: 1994*, table 5, pp. 38–39.

50. For sales data, see the following Commerce Department publications: *U.S. FDI, 1957 Survey*, table 22, p. 110; *U.S. FDI, 1966 Benchmark*, table L-3, p. 199; *U.S. FDI, 1977 Benchmark*, table II.H.1, p. 318; *U.S. Direct Investment Abroad, 1988* (Washington, DC: USGPO, 1990), table 34, n.p.; hereafter cited as *U.S. FDI, 1988 Survey*. For trade data, see Commerce Department, "International Business Indicators," *Overseas Business Reports* (January 1973), table 5, p. 14; Commerce Department, *U.S. Foreign Trade Highlights* (various years).

51. For sales data, see U.S. Commerce Department, *U.S. Direct Investment Abroad: Operations of U.S. Parent Companies and Their Foreign Affiliates, Preliminary 1990 Estimates* (Washington, DC: USGPO, September 1992), table III.F.2, n.p.; for trade data, see Commerce Department, *U.S. Foreign Trade Highlights: 1992*, p. 88.

52. For sources, see note 23.

53. For sales data, see MITI, *Japanese FDI, 8th Survey*, table 51, p. 54; for trade data, see IMF, *Direction of Trade Statistics Yearbook: 1980*, p. 242. Specifically, in the United States, 1974 estimates of Japanese manufactured exports ranged as high as 10 times the value of local production.

54. MITI, *FDI in Japan, 25th Survey*, table 24-4, p. 80.

55. 1982 survey; 1988 DOT stats.

56. For 1992 data, see table 3.4; for 1982 data, see Commerce Department, *U.S. FDI, 1982 Survey*, table III.D.3, p. 215; Commerce Department, *U.S. Foreign Trade Highlights: 1988*, table V.1, pp. 82–86.

57. For 1992 data, see table 3.4; for 1982 data, see MITI, *The First Comprehensive Survey of Foreign Investment Statistics*, 1983, table II.53.3, p. 330; IMF, *Direction of Trade Statistics*, various years.

58. For sources, see table 3.4.

59. For sources, see table 3.4.

60. Commerce Department, *U.S. FDI, 1982 Survey*, table III.D.3, p. 215; Commerce Department, *U.S. Foreign Trade Highlights: 1988*, table V.1, pp. 82–86.

61. For citations, see table 3.4.

62. According to Yoshihara (*Japanese Investment*, pp. 124–125), writing at the height of Japanese FDI in East Asian textiles: "If investment was to establish a

spinning mill, the participating trading company wanted to be its chief supplier of fiber; if it was to set up a fiber plant, the trading company wanted to be its chief supplier of chemical raw materials; if investment was to build an export base, it wanted to market the goods."

63. Again, according to Yoshihara (*Japanese Investment*, pp. 169–170), the trading company is little involved in the marketing of electrical machinery, automobiles, and general machinery, and its overseas investment in these products is small. But in such homogeneous products as textiles, iron and steel, and chemicals, whose marketing it handles, overseas investment is large. *Contrary to the widely held view that the trading company is an active investor in most industries, its investment is highly selective.* In the field of products that differentiated or require customer service, involvement as either marketer or investor tends to be small.

64. For an early survey of these barriers, see Michael Yoshino, *The Japanese Marketing System: Adaptations and Innovations* (Cambridge, MA: MIT Press, 1971); for more recent surveys, see the following chapters in Paul Krugman, ed., *The U.S. and Japan: Trade and Investment* (Cambridge, MA: MIT Press for the National Bureau of Economic Research, 1991): Itoh Motoshige, "The Japanese Distribution System and Access to the Japanese Market," and Ito Takahashi and Maruyama Masayoshi, "Is the Japanese Distribution System Really Inefficient?"

65. This subject had attracted much recent attention among scholars and policy makers; see, for example, Robert Z. Lawrence, "Efficient or Exclusionist? The Import Behavior of Japanese Corporate Groups," a paper prepared for the Brookings Panel on Economic Activity, April 4–5, 1991.

66. Bank of Korea, *Overseas Direct Investment Statistics: 1994*, table 5, pp. 38–39.

67. Commerce Department, *U.S. FDI, 1957 Survey*, table 22, p. 110; Commerce Department, *U.S. FDI, 1966 Benchmark*, table L-1, p. 197.

68. Commerce Department, *U.S. FDI, 1977 Benchmark*, table II.H.1, p. 318; Commerce Department, *U.S. FDI, 1988 Survey*, table 34, n.p.; Commerce Department, *U.S. FDI, 1992 Survey*, table III.F.2, n.p.

69. For 1971, see Japan, Ministry of International Trade and Industry, Industrial Policy Bureau, *Overseas Business Activities of Japanese Enterprises: Current Situation and Problems* [*Wagakuni kigyo no kaigai jigyo katsudo: sono gendai to mondaiten*] (Tokyo: MITI, 1973), table 4-2-2, pp. 86–87. For 1988, see Japan, Ministry of International Trade and Industry, Industrial Policy Bureau, International Business Affairs Division, *The 19th Survey of the Overseas Business Activities of Japanese Enterprises* [*Dai jyuukyuu-kai wagakuni kigyou no kaigai jigyou katsudou*] (Tokyo: Ministry of Finance Printing Bureau, 1990), pp. 82–83. For 1990, see Japan, Ministry of International Trade and Industry, Industrial Policy Bureau, International Business Affairs Division, *The 22nd Survey of the Overseas Business Activities of Japanese Enterprises* [*Dai nijyuuni-kai wagakuni kigyou no kaigai jigyou katsudou*] (Tokyo: Ministry of Finance Printing Bureau, 1990), pp. 88–89.

70. Commerce Department, *Foreign Direct Investment in the United States: 1992*, tables G-2 and G-24, n.p.

71. MITI, *FDI in Japan, 25th Survey*, table 24-4, p. 80.

72. For sources, see note 2.

73. See, for example, Encarnation, *Rivals beyond Trade*, esp. pp. 26–31, 190–197.

74. U.S. Commerce Department, *Direction of Trade Statistics: 1992*, pp. 11, 15, 79; U.S. Commerce Department, Bureau of Economic Analysis, *Foreign Direct*

Investment in the United States: 1987 Benchmark Survey, Final Results (Washington, DC: USGPO, August 1990), table G-31, p. 149; hereafter cited as Commerce Department, *FDI in U.S.: 1987 Benchmark*.

75. For U.S. exports to U.S. affiliates abroad, and overall sales data, see Commerce Department, *U.S. FDI, 1992 Survey*, tables II.E.3, II.H.5, II.H.22, III.E.3, III.H.2, n.p.; for overall U.S. exports, see Commerce Department, *U.S. Foreign Trade Highlights: 1992*, table 2, p. 11.

76. For sources, see note 58.

77. Commerce Department, *U.S. Foreign Trade Highlights: 1991*, pp. 15, 89; Commerce Department, *FDI in U.S.: 1987 Benchmark*, table G-31, p. 149.

78. For sources, see table 3.6.

79. For sources, see table 3.6.

80. For sources, see table 3.6.

81. See Encarnation, *Rivals beyond Trade*, esp. pp. 1–35.

PART II

FOREIGN DIRECT INVESTMENT
AND TRADE FLOWS

4

Foreign Direct Investment Outflows and Manufacturing Trade

A Comparison of Japan and the United States

Edward M. Graham

Introduction

This chapter presents empirical evidence on whether outward foreign direct investment (FDI) and international trade are substitutes or complements, that is, whether a nation's greater stock of FDI is associated with decreases or increases of its exports and imports.[1] This issue has long concerned policy makers, who have worried about possible negative effects of outward FDI upon a nation's balance of payments and employment of its work force. In this chapter, I report results pertaining to two nations that are home to large stocks of FDI: the United States and Japan.

In principle, either relationship between FDI and exports could hold. When investors, usually multinational firms, based in one nation (the "home" nation) establish operations under their managerial control in some other nation (the "host" nation), FDI occurs. Often, the motivation is to produce locally in the host nation products that had previously been exported from the home nation, and, when this happens, FDI and home nation exports function as substitutes. But the home nation operations of a multinational firm also can be vertically linked with host nation operations, such that an increase in the activity in the latter generates increased demand for intermediate products (including capital goods) from the former. Also, marketing and distribution capabilities created by FDI might enable the home nation operations to export final goods and services to customers who would not be reached in the absence of FDI. If either of these possibilities happens, home country FDI and exports will be complements.

Because the value of intermediate products is a component of the value-added of final goods, it could be argued that FDI and exports must be net substitutes in some long-run sense; that is, if exports of final goods from a home nation are displaced by local production, there will be a net loss of export value even if the gross loss is offset in part by export of capital and intermediate goods. This is true in a trivial sense because the value of final goods must be greater than or equal to the value of all inputs used to produce those goods. However, this line of argument supposes that a host nation's demand for a particular good will always be fulfilled by exports from the home country, which might not be the case. Changes in the relative cost of production might imply that, with the passage of time, a home nation's exports will be displaced by local production, whether the displacement is done by multinational firms shifting production from the home to the host nation or by local firms operating entirely within the host nation.

Indeed, over time, the relationship between FDI and exports could very well change. If, first, the host nation were to become relatively more efficient in the production of a particular class of final goods and the home nation were to become relatively more efficient in the production of intermediate goods used to produce these final goods, and, second, if multinational firms were to hold specialized skills enabling the realization of internal economies associated with a vertical link in the production of the two sets of goods, the relationship between additional FDI and exports by these firms could become increasingly complementary, even if initial FDI served to displace home country exports.

Even more complex relationships between FDI and international trade have been noted. Urata (1995) examined the growth of the electronics industry in East Asia and found that direct investment and trade in electronics goods have grown hand-in-hand in the region. The electronics industry worldwide has been marked by rapid overall growth and by rapid rates of new product development and cost reduction. Urata found that FDI by Japanese firms in the East Asian region has been driven both by growth of host nation demand and by complex patterns of shifting relative costs, causing firms to seek new production sites and to create complex patterns of cross hauling of both final goods and intermediate products. Urata notes that as these Japanese multinational enterprises (MNEs) have, over time, placed new direct investments in countries where they were previously absent (for example, China), these firms have not stopped or even curtailed production in countries with older-vintage FDI.

A further reason for complementarity between international trade and activity of multinational firms is explored by Brainard (1995b), notably that multinational firms typically hold intellectual property advantages (e.g., technologies and trademarks) that might enable larger market shares and hence increase both trade and investment in markets where these firms operate. Brainard hypothesized that a firm's share of trade in total sales to a particular market will be negatively affected by transport costs and trade barriers but positively affected by investment barriers and firm-level scale economies. Using U.S. Commerce Department data for U.S. direct investment abroad and foreign direct investment in the United States, she found that trade and FDI barriers and scale economies are robust explanators, but transportation costs are not. In a related work, Brainard shows that relative factor proportions are not a robust explanator of multinational firm activity (Brainard 1995a).

In fact, most studies of FDI and exports as net substitutes or net complements tend to indicate that the relationship is complementary, that more FDI is associated with more, rather than fewer, exports. Thus, the issue, as a practical matter, becomes empirical.

In both the United States and in the United Kingdom during the late 1960s, for example, there was official concern over the effects of outward FDI on the overall balance of payments on a current account basis. Central to this concern was the question of the impact of outward FDI on trade flows. In response, two studies of these effects were carried out under official auspices (Reddaway et al. 1967 and Hufbauer and Adler 1968) and remain among the best empirical studies of the effects of FDI.

Using somewhat different methodologies and coverage, both studies arrived at roughly similar conclusions: if future cash flows are not discounted, the overall long-term effects of outward FDI on the balance of payments are positive. The positive effects of financial flows alone should be no surprise because a firm undertakes an investment of any sort on the expectation that it will yield a positive return for the firm's shareholders, and ultimately that return must be reflected in dividend payments by the parent organization to those shareholders. Thus, if the shareholders of the firm are nationals of the home country, the returns accruing to the foreign affiliates of a firm must ultimately accrue to home country nationals funded through the parent organization. However, both studies also indicated that outward FDI tended to stimulate exports (mostly of capital goods and intermediate goods) without stimulating imports in equal magnitude.

Later studies yielded results generally consistent with these findings. Bergsten, Horst, and Moran (1978), for example, found that the growth of U.S. affiliates abroad had a significantly positive effect on the growth of exports of the U.S. parent firms. Lipsey and Weiss (1981) also found that outward U.S. FDI was associated with increased U.S. exports, even after controlling for other effects (firm size, expenditures on research and development (R & D) and marketing, etc.), but that the production of U.S. affiliates abroad substituted for exports to the host country or third countries. In a later study, the same authors (Lipsey and Weiss 1984) analyzed unpublished U.S. Commerce Department data at the level of the individual firm to examine foreign production and U.S. exports in 14 industries in the manufacturing sector. They reported positive and significant relationships in 11 of these industries.

In 1988 Blomström, Lipsey, and Kulchyck published a study of the effects of offshore production of Swedish-owned firms on Sweden's export of manufactured goods. Sweden is an advanced industrial economy located close to other advanced economies, and most of Sweden's direct investment is located either elsewhere in Western Europe or in North America. Blomström et al. found that increases in the production of affiliates of Swedish firms are positively related to increases in exports for the seven industrial categories studied. Furthermore, there was no propensity for this positive relationship to change as the foreign production grew.

Pearce (1990), following an approach similar to that of Blomström et al., examined the exports and foreign production of 458 of the world's largest industrial MNEs for 1982. According to him, increases in foreign production are generally positively related to increases in exports, especially for intrafirm (as opposed to interfirm) exports, underscoring the importance of vertical relationships among the international affiliates of this sample of MNEs.

Buigues and Jacquemin (1994) examine complementarity versus substitution between FDI and exports for both U.S. and Japanese direct investment in the European Union (EU). The basic assumption is that if the EU share of the total exports from each of these countries is positively related to the EU share of FDI adjusted for control of three additional variables, the relationship is complementary. The variables are intra–EC nontariff trade barriers, rate of growth of final demand, and the EC's sectoral specialization, all assumed to be positively related to FDI. Buigues and Jacquemin's sample is pooled cross-sectionally across seven industries (six for the United States) and ten years. They find a complementary relationship between FDI and exports for both the United States and Japan.

Industry Canada (1994) found that FDI from Canada as well as in Canada is associated with increases of both Canada's exports and imports. The findings are aggregate and (apparently) based on time series analysis. Estimates are made of the elasticities of exports and imports for Canada's outward investment, and the latter are higher than the former. These estimated elasticities of trade with respect to investment stocks (see Industry Canada 1994, table 7) are not, however, controlled for the influence of factors such as economic activity, comparative costs, or other variables that could affect the outcomes.

Thus, all of the studies cited conclude that the relationship between FDI and exports is complementary. As I explain in the next section, the results of my empirical investigations point to a consistent result, but with some twists.

Empirical Results

Most of the studies just described could be criticized for ignoring the possible effects of simultaneous determination of FDI and exports, which could be causing a spurious correlation and hence lead to an erroneous interpretation of complementarity.[2] This would be the case if both FDI and exports were responding to a common, unspecified causal element. For example, suppose that income or size of market alone determined both direct investment abroad and exports—that is, both exporters and direct investors put their energies into developing large markets or those with high per capita incomes but ignored small or low per capita income markets.[3] Then simply showing a large share of exports associated with markets where the share of direct investment was also large would not be sufficient to show that exports and direct investment abroad were complementary. They could still be substitutes once the effects of market size were taken into account.[4] Likewise, elements of simultaneous determination could distort results of studies based on differences across industries.

Thus, in the results reported here I tried to remove factors that might simultaneously determine exports and FDI and then to examine the relationship between these two latter variables with the source of the simultaneity bias removed. Specifically, I used a gravity model first to estimate the effects of three variables deemed to be very important determinants of both FDI and exports: (1) per capita income in each host nation market (for which gross domestic product [GDP] per capita was used), (2) total size of this market (for which total population was used), and (3) distance from the host to the home country. The model was used to test determinants of FDI and exports for two home countries, the United States and Japan. The "distance" from the home country to the host country was, for the United States, the great circle distance from Indianapolis (approximately the center of economic activity of the United States) to the host nation capital and, for Japan, from Tokyo to the capital.[5] The gravity specification was multiplicative; that is, the assumed relationship was

$$y = \log(\alpha x_1^{\beta_1} x_2^{\beta_2} x_3^{\beta_3} \varepsilon),$$

where y is the logarithm of the dependent variable (FDI or exports), x_1, x_2, and x_3 are the three independent variables, and ε is an error term (assumed, as usual, to be log-normally distributed with mean 1). The expected signs of β_1 and β_2 are positive (both home nation exports and FDI would be expected to be positive functions of per capita income and market size); the expected sign of β_3 is negative for exports (the further the market is from the home nation, the higher transport costs, and hence the less likely that firms would export from the home nation) but indeterminate for direct investment (for example, if direct investment were to be a substitute for exports, then arguably the substitution would be most likely in those markets for which transactions costs associated with exports were high, and the expected sign of β_3 would be positive, but one can envisage circumstances where direct investment would occur in geographically proximate markets [see, e.g., Graham 1995]).

The residuals from each of the two estimations (exports and FDI as a function of the three variables) were then regressed on one another. The presumption was that if the gravity models have succeeded in removing simultaneity bias, then any correlation of the residuals would reflect some other causal relationship between FDI and exports—such as that due to sourcing substitution or to complementarities in production or distribution and marketing. A positive correlation coefficient would suggest complementarity and a negative coefficient substitutability.

I also performed similar two-stage analyses between imports and direct investment abroad.

Results for the United States

For the United States, the sample included 40 individual countries that were destinations of both U.S. exports and U.S. direct investment. These 40 countries accounted in 1991 for over 96 percent of the stock of U.S. direct investment abroad and over 95 percent of U.S. manufactured goods exports. The analyses were completed for three different years (1991, 1988, and 1983), and the results were roughly consistent for each year. Only the results for 1991 are reported here. Separate analyses were performed using (1) the data for all 40 countries (reported in the tables as "World"), (2) only those countries located in Europe, (3) only those countries located in the Western hemisphere, and (4) only those countries located in East Asia. It should be noted that some countries in the sample are not in Europe, the Western hemisphere, or East Asia; thus, the world sample contains more observations than the sum of those in each of the three identified regions.

Summary results[6] of the gravity analyses appear in table 4.1. As can be seen, the specification led to overall good fits for the whole sample (world) and for the subsamples subsuming Europe and the Western hemisphere: for all of these, the F tests were significant at the ≥ 99 percent confidence level, and the R^2s all exceed 50 percent. Thus, it would appear that the three independent variables—income per capita, population, and distance—"explain" fairly robustly cross-country patterns of U.S. exports, imports, and outward direct investment in the manufacturing sector. The overall fit for the East Asian subsample is substantially less good than for the other two subsamples, with the fit particularly poor for U.S. imports, where the F test is significant at only the 90 percent level and the R^2 statistic suggests that only 31 percent of the total variance of the dependent variable is explained by the three independent variables. For U.S. exports and U.S. direct investment to Asia, the overall fit is better, but the F test is still only significant at

Table 4.1 Gravity Model Results, U.S. Data, 1991

Dependent variable	F test	Coefficients of independent variables (standard error in parentheses)			
		Income/cap	Population	Distance	R^2
U.S. exports					
World	***	0.66 (.11)	0.11 (.10)	−0.38 (.22)	0.54
Europe	***	0.29 (.88)	0.60 (.64)	−1.56 (2.3)	0.63
W. Hemisphere	***	0.46 (.61)	0.41 (.42)	−0.98 (.31)	0.93
East Asia	**	0.89 (.50)	−0.23 (.46)	−0.77 (2.4)	0.40
U.S. imports					
World	***	0.94 (.08)	−0.00 (.07)	0.27 (.16)	0.80
Europe	***	0.82 (.15)	0.27 (.13)	−1.33 (1.2)	0.87
W. Hemisphere	***	1.15 (.20)	−0.24 (.19)	−0.14 (.26)	0.93
East Asia	*	0.53 (.26)	−0.07 (.14)	−0.61 (2.1)	0.31
U.S. direct investment abroad					
World	***	0.92 (.14)	0.17 (.13)	−0.77 (.29)	0.60
Europe	***	0.86 (.47)	0.80 (.39)	−9.57 (3.6)	0.66
W. Hemisphere	***	1.31 (.22)	0.10 (.20)	−0.31 (.28)	0.96
East Asia	**	0.93 (.30)	−0.15 (.16)	1.09 (2.5)	0.49

*Significant at 90 percent confidence level.
**Significant at 95 percent confidence level.
***Significant at 99 percent confidence level.

the 95 percent level and the R^2 statistics indicate that the relationships explain less than 50 percent of the total variance of the dependent variables.

The coefficients on the independent variables mostly indicate the expected sign (recalling that the expected sign of the coefficient of the distance variable is indeterminate in the investment equation) but in many cases are not statistically significant. There are a few anomalies. The biggest of these is that the coefficient of the size of market variable (as measured by population) often does not represent the expected sign but also is not significant (except for U.S. direct investment in Europe, where the sign is as expected). A second anomaly is that none of the coefficients of the independent variables for the U.S. exports to Europe is significant, even though the overall relationship is. This suggests the possibility of multicollinearity among the independent variables and hence that additional tests for joint significance of the three variables would be appropriate (e.g., calculation of joint confidence intervals for the variables taken two at a time).

It is perhaps noteworthy that the coefficient on the income per capita variable is highly significant for U.S. imports with the expected (positive) sign for the world sample and for all three of the subsamples. Thus, the "pauper labor" argument so often heard these days in the United States is not supported by this result because U.S. imports are associated with high-income—hence high-wage—source countries, not low-wage countries.

Likewise, the coefficient for income per capita is highly significant for U.S. direct investment abroad, with the exception of Europe, suggesting that the "runaway plant" argument is not supported by the analysis. The income per capita coefficient for Europe is not significant perhaps because U.S. firms have concentrated a disproportionate amount of direct investment in the United Kingdom (UK), a country whose per capita income is not high relative to the rest of Europe. However, the UK per capita income is high by world standards, and, thus, this concentration probably does not distort the results for the world sample. The variance in per capita incomes in Europe is in fact not as great as in the other regions. Perhaps this explains why for Europe alone market size appears to be a more important determinant of direct investment than does per capita income: most European nations are in the "advanced industrial" category, and nations with large populations likely would receive more U.S. direct investment abroad in the manufacturing sector than nations with smaller populations.

It is worth noting that the first-stage results were most robust for the Western hemisphere. For this subsample, the R^2 statistic was in excess of 0.9 for all three dependent variables, suggesting that over 90 percent of the variance in the dependent variables was explained by the independent variables.

Table 4.2 presents the results of the second-stage regressions. As can be seen, the relationship between the remaining unexplained variation in U.S. outward direct investment in the manufacturing sector and the remaining unexplained variation in U.S. exports of manufactured goods for the world sample was positive and significant at the 95 percent level. The relationship between these variables was also positive and significant for both the Europe and East Asia subsamples, but it was negative and significant for the Western hemisphere subsample. These results suggest that U.S. outward direct investment and exports are complements globally and in the European and East Asian regions but that they are substitutes in the Western hemisphere. I will revisit this Western hemisphere result shortly.

Table 4.2 Regressions of Residuals on Residuals of Gravity Equations, U.S. Data, 1991

	Coefficient	Standard error	Significance
U.S. FDI and U.S. exports			
World	0.486	0.207	**
Europe	0.479	0.126	***
W. Hemisphere	−0.866	0.253	**
East Asia	0.524	0.228	**
U.S. FDI and U.S. imports			
World	0.282	0.138	**
Europe	0.174	0.080	*
W. Hemisphere	−0.392	0.303	NS
East Asia	0.208	0.261	NS

*Significant at 90 percent confidence level.
**Significant at 95 percent confidence level.
***Significant at 99 percent confidence level.

Table 4.2 also reports the results of second-stage regressions of the relationship between U.S. outward direct investment in the manufacturing sector and U.S. imports of manufactured goods. The coefficient is positive but only significant at a 95 percent level for the world sample. The coefficients are not significant for either the East Asian subsample or the Western hemisphere subsample, although the signs of the coefficients are consistent with those reported earlier for outward direct investment and exports. For the European subsample, the coefficient is positive and marginally significant. Thus, the residual relationship between FDI and imports is weak if there is one at all.

Why are the signs of the coefficients for the Western hemisphere different from those of the remainder of the sample? My guess is that these results are a fallout of the import substitution policies pursued throughout much of Latin America during the 1970s and early 1980s, whereby multinational corporations often were induced to establish local production facilities that would then operate behind protectionist walls and enjoy quasi-monopolistic status in the relevant market. Because such operations were frequently inefficient, most governments that pursued such policies have in recent years begun a process of policy reform (see, e.g., the various national studies in Williamson 1993). Nonetheless, the legacy of import substitution seems to have survived into the early 1990s. The possibility that the negative relationship between U.S. direct investment and U.S. exports in the Western hemisphere is the legacy of import substitution programs is reinforced by the results of a gravity model for the hemisphere with Canada removed from the subsample of countries. In this model, the coefficient on the second-stage regression for the direct investment abroad and U.S. exports variables increases in magnitude (but remains negative; it goes from −0.866 to −0.955) and becomes more significant (it now is significant at the ≥99 percent level of confidence).

However, one should note that the coefficient for the relationship between U.S. outward direct investment and U.S. imports for the Western hemisphere subsample is negative and not significant. This result runs contrary to the frequent claim that multinational firms are transferring production to low-wage areas south of the (U.S.) border in order to service the domestic U.S. market. If this claim were true, one would expect a positive and significant coefficient. Much the same statement can be made about East Asia. For this subsample, the sign of the coefficient is positive (which, other things being equal, would support the transfer of production story) but not statistically significant.

The results seem to support an overall positive relationship between U.S. outward direct investment and U.S. exports in the manufacturing sector. There is also weak evidence for a positive relationship between U.S. outward direct investment and U.S. imports in this sector. Thus, direct investment seems to enhance trade, but to create direct links to exports rather than to imports.

Results for Japan

The Japanese sample consisted of 36 nations accounting for all of Japan's reported stocks of outward direct investment in the manufacturing sector and about 90 percent of Japan's manufacturing exports. The two-stage regressions were run on the sample as a whole and on partitions where the 36 nations were partitioned into

East Asia and non–East Asia. Australia and New Zealand were included in the East Asian subsample.

As can be seen in table 4.3, the gravity model is quite robust in terms of its ability to explain both Japanese exports and imports of manufactured goods (as was the case for the United States). Unlike the case of the United States, the distance variable for Japan is a statistically significant explanator of exports and imports for the world and for non–East Asian nations (but not for the East Asian nations). However, the gravity model, for Japan, does *not* appear very robust to explain outward direct investment.

The second-stage least square results for Japan are indicated in table 4.4. For the relationship between Japanese outward FDI and exports in the manufacturing sector, the sign of the coefficient is positive, consistent with complementarity between FDI and exports, and is significant for both the world sample and the non–East Asia subsample. For the East Asia subsample, the sign is positive, but the result is not statistically significant, a result addressed later.

For Japanese outward direct investment and imports in the manufacturing sector, the two-stage model does not seem to offer robust explanatory power. The signs on all of the coefficients are positive as expected, but none of these coefficients is statistically significant, save for that for the world sample, which is significant only in the 90 percent confidence interval.

The lack of significance for Japanese outward FDI and exports for the East Asian nations is puzzling. This result, it would seem, is driven by the presence in the

Table 4.3 Gravity Model Results, Japanese Data, 1993

Dependent variable	F test	Coefficients of independent variables (standard error in parentheses)			R^2
		Income/cap	Population	Distance	
Japanese exports					
World	***	0.81 (.13)	0.62 (.13)	−1.39 (.29)	0.61
Non–East Asia	***	0.89 (.18)	0.88 (.18)	−0.37 (1.11)	0.69
East Asia	***	0.83 (.22)	0.42 (.21)	−0.98 (.41)	0.74
Japanese imports					
World	***	1.09 (.16)	0.95 (.16)	−1.62 (.35)	0.67
Non–East Asia	***	1.45 (.16)	1.00 (.20)	−0.86 (1.28)	0.75
East Asia	*	1.04 (.33)	−0.90 (.07)	−1.02 (.60)	0.67
Japanese direct investment abroad					
World	*	0.48 (.20)	0.45 (.20)	0.01 (.45)	0.18
Non–East Asia	**	0.66 (.34)	0.63 (.33)	3.44 (2.05)	0.41
East Asia		0.32 (.33)	0.31 (.47)	0.61 (1.02)	0.09

*Significant at 90 percent confidence level.
**Significant at 95 percent confidence level.
***Significant at 99 percent confidence level.

Table 4.4 Regressions of Residuals on Residuals of Gravity Equations,
Japanese Data, 1991

	Coefficient	Standard error	Significance
Japanese FDI and exports			
World	0.97	0.20	***
Non–East Asia	1.35	0.28	***
East Asia	0.31	0.39	NS
Japanese FDI and imports			
World	0.37	0.21	*
Non–East Asia	0.54	0.34	NS
East Asia	0.16	0.28	NS

*Significant at 90 percent confidence level.
***Significant at 99 percent confidence level.
NS = Not significant.

sample of Indonesia, long a recipient of large amounts of Japanese direct investment in the manufacturing sector. Like much U.S. direct investment in the Western hemisphere, historically Japanese direct investment in Indonesia has been in
response to import substitution policies.

Tables 4.5 and 4.6 indicate the first- and second-stage regression results for the
East Asian sample without Indonesia. The gravity model without Indonesia remains robust enough to explain both exports and imports of manufactured goods,
and, in addition, it becomes robust enough to explain Japanese outward direct
investment in the manufacturing sector. The second-stage results become highly
significant, with the coefficients on both Japanese outward FDI and exports and
outward FDI and imports statistically significant. Apparently, in terms of relationships between Japanese outward FDI and traded manufactured goods, Indonesia
is an outlier of significant proportion.

Exactly why Indonesia should be an outlier is not known for certain, but a likely
hypothesis is virtually the same as for the anomalies reported in the analysis of
the U.S. data for the Western hemisphere. For a considerable period of time, Indonesia pursued import substitution policies, and Japanese firms responded by
directly investing in the Indonesian economy to create affiliates that served the

Table 4.5 Gravity Model Results, East Asian Sample without Indonesia,
Japanese Data, 1993

Dependent variable	F test	Coefficients of independent variables (standard error in parentheses)			R^2
		Income/cap	Population	Distance	
Japanese exports	***	1.06 (.28)	0.47 (.22)	−0.45 (.55)	0.82
Japanese imports	**	1.26 (.39)	0.87 (.31)	−0.41 (.75)	0.74
Japanese FDI	**	0.86 (.39)	0.42 (.31)	−0.44 (.75)	0.62

**Significant at 95 percent confidence level.
***Significant at 99 percent confidence level.

Table 4.6 Regressions of Residuals on Residuals of Gravity Equations, East
Asian Sample without Indonesia, Japanese Data, 1993

	Coefficient	Standard error	Significance
Japanese FDI and exports	1.15	0.23	***
Japanese FDI and imports	0.70	0.22	***

***Significant at 99 percent confidence level.

local market behind protectionist barriers. However, for both Japan and the Western hemisphere, this explanation serves only as an hypothesis. Future work seems
to be indicated.

Conclusions

The empirical evidence presented in the previous section is generally consistent
with that of earlier studies reviewed earlier in the chapter. The evidence tends to
suggest that U.S. outward direct investment (or, more properly, the output of
affiliates of U.S.–based firms enabled by this investment) and U.S. exports in manufacturing are complements and not substitutes. An exception may be the Western
hemisphere nations, which in this sample are predominantly developing or newly
industrializing ones (with the exception of Canada). For the Western hemisphere
nations, the results of this study were inconclusive. The sign of the relevant coefficient from the gravity model specification was negative, consistent with a sub-
stitutive relationship, and was statistically significant at a 95 percent level of
confidence but not at a 99 percent level. The same complementarity appears in
the Japanese data; however, Indonesia would appear to be an outlier, in that robust results are obtained for relationships between Japanese outward FDI and both
exports and imports for the East Asian nations only if Indonesia is dropped from
the sample.

When direct investment and exports indeed are complements, this result does
not support the claim that direct investment abroad is associated with loss of
jobs or deindustrialization of the United States or Japan.[7] In particular, the analyses do not support contemporary variants of the pauper labor hypothesis (e.g.,
that multinational firms locate foreign direct investment primarily in nations
where workers are highly productive but are paid low wages). The analysis presented here, consistent with that of Brainard (1995b), suggests that for FDI from
both the United States and Japan, high per capita income is a drawing factor,
even though much FDI from both nations is located in newly industrializing
nations, where wages are significantly lower than in Japan or the United States.

More important, however, the complementarity between FDI and exports
suggests that outward direct investment from neither country is associated with
"hollowing out" or deindustrialization, as is often claimed. Rather the opposite would appear to be true: that as direct investment abroad expands, the
affiliates of both U.S. and Japanese multinationals created by this investment
acquire large appetites for goods produced in the home economies, and thus that

expansion abroad is associated with increased, rather than decreased, export possibilities.

It is, however, also true that the same expansion abroad is associated, if more weakly, with increased imports of manufactured goods into the home economies. Are these expanded imports associated with job loss or deindustrialization?

This last issue cannot be answered on the basis of the evidence provided here. A reasonable (but, on the basis of the evidence here, untestable) hypothesis would be that the imports associated with multinational activity embody a higher percentage of unskilled or semiskilled labor, and a lower percentage of higher skilled labor, than do the associated exports. If this hypothesis is correct, the implication would be that expansion of multinational activity does put wage or unemployment pressure on low-skilled labor in the home countries (the United States and Japan) but creates additional demand for high-skilled labor. This in turn would cause the wages of the latter class of workers to rise relative to the former, and thus it is not out of the question that multinational activity has contributed to the growing disparities in income distribution observed to be occurring in the United States (but apparently not in Japan). However, this possiblity is conjectural and is not the only possible interpretation of the empirical results presented here. As is so often the case, apparently more research is necessary to test these propositions.

Notes

I am grateful to Mun Ho, Raymond Vernon, Dennis Encarnation, Robert Lawrence, Antonio Fatas, Robert Kennedy, Raymond Mataloni, Catherine Mann, and Steve Saeger for helpful comments and suggestions. I also benefited from the comments I received on this research at an INSEAD brown-bag seminar. Finally, I thank Ishtiaq Mahmood for research assistance.

1. Put more properly, the issue is whether the outputs of affiliates of U.S. firms created through FDI and trade are substitutes or complements; thus, the stock of FDI should be interpreted as a surrogate for this output.

2. The major exception is Brainard (1995b), which is not an effort directly to test the complementarity/substitutability issue.

3. Brainard (1995b) in fact shows that high income levels in countries are associated with both increased multinational sales and increased trade.

4. That is, in any market, an increase in FDI could at the margin reduce U.S. exports.

5. One problem arises with this last variable in relation to Canada and Mexico, because much commerce between the United States and each of these nations originates very close to the border. Hence, the distance measure might overstate the effective distance. However, as reported later in the text, the variable did not appear significant for the estimations on the North American nations.

6. The U.S. results also appear in Edward M. Graham, "U.S. Direct Investment Abroad and U.S. Exports in the Manufacturing Sector: Some Empirical Results Based on Cross-Sectional Analysis," in Peter J. Buckley and Jean-Louis Mucchielli, eds., *Multinational Firms and International Relocation* (Wokingham, England: Edward Elgar, 1996).

7. Articulated by, among others, the U.S. organized labor movement; Goldfinger (1971) remains one of the best statements of the attitude of organized labor toward international trade and investment.

References

Bergsten, C. Fred, Thomas Horst, and Theodore H. Moran (1978). *American Multinationals and American Interests*. Washington, DC: Brookings Institution.

Blomström, M., R. E. Lipsey, and K. Kulchyck (1988). "U.S. and Swedish Direct Investment and Exports," in Robert E. Baldwin, ed., *Trade Policy Issues and Empirical Analysis*. Chicago: University of Chicago Press, for the National Bureau of Economic Research.

Brainard, S. Lael (1995a). *An Empirical Assessment of the Factor Proportions Explanation of Multinational Sales*, National Bureau of Economic Research Working Paper No. 4583.

Brainard, S. Lael (1995b). *An Empirical Assessment of the Proximity-Concentration Tradeoff between Multinational Sales and Trade*, National Bureau of Economic Research Working Paper No. 4580.

Buigues, Pierre, and Alexis Jacquemin (1994). "Foreign Direct Investment and Exports to the European Community," in Mark Mason and Dennis Encarnation, eds., *Does Ownership Matter: Japanese Multinationals in Europe*. Oxford: Oxford University Press.

Goldfinger, Nat (1971). "A Labor View of Foreign Investment and Trade Issues," Commission on International Trade and Investment Policy, *United States International Economic Policy in an Interdependent World*. Washington, DC: U.S. Government Printing Office.

Graham, Edward M. (1995). "Canadian Direct Investment Abroad and the Canadian Economy: Some Theoretical and Empirical Considerations," in Steven Globerman, ed., *Canadian-Based Multinationals*. Calgary: University of Calgary Press for Industry Canada.

Hufbauer, Gary C., and F. M. Adler (1968). *Overseas Manufacturing Investment and the Balance of Payments*, U.S. Treasury Department Tax Policy Research Study No. 1. Washington, DC: U.S. Government Printing Office.

Industry Canada (Micro-Economic Policy Branch) (1994). "Canadian-Based Multinational Enterprises: An Analysis of Activities and Performance," in Steven Globerman, ed., *Canadian Direct Investment Abroad*. Calgary: University of Calgary Press.

Lipsey, R. E., and M. Y. Weiss (1981). "Foreign Production and Exports in Manufacturing Industries," *Review of Economics and Statistics* 63: 488–494.

Lipsey, R. E., and M. Y. Weiss (1984). "Foreign Production and Exports of Individual Firms," *Review of Economics and Statistics* 66: 304–308.

Pearce, R. D. (1990). "Overseas Production and Exporting Performance: Some Further Investigations," University of Reading Discussion Papers in International Investment and Business Studies, No. 135.

Reddaway, W. B., J. O. N. Perkins, S. J. Potter, and C. T. Potter (1967). *Effects of U.K. Direct Investment Overseas*. London: HMSO.

Urata, Shujiro (1995). *Emerging Patterns of Production and Foreign Trade in Electronics Products in East Asia: An Examination of a Role Played by Foreign Direct Investment*. Paper presented to the conference, "Competing Production Networks in Asia: Host Country Perspectives," Asia Foundation, San Francisco, California, April 27–28.

Williamson, John, ed. (1993). *The Political Economy of Policy Reform*. Washington, DC: Institute for International Economics.

5

Do Multinationals Shift Production in Response to Exchange Rate Changes?

Evidence from 1977 to 1993

Subramanian Rangan

> No matter what the risk profile, the firm that is
> able to exploit . . . volatility possesses a competi-
> tive advantage gained by its ownership of a glo-
> bal network. . . . In the case of . . . multinational[s
> this advantage] . . . might potentially consist of
> production shifting.
>
> Bruce Kogut, "Designing Global Strategies:
> Profiting from Operational Flexibility"

Exchange rate changes do not figure high on the list of reasons why multinational enterprises (MNEs) locate operations abroad. But as the epigraph suggests, once they locate operations in two or more currency areas, MNEs may in many respects be well positioned to exploit changes in exchange rates. In addition to hedging in currency markets, flexing profit margins, and improving productivity, MNEs may respond to exchange rate changes by also shifting production within their networks to areas made more competitive by the exchange rate change.

Although this simple concept has long held appeal to economists and management scholars, skeptics have wondered whether multinational enterprises really shift production—say, between home and abroad—in response to currency swings. After all, these skeptics note, even at the margin, economic, institutional, and organizational factors (such as plant scale economies and insufficient coordination) may make such switching suboptimal or unfeasible. Moreover, considering the many well-established differences in the average operating practices of MNEs headquartered in different countries, many observers, including policy makers, wonder whether U.S., European, and especially Japanese MNEs respond equally flexibly to exchange rate changes.

I have been exploring these questions with a data set constructed from U.S. Bureau of Economic Analysis (BEA) annual surveys on the operations between 1977 and 1993 of U.S. multinationals abroad and foreign multinationals in the United States. To anticipate, let me summarize the key findings that emerge from this analysis. (1) Across the board, MNEs from the United States, Europe, and Japan exhibit systematic and statistically significant responsiveness in the anticipated manner to exchange rate changes. (2) In terms of magnitude, the exchange rate responses of Japanese MNEs are as vigorous as those of MNEs headquartered in Europe and the United States. (3) Finally, as one might expect, responsiveness varies sharply across the subindustries within manufacturing. Accordingly, the chapter concludes that when it comes to exchange rate–induced production shifting within MNE networks, industry matters but nationality does not.

I will present and discuss these findings after elaborating on the research questions and hypotheses, the data and methodology, and the model that I estimate empirically.

Production Shifting within MNEs

Multinational enterprises, like most firms, seek to maximize their profits, market share, and longevity. Because exchange rate changes can influence all three of these goals, it therefore stands to reason that MNEs should respond to them. Indeed, in perfectly competitive markets, the question may be moot. But as Stephen Hymer (1976[1960]) argued in his pioneering work, MNEs operate in imperfectly competitive markets, where, by virtue of certain firm-specific advantages, these enterprises enjoy rents. Add to the presence of rents uncertainty over the future course of exchange rate changes, and institutional inertia becomes a feasible option. Therefore, it is legitimate from a research standpoint to ask if MNEs shift production in response to exchange rate changes.

Nearly three decades ago, Raymond Vernon (1966: 198) noted that multinational enterprises with multiplant locations might source from low-cost facilities when it became apparent that such facilities were cheaper net of transport costs and tariffs. More recently, Jane Little (1987) has written that

[f]irms with production and marketing facilities on both sides of an exchange rate possess an extra degree of flexibility in adjusting to a new competitive situation. These multinationals can turn to existing plants in countries where the currency is depreciating and, with comparative ease, expand output where relative production costs are falling. (46)

Although this proposition has long held appeal to economists and management scholars (see Adler and Stevens 1974; Caves 1982; Dunning and Rugman 1985; Ghoshal 1989; Knetter 1992 and 1993; Kogut 1985; Lessard 1986; Lipsey and Kravis 1986; Vernon 1966), there has been considerable skepticism surrounding its feasibility. For instance, Bruce Kogut (1985: 32) has asked rhetorically, "Do managers perceive and identify potential options generated by being multinational? . . . Are there organizational mechanisms that permit the coordination of the international activities essential to the exploitation of flexibility?" David Goldsbrough (1981: 573 and 580) has argued that because "integrated plants" within a multinational firm's network might produce specialized outputs that "have fewer close substitutes . . . trade flows generated by the location decisions of a firm with large fixed investments in several countries may not respond as rapidly to shifts in relative prices as those of an independent producer." What is the reality? Do multinational enterprises respond flexibly to exchange rate changes? Do they shift production within their internal networks—say, between home and abroad—in response to currency swings? If one controls for other economic factors, do MNEs headquartered in different countries respond differently to exchange rate changes? Does their at-the-margin behavior reflect well-established differences in average tendencies?

Does ownership matter? That question is raised here in two important ways. In the first instance, MNEs are networks of affiliated companies linked by ties of common "ownership." Thus, trade between affiliates in an MNE network has been dubbed "hierarchical" trade, and many scholars have been interested in contrasting this trade to that conducted in arm's-length "markets" between unaffiliated firms. Accordingly, scholars have pursued the question from an institutional angle by asking whether hierarchies are as responsive as arm's-length markets in adjusting to exchange rate changes.

The presumption has been that trade in arm's-length markets is more responsive because hierarchical or intrafirm trade "usually . . . [takes] place in consequence of central commands rather than in response to price signals" (Helleiner 1981: 3). If this indeed is the case, then ownership matters in the sense that governance through internalization impedes flexibility and adjustment to relative price changes. The implications for both firms and nations are obvious and important.

But in the context of examining MNE responsiveness to exchange rate changes, the question about ownership may also be asked with an emphasis on firms' nationality. Do national factors influence the extent of production shifting that MNEs undertake in response to exchange rate changes? In particular, do MNEs headquartered in Europe and especially Japan respond as vigorously to exchange rate changes as MNEs headquartered in the United States (even when what is called for is a substitution away from home content into foreign content)?

The focus on Japan is important and interesting for at least two reasons. First, as Paul Krugman (1991) points out, "There is . . . a widespread sense that as Japan has moved from the periphery to the center of the world economy, it has continued to play the game by somewhat different rules than other advanced nations" (1). This impression is based partly on casual empiricism, partly on some careful studies that document significant differences in the operating practices of Japanese enterprises (see Kreinin 1988; and Lawrence 1991), and partly on some well-known facts.

For instance, it is well known that for a variety of reasons, including the recency of their expansion abroad, the foreign affiliates of Japanese multinationals rely, on average, more heavily on home operations than do their European and U.S. counterparts. But considering the rise in global competition and the heightening of trade tensions, managers and policy makers alike want to know whether such reliance is, even at the margin, relatively more sticky and inflexible. Peter Petri (1991) has pointed out that some observers believe that the answer will turn out to be affirmative:

[There is a thesis that] is challenging the view that Japan has become more open with *endaka*. It emphasizes the relatively slow adjustment of the Japanese . . . bilateral trade surplus with the United States . . . notwithstanding sharp improvements in U.S. price competitiveness. The proponents of this view have argued that exchange rate adjustments, no matter how large, cannot satisfactorily open Japan. (52)

Second, a focus on Japan also permits us to explore whether Japanese, European, and U.S. MNEs respond differently to exchange rate changes so that we can infer something about the relative influence of market versus institutional forces. The logic goes as follows: exchange rate changes are a market-driven exogenous force that buffets all MNEs regardless of their nationality. What is different between Japanese and Western, especially U.S. enterprises, is the set of institutional arrangements under which they operate. Therefore, if after one takes product mix differences into account, Japanese, European, and U.S. firms respond differently to exchange rate changes, then the presumption is strengthened that institutional forces matter even at the margin. If significant differences are not found, we may conclude that, at least at the margin, certain market forces (exchange rate changes in this case) supersede institutional ones. Such a finding will weaken the importance of the notion of path dependence in international business and also imply that sufficiently large shifts at the margin may bring about convergence even at the mean.[1]

In the remainder of this chapter, I want to focus on the question of whether and to what extent MNEs shift production in response to exchange rate changes and whether there are systematic and significant national differences in the vigor with which they respond. I have addressed more directly elsewhere (Rangan 1994) the question of whether markets respond more flexibly than hierarchies to common exchange rate changes.

In thinking conceptually about the issue of production shifting within MNEs, I find it useful to work with the following simple but not atypical scenario. Suppose there is a U.S.–headquartered MNE engaged in the manufacture and sale of products in the United States and Europe. For a variety of well-known reasons, including transport costs and immovability of certain value-added activities (such as distribution and service), the MNE co-locates the bulk of its operations near its markets. In other words, what the MNE sells in Europe it produces, for the most part, in Europe. But there remain some intermediate inputs that the European affiliates of this MNE source from the United States—almost exclusively from the parent unit. The net result is that the products that this MNE (or strictly speaking, its foreign affiliate) sells in Europe contain a mix of local (European) and home (U.S.) content, and the question at hand is this: how do changes in real exchange rates influence the composition of this mix?

Factors in the Decision

From a managerial-microeconomic perspective, several obvious factors over and above changes in real exchange rates are likely to determine whether and how much the mix between local and home content will shift. At the top of the list may be the availability and lumpiness of suitable capacity in the location favored by the exchange rate change. A second factor may be the importance of scale economies. In the presence of sizable plant scale economies in the area where the currency is appreciating, exchange rate changes must be sufficiently large before switching becomes optimal.

Further, switching costs, such as severance payments and redesign charges, are undoubtedly part of the equation. The magnitude of switching costs will likely differ across industries (larger in autos than in electronics) and even host countries (depending on local regulations regarding layoffs, local content, and export performance requirements). Like plant scale economies, switching costs will tend to make production shifting optimal only in response to relatively large shifts in exchange rates.

A factor that may enable MNEs headquartered in Europe and Japan to be more responsive to exchange rate changes than MNEs headquartered in the United States is the relative ease of "exit" in the United States. Consider what might happen when the dollar appreciates. European and Japanese MNEs might shrink their U.S. operations and shift production to existing facilities at home. Because they dominate home markets, existing facilities at home are likely to be better placed to accommodate the increased demand, but, in some cases, marginal expansion may be called for. But the response of U.S.–based MNEs to a dollar appreciation may appear more sticky because expansion in Europe or Japan to serve the home (i.e., U.S. market) is fraught with the risk of strained and costly exit (should the need arise). That is, getting in may be easy, but getting out may not be. Mindful of a dampened ability to respond to future depreciations in the U.S. dollar, U.S. MNEs may not exhibit vigorous production-shifting responses to appreciations in the dollar. Or they may exhibit a relatively sluggish or lagged response.

Another important factor that may matter in a few cases is whether the firms' competitive advantages are bound to a unique location (such as Silicon Valley, for instance). For firms and industries affected, even large appreciations in the region's currency may not elicit a vigorous switching response. In the strategy vocabulary popularized by Michael Porter, such firms compete on "differentiation" not "cost," and introducing newer, more sophisticated products might be their best response to low-cost competitors based in regions where currencies have depreciated. Of course, such a strategy typically entails staying where the innovation occurs. Consequently, little or no production shifting may be observed.

Of course, even in such circumstances, if the real exchange rate continues to appreciate over a prolonged period, eventually, the changed competitive position is likely to influence the sourcing patterns of these "location-bound" MNEs. Presumably, such lagged adjustment also occurs when an MNE has plants in two or more currency areas but is unable to shift production readily among them because the plants are specialized.

Helen Junz and Rudolf Rhomberg, in a seminal article written over two decades ago (1973), discussed the issue of lags in international trade adjustment. They suggest a temporal taxonomy of lags consisting of recognition lags (the time taken to "become aware of the changed competitive situation"), decision lags ("the time taken for new business connections to be formed and new orders to be placed"), delivery lags (self-explanatory), replacement lags (the time taken to wear out or deplete existing stocks before new orders can be placed), and production lags (the time taken by producers to decide to switch old or add new capacity to service foreign markets) (413).

In this taxonomy, it would appear that, in terms of the *speed* with which they can respond to common exchange rate changes, MNEs ought to be better placed than arm's-length traders who operate in international markets. In particular, Junz and Rhomberg's "decision" lags (the time taken for "new business connections to be formed and new orders to be placed") and "production" lags (the time it might take "producers . . . to become convinced that a profit opportunity which they perceive in certain markets is sufficiently large and permanent to warrant the expense and effort of shifting from supplying one market to another or adding capacity in order to supply the other market") ought to be shorter for multinational enterprises than for their solely national counterparts (413).

Considering the information and scanning advantages that MNEs enjoy over arm's-length traders, we might anticipate that when MNEs shift production in response to exchange rate changes, they do so with shorter lags than those reported in traditional empirical studies of trade adjustment. Indeed, in related previous work (Rangan 1994), I found that this hypothesis does receive support in the data.[2]

Conceptual Models

Based on the preceding discussion, we can formulate three models of multinational sourcing adjustment to exchange rate changes. I have portrayed these models in the three panels in figure 5.1, which is drawn from the viewpoint of a foreign affiliate of an MNE parent. For illustrative purposes, let us suppose these pictures are drawn from the perspective of a German affiliate of an MNE headquartered in the United States.

In each panel, the *x* axis depicts changes in the bilateral dollar-mark real exchange rate. Real depreciations in the dollar are indicated by shifts to the right of zero, and real appreciations by shifts to the left of zero. That is, to the right of zero, U.S. capacity is becoming relatively more competitive, and to the left it is becoming less competitive. The *y* axis depicts the U.S. (or home) content level in products sold in Germany by the German affiliate of the U.S. MNE. With this context in mind, I will consider each model in turn.

The Complete Adjustment Model

The complete adjustment model posits that firms will not shift production in response to small exchange rate changes because of plant scale economies and switching costs. But if the magnitude of the exchange rate change is large enough to push the rate across a certain threshold (which is likely to vary by firm, industry, and country), then, even after factoring in switching costs and lost plant scale economies, firms will completely shift production. Clearly, this model emphasizes factor costs and predicts that multinationals will adjust completely and symmetrically threshold breaching changes in real exchange rates.

Thus, when the dollar depreciates in real terms and crosses the switching cost threshold, foreign production ceases altogether, and the foreign market is served from facilities at home. In this extreme case, U.S.–content level in products sold abroad by U.S.–based MNEs rises to 100 percent. The converse holds when the dollar appreciates beyond the switching threshold. The pattern of adjustment is

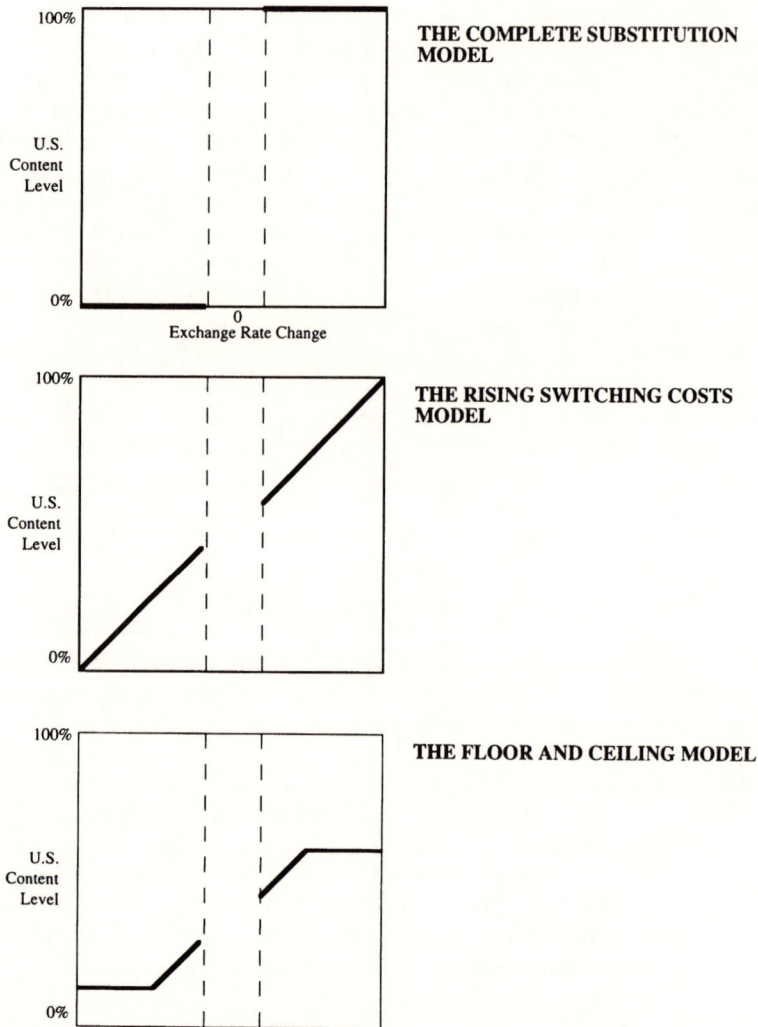

Figure 5.1 Conceptual Models of Multinational Sourcing Responses to Exchange Rate Changes.

shown in the top panel in figure 5.1. Of course, in reality, the complete substitution model of unbounded adjustment does not fully represent MNEs' production shift because switching costs are unlikely to be fixed and (due to re-entry costs) complete exit is likely to be rare.

The Rising Switching Costs Model

This model, which goes some distance toward closing the gap between model and reality, posits that switching costs are likely to be a rising and perhaps convex function of the degree to which switching takes place. In other words, there is likely to be a sequence of switching thresholds, each breached successively as the exchange rate moves secularly in a particular direction away from the initial rate. So a 10 percent change in the exchange rate may lead to a small adjustment, a 20 percent change leads to a larger adjustment, and a 40 percent change to an even larger adjustment. This pattern of adjustment is depicted in the second panel in figure 5.1.

But like the complete substitution model, this model also assumes that adjustment can be unbounded (i.e., reach 100 percent). Of course, solely in response to changes in exchange rates, an MNE would not likely completely abandon its operations in countries that have become relatively less cost-competitive. This notion of bounded responses motivates the final model.

The Floor and Ceiling Model

The floor and ceiling model maintains the notion of thresholds and rising switching costs, but it also assumes a certain level—call it the "floor"—below which home-country content cannot be reduced in the medium run (i.e., over the average exchange rate cycle). For instance, a critical or highly scale-intensive input may have to be fabricated in a single facility that, for historical and market size–related reasons, is located at home. Or it may be that because of relative newness, the input has to be fabricated near the site of innovation and ongoing research—home. Under such circumstances, changes in exchange rates may not trigger a shift in the locus of production of these inputs.

Likewise, there is also a "ceiling," above which the home-country content level cannot rise in the medium run, because, say, certain value-added activities (such as packaging, distribution, sales, and service) have to remain local. Among other factors, value-to-weight ratio of inputs, tariffs, the degree to which value is added in the provision of services, and local content regulations may all determine the height of the ceiling.

This model suggests a discontinuous adjustment curve with kinks on either side where the slope of the adjustment curve goes from positive to zero. The kinks imply first that the responses are bounded. That is, in the time horizon contemplated here, the home-local mix cannot go to 1:0 or 0:1 proportions. Second, given certain initial home content levels, responses may be asymmetric between appreciations and depreciations. For instance, if the initial home content level is near or at the floor, then even a relatively large appreciation in the home currency is unlikely to elicit switching responses. But threshold breaching depreciations will trigger a rise in home content. Likewise, if the initial home content level is near or at the ceiling, then even relatively large depreciations in the home currency will not elicit much of a response, but threshold-breaching appreciations will.

Among the three models sketched here, it would appear that the floor and ceiling is most plausible, especially if one thinks of the floors and ceilings as endogenous over longer time horizons. Of course, it will be difficult from an empirical standpoint to distinguish between the rising switching costs model and the floor and ceiling model because (1) the shortest time window over which changes can be examined in the BEA data is one year—a period whose length may be sufficient for firms to shift floors and ceilings and (2) in the sample interval (1977–

1993) firms may be operating within the adjustment band—the positive-sloped area that is away from either floor or ceiling—and may not brush up against either the upper or lower bounds.

The Role of Competition, Liberalization, and Technology

Beyond the factors considered in these simple models, three other factors are likely to affect the phenomenon, all likely to increase elasticities of substitution. First, the intensity of international competition has risen considerably over the period covered in this study—1977 to 1993. Second, over the last 15 years many countries have liberalized their trade regulations and taken other steps that make the transshipment of intermediate and final goods relatively more attractive and feasible. Finally, considering the steep fall over the last 15 years in transportation and, particularly, telecommunications costs, it ought to have become easier and less expensive for multinationals to coordinate their production networks.

The Empirical Specification

Accordingly, the specifications I estimate are variations of the following:

$$\Delta C_{ijt} = \alpha_{ij} + \beta_{ij}\Delta e_{ijt} + \gamma_{ij}T_t + \varepsilon_{ijt},$$

where ΔC_{ijt} denotes changes in home content level in products sold by MNE affiliates operating in industry i, country j, in period t; α_{ij} is the intercept; Δe_{ijt} denotes changes in the industry-specific bilateral real exchange rate (explained later); T_t is a time trend variable whose coefficient is meant to capture the role of rising competition, liberalization, and falling telecommunications costs; and ε_{ijt} is an error term. Of course, β_{ij} is the exchange rate elasticity of the home content level and it can be estimated with lags.

Considering the breadth of the earlier discussion, this specification is clearly "parsimonious." I want, therefore, to say a word about omitted variable bias and choice of functional form. First, firms do not report and the BEA does not gather data on switching costs or plant scale, or mention floors and ceilings. Further, I am not aware of another source that provides these data specifically for multinational enterprises. Ergo, the reduced form specification.

Having acknowledged this, let me point out that the omitted variables—including unavailability of capacity, switching costs, plant scale economies, location-boundedness, and proximity to a floor or ceiling—only impede or dampen responsiveness. This implies that any bias to the estimate of β_{ij} is likely to be downward. Consequently, if β_{ij} turns out to be positive and statistically significant, then we have a strong indication that the MNEs in the sample do actually shift production in response to exchange rate changes. In this sense, the parsimonious specification provides a strong test of the hypothesis that MNEs shift production in response to exchange rate changes.

On the issue of functional form, I note three points. First, in the absence of formal modeling on which to base a choice of alternatives, it is sensible to stick with a linear specification. Second, in existing trade literature the linear model is conventional.[3] Finally, the key dependent and independent variables are measured in percentage changes, and this too supports the choice of a linear specification.

Variables, Methodology, and Data

As noted before, I examine the production-shifting responses for two sets of MNE affiliates—the majority-owned foreign affiliates of MNEs headquartered in the United States, and the U.S. (minority and majority) affiliates of MNEs headquartered in Canada, Europe, and Japan. Consequently, there are two sets of dependent variables in my analysis.

In my analysis of the production-shifting responses of U.S. MNEs, the dependent variable is the percentage change in U.S. content levels in sales made abroad by their majority-owned foreign affiliates. The dependent variable in my analysis of European and Japanese MNEs is the percentage change in the foreign (primarily home) content levels in sales made in the United States by their U.S. affiliates.

Thus, in both cases I examine changes from the viewpoint of affiliates as opposed to parents (mainly because the estimation process is less prone to measurement error).[4] The changes in content levels are volume, not value, measures. To clarify, let me explain briefly how I estimate volume changes in content. Take the U.S. content level in sales made abroad by U.S. majority-owned foreign affiliates (MOFAs). For the base year of the study, I estimate U.S. content by dividing the U.S. exports made to MOFAs in a particular country in a particular industry by the sales made by MOFAs in that country in that industry in the same year.

For subsequent years, I estimate U.S. content levels in the same manner except that I first deflate export values by the industry-specific U.S. export price and likewise deflate foreign sales values by the industry-specific producer price in the host country. Then, to remove currency translation effects, I convert back into national currencies all MOFA sales figures (which are reported in current U.S. dollars), and rescale these national currency figures back into U.S. dollars at the nominal exchange rate in effect during the base year. This procedure assures that pure currency, pure price, and equivalent but opposing currency and price changes will not influence the U.S. content measure.[5]

The key independent variable in my analysis is, of course, the percentage change in industry-specific real exchange rates, which I estimate based on changes in bilateral nominal exchange rates and changes in industry-specific producer prices in the United States and the partner countries in the study.

The industries covered in this study include manufacturing and food, chemicals (including pharmaceuticals), metals, nonelectrical machinery, electrical machinery, and motor vehicles and parts. Country coverage is guided by relative importance of countries as homes or hosts of MNEs and by the availability of data. Thus, I examine the production-shifting responses of U.S. MOFAs in nine countries: Canada, France, Germany, Italy, the Netherlands, Switzerland, the United Kingdom, Japan, and Australia. And, on the flip side, I examine the production-shifting responses of the U.S. affiliates of Canadian, French, German, Dutch, Swiss, British, and Japanese multinational parents.

The unit of analysis varies based on the question being addressed, but period-industry-country triplets form the basic units of observation. For example, the percentage change between 1985 and 1986 in real exchange rates and U.S. content levels in sales made by U.S. majority-owned foreign affiliates in the chemical industry in France is one such observation.

Exchange rate data and national price deflators come from the International Monetary Fund's (IMF) *International Financial Statistics*, the Organization for Economic Cooperation and Development's *Indicators of Industrial Activity*, and the U.S. Bureau of Labor Statistics' U.S. Export and Producer Price series. Data for estimating content levels come primarily from the U.S. Bureau of Economic Analysis' annual surveys of United States multinationals abroad and foreign multinationals in the United States. To date, annual surveys of foreign multinationals' operations in the United States are available for 17 years, from 1977 through 1993. Annual surveys of U.S. multinationals' operations abroad are available for 12 years, from 1982 through 1993. I supplement this latter series with the BEA's 1977 benchmark survey.

Although this is not a very long series, the coverage here (based on support from the existing data) in terms of time, countries, and industries is wider than that in any previous study that has considered these issues. Besides, as figure 5.2 shows, the 1977–1993 time interval encompasses at least one prolonged episode each of dollar appreciation and depreciation, along with other less pronounced shifts in the exchange rate. So the results ought to be robust and generalizable.

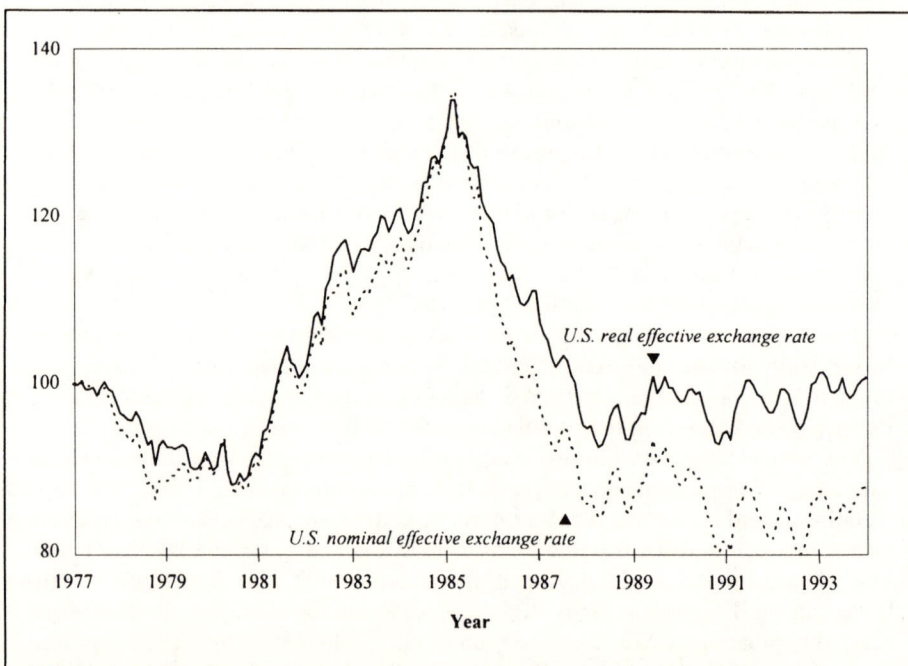

Figure 5.2 Index of U.S. Dollar's Trade Weighted Exchange Rate, 1977–1993.
Source: J.P. Morgan.

Empirical Results

U.S. MNEs Abroad   Let us begin by looking at how exchange rates and home content levels have moved over the course of the study period. Figure app. A in the appendix plots exchange rate movements and sourcing patterns within the Canadian affiliates of U.S.–headquartered MNEs.

In the center of figure A, in the panel entitled "Chemicals and allied products," the solid line plots the course of the real exchange rate that is specific to the chemical and drug industry, and the dotted line tracks U.S. content levels in sales made by the Canadian chemical and drug affiliates of U.S. MNEs. Both the exchange rate, which is stated in terms of U.S. dollars per Canadian dollar, and the home content levels are plotted as indexes. The scale on the left pertains to exchange rates (1980 = 100) and the scale on the right pertains to home content levels (1982 = 100).

Examining the solid line in this panel, we can identify roughly three exchange rate episodes over the 1977–1993 period between the U.S. and the Canadian dollar. First, between 1977 and 1981, the U.S. dollar appreciated by about 10 percent; then between 1981 and 1991 it depreciated by about 30 percent; and finally between 1991 and 1993 it appreciated by about 10 percent. So in the index, we see a down-up-down pattern.

Likewise, remembering that estimates of U.S. content levels between 1978 and 1981 are missing because the BEA did not conduct annual surveys on the foreign operations of U.S. MNEs during those years, we can follow the dotted line in this panel to see the shifts in the U.S. content levels in sales made by Canadian chemical and drug affiliates of U.S. MNEs. We can see that when the dollar was appreciating (between 1977 and 1982) U.S. content levels fell by about 30 percent; then when the dollar was depreciating sharply (between 1982 and 1990) U.S. content levels rose by about 125 percent; finally, when the dollar was again appreciating (between 1990 and 1993), U.S. content levels fell by about 10 percent.

The pattern is clear enough to suggest that at least in the chemicals and allied products industry, the Canadian affiliates of U.S. MNEs were shifting production quite vigorously in accord with exchange rate changes. Moreover, they were doing so systematically and contemporaneously.

The table on the right-hand top corner of figure app. A demonstrates the absolute magnitudes of U.S. content. The table contains two columns of information—one indicating the industry structure of U.S. multinational operations in Canada, and the other indicating U.S. content levels in 1982, the year for which the U.S. content index is set to 100. As we can see from this table, chemicals and allied products have on average accounted for 13 percent of the total sales made by the Canadian manufacturing affiliates of U.S. multinational parents. And, in 1982, U.S. content levels in sales made by Canadian chemicals and allied products affiliates stood at 11.9 percent. Now, following the dotted line in the center panel, we can tell that in the intervening years, especially between 1982 and 1990 when the dollar was depreciating sharply, U.S. content levels in this industry rose to about 27 percent. So during a period when the dollar fell by 30 percent, the U.S. content levels in this industry rose by more than 100 percent (rising from 12 to 27 percent).

Contrast the patterns in the "Chemicals and allied products" panel with those in the "Motor vehicles and equipment" panel. In the latter case, there is virtually no movement in either the real exchange rate or the U.S. content level. The U.S. content level in motor vehicles and parts was 62 percent in 1982, and it remained virtually unchanged in 1993. Not only is this pattern unlike the one we saw in chemicals and allied products, but it also shapes the industry share–weighted aggregate pattern shown in the panel on the center top of the exhibit. This is because (at 43 percent of the total) motor vehicles and parts dominate overall sales made by the Canadian manufacturing affiliates of U.S. parents.

Scanning the other panels, we can see coterminous movements in exchange rates and U.S. content levels in "Food and kindred products," and perhaps in "Primary and fabricated metals." But, in "Machinery, except electrical," and "Electric and electronic equipment," no particular relationship is apparent. And as noted earlier, the panel entitled "MOFA industry shares–weighted manufacturing" (in the top center of the page) provides a summary picture in which the weights reflect the six subindustries' shares in total manufacturing sales.[6]

Figures app. B through app. I in the appendix show how exchange rates and U.S. content levels moved in the other countries studied (i.e., France, Germany, Italy, the Netherlands, the United Kingdom, Switzerland, Japan, and Australia— all countries where U.S. multinational enterprises have sizable foreign operations). The center top panel particularly shows the industry share-weighted aggregate patterns. Although there are wide variations by industry, and some panels do not show content levels due to missing data, by and large, real exchange rates and U.S. content levels move together as predicted.

Figures 5.3A and B show scatterplots of movements in exchange rates and U.S. content levels. If the foreign affiliates of U.S. MNEs were flexing their U.S. content levels in response to shifts in real exchange rates, we would expect the points in the plot to be arrayed in an upward-sloping pattern.

Overall in figure 5.3A there appears to be a positive correlation. During the dollar appreciation period of 1980 to 1985 U.S. content fell (see points in the lower left quadrant), and during the dollar depreciation period of 1985 to 1989 U.S. content rose (see points in the upper right quadrant). But it appears that the responses during the dollar depreciation period are more systematically related to exchange rate changes than those during the dollar appreciation period. Indeed, a regression line through the points on the top right quadrant is positively sloped and statistically meaningful.

But the points on the bottom left quadrant of figure 5.3A differ. These points are estimates from the first half of the 1980s, when the U.S. dollar was appreciating. On the x axis, we can see that between 1980 and 1985 the dollar had appreciated by between 20 and 40 percent against the currencies of the countries considered. How did U.S. content levels move? Clearly, because all the points except the one for Germany fall to the south of the zero mark on the y axis, we know that U.S. content levels fell over this period. But the extent to which content fell in each country shows no relationship to the extent to which exchange rates changed. For instance, whereas the Swiss manufacturing affiliates of U.S. MNEs dropped their U.S. content by about 50 percent, the German manufacturing affiliates, which faced an even steeper dollar, appear to have raised their U.S. content over this period.

Clearly, unless unobserved country effects dominate (and they are unlikely to), there is no systematic relationship between changes in exchange rates and U.S.

content levels during this dollar appreciation period. I want to suggest two possibilities that might explain the pattern or lack thereof. First, because annual data
on U.S. content levels are available only after 1982, I do not know how content
levels moved between 1979 and 1982 when the dollar appreciated most steeply.
If firms' responses were contemporaneous and thus "front loaded," I would have
missed it. I believe this is likely a major contributing factor.

Second, the little tables in appendix figures app. A through app. I show that
the absolute level of the U.S. content was already quite low in Germany (3.9 percent), the United Kingdom (5.8 percent), and Italy (4.1 percent)—countries that
showed the least response. It is plausible that U.S. MNEs, given their long history
of being multinationals, had localized all but the most critical inputs. Thus, they
were operating at or near the floor.

In any event, figure 5.3B, which covers the 1989–1993 period, shows how with
the exception of Japan, appreciations and depreciations are unmistakably correlated positively with drops and rises, respectively, in U.S. content. I will present
results of regressions after reviewing the production-shifting patterns of the U.S.
affiliates of MNEs headquartered in Europe and Japan.

Foreign MNEs in the United States   Before reviewing the sourcing patterns of the U.S.
affiliates of foreign multinational enterprises, I must note two differences driven
by data availability. The helpful difference is that, unlike in the case of U.S. MNEs
abroad, here the BEA data allow us to estimate content levels for the entire sample
period including 1978–1981.[7] So a more complete picture emerges here.

The second difference is that the content level tracked here is the foreign or
non–U.S. content level. Strictly speaking, since the independent variable is a bilateral real exchange rate, one would like to track just the home content level. But
the BEA data do not allow us to decompose by country of origin imports made by
the U.S. affiliates of foreign MNEs. Fortunately, the damage done ought to be
limited because between 60 and 80 percent of the imports made by these affiliates are sourced from their parents.[8]

Figure app. AA in the appendix shows the movements in foreign content levels in sales made by the U.S. affiliates of British multinationals. This figure is set
up exactly as figure app. A. And, like the foreign affiliates of U.S. multinationals,
the food and chemical industries show the most noticeable patterns, but as the
center top panel entitled "Affiliates' Industry Shares-Weighted Manufacturing"
suggests, even overall, the patterns are remarkable and the story is clear—foreign
content and exchange rates move in tandem.

Figure app. BB illustrates the movements in foreign content levels in sales made
by the U.S. affiliates of Japanese multinationals. Although there are several patches
of missing data, the pattern is again clearly noticeable. Indeed, examining figures
app. CC through GG (in the appendix), one gets the sense that the patterns are rather
robust and consistent. Last, figure app. 5.4 shows scatterplots for the U.S. affiliates
of foreign MNEs and demonstrates quite clearly the anticipated relationship.

Regression Results   So do Japanese MNEs shift production in response to exchange
rate changes? Has their response been less elastic than those of their European
and U.S. counterparts? Based on the discussion so far, the answer to the first question ought be yes, and, indeed, this is what the regression results in table 5.1 show.

**Percentage change in U.S. content levels
in sales made by U.S. MOFAs**

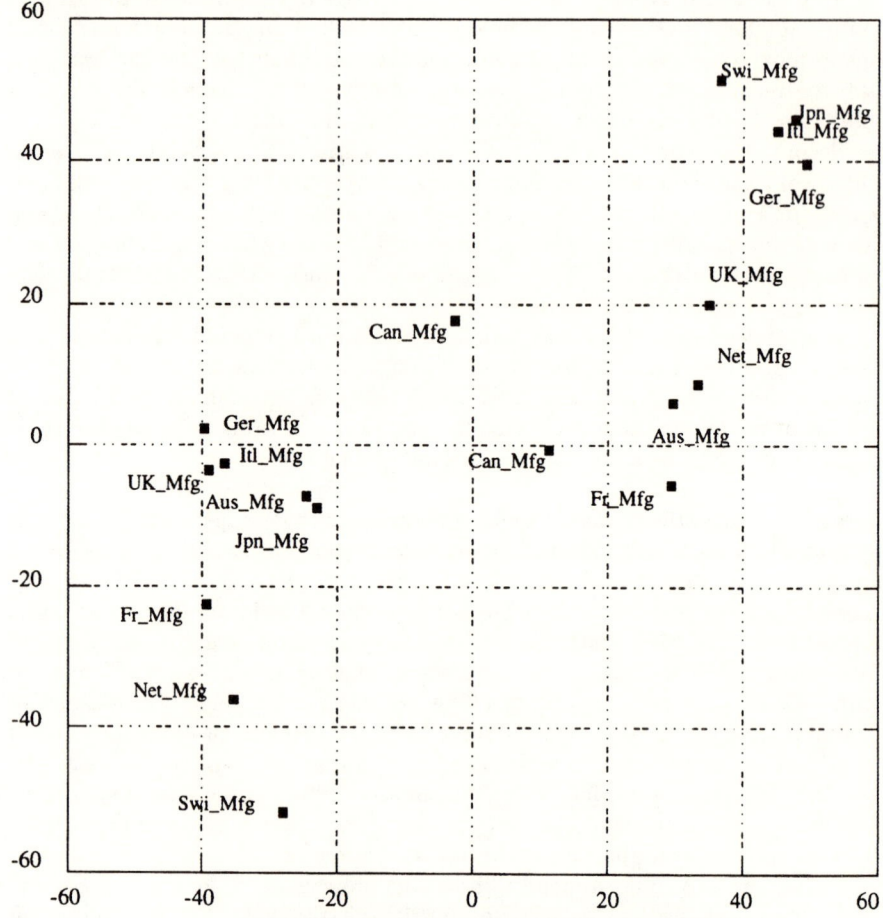

Percentage change in U.S. real exchange rates
Changes < 0 are dollar appreciations between 1980 and 1985;
Changes > 0 are dollar depreciations between 1985 and 1989

Figure 5.3A Change in U.S. Content Levels in Sales Made by All U.S. Majority-Owned Foreign Affiliates in Manufacturing, 9 countries, 1982–1985 and 1985–1989. *Sources*: Author's estimates based on data obtained from the U.S. Bureau of Economic Analysis, *U.S. Direct Investment Abroad*; IMF, *International Financial Statistics*; OECD, *Indicators of Industrial Activity*; U.S. Bureau of Labor Statistics, "U.S. Export Prices." For reasons stated in the text (lack of data), changes in U.S. content levels between 1982 and 1985 are plotted against changes in real exchange rates between 1980 and 1985.

**Percentage change in U.S. content levels
in sales made by U.S. MOFAs**

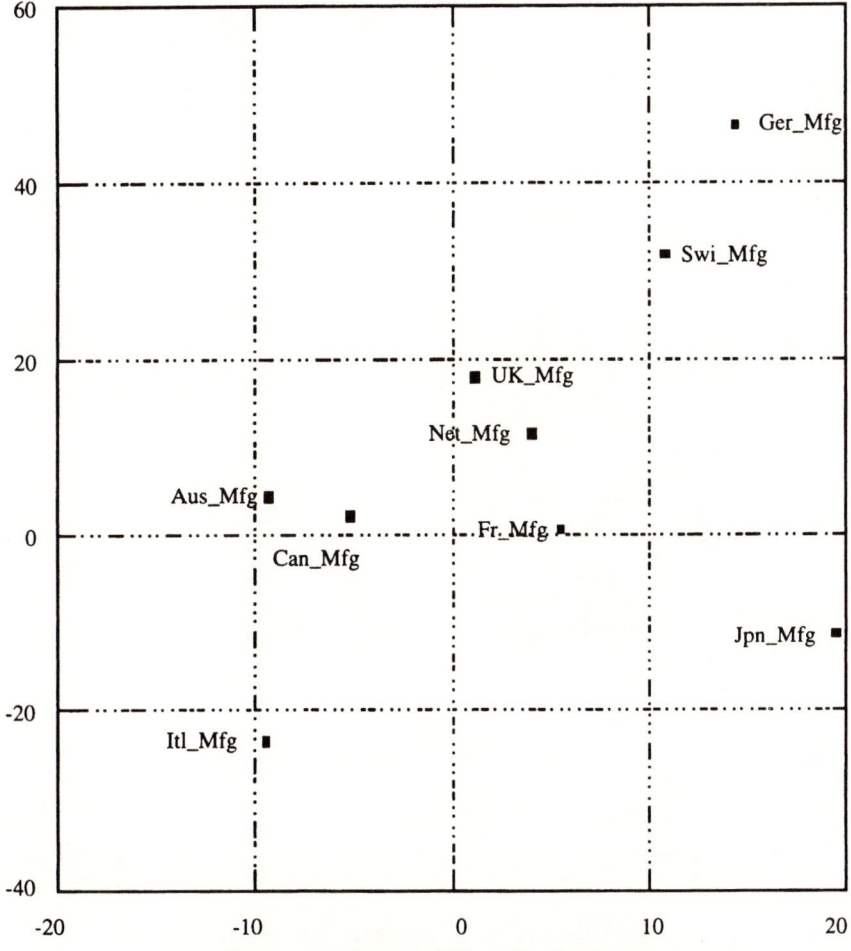

Percentage change in U.S. real exchange rates
Changes < 0 are dollar appreciations between 1989 and 1993;
Changes > 0 are dollar depreciations between 1989 and 1993

Figure 5.3B Change in U.S. Content Levels in Sales Made by All U.S. Majority-Owned Foreign Affiliates in Manufacturing, 9 countries, 1989–1993. *Sources*: Author's estimates based on data obtained from the U.S. Bureau of Economic Analysis, *U.S. Direct Investment Abroad*; IMF, *International Financial Statistics*; OECD, *Indicators of Industrial Activity*; U.S. Bureau of Labor Statistics, "U.S. Export Prices."

Percentage change in foreign content levels in sales made by the U.S. affiliates of foreign multinationals

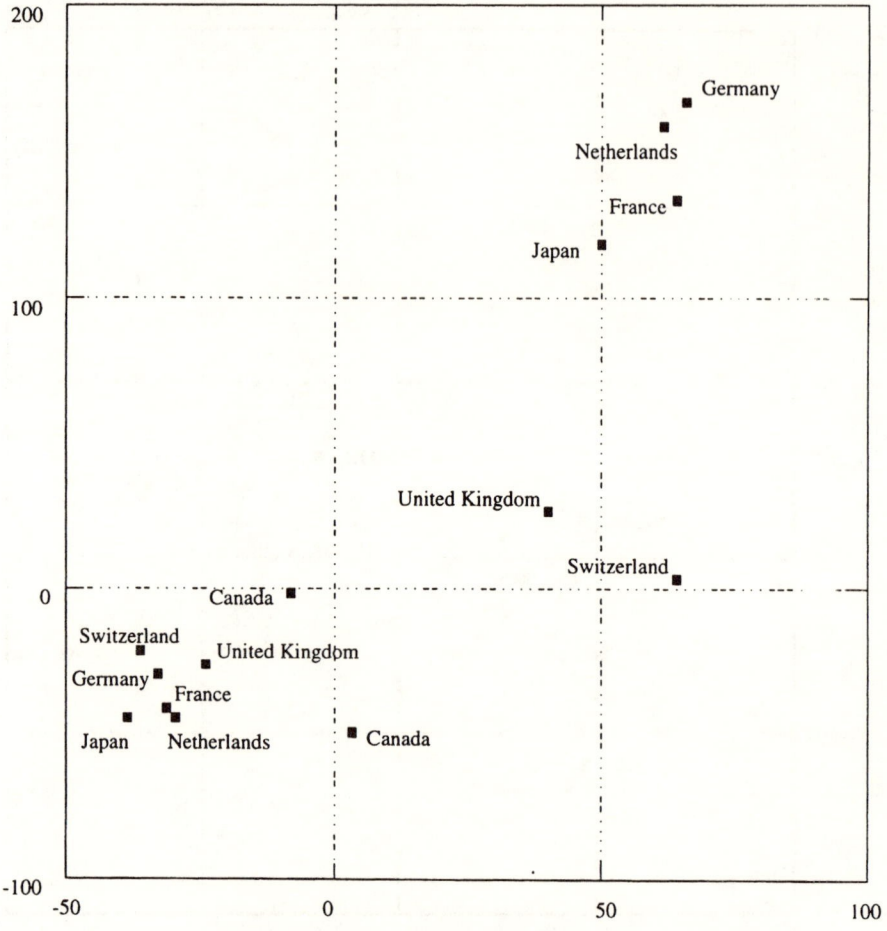

Percentage change in home-country real exchange rates
Changes > 0 are depreciations in home country currency between 1979 and 1985
Changes < 0 are appreciations in home country currency between 1985 and 1989

Figure 5.4A Changes in Foreign Content Levels in Sales Made by the U.S. Affiliates of Foreign Multinationals in Manufacturing, 7 countries, 1979–1985 and 1985–1987. *Sources*: Author's estimates based on data obtained from the U.S. Bureau of Economic Analysis, *U.S. Direct Investment Abroad*; IMF, *International Financial Statistics*; OECD, *Indicators of Industrial Activity*; U.S. Bureau of Labor Statistics, "U.S. Export Prices." For Japan, the yen depreciation period begins in 1978 and goes through 1985.

**Percentage change in foreign content levels in sales
made by the U.S. affiliates of foreign multinationals**

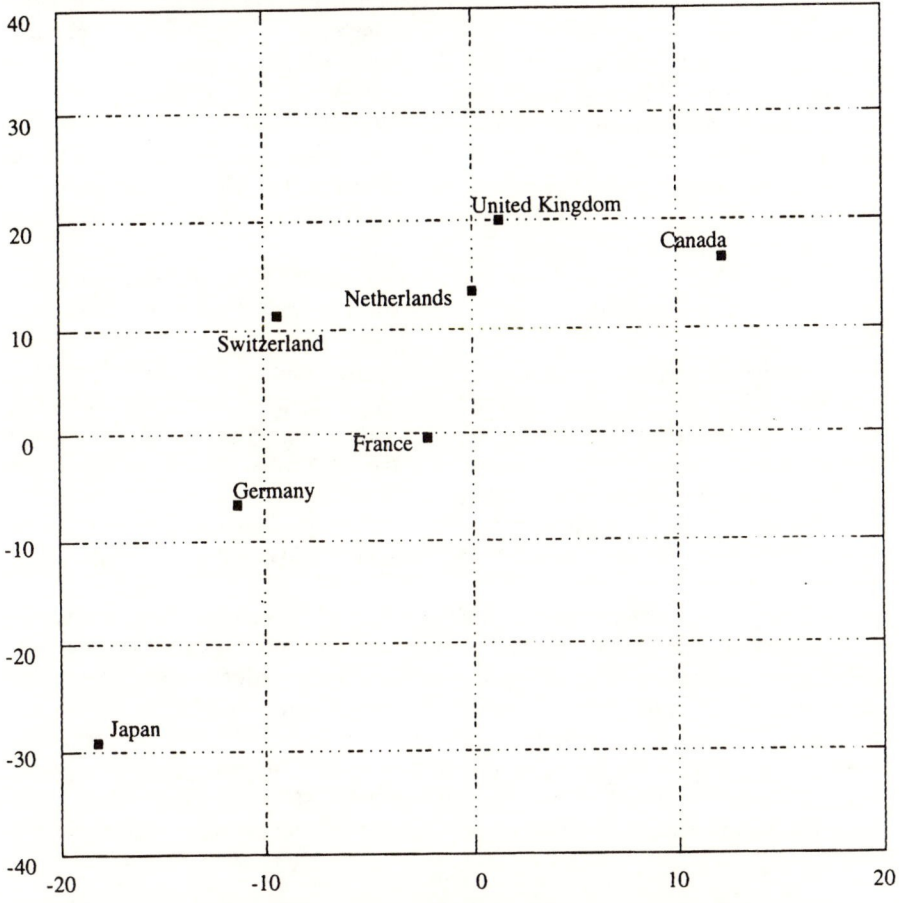

Percentage change in home-country real exchange rates
Changes > 0 are depreciations in home country currency between 1979 and 1985
Changes < 0 are appreciations in home country currency between 1985 and 1989

Figure 5.4B Changes in Foreign Content Levels in Sales Made by the U.S. Affiliates of Foreign Multinationals in Manufacturing, 7 countries, 1979–1985. *Sources*: Author's estimates based on data obtained from the U.S. Bureau of Economic Analysis, *U.S. Direct Investment Abroad*; IMF, *International Financial Statistics*; OECD, *Indicators of Industrial Activity*; U.S. Bureau of Labor Statistics, "U.S. Export Prices." For Japan, the exchange rate change episode begins in 1990 and goes through 1993.

The coefficient on exchange rates for Japan is positive and passes easily the conventional test for statistical significance. And because the exchange rate coefficients in the table are elasticities, the results for Japan imply that for every 1 percent appreciation (depreciation) in the yen-dollar real exchange rate, the U.S. affiliates of Japanese MNEs drop (raise) by 1.3 percent their foreign content level.

In terms of comparison, one can see from the other columns in the table that Japanese MNEs respond at least as elastically as the British, French, or German firms. In fact, as the first column in table 5.1 shows, the average exchange rate elasticity is around 1.06, which is not statistically different from the number for Japan alone.

Before moving to look at the results for U.S. MNEs, I would like to mention lags and the time trend variable. The inclusion of lagged exchange rates produced no change in the results, and the lagged variables themselves took neither sizable nor even moderately significant coefficients. These results imply that the U.S. affiliates of foreign multinational enterprises not only shift production contemporaneously with exchange rate changes, but their response is also complete in the same year. Because these are annual data, absence of lags in these data is not implausible. A survey of the literature on lags in trade concludes that "while adjustment is not instantaneous, the lags are fairly short, with most of the effect occurring within four quarters or so" (Goldstein and Khan 1985: 1067).

Similarly, the coefficient on the time trend variable is neither large nor statistically significant. Entering time as an interaction term with the exchange rate does not change the results. This finding is consistent with results shown in table 5.2, which reports the results for multiyear windows. Column 1 of table 5.2 shows that between 1979 and 1985—a period when the home currencies were depreciating vis-à-vis the dollar—the production-shifting elasticity of foreign multinationals in the United States was 2.8. Then during the 1985–1987 period, when their home currencies appreciated sharply against the U.S. dollar, foreign multinationals

Table 5.1 Regressions Explaining Year-to-Year Changes in the Foreign-Content Levels in Sales Made by the U.S. Affiliates of Japanese, British, French, and German Multinationals, Aggregate Manufacturing, 1977–1993

			Country of headquarters		
Independent variables	All foreign	Japan	United Kingdom	France	Germany
Constant	2.24	3.24	0.17	4.67	3.00
	(1.47)	(1.17)	(0.06)	(0.80)	(1.03)
Changes in real exchange rates	1.06	1.31	0.89	1.31	0.96
	(7.25)	(5.34)	(3.19)	(2.35)	(3.91)
Summary statistics					
Adjusted R^2	.32	.65	.38	.23	.49
Number of observations	112	16	16	16	16

T statistics in parentheses.

Table 5.2 Regressions Explaining Changes in the Home-Content Levels in Sales Made by Foreign Affiliates of U.S. Multinationals and the U.S. Affiliates of Foreign Multinationals, Aggregate Manufacturing, 1979–1993

Independent variables	Foreign multinationals' U.S. affiliates			U.S. multinationals' foreign affiliates	
	Home currencies depreciating 1979–1985[a]	Home currencies appreciating 1985–1987	Home currencies appreciating and depreciating 1989–1993	Dollar depreciating 1985–1989	Dollar appreciating and depreciating 1989–1993[b]
Constant	-60.80	3.30	8.95	-28.51	9.345
	(-0.99)	(0.25)	(1.96)	(-1.65)	(2.13)
Changes in real exchange rates	2.80	1.17	1.39	1.49	1.88
	(2.46)	(2.61)	(3.07)	(3.19)	(3.83)
Summary statistics					
Adjusted R^2	.46	.49	.58	.51	.67
Number of observations	7	7	7	9	8

T statistics in parentheses.

[a]For Japan, the yen depreciation is measured from 1978.

[b]Results shown are without Japan. With Japan, the coefficient on exchange rates is 0.45 with a t statistic of 0.66.

exhibited a production-shifting elasticity of 1.17 (which if anything appears lower than the elasticity of the previous years). And finally, between 1989 and 1993, the production-shifting elasticity for these entities was 1.39. These results suggest that the exchange rate elasticities have remained largely unchanged over these last years.

Table 5.2 also shows (in columns 4 and 5) the regression results for U.S. multinationals. At 1.49 and 1.88, little distinguishes the U.S. results from the ones already reviewed.

Conclusion

During the previous decade and a half, real exchange rates have moved quite dramatically. Between the late 1970s and mid-1980s, the U.S. dollar rose sharply and then tumbled against major currencies (especially the Japanese yen). Using these exchange rate episodes as a natural test bed, this chapter has examined whether multinational enterprises respond by shifting their sourcing and, if they do so, whether their responsiveness differs by nationality of the parent firm.

The results just reviewed provide compelling evidence that multinational firms shift production systematically in response to exchange rate changes and that the vigor with which they do so is unaffected by the country in which they are headquartered. In particular, Japanese multinationals respond at least as elastically to exchange rate changes as MNEs headquartered in Europe and the United States. Indeed, the appreciation of the yen over the last decade has decreased sharply the reliance of the U.S. affiliates of Japanese MNEs on their home operations.

This finding is consistent with the conclusion reached by other empirical studies (see Lawrence 1991; and Petri 1991) "that access to the Japanese market is not completely insensitive to incentives—that the implicit barriers to imports are more like tariffs than quotas" (Krugman 1991: 4).

An equally noteworthy finding of this study is the absence of lags in the sourcing adjustment of European and Japanese multinationals. Why U.S. MNEs exhibit lags in adjustment while foreign MNEs do not is a puzzle that remains to be explored. One plausible reason is that U.S. MNEs face an asymmetric disadvantage in entering and especially exiting European and Japanese labor markets. There may also be factors related to the degree to which firms outsource in responding to exchange rate changes. But more work remains to be done before these hypotheses can be sorted out. Moreover, future work should distinguish between responsiveness that is wholly internal to the MNE's own network and that which relies on outsourcing.

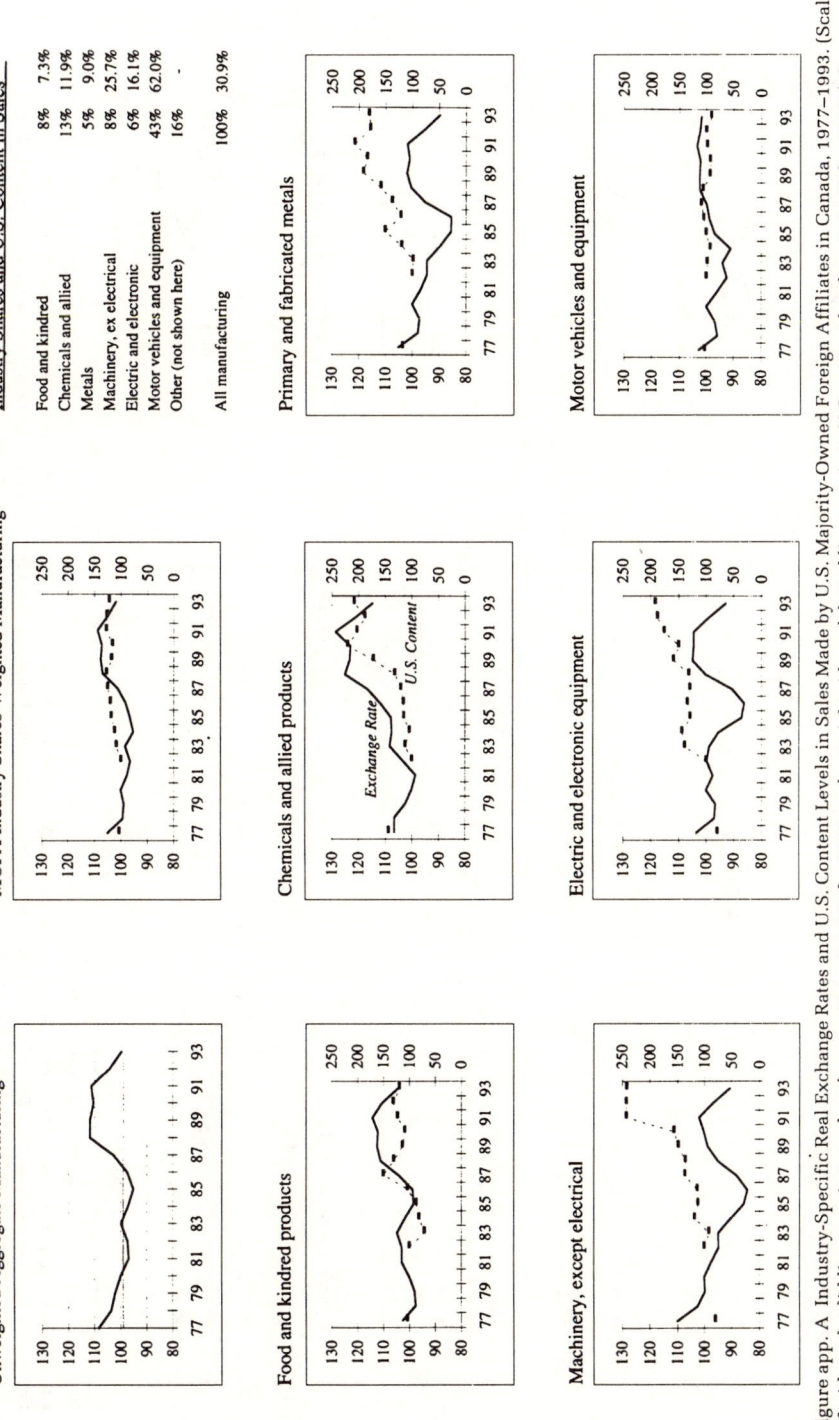

Industry Shares and U.S. Content in Sales[b]

Food and kindred	8% 7.3%
Chemicals and allied	13% 11.9%
Metals	5% 9.0%
Machinery, ex electrical	8% 25.7%
Electric and electronic	6% 16.1%
Motor vehicles and equipment	43% 62.0%
Other (not shown here)	16% -
All manufacturing	100% 30.9%

Figure app. A Industry-Specific Real Exchange Rates and U.S. Content Levels in Sales Made by U.S. Majority-Owned Foreign Affiliates in Canada, 1977–1993. (Scale on left side and solid line pertain to real exchange rates, set at 100 for 1980; scale on right side and dotted line pertain to U.S. content levels, set at 100 for 1982.[a]) Sources: U.S. Bureau of Economic Analysis, U.S. Direct Investment Abroad; IMF, International Financial Statistics; and OECD, Indicators of Industrial Activity. [a]Industry-specific real exchange rate = ((U.S. $/Foreign Currency Unit) × (P * i/Pi)); U.S. content levels estimated as described in the text. U.S. content levels for years 1978–1981 are not available. [b]Industry shares are based on MOFAs' cumulative sales in 1977, and 1982 through 1993; U.S. content figures are for 1982 unless otherwise indicated; na = not available.

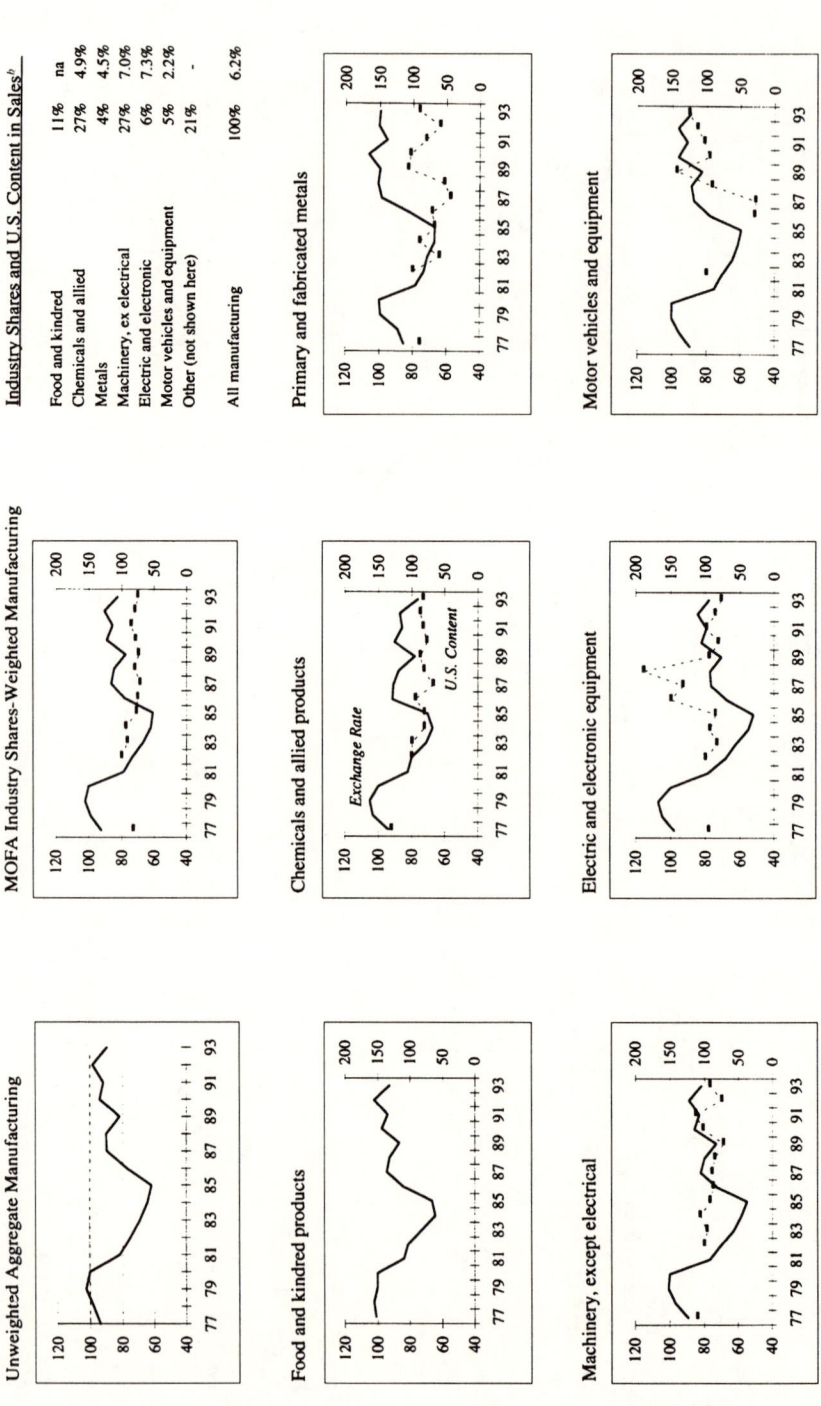

Figure app. B Industry-Specific Real Exchange Rates and U.S. Content Levels in Sales Made by U.S. Majority-Owned Foreign Affiliates in France, 1977–1993. (Scale on left side and solid line pertain to real exchange rates, set at 100 for 1980; scale on right side and dotted line pertain to U.S. content levels, set at 100 for 1982.ª) *Sources:* U.S. Bureau of Economic Analysis, *U.S. Direct Investment Abroad;* IMF, *International Financial Statistics;* and OECD, *Indicators of Industrial Activity.* ªIndustry-specific real exchange rate = ((U.S. $/Foreign Currency Unit) × (P * i/Pi)): U.S. content levels estimated as described in the text. U.S. content levels for years 1978–1981 are not available. ᵇIndustry shares are based on MOFAs' cumulative sales in 1977, and 1982 through 1993; U.S. content figures are for 1982 unless otherwise indicated; na = not available.

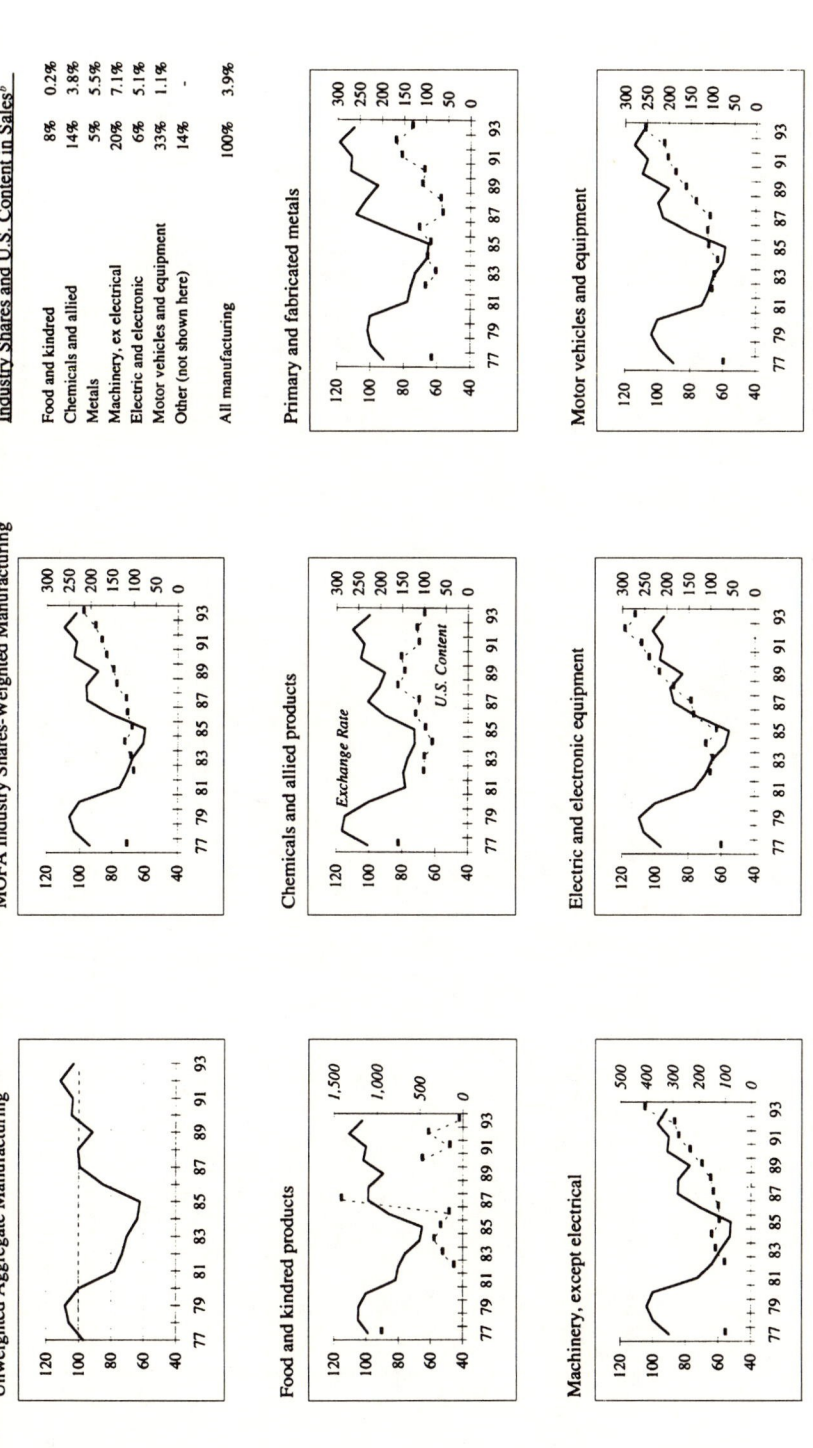

Industry Shares and U.S. Content in Sales[b]

Food and kindred	8%	0.2%
Chemicals and allied	14%	3.8%
Metals	5%	5.5%
Machinery, ex electrical	20%	7.1%
Electric and electronic	6%	5.1%
Motor vehicles and equipment	33%	1.1%
Other (not shown here)	14%	-
All manufacturing	100%	3.9%

Figure app. C Industry-Specific Real Exchange Rates and U.S. Content Levels in Sales Made by U.S. Majority-Owned Foreign Affiliates in Germany, 1977–1993. (Scale on left side and solid line pertain to real exchange rates, set at 100 for 1980; scale on right side and dotted line pertain to U.S. content levels, set at 100 for 1982.[a]) *Sources:* U.S. Bureau of Economic Analysis, *U.S. Direct Investment Abroad;* IMF, *International Financial Statistics;* and OECD, *Indicators of Industrial Activity.* [a]Industry-specific real exchange rate = ((U.S. $/Foreign Currency Unit) × (P * i/Pi)); U.S. content levels estimated as described in the text. U.S. content levels for years 1978–1981 are not available. [b]Industry shares are based on MOFAs' cumulative sales in 1977, and 1982 through 1993; U.S. content figures are for 1982 unless otherwise indicated; na = not available.

123

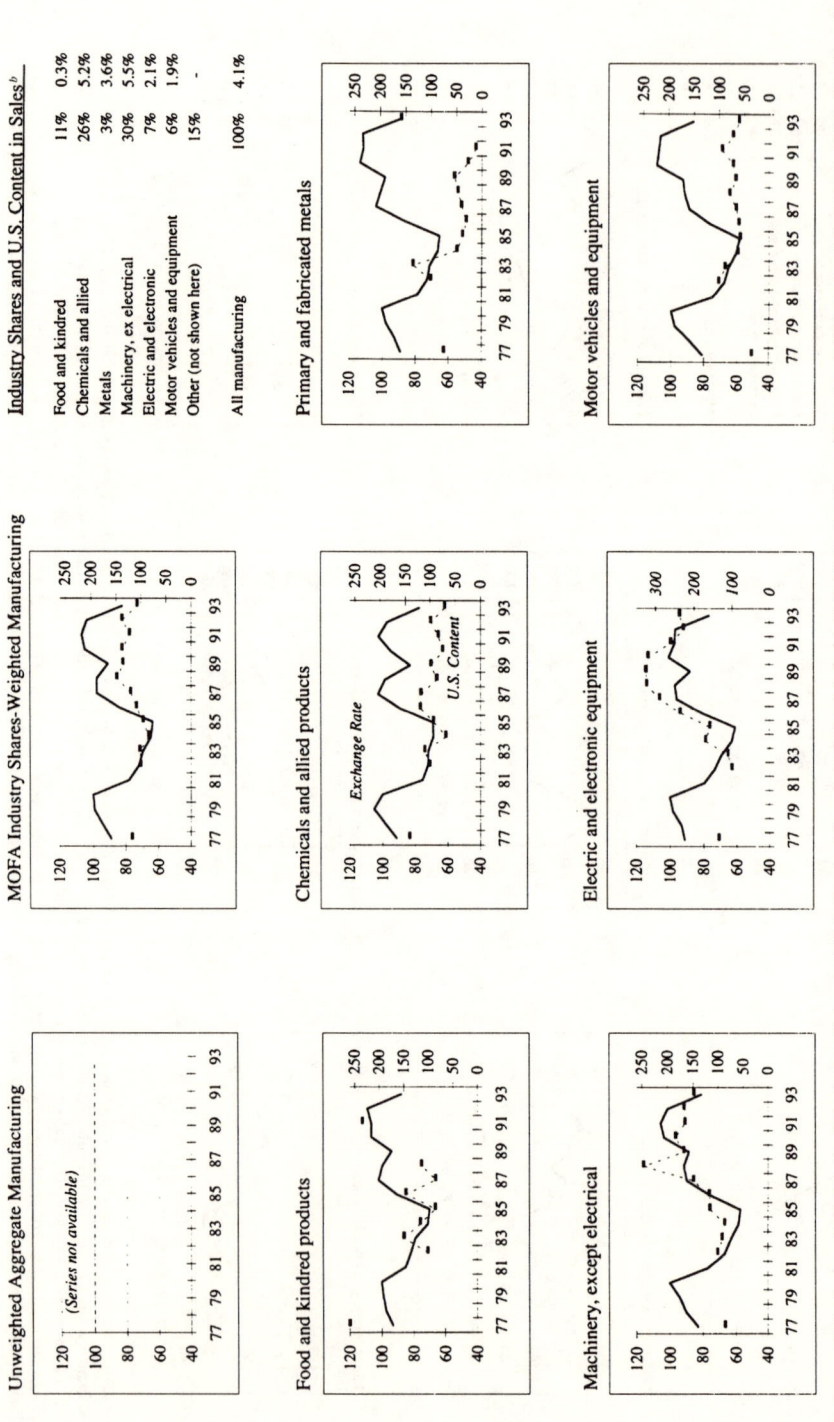

Figure app. D Industry-Specific Real Exchange Rates and U.S. Content Levels in Sales Made by U.S. Majority-Owned Foreign Affiliates in Italy, 1977–1993. (Scale on left side and solid line pertain to real exchange rates, set at 100 for 1980; scale on right side and dotted line pertain to U.S. content levels, set at 100 for 1982.[a]) Sources: U.S. Bureau of Economic Analysis, U.S. Direct Investment Abroad; IMF, International Financial Statistics; and OECD, Indicators of Industrial Activity. [a]Industry-specific real exchange rate = ((U.S. $/Foreign Currency Unit) × (P * i/Pi)); U.S. content levels estimated as described in the text. U.S. content levels for years 1978–1981 are not available. [b]Industry shares are based on MOFAs' cumulative sales in 1977, and 1982 through 1993; U.S. content figures are for 1982 unless otherwise indicated; na = not available.

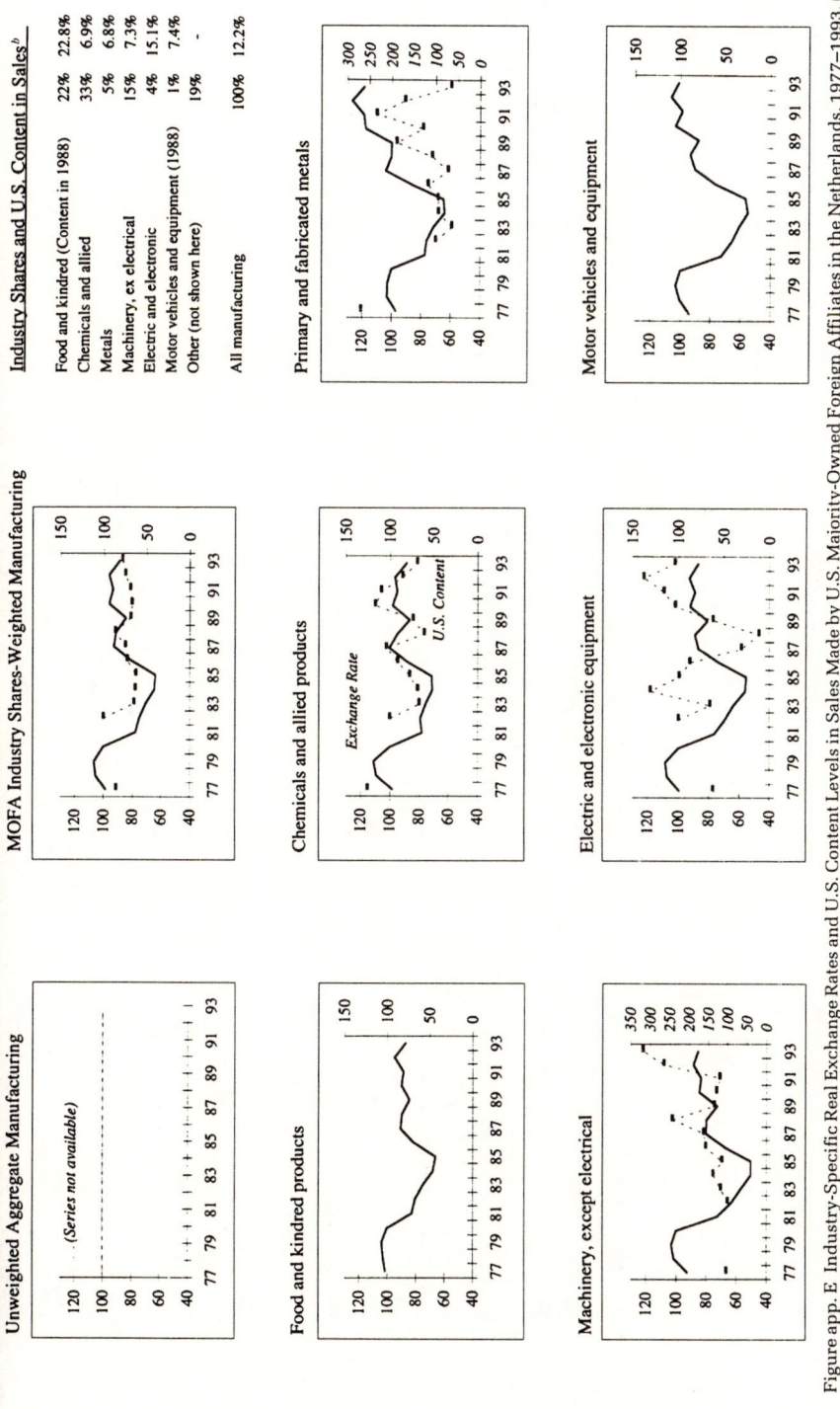

Industry Shares and U.S. Content in Sales[b]

Food and kindred (Content in 1988)	22%	22.8%
Chemicals and allied	33%	6.9%
Metals	5%	6.8%
Machinery, ex electrical	15%	7.3%
Electric and electronic	4%	15.1%
Motor vehicles and equipment (1988)	1%	7.4%
Other (not shown here)	19%	-
All manufacturing	100%	12.2%

Figure app. E Industry-Specific Real Exchange Rates and U.S. Content Levels in Sales Made by U.S. Majority-Owned Foreign Affiliates in the Netherlands, 1977–1993. (Scale on left side and solid line pertain to real exchange rates, set at 100 for 1980; scale on right side and dotted line pertain to U.S. content levels, set at 100 for 1982.[a]) *Sources:* U.S. Bureau of Economic Analysis, *U.S. Direct Investment Abroad;* IMF, *International Financial Statistics;* and OECD, *Indicators of Industrial Activity.* [a]Industry-specific real exchange rate = ((U.S. $/Foreign Currency Unit) × (P * i/Pi)); U.S. content levels estimated as described in the text. U.S. content levels for years 1978–1981 are not available. [b]Industry shares are based on MOFAs' cumulative sales in 1977, and 1982 through 1993; U.S. content figures are for 1982 unless otherwise indicated; na = not available.

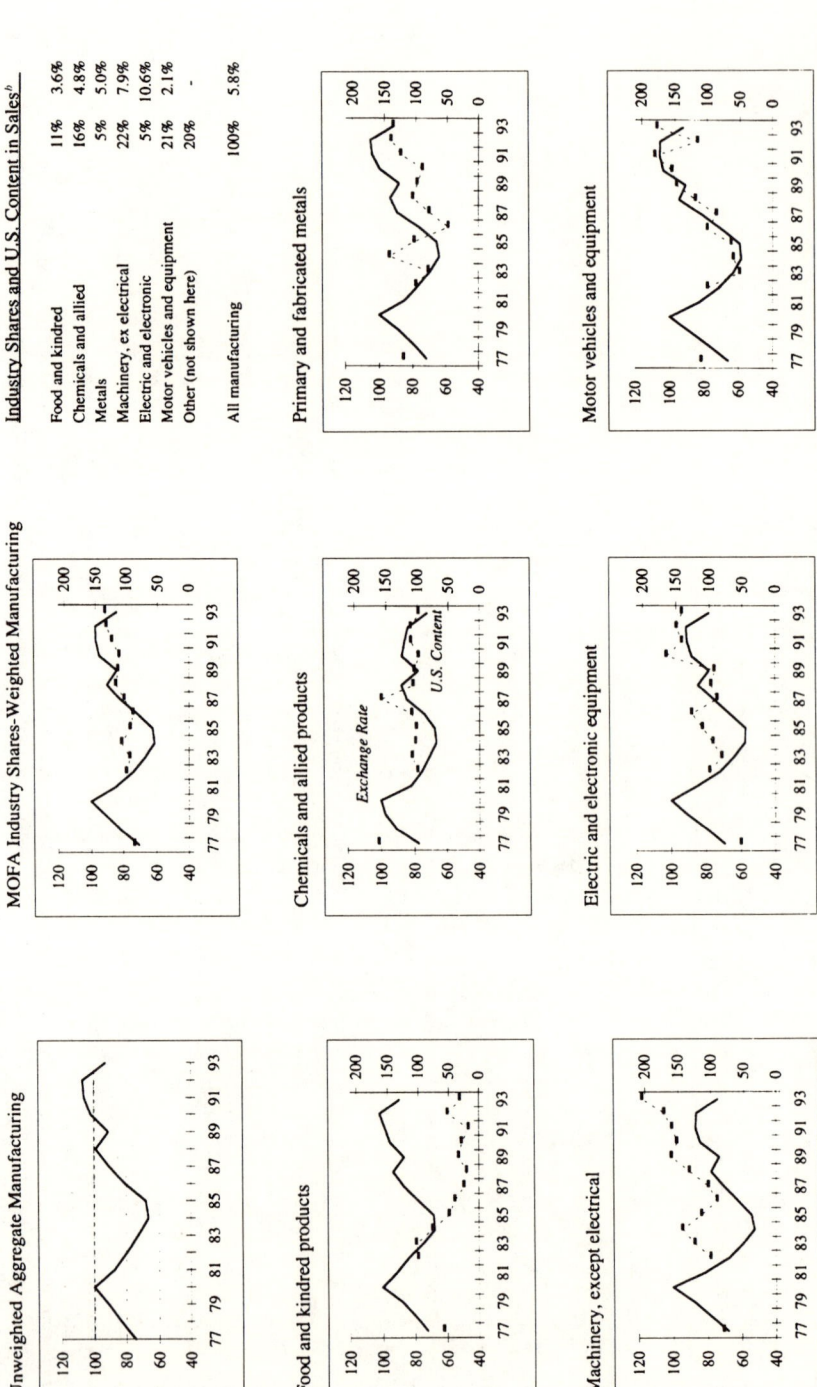

Figure app. F Industry-Specific Real Exchange Rates and U.S. Content Levels in Sales Made by U.S. Majority-Owned Foreign Affiliates in the United Kingdom, 1977–1993. (Scale on left side and solid line pertain to real exchange rates, set at 100 for 1980; scale on right side and dotted line pertain to U.S. content levels, set at 100 for 1982.[a]) *Sources:* U.S. Bureau of Economic Analysis, *U.S. Direct Investment Abroad;* IMF, *International Financial Statistics;* and OECD, *Indicators of Industrial Activity.* [a]Industry-specific real exchange rate = ((U.S. $/Foreign Currency Unit) × (P * i/Pi)); U.S. content levels estimated as described in the text. U.S. content levels for years 1978–1981 are not available. [b]Industry shares are based on MOFAs' cumulative sales in 1977, and 1982 through 1993; U.S. content figures are for 1982 unless otherwise indicated; na = not available.

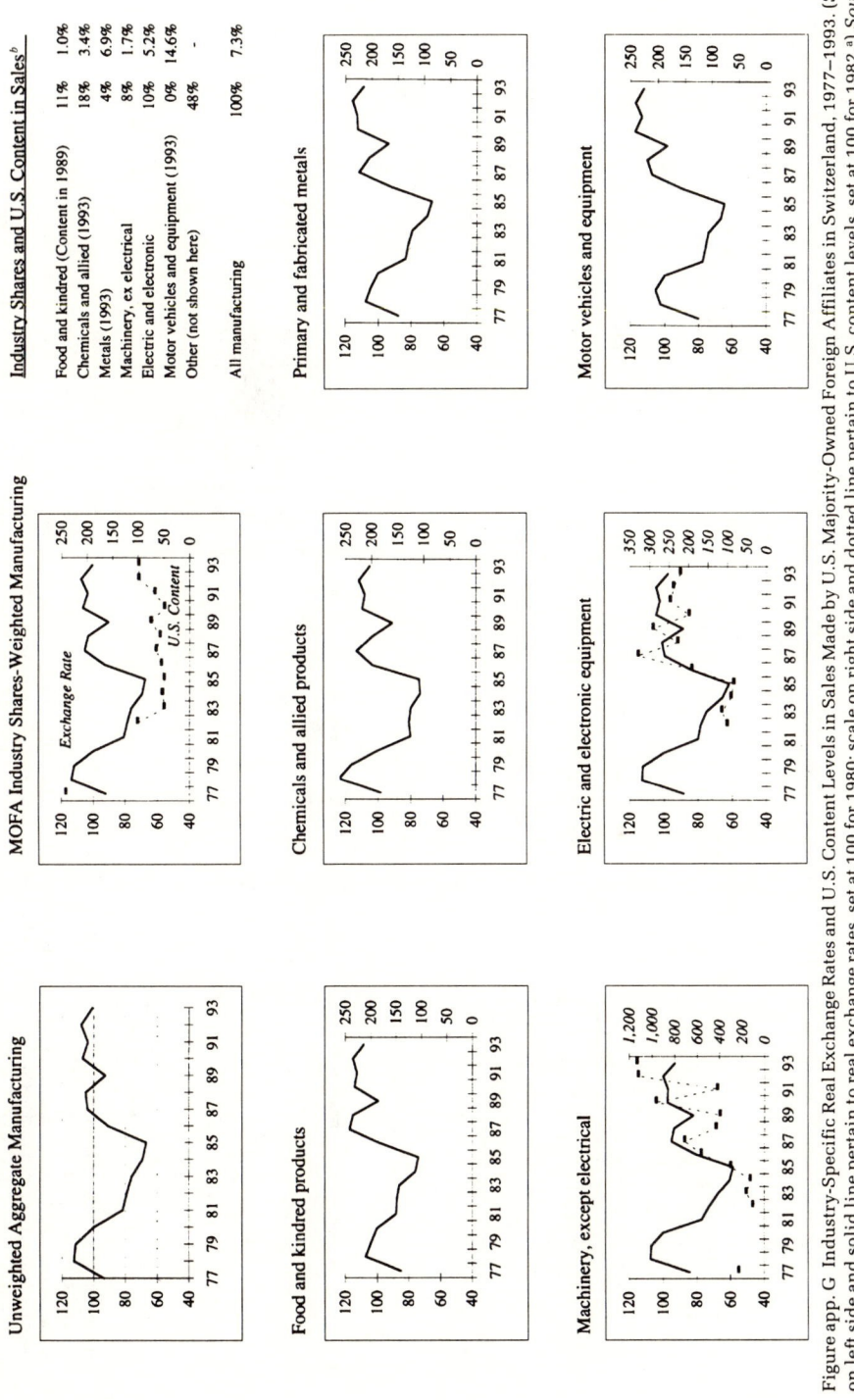

Figure app. G Industry-Specific Real Exchange Rates and U.S. Content Levels in Sales Made by U.S. Majority-Owned Foreign Affiliates in Switzerland, 1977–1993. (Scale on left side and solid line pertain to real exchange rates, set at 100 for 1980; scale on right side and dotted line pertain to U.S. content levels, set at 100 for 1982.[a]) *Sources:* U.S. Bureau of Economic Analysis, *U.S. Direct Investment Abroad;* IMF, *International Financial Statistics;* and OECD, *Indicators of Industrial Activity.* [a]Industry-specific real exchange rate = ((U.S. $/Foreign Currency Unit) × (P * i/Pi)): U.S. content levels estimated as described in the text. U.S. content levels for years 1978–1981 are not available. [b]Industry shares are based on MOFAs' cumulative sales in 1977, and 1982 through 1993; U.S. content figures are for 1982 unless otherwise indicated; na = not available.

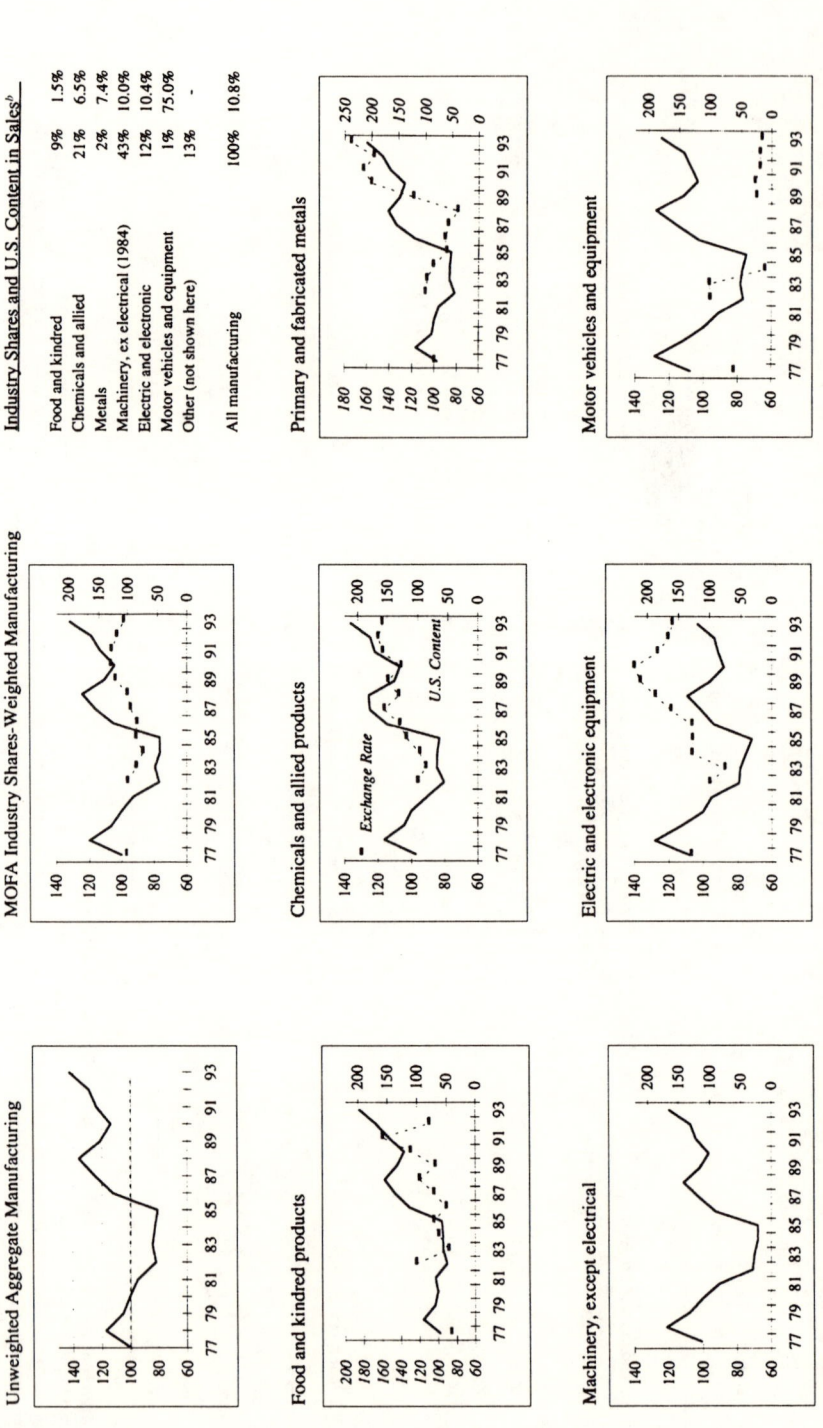

Figure app. H Industry-Specific Real Exchange Rates and U.S. Content Levels in Sales Made by U.S. Majority-Owned Foreign Affiliates in Japan, 1977–1993. (Scale on left side and solid line pertain to real exchange rates, set at 100 for 1980; scale on right side and dotted line pertain to U.S. content levels, set at 100 for 1982.ᵃ) *Sources:* U.S. Bureau of Economic Analysis, *U.S. Direct Investment Abroad;* IMF, *International Financial Statistics;* and OECD, *Indicators of Industrial Activity.* ᵃIndustry-specific real exchange rate = ((U.S. $/Foreign Currency Unit) × (P * i/Pi)); U.S. content levels estimated as described in the text. U.S. content levels for years 1978–1981 are not available. ᵇIndustry shares are based on MOFAs' cumulative sales in 1977, and 1982 through 1993; U.S. content figures are for 1982 unless otherwise indicated; na = not available.

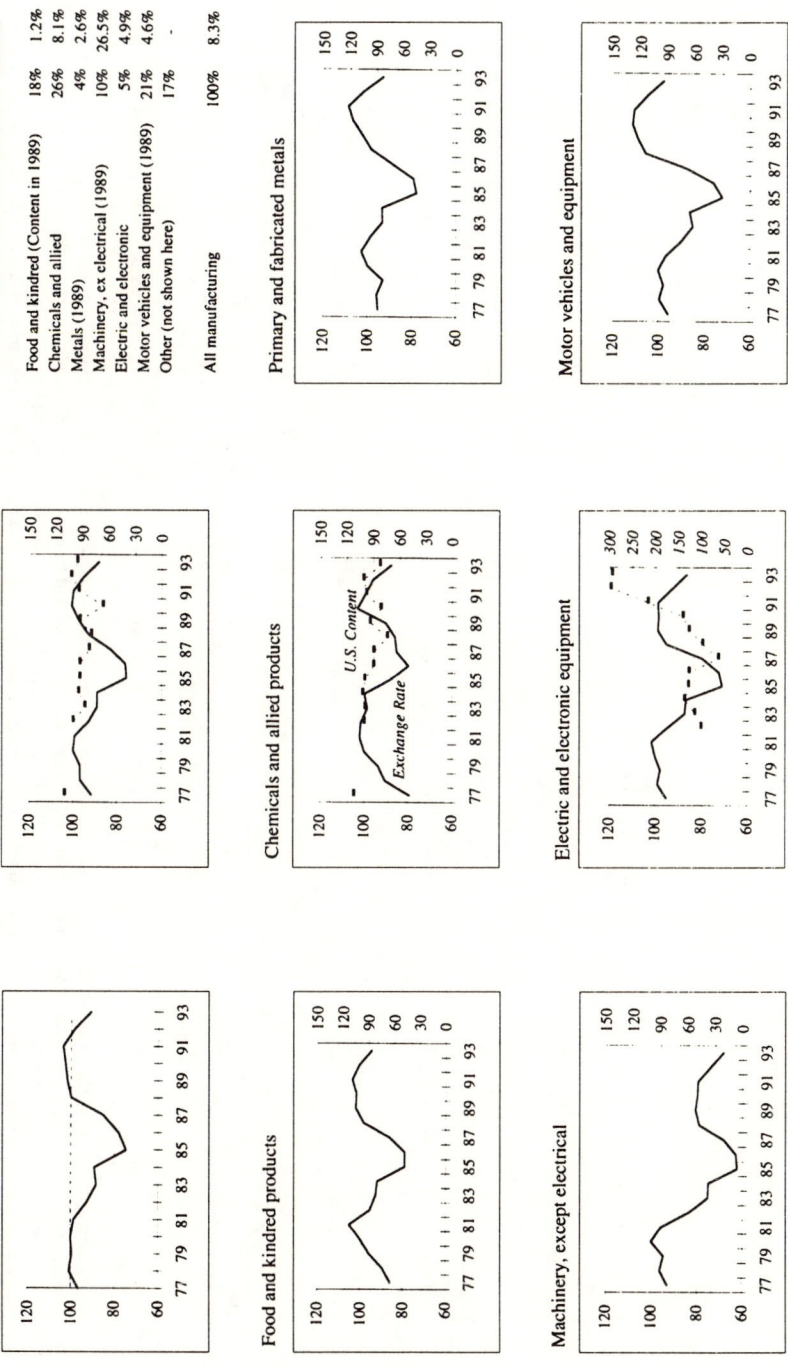

Figure app. I Industry-Specific Real Exchange Rates and U.S. Content Levels in Sales Made by U.S. Majority-Owned Foreign Affiliates in Australia, 1977–1993. (Scale on left side and solid line pertain to real exchange rates, set at 100 for 1980; scale on right side and dotted line pertain to U.S. content levels, set at 100 for 1982.[a]) *Sources:* U.S. Bureau of Economic Analysis, *U.S. Direct Investment Abroad*; IMF, *International Financial Statistics*; and OECD, *Indicators of Industrial Activity.* [a]Industry-specific real exchange rate = ((U.S. $/Foreign Currency Unit) × (P * i/Pi)); U.S. content levels estimated as described in the text. U.S. content levels for years 1978–1981 are not available. [b]Industry shares are based on MOFAs' cumulative sales in 1977, and 1982 through 1993; U.S. content figures are for 1982 unless otherwise indicated; na = not available.

129

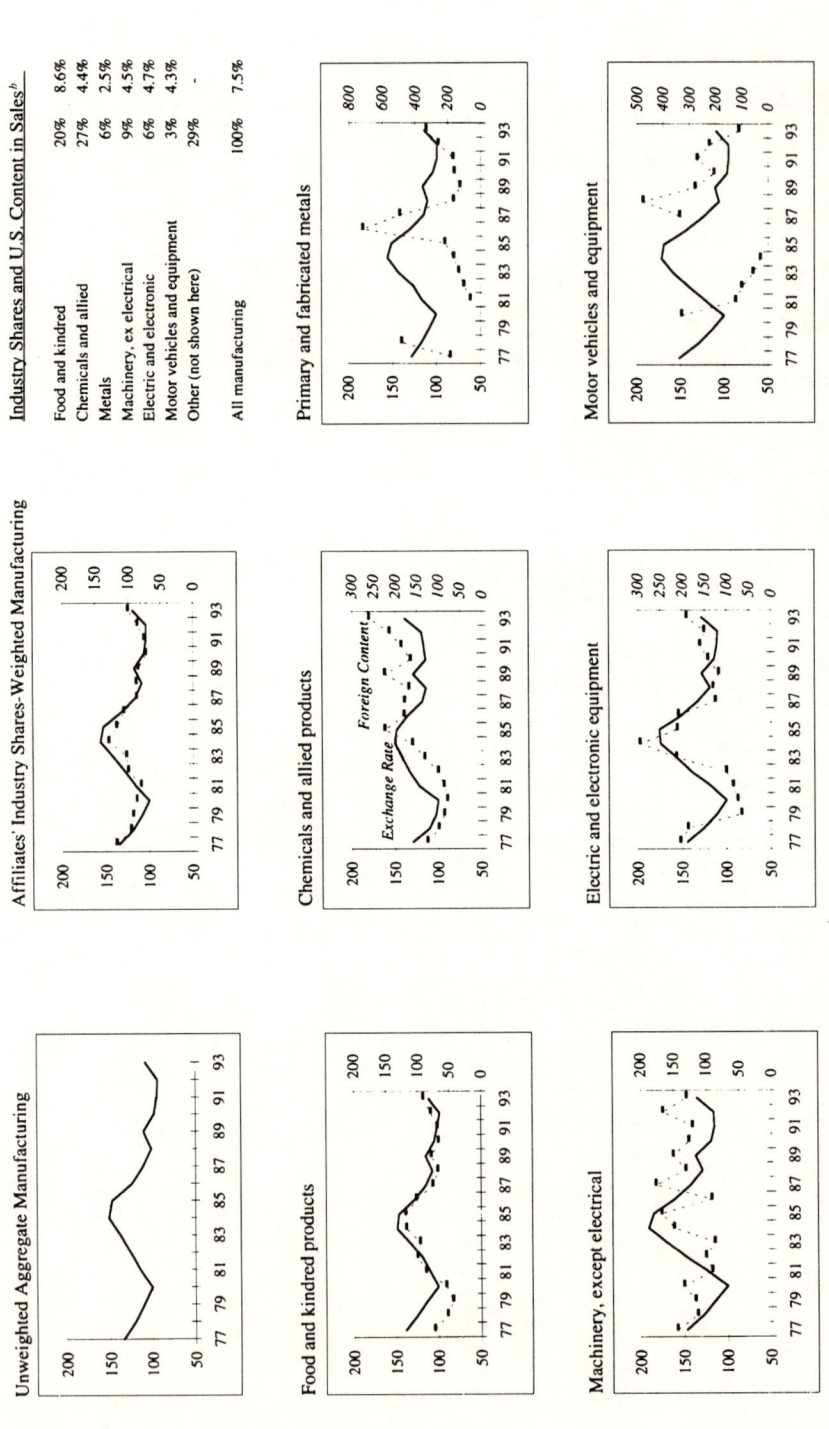

Figure app. AA Industry-Specific Real Exchange Rates and Foreign Content Levels in Sales Made by the U.S. Affiliates of British Multinationals, 1977–1993. (Scale on left side and solid line pertain to real exchange rates, set at 100 for 1980; scale on right side and dotted line pertain to U.S. content levels, set at 100 for 1982.[a]) *Sources:* U.S. Bureau of Economic Analysis, *Foreign Direct Investment in the United States;* IMF, *International Financial Statistics;* and OECD, *Indicators of Industrial Activity.* [a]Industry-specific real exchange rate = ((Foreign Currency Units/U.S. $) × (Pi/P * i)); foreign content levels estimated as described in the text. [b]Industry shares are based on affiliates' cumulative sales between 1977 and 1993; foreign content figures shown are for 1982, the base year; na = not available.

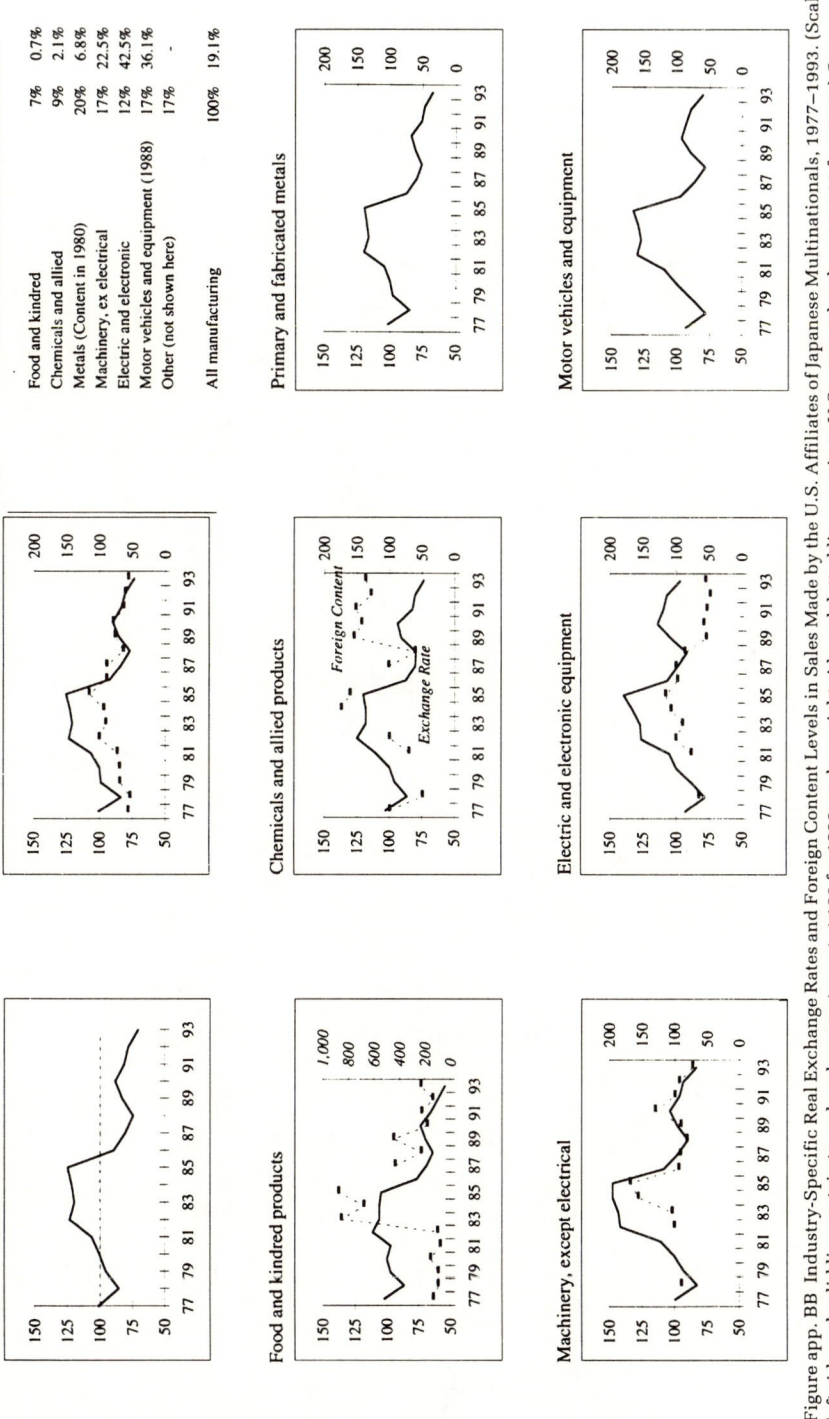

Unweighted Aggregate Manufacturing

Affiliates' Industry Shares-Weighted Manufacturing

Food and kindred products

Chemicals and allied products

Primary and fabricated metals

Machinery, except electrical

Electric and electronic equipment

Motor vehicles and equipment

Figure app. BB Industry-Specific Real Exchange Rates and Foreign Content Levels in Sales Made by the U.S. Affiliates of Japanese Multinationals, 1977–1993. (Scale on left side and solid line pertain to real exchange rates, set at 100 for 1980; scale on right side and dotted line pertain to U.S. content levels, set at 100 for 1982.[a]) Sources: U.S. Bureau of Economic Analysis, Foreign Direct Investment in the United States; IMF, International Financial Statistics; and OECD, Indicators of Industrial Activity. [a]Industry-specific real exchange rate = ((Foreign Currency Units/U.S. $) × (Pl/P * i)): foreign content levels estimated as described in the text. [b]Industry shares are based on affiliates' cumulative sales between 1977 and 1993; foreign content figures shown are for 1982, the base year; na = not available.

131

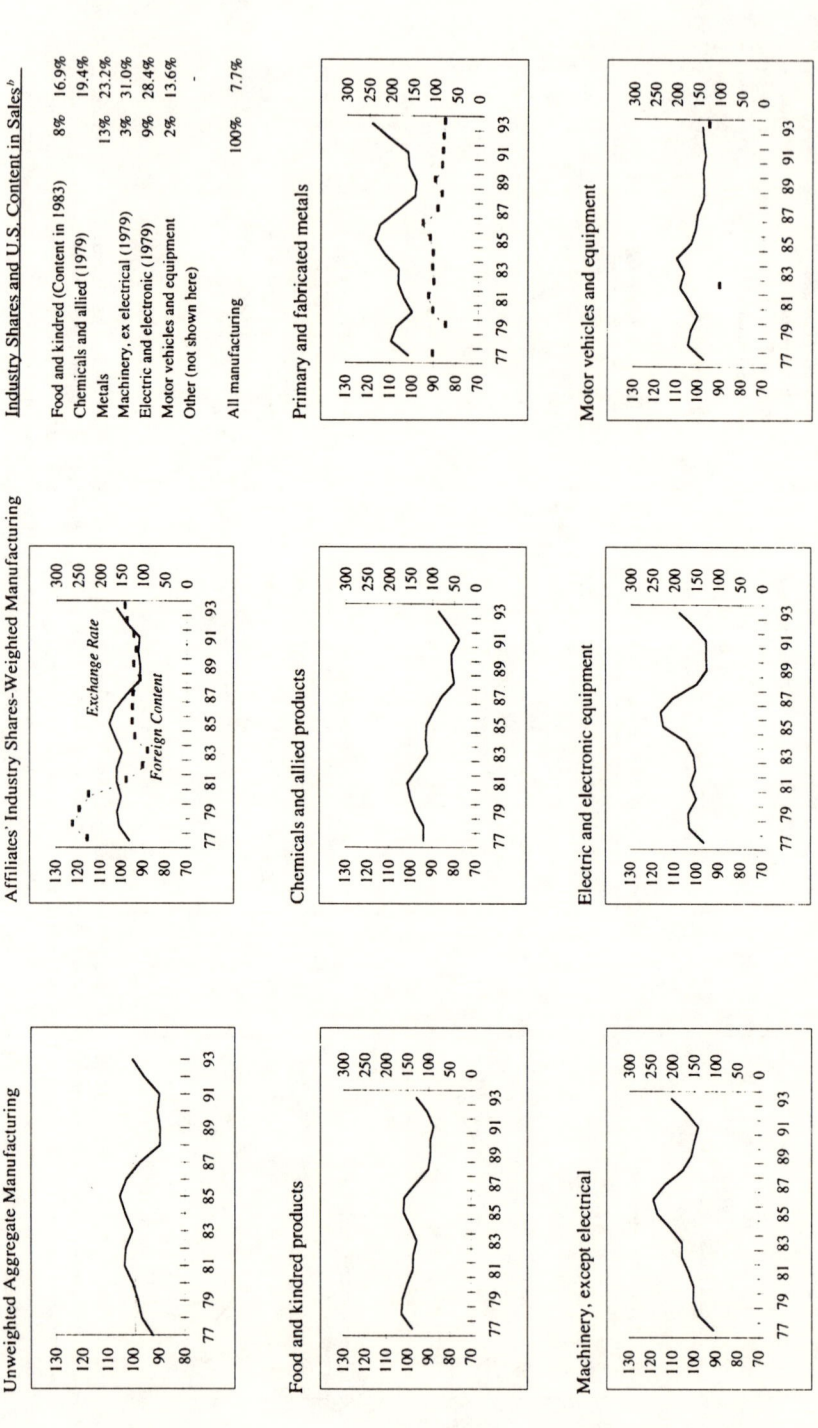

Figure app. CC. Industry-Specific Real Exchange Rates and Foreign Content Levels in Sales Made by the U.S. Affiliates of Canadian Multinationals, 1977–1993. (Scale on left side and solid line pertain to real exchange rates, set at 100 for 1980; scale on right side and dotted line pertain to U.S. content levels, set at 100 for 1982.[a]) *Sources*: U.S. Bureau of Economic Analysis, *Foreign Direct Investment in the United States*; IMF, *International Financial Statistics*; and OECD, *Indicators of Industrial Activity.* [a]Industry-specific real exchange rate = ((Foreign Currency Units/U.S. \$) × (Pi/P * i)); foreign content levels estimated as described in the text. [b]Industry shares are based on affiliates' cumulative sales between 1977 and 1993; foreign content figures shown are for 1982, the base year. na = not available.

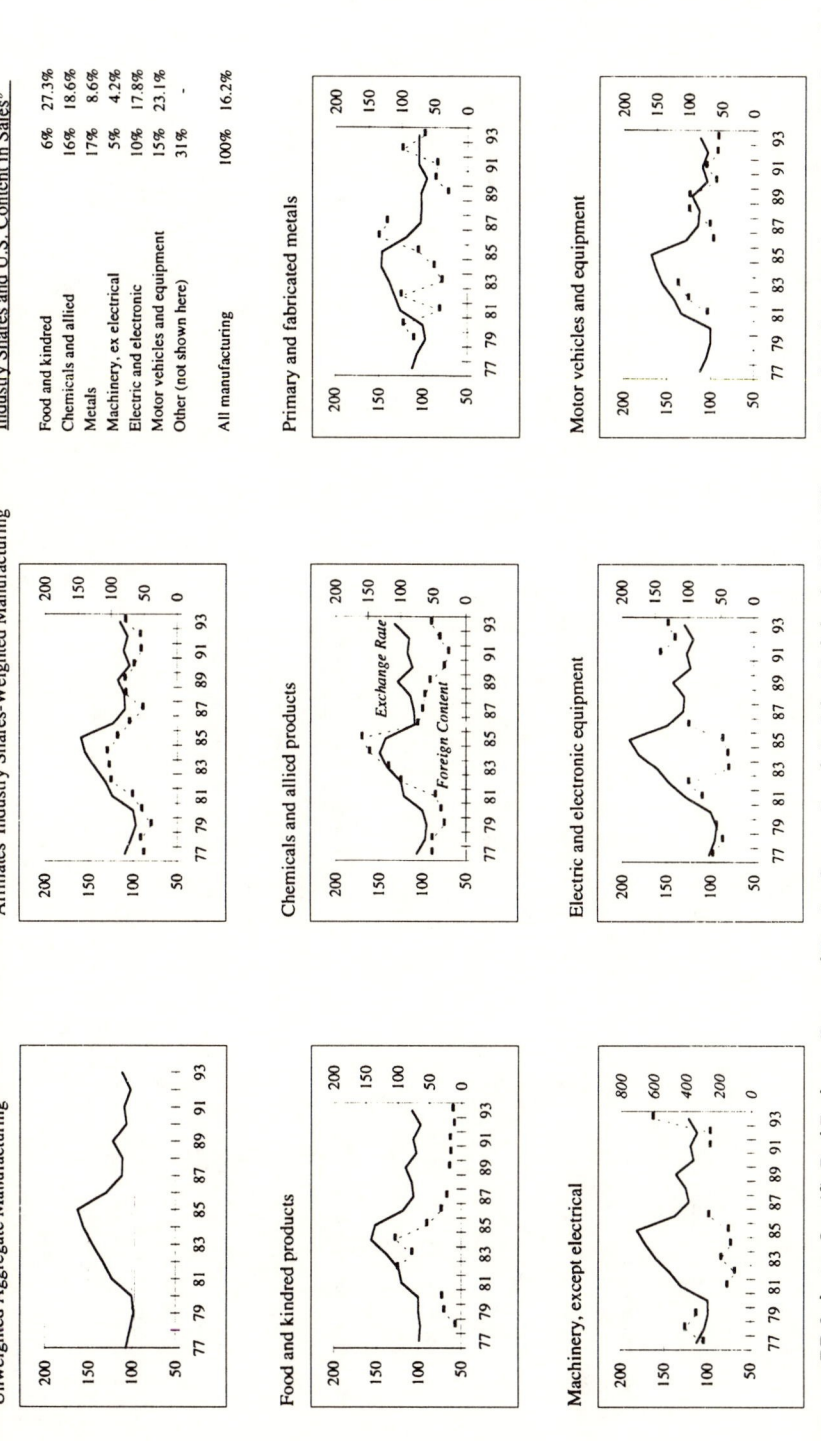

Figure app. DD Industry-Specific Real Exchange Rates and Foreign Content Levels in Sales Made by the U.S. Affiliates of French Multinationals, 1977–1993. (Scale on left side and solid line pertain to real exchange rates, set at 100 for 1980; scale on right side and dotted line pertain to U.S. content levels, set at 100 for 1982.[a]) Sources: U.S. Bureau of Economic Analysis, Foreign Direct Investment in the United States; IMF, International Financial Statistics; and OECD, Indicators of Industrial Activity. [a]Industry-specific real exchange rate = ((Foreign Currency Units/U.S. $) × (Pi/P * i)); foreign content levels estimated as described in the text. [b]Industry shares are based on affiliates' cumulative sales between 1977 and 1993; foreign content figures shown are for 1982, the base year; na = not available.

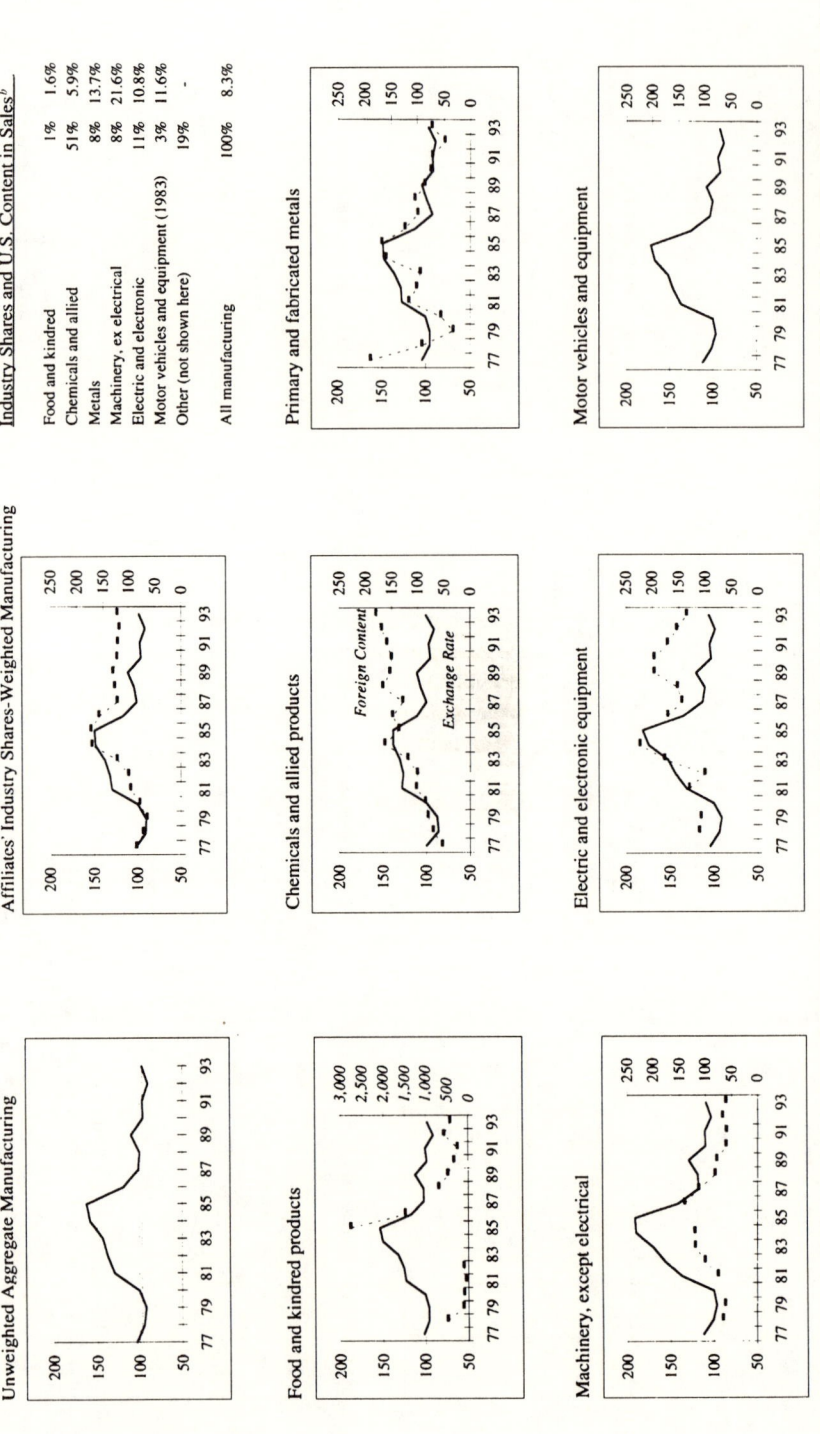

Figure app. EE Industry-Specific Real Exchange Rates and Foreign Content Levels in Sales Made by the U.S. Affiliates of German Multinationals, 1977–1993. (Scale on left side and solid line pertain to real exchange rates, set at 100 for 1980; scale on right side and dotted line pertain to U.S. content levels, set at 100 for 1982.[a]) *Sources:* U.S. Bureau of Economic Analysis, *Foreign Direct Investment in the United States*; IMF, *International Financial Statistics*; and OECD, *Indicators of Industrial Activity.* [a]Industry-specific real exchange rate = ((Foreign Currency Units/U.S. $) × (Pi/P * i)); foreign content levels estimated as described in the text. [b]Industry shares are based on affiliates' cumulative sales between 1977 and 1993; foreign content figures shown are for 1982, the base year; na = not available.

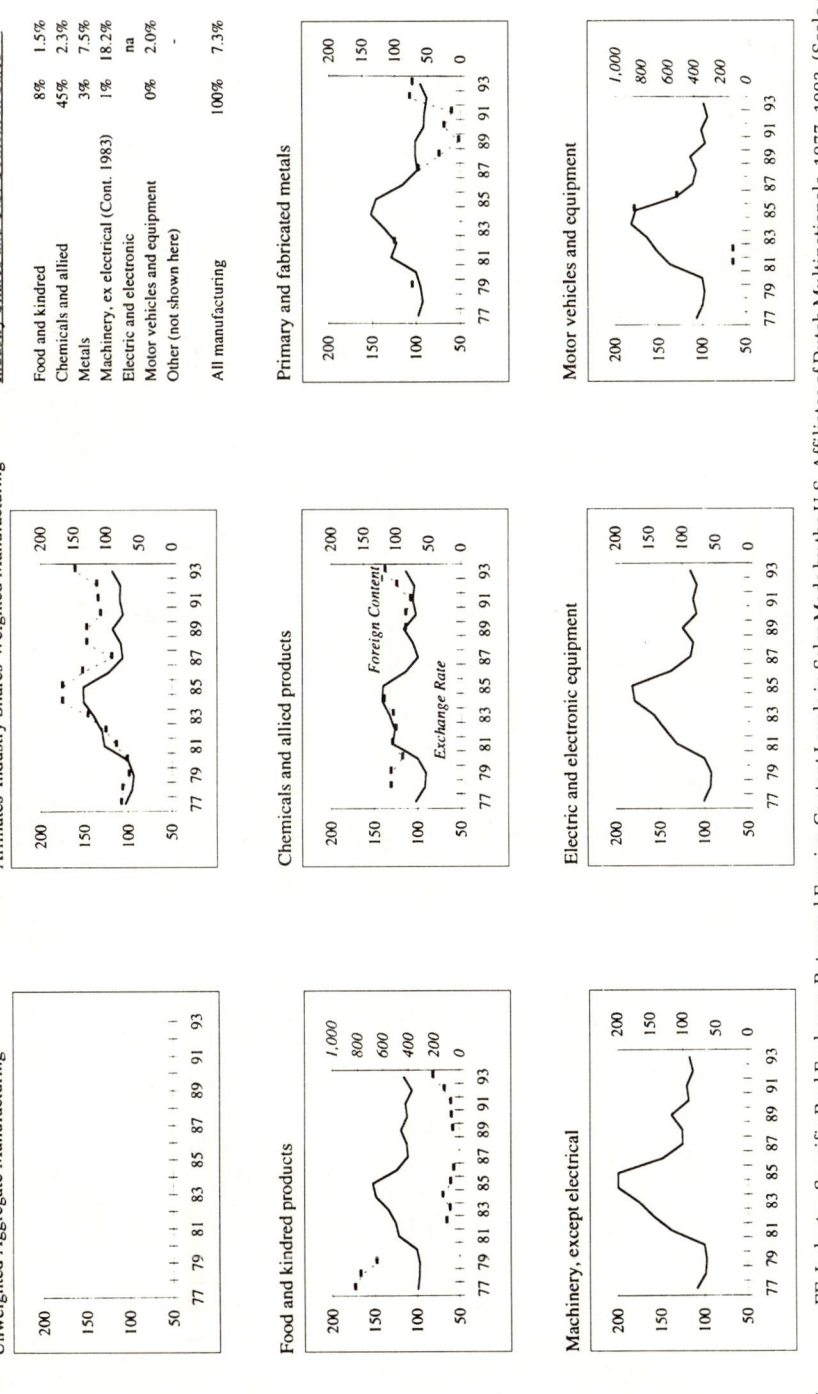

Unweighted Aggregate Manufacturing

Affiliates' Industry Shares-Weighted Manufacturing

Industry Shares and U.S. Content in Sales[b]

Food and kindred	8%	1.5%
Chemicals and allied	45%	2.3%
Metals	3%	7.5%
Machinery, ex electrical (Cont. 1983)	1%	18.2%
Electric and electronic		na
Motor vehicles and equipment	0%	2.0%
Other (not shown here)		-
All manufacturing	100%	7.3%

Food and kindred products

Chemicals and allied products

Primary and fabricated metals

Machinery, except electrical

Electric and electronic equipment

Motor vehicles and equipment

Figure app. FF Industry-Specific Real Exchange Rates and Foreign Content Levels in Sales Made by the U.S. Affiliates of Dutch Multinationals, 1977–1993. (Scale on left side and solid line pertain to real exchange rates, set at 100 for 1980; scale on right side and dotted line pertain to U.S. content levels, set at 100 for 1982.[a]) *Sources*: U.S. Bureau of Economic Analysis, *Foreign Direct Investment in the United States*; IMF, *International Financial Statistics*; and OECD, *Indicators of Industrial Activity*. [a]Industry-specific real exchange rate = ((Foreign Currency Units/U.S. $) × (Pi/P * i)): foreign content levels estimated as described in the text. [b]Industry shares are based on affiliates' cumulative sales between 1977 and 1993; foreign content figures shown are for 1982, the base year; na = not available.

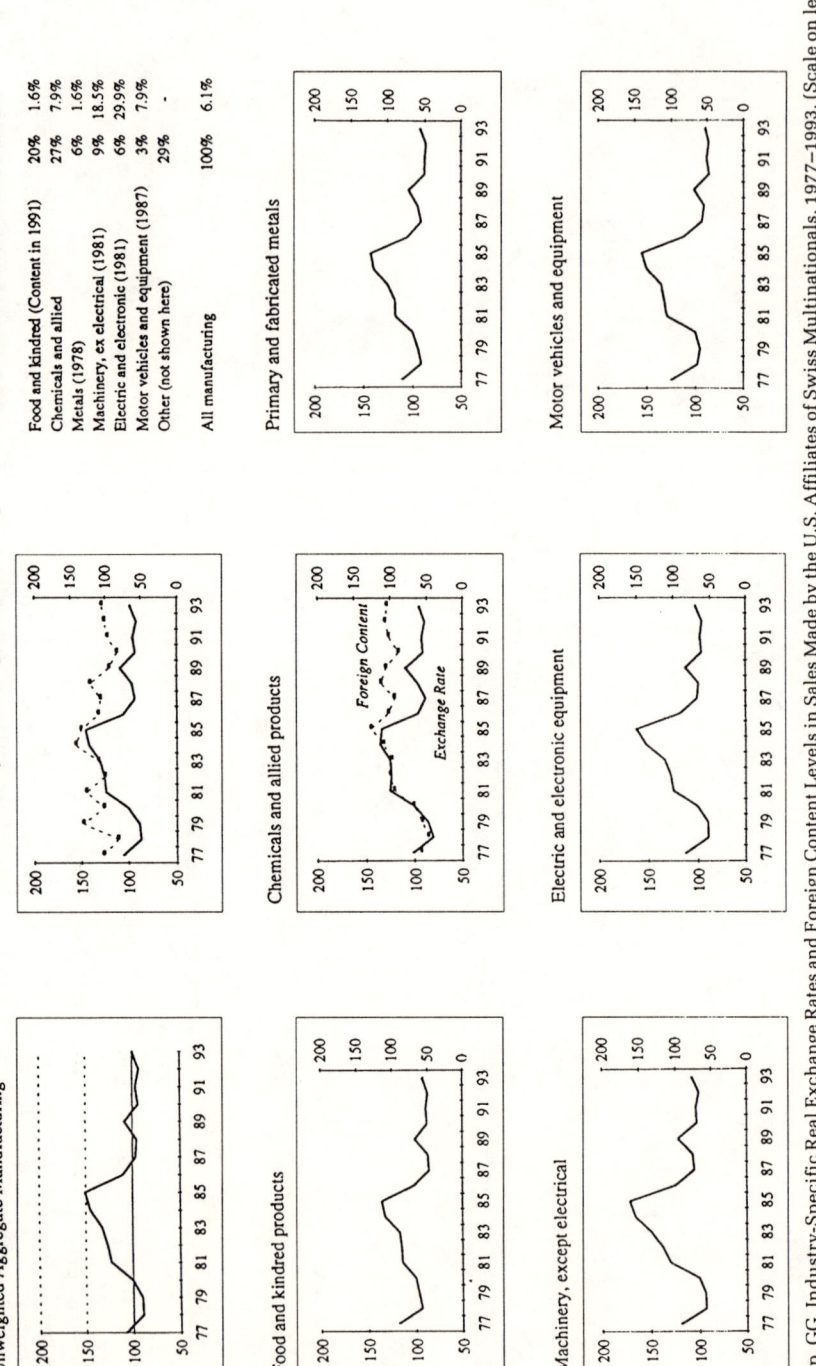

Figure app. GG Industry-Specific Real Exchange Rates and Foreign Content Levels in Sales Made by the U.S. Affiliates of Swiss Multinationals, 1977–1993. (Scale on left side and solid line pertain to real exchange rates, set at 100 for 1980; scale on right side and dotted line pertain to U.S. content levels, set at 100 for 1982.ª) *Sources*: U.S. Bureau of Economic Analysis, *Foreign Direct Investment in the United States*; IMF, *International Financial Statistics*; and OECD, *Indicators of Industrial Activity*. ªIndustry-specific real exchange rate = ((Foreign Currency Units/U.S. \$) × (Pi/P * i)); foreign content levels estimated as described in the text. ᵇIndustry shares are based on affiliates' cumulative sales between 1977 and 1993; foreign content figures shown are for 1982, the base year; na = not available.

Industry Shares and U.S. Content in Salesᵇ

Food and kindred (Content in 1991)	20% 1.6%
Chemicals and allied	27% 7.9%
Metals (1978)	6% 1.6%
Machinery, ex electrical (1981)	9% 18.5%
Electric and electronic (1981)	6% 29.9%
Motor vehicles and equipment (1987)	3% 7.9%
Other (not shown here)	29% -
All manufacturing	100% 6.1%

Notes

1. As the text indicates, in this research I treat exchange rate changes as exogenous. I assume that the sourcing responses and strategies of MNEs do not cause exchange rate changes, but, rather, that the chain of causality runs the other way. Also, consistent with a "random walk" characterization of exchange rate movements, all changes in rates are considered permanent.

2. Readers may refer to that article for a fuller discussion of the issue of lags.

3. See Stern and colleagues 1976; Hooper and Mann 1989; and Lawrence 1990.

4. To estimate production-shifting responses from an MNE parent's point of view, we would need quite detailed information on each of the many countries from which MNE parents source inputs. Such information is not available annually on an industry by country basis, and extrapolating based on available information is not only a challenging task but also likely to aggravate measurement error.

5. On request I will be happy to furnish details and some examples of how I estimate the content levels.

6. The category called "Other" includes manufacturing sales that occur outside the six product categories shown here. As the table on the top right-hand corner of the figure indicates, this "Other" category accounts for only 16 percent of the sales made by the Canadian manufacturing affiliates of U.S. MNEs.

7. The BEA extrapolates its data for 1977, 1978, and 1979 from the 1980 benchmark survey. And even here in some years the data are missing for one or another industry.

8. Two points on this. First, between 1977 and 1993, the dollar has moved in roughly the same direction against other major currencies. This correlation between bilaterals (dollar-pound, dollar-DM, etc.) ought to ameliorate to a great extent the problem just described. Second, the estimates of foreign content have been made after taking into account all available information. For instance, in deflating the import values, the share of imports sourced from parents are deflated by the industry-specific export price in the home country of the U.S. affiliate, and the balance is deflated by the industry-specific U.S. import price.

References

Adler, Michael, and Guy V. G. Stevens (1974). "The Trade Effects of Direct Investment," *Journal of Finance* 29(2): 655–676.

Caves, Richard E. (1982). *Multinational Enterprise and Economic Analysis*. Cambridge: Cambridge University Press.

Dunning, John H., and Alan Rugman (1985). "The Influence of Hymer's Dissertation on Theories of Foreign Direct Investment," *American Economic Review* 75 (May): 228–232.

Ghoshal, Sumantra (1987). "Global Strategy: An Organizing Framework." *Strategic Management Journal* 8: 425–440.

Goldsbrough, David. J. (1981). "International Trade of Multinational Corporations and Its Responsiveness to Changes in Aggregate Demand and Relative Prices," *International Monetary Fund Staff Papers* 28(3): 573–599.

Goldstein, Morris, and S. Khan Moshin (1985). "Income and Price Effects in Foreign Trade," in Ronald W. Jones and Peter B. Kenen, eds., *Handbook of International Economics, Volume II*. Amsterdam: Elsevier. 1041–1105.

Helleiner, Gerald K. (1981). *Intra-firm Trade and the Developing Countries*. New York: St. Martin's Press.

Hymer, Stephen H. (1976 [1960]). *The International Operations of National Firms: A Study of Direct Foreign Investment*. Cambridge, MA: MIT Press.

International Monetary Fund (1991). *International Financial Statistics*, Yearbook. Washington, DC: IMF.

Junz, Helen B., and Rudolf R. Rhomberg (1973). "Price Competitiveness in Export Trade Among Industrial Countries," *The American Economic Review* 63(2): 412–418.

Kogut, Bruce (1985). "Designing Global Strategies: Profiting from Operational Flexibility," *Sloan Management Review* 27: 27–38.

Knetter, Michael M. (1992). "Multinationals and Pricing to Market Behavior," in Michael W. Klein and Paul J. J. Welfens, eds., *Multinationals in the New Europe and Global Trade*. Berlin: Springer Verlag. 65–87.

Knetter, Michael M. (1993). "International Comparisons of Pricing-To-Market Behavior," *American Economic Review* 83(3): 473–486.

Kreinin, Mordechai (1988). "How Closed Is Japan's Market? Additional Evidence," *World Economy* 11(4): 529–542.

Krugman, Paul (1991). "Introduction," in *Trade with Japan: Has the Door Opened Wider?* Chicago: University of Chicago Press for the National Bureau of Economic Research.

Lawrence, Robert Z. (1990). "U.S. Current Account Adjustment: An Appraisal," *Brookings Papers on Economic Activity* 2: 343–392.

Lawrence, Robert Z. (1991). "How Open Is Japan?" in Paul R. Krugman, ed., *Trade with Japan: Has the Door Opened Wider?* Chicago: University of Chicago Press. 9–37.

Lessard, Donald R. (1986). "Finance and Global Competition: Exploiting Financial Scope and Coping with Volatile Exchange Rates," in Michael E. Porter, ed., *Competition in Global Industries*. Boston: Harvard Business School Press. 147–184.

Lipsey, Robert E., and Irving B. Kravis (1986). "The Competitiveness and Comparative Advantage of U.S. Multinationals, 1957–1983," NBER Working Paper Series, no. 2051, October.

Little, Jane Sneddon (1987). "Intra-Firm Trade: An Update," *New England Economic Review* May/June: 46–51.

Organisation for Economic Co-operation and Development (1992a). *Historical Statistics: 1960–1990*. Paris: OECD.

Organisation for Economic Co-operation and Development (1992b). *Indicators of Industrial Activity: 1992/2*. Paris: OECD.

Organisation for Economic Co-operation and Development (1992c). *Technology and the Economy*. Paris: OECD.

Organisation for Economic Co-operation and Development (1992d). "The International Sourcing of Manufactured Intermediate Inputs: By Canada, France, Germany, Japan, the United Kingdom and the United States," June, DSTI/STII/IND/92(1).

Petri, Peter A. (1991). "Market Structure, Comparative Advantage, and Japanese Trade under the Strong Yen," in Paul R. Krugman, ed., *Trade with Japan: Has the Door Opened Wider?* Chicago: University of Chicago Press. 51–84.

Rangan, Subramanian (1994). "Are Transnational Corporations an Impediment to Trade Adjustment," *Transnational Corporations* 3(3): 52–80.

U.S. Department of Labor, Bureau of Labor Statistics (1990). *Handbook of Labor Statistics*, August 1989, Bulletin no. 2340.

U.S. Department of Labor, Bureau of Labor Statistics (1992a). "U.S. Export Dollar Price, Average Exchange Rate, and Foreign Currency Price Indexes—Nominal." (Printout of *SIC* classified export prices obtained from the department's Division of International Prices.)

U.S. Department of Labor, Bureau of Labor Statistics (1992b). "U.S. Export Dollar Price, Average Exchange Rate, and Foreign Currency Price Indexes—Nominal." (Printout of *SITC* classified export prices obtained from the department's Division of International Prices.)

U.S. Department of Labor, Bureau of Labor Statistics (1992c). "U.S. Export Price Indexes for Selected Categories of Goods." (Printout of *SIC* classified export prices and relative *weights* obtained from the department's Division of International Prices.)

Vernon, Raymond (1966). "International Investment and International Trade in the Product Cycle," *Quarterly Journal of Economics* 83(2): 190–207.

PART III

FOREIGN DIRECT INVESTMENT AND TECHNOLOGY FLOWS

6

Intrafirm Technology Transfer by Japanese Multinationals in Asia

Shujiro Urata

Introduction

Foreign direct investment (FDI) in the world has increased rapidly in recent years. One of the main interests on the part of the countries hosting FDI is to acquire technologies that would contribute to their economic growth. Among various means of international technology transfer, including international trade in technology through patents and in capital goods embodying technology, FDI has increased in significance as multinational enterprises (MNEs) have expanded their FDI activities rapidly. Technology transfer is also a main concern for MNEs, for its success or failure determines the outcome of their overseas operations.

This chapter attempts to examine the following two issues involving technology transfer and FDI in recent years: the patterns of technology transfer through FDI and the determinants of successful technology transfer. This analysis will be of interest not only to academics but also to both MNEs undertaking FDI and policy makers formulating FDI policies and technology policies.

My analysis will be conducted on Japanese firms in four machinery industries (general machinery, electric machinery including electronics, automobiles, and precision instruments) in East Asia, since a unique set of detailed information on technology transfer by Japanese firms in these industries has become available. Japanese firms as a subject of analysis are of interest for at least two reasons. First, Japanese firms have undertaken FDI actively in East Asia, and consequently their impact on the economic activities of the host countries has grown. Second, the pattern of technology transfer by Japanese firms is arguably different from that by firms of other countries. This chapter undertakes an in-depth analysis of the patterns of technology transfer by Japanese firms based on available data and makes comparisons based on casual observations made by local workers with experience working for foreign firms.

The second section of the chapter discusses the recent development of Japanese outward FDI with a focus on East Asia, with the purpose of presenting background information for the analysis in the third section, which examines the pattern of technology transfer by Japanese firms in East Asia and identifies the factors that influence its success or failure. The final section presents concluding comments.

Japanese Foreign Direct Investment in Asia

Japanese FDI increased on a large scale and underwent major changes in its regional and sectoral composition in the latter half of the 1980s (figs. 6.1 and 6.2). The scale of FDI during the 4-year period from 1986 to 1989 was unprecedented, far exceeding the total FDI from all previous years combined. Equally as dramatic as the size of the boom was the pace at which Japanese FDI declined after reaching a peak in 1989.

According to Kawai and Urata (1995), from whom much of this section was drawn, several factors may be responsible for such changes in Japanese FDI in the latter half of the 1980s. First, the recent globalization of business activities, made possible by a general rise in Japanese firms' managerial and technological capabilities, was a natural underlying factor behind the surge of Japanese FDI. Needless to say, the rapid and steep appreciation of the yen against the major international currencies was the most important macroeconomic factor leading to the expansion of FDI in the second half of the 1980s and also in the early 1990s.

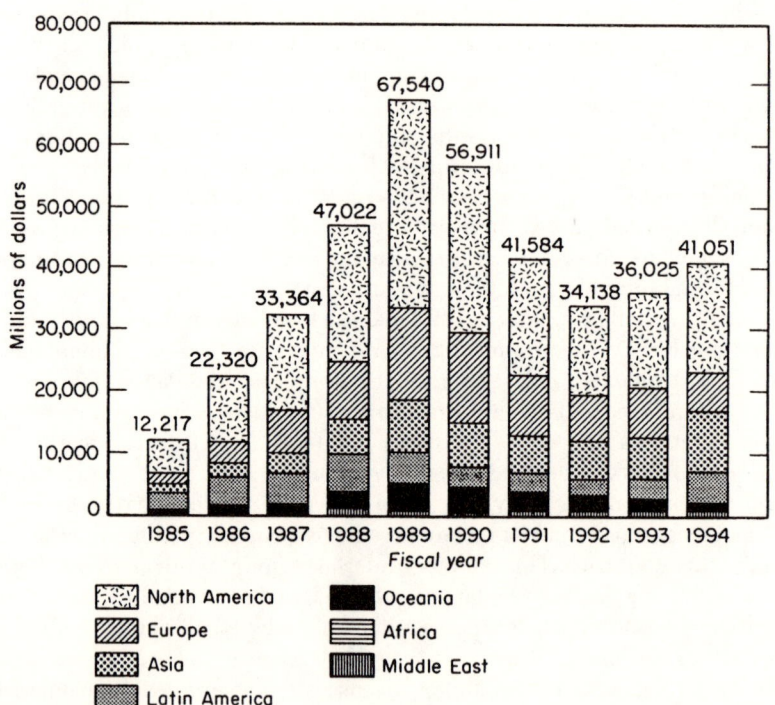

Figure 6.1 Japan's Foreign Direct Investment by Region. *Source:* Ministry of Finance.

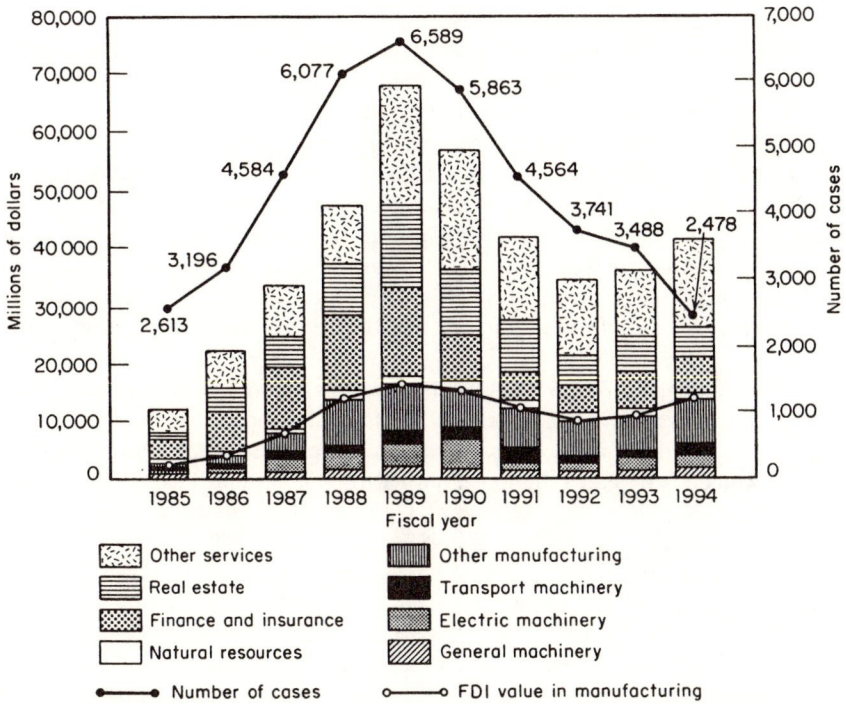

Figure 6.2 Japan's Foreign Direct Investment by Sector. *Source:* Ministry of Finance.

The drastic yen appreciation stimulated Japanese FDI in two ways. The first was the dramatic "relative price" effect. The yen appreciated by 37 percent between 1985 and 1988 on a real, effective basis. These relative price effects substantially reduced Japan's international price competitiveness. To cope with the new international price structure, a number of Japanese firms moved their production base to foreign countries, especially to East Asia, where production costs are lower.

Second, yen appreciation had a positive impact on Japanese FDI through the "liquidity" or "wealth" effect. To the extent that yen appreciation made Japanese firms relatively more "wealthy" in the sense of increased collateral and liquidity, it enabled them to finance FDI relatively more cheaply than their foreign competitors. Liquidity was also injected into the economy by the Bank of Japan in the second half of the 1980s, pushing up the prices of shares, stock, and land, to result in the "bubble economy." Such an increase in liquidity and the subsequent asset-price inflation also had a positive impact on Japan's FDI.

Japanese FDI in the 1980s was directed largely to North America and Europe, mainly in services and manufacturing. These two developed regions together absorbed two thirds of Japan's FDI outflows. Although a smaller share of Japan's FDI went to East Asia in the 1980s, investments in manufacturing were relatively active. The 1990s have seen some changes in the patterns of Japan's FDI. First, Japan's FDI to East Asia started to rise, resulting in an increase in its share in Japan's

FDI. Major factors behind Japan's FDI in East Asia include the region's robust economic growth, low unit labor costs, liberalization and pro–FDI policies, and yen-rate appreciation. Another noticeable change was that manufacturing firms have been undertaking FDI actively, particularly in East Asia.

Since the mid-1980s, geographical distribution of Japan's FDI to Asia has changed significantly, from the Asian NIEs (newly industrializing economies) to ASEAN (Association of Southeast Asian Nations), and then to China and other Asian countries.[1] The NIEs attracted FDI until the late 1980s through FDI promotion policies. Policy makers in Korea, Taiwan, and Singapore, in particular, promoted inward FDI in their pursuit of high-tech industrialization. These countries enjoyed positive growth brought about by the simultaneous expansion of trade and inward FDI.

However, Japanese FDI in the Asian NIEs reached a peak in the late 1980s just as its overall FDI also peaked. The Asian NIEs started to lose some of their cost advantages due to rapid wage increases and currency appreciation. Firms in Japan and other advanced economies therefore started to look at other East Asian countries such as ASEAN as hosts for investment. One important factor in attracting FDI in manufacturing to ASEAN has been the ASEAN countries' shift from inward-oriented to outward-oriented strategies, the latter carried out through their unilateral liberalization of trade and FDI inflows. Such regime changes were prompted by the earlier success of outward-oriented policies in the NIEs.

Since 1988 and 1989, FDI inflows to China have also grown quickly because of China's gradual but persistent economic reforms, open-door liberalization policy, and its political and social stability despite the Tiananmen Square incident in 1989. As of 1994, China was the largest recipient of Japanese FDI in Asia. The attractiveness of China as a host to FDI has increased recently because some ASEAN countries have lost their attractiveness in the emergence of serious bottlenecks in conducting businesses in these countries, such as underdevelopment of infrastructure and shortage of skilled manpower. In recent years, despite a significantly lower scale, Japanese FDI to other Asian countries, such as Vietnam and India, has begun to increase.

Since the 1980s, Japanese FDI in East Asia has primarily been aimed at the manufacturing and services sectors. A distinct characteristic of Japanese FDI in Asia is the relatively large share in manufacturing in comparison to other regions. The magnitude of Japanese manufacturing FDI increased more than sevenfold in eight years from $0.5 billion in 1985 to $3.7 billion in 1993. The rate of increase in Japanese manufacturing FDI in East Asia during the period was greater than the corresponding FDI to the world, and the share of East Asia in Japanese manufacturing FDI rose from 19.6 percent in 1985 to 32.9 percent in 1993. The share of manufacturing in overall Japanese FDI in East Asia also rose from 32 percent to 55 percent over the 1985 to 1993 period. The geographical shift of Japanese manufacturing FDI away from the NIEs to ASEAN and then to China is pronounced.

Sectoral composition of Japanese manufacturing FDI in East Asia has changed notably since the latter half of the 1980s. The most remarkable development is that Japanese FDI in electric machinery (including electronics) has expanded sharply. At the end of 1991 the share of electric machinery in total Japanese FDI in Asia stood at 9.4 percent, the largest share among manufacturing sectors (table 6.1).[2] Significantly, electric machinery's share in Japanese FDI in Asia is signifi-

Table 6.1 Japanese Foreign Direct Investment in Asia and in the World, $ Value (in millions) and % Share

	Asia				World			
	1991		Cumulative through 1991		1991		Cumulative through 1991	
Sector	Value	Share	Value	Share	Value	Share	Value	Share
Food	158	2.7	1,325	2.5	632	1.5	4,717	1.3
Textiles	218	3.7	2,085	3.9	616	1.5	4,615	1.3
Wood and pulp	35	0.6	560	1.0	311	0.7	3,280	0.9
Chemicals	576	9.7	3,217	6.0	1,602	3.9	12,542	3.6
Metals	245	4.1	3,049	5.7	907	2.2	11,215	3.2
General machinery	255	4.3	1,904	3.6	1,284	3.1	9,216	2.6
Electric machinery	872	14.7	5,047	9.4	2,296	5.5	22,656	6.4
Transport machinery	191	3.2	1,890	3.5	1,997	4.8	12,877	3.7
Other manufacturing	377	6.4	2,509	4.7	2,666	6.4	12,804	3.6
Manufacturing total	2,928	49.3	21,587	40.4	12,311	29.6	93,924	26.7
Agriculture-forestry	27	0.5	357	0.7	277	0.7	1,635	0.5
Fishing	24	0.4	219	0.4	71	0.2	810	0.2
Mining	260	4.4	7,617	14.2	1,003	2.4	17,542	5.0
Construction	96	1.6	336	0.6	429	1.0	2,818	0.8
Commerce	711	12.0	4,503	8.4	5,249	12.6	36,564	10.4
Finance	800	13.5	5,031	9.4	4,971	12.0	70,290	19.9
Services	521	8.8	6,224	11.6	5,412	13.0	40,079	11.4
Transportation	96	1.6	1,191	2.2	2,489	6.0	19,927	5.7
Real estate	357	6.0	3,348	6.3	8,899	21.4	54,748	15.5
Others	1	0.0	1,639	3.1	10	0.0	7,533	2.1
Nonmanufacturing	2,893	48.7	30,967	57.9	28,815	69.3	251,946	71.5
Branches	116	2.0	866	1.6	464	1.1	5,928	1.7
Real estate	0	0.0	37	0.1	0	0.0	595	0.2
Total	5,936	100.0	53,455	100.0	41,584	100.0	352,392	100.0

Source: Ministry of Finance.

cantly greater than the corresponding share in Japanese FDI in the world (6.4 percent). Among other manufacturing sectors, chemicals and metals have relatively large shares in Japanese FDI in Asia. The shares for general machinery, transport machinery, and other manufacturing, in which precision instruments are included, are 3.6, 3.5, and 4.7 percent, respectively.

Technology Transfer by Japanese Firms in East Asia

This section investigates the pattern of technology transfer from Japanese workers to local workers at Japanese firms in East Asia, using the results of a questionnaire survey conducted by the Nikkei Research Institute of Industry and Market. The main purpose of this exercise is to identify the effective strategies for transferring technologies.[3] In addition, where possible, an attempt is made to compare the patterns of technology transfer by Japanese firms and by U.S. firms;

such comparisons rely on interviews with local workers employed by foreign firms in several Asian countries.

Characteristics of Japanese Firms Surveyed

A questionnaire was conducted on Japanese firms in October 1991.[4] In addition to questions regarding the patterns of technology transfer, a number of questions were asked regarding the characteristics of the firm and the methods used to facilitate technology transfer.

Table 6.2 presents characteristics of the surveyed firms. Of 133 firms, electric machinery has the largest representation, followed by general machinery, automobiles, and precision machinery. These shares among the machinery sectors are similar to those reported in the official statistics (table 6.1). As for the year of start-up, the sample is almost evenly distributed among firms starting operation before 1985 and after 1986. As for the type of ownership, for approximately 70 percent of the firms the Japanese hold majority ownership, whereas for the remaining 30 percent they have minority ownership.

I investigated the rate of job separation over a 1-year period for each job rank, thinking that technology transfer would be undertaken effectively in a stable employment environment. The average job separation rate for managers of the executive class or higher was a mere 0.6 percent. Evidently, the people who serve in positions where local management policy is determined stay with the company. Even at the middle-management level of section chief or higher, the separation rate on average was no more than 4.1 percent. This finding counters a popular perception of a high job separation rate, characterized as "job-hopping."

On the other hand, the job separation rate among personnel who work at production sites was as high as 16.9 percent and would lead to a complete turnover of personnel within about 6 years. For industries, the job separation rate is low for automobiles. And among the countries under study, Hong Kong, unlike China and Indonesia, has a particularly high turnover rate. The job separation rate for engineers, who are generally involved in technology transfer, was 4.7 percent, which roughly equals that of middle management.

Japanese corporations often maintain that transfer of technology does not benefit the company because the local personnel who acquire the technology soon quit the company. Yet from the results of the survey, it seems that this belief does not hold true, at least not for engineers.

Adoption of the Japanese management style by Japanese firms in their overseas operations is an interesting point.[5] It is often argued that the success of Japanese firms in the post–World War II period reflects Japanese management style, generally characterized by such features as a lifetime employment system, labor-management conferences, job rotation, and a multitask operation.[6] The lifetime employment system and labor-management conferences lead to an environment in which both workers and management can have mutually agreeable long-term plans for themselves as well as the firm, a system that would maximize the firm's profits as well as workers' benefits. Job rotation and multitask operations are likely to improve workers' technological capability, as both of these systems enable workers to increase their understanding of the technologies used in the firm. One would assume that the success of overseas affiliates of Japanese firms may depend on their successful adoption of Japanese management style in their overseas operations.

According to the results of the survey, adoption of Japanese management style by Japanese firms in their East Asian operation appears to be limited, as the share of firms that practice it is less than 50 percent. Specifically, firms adopted various components of Japanese management style: the lifetime employment system (30.8 percent), labor-management conferences (40.6 percent), job rotation (35.3 percent), and multitask operations (47.4 percent). Among the industries considered, a large proportion (nearly 70 percent) of Japanese firms in automobiles has adopted job rotation and multitask operation systems. Production of automobiles requires a large number of processes and technologies; accordingly, the need for and the usefulness of job rotation and a multitask operation are high.

As for the geographical destinations of the sales of the firms surveyed, on average 46.6 percent of their sales were exported and the remaining 53.4 percent were sold in the local market. There are wide variations in the export ratios (exports/total sales) for the firms in different sectors and for those located in different countries. Among the industries surveyed, the export ratio is high for electric machinery and precision machinery. These findings largely reflect the types of policies pursued for different industries by the host country governments. Specifically, protective measures are applied to automobiles and general machinery for their promotion, resulting in a greater emphasis on local sales, whereas such measures are not applied to electric machinery and precision instruments, leading to greater sales orientation toward the export market.

As for the firms located in different countries, the export ratio is high for firms in Hong Kong, Singapore, Malaysia, the Philippines, and Thailand but low for the firms in Indonesia, Korea, and Taiwan. These observed patterns largely reflect the types of trade policies pursued by these countries and the size of the local market; the export ratio of firms in countries where export promotion policy is applied or where the local market is small tends to be high, whereas the export ratio of firms in countries where import substitution policy is applied or where the local market is large tends to be low.

The differences in the geographical patterns of sales destinations by Japanese firms in different industries and in different countries clearly reflect the motives behind their FDI, export sales, or local sales (table 6.3). In addition to the consideration for sales, availability of cheap labor was an important motive for the firms in general machinery, electric machinery, and precision machinery. More than 50 percent of firms in the automobile industry were motivated to undertake FDI by the FDI undertaken by their business partners. This observation reflects the importance of the subcontracting production system, or *shitauke*, in automobile production, under which parent firms, assemblers of final products, and subcontractors supplying components have close business ties. As for the role of FDI promotion policy in attracting FDI, approximately 30 percent of Japanese firms considered the incentives given by FDI promotion policies an important factor in making their decision on FDI, indicating FDI promotion policies. It is interesting to find variation in the importance of FDI promotion policies as an effective motivation for FDI among host countries. For as many as 50 percent of

Table 6.2 Characteristics of Sample Firms

	Number of firms	Initial year of operation $(n)^a$		Foreign ownership $(n$ of firms$)^a$		Job separation in 1990 (%)	
		Before 1985	After 1986	<50%	>50%	Executives	Middle management
Total	133	57	63	41	90	0.6	4.1
Industry							
General machinery	32	12	13	13	19	1.5	3.1
Electric machinery	61	25	34	14	46	0.4	6.1
Transport machinery	30	14	12	11	19	0.0	2.0
Precision instruments	10	6	4	3	6	0.5	1.4
Host country							
Korea	17	5	10	4	12	3.3	4.5
Taiwan	32	13	15	12	20	0.3	3.4
Hong Kong	4	2	2	0	4	0.0	5.0
Singapore	16	10	3	6	10	1.2	2.1
Thailand	32	11	18	9	22	0.0	6.1
Indonesia	13	9	4	5	8	0.1	0.9
Malaysia	14	6	7	2	12	0.0	5.1
Philippines	3	1	2	2	1	0.0	6.0
China	2	0	2	1	1	0.0	0.0

Source: Nikkei Research Institute of Industry and Market (1992).

^{a}Because not all firms responded to every question, the sum of the responses on some questions does not equal to the total number of firms.

Japanese firms in Thailand and in Malaysia, whose governments are active in FDI promotion, the incentives given to FDI played an important role in deciding on FDI.

Technology Transfer by Japanese Firms

To reveal the current status of technology transfer, I use two indicators in the survey. One indicator measures the extent of the targeted level of technology transfer that has been achieved so far by drawing on the response to the following question: to what extent (in percentage terms) has the level of technology transfer targeted at the time of start been completed. This indicator is commonly used by other researchers, but it suffers from its subjectivity (see, for example, Yamashita 1991). The targeted level of technology transfer is usually not explicitly specified by investing firms, and moreover, the judgment as to the extent of technology transfer being accomplished is often not based on observable indicators but on an impressionistic evaluation of the person responding to the questionnaire. To remedy the shortfall associated with the indicator just discussed, I devised a more objective indicator, which attempts to determine the extent of technology transfer being accomplished by identifying the individuals

Table 6.2 (continued)

| Production workers | Technicians | Japanese management style | | | | Exports as a share of sales (%) |
		Lifetime employment	Labor-management conferences	Job rotation	Multitask operation	
16.9	4.7	30.8	40.6	35.3	47.4	40.6
20.0	5.2	21.9	37.5	12.5	43.8	28.6
18.5	4.8	36.1	41.0	29.5	39.3	69.6
9.5	3.9	30.0	50.0	70.0	66.7	13.0
19.1	5.7	30.0	20.0	40.0	50.0	76.2
19.0	7.5	35.3	58.8	23.5	41.2	20.5
18.2	4.8	28.1	46.9	37.5	50.0	34.1
36.3	11.3	25.0	25.0	0.0	0.0	77.7
22.7	3.2	18.8	31.3	37.5	43.8	67.1
11.7	4.3	37.5	28.1	34.4	56.3	59.2
3.9	2.2	38.5	53.8	61.5	53.8	5.8
26.6	6.2	35.7	35.7	35.7	28.6	81.2
6.3	0.3	0.0	66.7	33.3	66.7	67.0
0.5	0.0	0.0	0.0	0.0	100.0	50.0

responsible for specific operations. If the local staff, not expatriates, are responsible, technology transfer is deemed complete.

In the survey, technologies are divided into 10 different types, and the extent of technology transfer to local workers achieved for each technology is shown in table 6.4.[7] According to the results, more than 70 percent of the Asian affiliates of Japanese firms transferred the four types of technologies: operations technology, maintenance and inspection, process control, and quality control. These observations indicate that Japanese firms have rigorously transferred the types of technologies required for manufacturing or assembly operations. The proportion of the firms that completed technology transfer to the total number of firms decreases significantly for the other types of technologies. Specifically, less than 50 percent of firms have transferred the technology for the development of molds and tools. For technological improvements and development of manufacturing processes, approximately one out of three firms has completed technology transfer. The proportion of firms completing technology transfer decreases to around 20–30 for design technology, the introduction and development of new products. These observations clearly show that Japanese firms have not successfully transferred more sophisticated technologies such as those that require modification or new development.

Table 6.3 Motives Behind Foreign Direct Investment

	Local Sales	Exports to Japan	Exports to Others	Local labor	Follow business partners	FDI promotion policies in hosts
Total	46.6	18.8	45.1	58.6	31.6	31.6
Industry						
General machinery	65.6	21.9	43.8	71.9	12.5	21.9
Electric machinery	31.1	26.2	55.7	65.6	34.4	34.4
Transport machinery	56.7	3.3	20.0	26.7	53.3	36.7
Precision instruments	50.0	10.0	60.0	70.0	10.0	30.0
Host country						
Korea	76.5	23.5	23.5	41.2	29.4	17.6
Taiwan	56.3	12.5	43.8	50.0	34.4	9.4
Hong Kong	0.0	50.0	100.0	75.0	50.0	25.0
Singapore	37.5	25.0	81.3	56.3	12.5	37.5
Thailand	37.5	18.8	43.8	71.9	28.1	53.1
Indonesia	53.8	7.7	7.7	46.2	46.2	30.8
Malaysia	28.6	7.1	50.0	71.4	50.0	50.0
Philippines	33.3	33.3	66.7	66.7	0.0	33.3
China	50.0	100.0	50.0	100.0	0.0	0.0

Source: Nikkei Research Institute of Industry and Market (1992).

The figures indicate the percentage of firms with the corresponding motives.

One observes interesting variations in the extent of technology transfer under-taken among the affiliates of Japanese firms in different economies. For most tech-nologies, transfer has advanced further for the affiliates in the NIEs than for those in ASEAN countries. The difference is particularly notable for the relatively more sophisticated technologies and for the introduction and development of new tech-nologies. These differences reflect the differences in the technological capability of the host countries. Technology transfer may be performed relatively smoothly in the NIEs because their technological capability is higher than that in ASEAN countries.

It may be useful to note here the differences in the patterns of technology transfer undertaken by Japanese firms and by non-Japanese firms. It is often argued that Japanese firms are slower or more hesitant in transferring technologies than firms of other nationals. More explicitly, Western firms are said to be more active in transferring technologies than Japanese firms (for example, see chapter 7 in this volume). Although one would need a detailed comparison between Western and Japanese firms to derive a reliable result, the following observations made by some local workers with work experience at both Western and Japanese firms[8] may be enlightening.

According to their observations, Western firms actively and effectively transfer operating technologies mainly with the help of manuals. That is, at Western firms local workers acquire technologies more or less by themselves, using manuals, so local workers learn to deal only with the problems discussed in the manuals. When

Table 6.4 Technology Transfer Achieved: Percentage of Firms Giving Responsibility to Local Workers

	Location			Industry				Overall
	NIEs	ASEAN	China	General machinery	Electric machinery	Automobiles	Precision instruments	
Operational technology	82.0	83.6	50.0	75.0	78.2	100.0	77.8	82.2
Maintenance/inspection	80.3	78.2	50.0	71.4	74.5	100.0	66.7	78.8
Process control	75.4	68.4	100.0	70.0	67.3	80.8	88.9	72.3
Quality control	75.4	66.7	100.0	63.3	70.9	80.8	77.8	71.7
Development of molds/tools	56.9	32.7	100.0	43.5	41.2	60.0	44.4	46.3
Technological improvements	40.7	26.0	50.0	34.6	23.1	62.5	22.2	34.2
Development of manufacturing processs	42.9	21.7	100.0	26.1	28.0	50.0	50.0	34.0
Design technology	38.6	14.9	100.0	28.0	19.6	48.0	22.2	28.6
Development of new products	30.2	11.6	100.0	22.7	18.2	31.8	22.2	22.7
Introduction of new technology	27.3	14.0	50.0	20.0	13.7	40.9	22.2	21.5

Source: Nikkei Research Institute of Industry and Market (1992).

a problem not discussed in the manuals arises, local workers call on engineers from the parent office. In contrast, Japanese firms rely more on on-the-job-training (OJT) for transferring technologies, so it takes longer for Japanese firms to transfer technologies. But once technology is transferred, local workers of Japanese firms acquire not only the operational technologies but also the ability to deal with problems. As a result, local workers can work more or less independently without assistance provided by Japanese workers.

If these observations are correct, one may argue that for Western firms technology transfer means transferring operational technologies, and therefore technology transfer is considered complete once operational technology is transferred. In contrast, for Japanese firms technology transfer means transferring not only operational technologies but also more complicated and sophisticated technologies, and therefore technology transfer is not complete unless all sorts of technologies are transferred. As noted earlier, because this is only a casual observation, it needs to be analyzed more in detail to reveal the differences and similarities in technology transfer among firms of different nationalities.

The Methods Used for Transferring Technologies

To transfer technologies expeditiously and effectively, a variety of methods, which may also be considered as a means to develop human resources, have been adopted by Japanese firms (table 6.5). Training workshops and OJT in local areas are two commonly used activities for transferring manufacturing technologies: that is, operational technology, maintenance, quality control, and process control. Indeed, approximately 60 percent of firms use these methods for transferring manufacturing technologies. As the level of technologies involved in transfer goes up, so does the relative importance of training workshops both in local areas and in Japan for technology transfer.

The emphasis on OJT and training workshops as a means of transferring manufacturing technologies indicates that actual practice at the workplace is considered more beneficial than classroom workshops for transferring relatively simple technologies. However, for transferring relatively sophisticated technologies, a classroom workshop is a main method of technology transfer, with OJT playing a subordinate role. It is interesting to note that the training workshop in Japan is commonly used as a major form of technology transfer for introduction of new technologies and new products, indicating that intensive training in transferring sophisticated technologies is provided at the parent office in Japan by inviting personnel from overseas offices. The use of small-group activities as a means of technology transfer is somewhat limited, compared to OJT or training workshops.

Training manuals written in different languages have different roles. Manuals written in local languages have a major role in transferring manufacturing technologies, whereas manuals written in English and Japanese have relatively greater roles in transferring sophisticated technologies. In particular, the use of manuals written in Japanese is high for transferring new technologies and new products. Consequently, local personnel get few opportunities to acquire sophisticated technologies.

Compared to Western firms, Japanese firms rely less on manuals and more on OJT as a means of technology transfer. Indeed, the manuals prepared and used by Western firms detail the directions for operating equipment. As a result, local

Table 6.5 Methods of Technology Transfer

	Local Language	Manual language		On-the-job training	Small-group activities	Training workshop	
		English	Japanese			Local	Japan
Operational technology	66.2	40.6	36.8	63.9	33.8	63.9	63.2
Maintenance/inspection	64.7	39.1	33.1	58.6	33.1	62.4	45.9
Quality control	61.7	42.9	36.8	59.4	48.1	63.2	55.6
Process control	56.4	41.4	36.8	55.6	35.3	58.6	36.8
Technological improvements	30.1	26.3	29.3	41.4	18.8	41.4	32.3
Introduction of new technologies	20.3	27.8	35.3	24.8	5.3	30.8	40.6
Design technology	18.0	30.8	37.6	29.3	7.5	28.6	39.1
Development of new products	14.3	19.5	29.3	10.5	2.3	18.8	28.6
Development of metal molds and machining tools	29.3	27.8	31.6	29.3	15.0	39.1	33.1
Development of manufacturing facilities	18.8	24.8	30.8	22.6	9.8	32.3	30.1

Source: Nikkei Research Institute of Industry and Market (1992).

The figures indicate the percentage of firms using the corresponding methods.

workers can learn how to operate the equipment without much difficulty. By contrast, the manuals prepared by Japanese firms suffer from a lack of detailed information. Japanese firms rely on OJT to overcome these shortcomings. This difference in the importance placed on manuals and OJT between Western and Japanese firms appears to be attributable to the difference in their perception of the meaning or definition of technology transfer. Thus, Western and Japanese firms differ in how they target and evaluate technology transfer, a point discussed in the final section.

Determinants of Successful Technology Transfer

In the previous section, I examined the patterns of technology transfer by Asian affiliates of Japanese firms and their characteristics, such as the motives behind foreign direct investment, length of operation, management practices, and the methods of technology transfer. This section investigates the determinants of technology transfer through a regression analysis. Such an analysis would be useful not only for academic researchers interested in the behavior of foreign firms and economic development but also for both policy makers and foreign firms involved in formulating effective methods for transferring technologies.

The dependent variable is the indicator reflecting the extent of technology transfer carried out, measured by the response to the question inquiring who is in charge of specified technological activities, local workers or Japanese workers. If the answer is local workers, then technology transfer is considered complete, and the value of 1 is given to the dependent variable. If the answer to the question is Japanese workers, then technology transfer is considered incomplete, and the value of 0 is given to the dependent variable. Independent variables, or explanatory variables, include various firm specific characteristics, FDI motives, management practices, and the methods used for facilitating technology transfer. Below I discuss the expected impact of explanatory variables on the dependent variable and the results of the analysis in turn.

The regression analysis was conducted for 10 different kinds of technologies. The results appear in table 6.6. As the dependent variable takes the value of 1 or 0, the Probit analysis is applied to deal with the statistical problems associated with a truncated dependent variable.

The length of operation in the host country has a positive impact on technology transfer, as the coefficient on the variable "year of operation" is positive in most cases. This finding is consistent with expectations and findings from earlier studies.[9] In particular, the positive impact is statistically significant for maintenance/inspection, quality control, and process control, indicating that the vintage effect is important for transferring manufacturing technologies. However, the vintage effect does not have a significant impact on transferring more sophisticated technologies. Apparently, accumulated experiences on the part of Japanese workers as well as local workers play an effective role in transferring manufacturing technologies, but not in transferring sophisticated technologies.

High local participation in equity holdings promotes transferring sophisticated technologies, as the coefficient for local ownership is positive and statistically significant for the transfer of sophisticated technologies. This result confirms the expectation, since high local participation may enable local management to pres-

	Operational technology	Maintenance/ inspection	Process control	Quality control	Development of molds/ tools	Technological improvements	Development of manufacturing processes	Design technology	Development of new products	Introduction of new technology
Firm characteristics										
Year of operation	+	+ **	+ ***	+ **	+	− *	+	+	−	−
Local ownership	− **	−	−	−	+	+	+	+ ***	+ ***	+ **
Local employees	+	+	+	+	−	+ **	−	−	−	−
Job separation ratio	+	−	− **	+	+	−	+	−	−	−
Export share	−	−	+	+	+	− **	−	−	+	− *
Motives										
Take advantage of cheap labor	−	−	−	−	− **	+	− ***	− **	− **	− *
Follow business customers	+ *	+	−	+	−	+	+	+	+	+
FDI promotion policies	+ **	+ *	+	+	− **	+	−	+	−	−
Japanese management style										
Lifetime employment	−	−	− **	+	+	−	+	−	−	−
Labor-management conferences	−	+	+	−	−	+	+	−	+	+ **
Job rotation	+	+	+	−	−	+ *	−	−	+	−
Multitask assignment	+ **	+	+	+	−	−	+	+ *	+	+
Technology transfer methods										
Manuals (local language)	−	+	− **	−	+ **	+	+ ***	+ ***	+ *	+
Manuals (English)	− **	−	− ***	+	+ *	−	+ ***	− ***	−	+
Manuals (Japanese)	−	−	−	+	− *	−	− ***	−	−	−
On-the-job training	−	−	−	+	+	+	− *	+	−	− *
Small-group discussion	−	+	+ **	+	+	−	+	−	+	+
Seminar in local areas	−	+	+	+	+	+ *	+	+ **	+ **	+
Seminar in Japan	+	+	+ *	−	+	−	−	−	+	−
Constant	+	+	+	+	+	− **	−	− **	− *	−
R^2	0.266	0.258	0.493	0.302	0.299	0.439	0.461	0.568	0.484	0.576
No. of observations	96	96	98	96	87	92	83	85	81	89
Percent correct predictions	0.833	0.802	0.837	0.837	0.736	0.815	0.831	0.835	0.877	0.91

These are my own estimates of determinants. Probit is used for the estimation, with "1" indicating that technology transfer was completed and "0" indicating that technology transfer was not completed on technology transfer. "+" indicates a positive impact on technology transfer. "−" indicates a negative impact on technology transfer.

*Significant at 90 percent confidence level.

**Significant at 95 percent confidence level.

***Significant at 99 percent confidence level.

sure Japanese firms to transfer technologies. Indeed, high correlation between local ownership and use of manuals in the local language may serve as evidence for this argument. This finding seems to indicate that ownership matters in determining the success or failure of technology transfer; the greater the influence of local management, expressed in the share of equity holding, the more advanced the firm in transferring technologies.

Similarly, one would expect that a high share of local workers in total workers would contribute to technology transfer. But this expectation is confirmed with statistical significance only in transferring technologies for technological improvement. In many cases it is not the number of local workers but the importance of managerial authority measured by equity holding that influences technology transfer. Related to the issue of workers in the Asian affiliates, high job mobility in Asian countries is often blamed as an obstacle for transferring technology by Japanese firms. The results here do not generally support this argument, as the coefficient on job separation ratio confirms the expected sign with statistical significance only in one case, transferring technologies for process control.[10]

Motivation behind FDI likely influences the degree of achievement of technology transfer. Firms motivated to set up an export base by FDI may be interested in undertaking technology transfer, because they are under pressure to produce competitive exportable products. However, this assertion is not supported by my results. Indeed, apparently technology transfer is not carried out by firms with a strong export orientation. Firms that have set up operations overseas in order to export their products have only a short time to manufacture competitive products to be sold in the international market. Under these circumstances, the firms have little time to transfer technology to local workers. To deal with the situation, they install the most up-to-date technologies but not transfer technologies. The finding that technology transfer is slow for the firms interested in exports is consistent with the result that technology transfer has not been carried out by the firms whose motive behind FDI was to take advantage of low-cost labor. The coefficient for cheap labor is negative in all the equations except one, and, moreover, in five cases the coefficient is statistically significant. This observation indicates that Japanese firms that invested in Asia to take advantage of low-wage labor in Asia are not interested in technology transfer.

Arguably, Japanese management style provides an environment conducive to the assimilation and improvement of technologies. Among the unique features of Japanese-style management, a lifetime employment system, joint labor-management conferences, job rotation, and multitask assignment are my choices here for analysis.[11] The lifetime employment system ostensibly promotes technology transfer. One would expect that, under the lifetime employment system, workers would not oppose adoption of new technologies, which tend to be labor-saving, because their positions in the firm are secure for life. But this expectation is not proven by the regression results. Indeed, technology transfer appears to be deterred under the lifetime employment system. One possible explanation may be that workers whose positions are secure under the lifetime employment system have little incentive to work hard or to learn about technology.

Joint labor-management conferences facilitate the introduction of new technologies, because acceptable conditions for the introduction of new technologies are sought and agreed on by both labor and management. Indeed, the results weakly confirm this argument, as the coefficient for labor-management conferences is positive in six cases and statistically significant in one case: the introduction of new technologies. Job rotation and multitask assignment also tend to promote technology transfer. For local workers, the experience at a variety of operations acquired through job rotation and multitask assignment not only fosters flexibility but also gives a worker the capacity to grasp the flow of the processes as a whole and thus facilitates local establishment of the technologies involved. The expected effect is observed with some statistical significance only in a few cases; job rotation leads to technological improvement, while multitask assignment facilitates transfer of operational technology and design technology.

Japanese management style is argued to have contributed to improving the technological capability of workers in Japan. However, my results show that the effectiveness of Japanese management style in technology transfer is limited.

Japanese firms have adopted various methods for promoting the localization of technology. The effectiveness of four methods has been investigated: manuals, OJT, small-group activities, and workshops. The results of the statistical analysis show that manuals written in local languages are extremely effective means of transferring technologies, especially such sophisticated technologies as design technology, development of new products, development of metal molds and machining tools, and development of manufacturing facilities. However, manuals in English and in Japanese turn out to be ineffective for transferring technologies. Indeed, the results show that the use of manuals in either English or Japanese tends to deter technology transfer. This somewhat unexpected result may not be surprising if the use of manuals in foreign languages is interpreted to reflect the backward-looking attitude of Japanese firms toward technology transfer.

Seminars in local areas are quite effective in improving technologies, designing technologies, and developing new products. Seminars in Japan are effective in transferring process control technologies but not in transferring other types of technologies. Considering the differences in the cost of hosting seminars in Japan and local areas, these observations indicate that the effectiveness of local seminars would be much greater.

Contrary to the expectation, OJT and small-group discussion, special features of Japanese practices, are generally not effective for transferring technologies; small-group discussion effective in transferring technologies for process control. Coupled with the earlier observation that Japanese management style does not promote technology transfer except for a few cases, the findings here seem to indicate one or both of the following two possibilities. First, special Japanese practices per se are not effective for transferring technologies at the Asian affiliates, and, second, these practices are not adopted in the same way as those adopted in Japan. Detailed information on the practices of Asian affiliates is needed to make a judgment on this point.[12]

Conclusions

Japanese firms have actively undertaken FDI since the mid-1980s. The survey conducted by the Nikkei Research Institute of Industry and Markets on technology transfer by Japanese firms in East Asia showed that a large part of manufacturing technologies, such as operational technologies, and maintenance and inspection technologies, has been transferred to the Asian affiliates of Japanese firms, but sophisticated technologies, such as design technology and development of new products, have not been transferred in many firms.

This analysis of the determinants of successful technology transfer by Japanese firms in East Asia leads to a number of interesting observations. First, the length of operation is an important factor in facilitating transfer of manufacturing technologies but not in transferring more sophisticated technologies. Second, localization of ownership leads to successful transfer of sophisticated technologies, suggesting that ownership matters. Third, transfer of sophisticated technologies is very slow in Japanese firms, which are set up to take advantage of cheap labor. Fourth, aspects of Japanese management style such as the lifetime employment system and Japanese technology transfer methods such as OJT and small-group discussion are in general not effective in transferring technologies. Fifth, among the methods used for technology transfer, manuals written in the local language and seminars in local areas are effective in transferring technologies.

The importance of technology transfer for Japanese firms undertaking FDI will increase in the future for several reasons. One is increasing competition among firms not only in the host country but also in the world market. Trade and FDI liberalization, under way in a number of countries in Asia, will intensify competition in these markets. Expansion of the activities by multinational enterprises has led to "mega-competition" among them on a global scale. Another factor that forces Japanese firms to speed up the process of technology transfer is the engineer shortage situation. The imminent reduction in the number of engineers in Japan will put Japanese firms in a difficult position to run their overseas operations as in the past. One way to run overseas operations efficiently is to transfer technologies, so that overseas operations may be run by local workers without much support from Japanese workers. It may not be an overstatement that the success or the failure of overseas operations of Japanese firms depends on technology transfer.

Technology transfer is equally important for the host countries to FDI, for successful technology transfer will benefit the recipient countries by improving technological capability, thereby leading to further economic growth. Only a sufficient supply of well-educated and well-trained personnel can facilitate technology transfer. Moreover, a well-functioning legal framework to protect intellectual property rights must be maintained, so that foreign firms may engage in active research and development (R & D) in the host countries.

These observations point to the need for further examination of the determinants of successful technology transfer by foreign firms. The important factors that have not been examined in this chapter, mainly because of a lack of reliable statistics, include information on the host countries such as educational level and industrial organization, including the level of competition in the host markets. More detailed information on parent offices of Japanese firms, such as their R & D activities, overseas operations outside of East Asia, and the industrial organization in which these firms operate, also must be considered. Finally, extension of this type of study on technology transfer by including non-Japanese foreign firms is very important.

Notes

I am grateful to the participants of the Conference on "Does Ownership Matter? Japanese Multinationals in Asia" at MIT, September 20–21, 1995 for helpful comments and discussions on the earlier version of this chapter presented there.

1. This observation applies to new FDI. A lack of data precludes one from obtaining accurate statistics, but there are signs showing that Japan's FDI undertaken with reinvested earnings has continued to grow in the ASEAN countries. See, for example, Okamoto and Urata (1994) for the case of Malaysia.

2. The discussions here refer to Japanese FDI in 1991 since the subsequent analysis on technology transfer is conducted on information in 1991.

3. The issue of technology transfer has been extensively analyzed theoretically and empirically. Empirical studies have analyzed technology transfer by Western firms and have been reviewed by several authors including Caves (1982) and Reddy and Zhao (1990). Empirical studies on Japanese firms published in English are very few; one is Yamashita (1991).

4. The survey was carried out by the Nikkei Research Institute of Industry and Market as part of a research project on technology transfer by Japanese multinationals. I participated in the project as a member. The results of the survey became available for independent research recently. The questionnaire was sent to 326 firms and 175 firms returned the questionnaire. Out of 175 firms, responses from 133 firms were considered reliable.

5. The issue of adoption of Japanese management style is closely related to the issue of "appropriate technology," which has been a central issue regarding technology transfer by foreign firms from developed countries to the recipient developing countries. According to the critics of the behavior of foreign firms, foreign firms bring with them technologies suited to developed countries but not suited for developing countries without modifying the technologies, thereby exacerbating the problems such as unemployment that host developing countries face. See, for example, Caves (1982) for more detailed discussion.

6. See Kawabe and Kimbara (1991) for concise discussions on Japanese management style.

7. In table 6.4 technologies are arranged in descending order in terms of the level of technology transfer achieved. It should be noted that the ordering based on the other indicator is identical except "introduction of new technologies" and "development of new products," whose orderings are reversed in comparison to the ordering shown in the table.

8. These observations were obtained from my discussions with local workers of Japanese and Western firms and with government officials in Malaysia, Thailand, and Indonesia.

9. In a study of foreign firms in Thailand, Sedgwick in this volume (chapter 7) finds that the extent of technology transfer by Japanese firms is limited in comparison with that of Western firms, and he attributes the limited extent of technology transfer by Japanese firms to an early stage of development of their operation.

10. It may be important to note that job-hopping is a problem for a firm, because it cannot recover the cost used for investing in workers who leave the firm. However, from the point of view of a society as a whole, job-hopping may be beneficial, as technologies are spread by these workers.

11. Many works have discussed Japanese management style with significantly different views. Kawabe and Kimbara (1991) present a concise review of these

works. Thong (1991) discusses evolutionary changes in Japanese management styles by analyzing Japanese firms in Malaysia.

12. Sedgwick (chapter 7 in this volume) gives some examples of the latter case from his study in Thailand.

References

Caves, Richard E. (1982). *Multinational Enterprise and Economic Analysis*. Cambridge: Cambridge University Press.

Kawabe, Nobuo, and Tatsuo Kimbara (1991). "Review of Studies on Japanese-Style Management," in S.Yamashita, ed., *Transfer of Japanese Technology and Management to the ASEAN Countries*. Tokyo: University of Tokyo Press. 123–133.

Kawai, Masahiro, and Shujiro Urata (1995). *Are Trade and Direct Investment Substitutes or Complements? An Analysis of the Japanese Manufacturing Industry*. Presented at the International Conference on Economic Development and Cooperation in the Pacific Basin, Berkeley, California, June.

Okamoto, Yumiko, and Shujiro Urata (1994). *Japan's Foreign Direct Investment in Malaysia in the 1990s*. Presented at the Third Annual Conference on Japan, "Revitalization of Japan's Economy: Implications for Malaysia," Kuala Lumpur, April.

Reddy, N. Mohan, and Liming Zhao (1990). "International Technology Transfer: A Review," *Research Policy* 19: 285–307.

Thong, Gregory T. S. (1991). "Foundations of Human Resources Management Practice in Japanese Companies in Malaysia." in S.Yamashita, ed., *Transfer of Japanese Technology and Management to the ASEAN Countries*. Tokyo: University of Tokyo Press. 135–152.

Yamashita, Shoichi (1991). "Economic Development of the ASEAN Countries and the Role of Japanese Direct Investment," in S.Yamashita, ed., *Transfer of Japanese Technology and Management to the ASEAN Countries*. Tokyo: University of Tokyo Press. 3–22.

7

Do Japanese Business Practices Travel Well?

Managerial Technology Transfer to Thailand

Mitchell W. Sedgwick

Introduction

We know from the many thorough studies of domestic Japanese firms that Japanese corporate "know-how" is more than technological innovation riding on financial clout.[1] Japanese corporations' organizational forms and managerial practices have been shown to be particular, powerful, and profitable. Expansion offshore, however, has naturally required substantial organizational and managerial modifications at Japanese firms as they move beyond their familiar—and apparently extremely consequential—domestic economic, political, and social environment. Host countries have gained important economic stimulus as a result of Japanese investment, but questions have arisen concerning the accomplishments of Japanese multinational corporations (MNCs) in implanting their powerful management technologies abroad. This issue may be even more relevant in Asia than in Europe or North America since in Asia the impact of Japanese foreign direct investment (FDI) on both national economies and the structure of industrialization has been far more pronounced.

Among Japanese MNCs, the urgency to change and adapt has been most acute at large, world-class manufacturing firms. Structural adjustments of the Japanese economy and intense competition between manufacturers have led to a rapid increase in the proportion and geographic diversity of their offshore production, especially since the revaluation of the yen in 1985. Thus, the combination of domestic economic pressures to move production offshore and generic characteristics of manufacturing, such as high density and breadth of interactions with the local environment, makes Japanese manufacturers abroad ideal subjects for the study of managerial adaptations. In addition, the proliferation of manufacturing by both Japanese and Western MNCs in Asia provides us with an extremely rich data set for comparing patterns of adaptation of firms from different home countries.[2]

Where one stands on the question "Does the ownership of MNCs matter?" may depend on where one collects information. Data in this chapter are grounded, first, on an examination of the broad set of linkages between Japanese headquarters and Thai subsidiaries—from the home office perspective—based on data collection and interviews with managers in Japan who oversee operations in Thailand and, second, on the overseas subsidiary perspective based on an extensive period of anthropological participant-observation inside subsidiaries of MNCs in Thailand. This chapter thus analyzes firm-level adaptations to the pressures of operating in foreign environments and specifically treats the means taken by Japanese manufacturers to move their local Thai staff toward "standardized" production. The chapter will also contrast managerial style at subsidiaries of Japanese and Western MNCs in Thailand. How might we proceed in understanding how MNCs manage know-how in foreign environments, why they do it differently, and the implications of those differences?

Multinational corporations attempt to fulfill their goal of profit seeking based on similar sets of external constraints and opportunities in each particular foreign environment. At a high level in the corporation, strategic decisions on foreign direct investment are taken that may allow MNCs to, for example, benefit from lower labor costs, avoid restrictions on foreign trade, capture local expertise and information, gain tax relief through transfer pricing, sell their locally produced goods in local or regional markets, reverse import products to their home markets, and so on. Once foreign investments are made, MNCs manufacturing abroad face a generic problem: how to overlay the varied environments in which they manufacture with a grid of training and tools that develops and maintains local skills so that goods are produced at standards acceptable to their sales market. Thus, for example, at Japanese-owned color picture tube subsidiaries in Mexico and Thailand, assuming machinery is similar, the same basic skills must be developed so that a standardized product can be assembled and sold in the United States. Or, from a different perspective, but demonstrating the same underlying principle, Japanese and Western manufacturers face similar local constraints at an industrial park in Malaysia, where they compete to produce micro-chips with similar specifications for personal computer manufacturers. The core problem in manufacturing abroad, then, is how to produce standardized output in unfamiliar local environments. Engineers may switch or alter machines to cope more easily with local worker capabilities, but over the long run this provides relatively marginal flexibility. The MNCs must successfully make "managerial technology transfers" so that machines are used efficiently.

While the terminology may suggest mechanical precision, managerial technology transfer concerns the processes of learning about the interplay of technical information and the social arrangements surrounding industrial production. Whether planned or not, managerial technology transfer will in practice reflect the local environment—the skills background of local staff, local organizational culture, locally available hardware—as local conditions intersect with know-how carried to the overseas subsidiary. All MNCs operating in the same foreign environment face broadly similar constraints then. However, at the point where managerial technology transfer enters, there appears to be considerable divergence in the practices of multinationals. And these differences are patterned according to home country origin of the multinational. In exploring this theme, I will support the view that ownership matters to managerial technology transfer.

I begin this chapter by explaining why I chose to conduct fieldwork in Thailand (including the relevance of the Thai case to analysis of FDI throughout Asia) and briefly describe my study sites and the methodology employed for field research. I then present a brief model of "Japanese manufacturing" as I believe it is understood by Japanese managers assigned to Japanese MNC subsidiaries abroad. To provide one kind of gauge on the success of managerial technology transfers, I report on the transfer of well-known Japanese shopfloor techniques in Thai subsidiaries. A measure of transfers at a particular factory at a particular moment in time, however, tells us little about the processes through which these transfers occur. Thus, my emphasis shifts from consideration of activity on the shopfloor to an examination of managerial aspects of the technology transfer process. Here, I underscore the interaction between expatriate and local engineers, which I argue is the most critical point in the technology transfer process in its overseas setting, and I contrast these interactions at Japanese and Western MNCs operating in Thailand. I argue that distinctive practices of managerial technology transfer at MNCs are based on the internal dynamics, or the organizational cultures, of those corporations as they developed in their home country setting. To yield insight into how Japanese managers think and act on the problems of production abroad, I propose some brief explanations of Japanese MNC behavior in Thailand within the conceptual logic of Japanese managers. I close with suggestions about the implications of variations in managerial technology transfer to both the development of MNCs and to patterns of industrialization among host countries in Asia.

Thai Study Sites and Methodology

I focused my study on subsidiaries of multinational corporations in Thailand for five reasons:

1. Compared with some of its Southeast Asian neighbors, Thailand has prepared the ground for substantial FDI through a relative preponderance of incentives and lack of formal restrictions. The combination of liberal economic policy and general flexibility in technocratic intervention on the ground makes the investment and operational environment comparatively laissez-faire. In terms of the research, this investment climate suggests that firm-level motivations—rather than responses to host government pressures—tend to guide changes in management practices of MNC subsidiaries in Thailand. Because I am essentially interested in generating conclusions about the behavior of multinationals abroad, Thailand is ideally positioned for my study.

2. Subsidiaries of MNCs in Thailand vary considerably as to product, size, and length of presence in the country. The research design captured many of these variations cross-sectionally and allows the analysis to address the relevance of these factors. In addition, I have a longitudinal data set on the firms I studied in detail.

3. The scale and impact of FDI on the Thai economy and society are enormous, so analyzing the Thai case is important in its own right.

4. Industrialization in Thailand raises several important issues in the general analysis of regional development in Asia. The Thai case has already been treated as a challenge to the "Asian developmental state" and "flying geese" explanations, by political scientists and economists, respectively, of economic success in the Asian newly industrialized economies (NIEs).[3] The Asian developmental state model proposes a pan-Asian pattern of industrialization modeled on the Japanese state's strong interventions in domestic economic affairs; the flying geese model posits the development of an Asian "product cycle" in which waves of industrial technologies developed and exploited by Japanese industry are later taken over by the NIEs, and in turn by the next set of industrializing countries in Southeast Asia. Although refined by the addition of the notion of "Asian industrial networks,"[4] the product cycle theory largely fits the Thai case. I agree, however, with critics of the Asian developmental state model that Thailand's dramatic economic growth in the 1980s evolved without, or in spite of, government intervention.[5] In any case, this discussion must be considered ongoing as Thailand, undermined by close neighbors with much lower labor costs, attempts to make its way up the technology ladder. Unlike its NIE predecessors, Thailand has a weak educational base and a tendency for the state to avoid serious intervention in economic affairs. At present its moves toward higher-technology manufacturing are strongly assisted, if not driven, by foreign direct investment. The following are relevant questions. Will the potency of FDI continue to be sufficient in terms of capital and, critically, skills development to sustain Thai industrial growth? If sufficient capital were available, does Thailand have the know-how to own and manage firms, such as those found in the Asian NIEs, which participate dynamically in world markets?[6] What lessons does Thailand provide in the "strong state-weak state" debate concerning economic growth?

5. And what are the implications of the Thai experience for other parts of Asia that are now turning to industrialization? The evolution of investment in Thailand may represent a pattern of new investment we can anticipate in other countries in Asia, especially those characterized by lower cost/lower skilled labor and rapidly expanding local markets. Here I am thinking of the "next wave" of Japanese investment in China, Indochina (especially Vietnam), and South Asia, all of which are recent recipients of multinational investment, especially by the Japanese. Only a few of these issues will be covered in this chapter, which focuses on management at the firm level. Nonetheless, they point to the relevance of the Thai case for generating cogent analyses of both the behavior of multinational corporations and their impact on host countries.

After fieldwork at the headquarters of several multinationals in Japan, I gathered data on the management of 15 wholly owned MNC subsidiary manufacturers, predominantly Japanese companies, in Thailand. I conducted detailed fieldwork at a consumer electronics plant, which assembled audio and video cassettes, and an automobile manufacturer, for 10 and 7 months, respectively. (Thai staff outnumbered Japanese managers 400:7 and 600:12 in these factories, though temporary Japanese "advisors" were also often present. Both plants had been manufacturing in Thailand for around five years at the time of the study.) For periods ranging from several days to 6 weeks, data were gathered at 13 other plants that differed from the reference plants in one parameter: same product but earlier establishment in Thailand, manufacture of a different product by same parent multi-national, same product but Western parent, and so forth.[7]

The research was thus designed to produce the generalizable findings expected of standard social science practice, while in-depth, anthropological methods characterized day-to-day fieldwork. To generate a background for the study, I collected data and conducted structured and open interviews with academics, government officials, and other specialists. At the reference companies themselves, in addition to interviewing, conducting surveys, and collecting an array of primary documents, I was intensively involved in participant-observation of activities in and outside the workplace, collected case studies as they unfolded, conducted content and other analyses of meetings, training sessions, shopfloor activities, and so on.

The "Japanese" Model

In brief, the strength of Japanese manufacturing in the postwar period has been characterized by its avoidance of "fordism"—the model associated with industrial production in the West—or the "atomization" of the workforce. In its most exaggerated form, the fordist image is of a worker defined as an input (like a machine or a raw material) to mass production, repetitively performing a simple and specified task without knowledge of the relationship of his work to either the product produced or, perhaps, to the overall organization itself. In contrast, organizational style in Japanese manufacturing stresses task flexibility and dependency between organizational components of the manufacturing process. The system is based on strong information flows throughout the organizational hierarchy generated by a workforce capable of communicating efficiently and accurately. Ideally the system devolves authority—over a limited sphere of activities—down to lower levels than would be the case in a traditional Western manufacturing model. Thus, workers, who are generally highly trained, appear to have a high degree of autonomy over their specific tasks and simultaneously push extensive information about those tasks into the system.

The Japanese model is relevant to this study because it fairly accurately represents the experience of Japanese managers transferred to overseas operations. The model is, of course, most powerfully articulated within the organizational systems and histories of the firms to which managers are attached. In addition, many of the so-called "Japanese" management techniques—often renamed in non-Japanese contexts—are now normative among manufacturers worldwide.[8] This broad acknowledgement of the strengths of Japanese management has reinforced the confidence of Japanese managers in their models, especially at firms with strong manufacturing traditions such as the ones I studied. This process has also been encouraged by the Japanese media, including a vast array of publications targeting an avid audience of business managers and engineers.

Japanese managers, then, carry to their overseas assignments a model of management that sits in a strong position within the public culture of Japan and the private cultures of their firms. This has generated an understandable expectation that the model should be perpetuated in the management of company subsidiaries abroad. So how successful are Japanese multinationals in transferring their model of management at Japanese subsidiaries in Thailand?

The Shopfloor

One way of gauging success may be to look at Japanese shopfloor activities. Often cited by industrial and academic researchers as "representative" activities, they may be a guide to measure the progress of a factory toward an ideal state of Japanese manufacturing.[9] Some of these researchers' claims (for example, that wearing similar uniforms in the factory implies that employees are unaware of hierarchical divisions) are problematic, and alert us that "Japanese manufacturing" and the "Japanese shopfloor" are complex systems that need to be treated with far more analytical care than they have to date. (This is, indeed, one of the goals of a larger work also using the field data from which this chapter is drawn.) Nonetheless, as markers to ground our discussion, here I will simply and briefly explain some common shopfloor techniques in Japan and contrast them with conditions observed in Thailand.[10]

Quality control circles (QC circles) are small-group activities in which, typically, assembly line workers share ideas about how to solve minor problems on their lines. Ideas are tested by gathering data from the line that can be analyzed using simple statistical techniques. Circles are based on the intuitive logic that a worker who is thinking could probably make valuable suggestions about how to work more productively. In the process of participating in circles, workers are assumed to become more interested in their jobs and more committed to their colleagues and the company.[11] While there are variations in Japan, QC circles regularly meet once or twice a week near the shopfloor, after work, for 30–40 minutes. Workers are not paid for their participation. In Thai plants, QC circles were conducted under overtime pay conditions. In many plants they were dropped altogether because of heavy production deadlines. Moreover, in all plants comparatively rudimentary analytical tools were utilized to identify the sources of production difficulties.

Muda-dori (time and resource management) is highly valued among Japanese manufacturers as a general paradigm under which waste, defined both in physical terms and in terms of time, is cut out of the production process. It includes *just-in-time* (JIT) delivery of parts by both external and in-house suppliers. In Thailand, plant layout reflected the scheme. For example, every tool, machine, and supply bin was positioned so it could be used most efficiently in the production process. However, complex measures were avoided. For example, the application of more than simple calculations to straight measurements in order to identify waste or "noise" on production lines—a common muda-dori activity within QC circles in Japan—was avoided. (Waste reduction on the lines in Thailand was the responsibility of production engineers, as in traditional Western systems.) The notion of earlier segments of the production line creating products for their "customers" further along in the production process was poorly developed. Just-in-time delivery by outside suppliers, even Japanese-owned suppliers, was not attempted. Indeed, the Japanese joked among themselves that one Japanese automobile assembler had a year's worth of supplies stockpiled on its huge lot.

Through *job rotation*, a typical worker at a large firm, who is likely to spend his entire working career in that firm, will change tasks and learn new skills such that he will eventually have worked on, or managed the work of, a number of lines or task areas. Over the course of his career his broad, hands-on knowledge of the factory will make him a more competent manager. In Thailand I observed almost no cases of job rotation among workers in the factories I studied. Thai workers were extremely reticent to change tasks, because they interpreted it as an indication that they were judged incompetent in their current jobs, and they did not want to separate themselves from the social relationships they had established with their co-workers. Japanese managers were satisfied with this arrangement, as it generated stability on the production line and did not require that they train workers for new tasks. The calculation by Japanese managers on how intensively to rotate Thai engineers was based essentially on whether it was best to spread out limited engineering manpower by frequent rotation or keep good engineers focused on tasks they could manage consistently. The latter option was viewed as safer and overwhelmingly prevailed.

On-the-job training (OJT) may be considered characteristic of Japanese manufacturing, forming part of a system in which workers in Japan are given the responsibility for quickly learning new tasks on a functioning line—where mistakes immediately affect output—under the tutelage of an individual or group of experienced co-workers. Awareness of the effect on all the line members of one's failure to quickly learn new tasks is deliberately used to motivate new line members. It should be recognized that in Japan the basic skills that even new recruits bring to the factory generally surpass those of workers in other industrialized countries. On-the-job training overwhelmingly predominated in Thai factories. However, this was explained in interviews as a response to high demand for output. Japanese managers felt that Thai workers had plenty of potential but were inexperienced and poorly trained. As a result, in addition to OJT, limited classroom work on assembly in the automobile plant was conducted by Japanese foremen flown in from Japan, with a Thai manager translating. With materials in Japanese or English, the experience was frustrating for all involved. In the consumer electronics plant, manuals had been translated into Thai and Thai midlevel managers conducted some training. However, they were insecure in their knowledge of Japanese methods, a topic I will explore below.

In practice, Japanese managers in Thailand were forced, or chose, to limit the use of Japanese shopfloor methods. Perhaps this is normal and explainable by the fact that the plants I studied in-depth were start-ups, in operation for around five years, with a largely inexperienced labor force. In these plants many Japanese managers told me that they fully expected that within 10–15 years shopfloor and production systems in their Thai factories would match those in place at "sister plants" in Japan. Therefore, the inclusion of a Japanese subsidiary that had been manufacturing locally for over 30 years was significant among my case studies. Whereas the average age of workers in the start-ups was 24 years, in the older plant the majority of workers "grew up with the company." They had joined young and stayed, averaging 37 years of age. The observation of serious limits on the extensiveness of Japanese management techniques was consistent in this older plant (and others) with an experienced labor force. The president of this company told me that, try as he might, he simply could not get these systems in place in Thailand to any degree that approached their use in Japan.

Because no product may be released from the factory at below standard quality, intense production pressures, combined with human and physical resources on the ground, have produced a set of manufacturing methods in Thai subsidiaries very much at odds with the Japanese ideal. The production system in Thailand is managed from above, with decisions controlled tightly by a centralized cadre of managers and engineers oriented to a top-down flow of information. It appears that Japanese multinationals in Thailand have reproduced the atomization of labor and strong centralization of decision-making authority—the fordism—that they managed to avoid in postwar Japan.

What Is Happening, or What Is Not Happening, at Japanese Subsidiaries in Thailand?

While there is a literature, largely focused on North American and European cases, addressing shopfloor activities at Japanese multinationals abroad,[12] very little is written on local management and their interactions with Japanese supervisors. The more I studied it, the more confident I became that exploring local management and its interactions with Japanese supervisors would ultimately yield the most comprehensive explanations of my specific observations concerning the shopfloor and my general analysis of how Japanese organizations go through the process of adjusting to cross-cultural conditions.

Expatriates at subsidiaries of MNCs manufacturing abroad are proportionately few in number and some occupy "advisor" positions on the margins of factory organizational charts, but they are in the highest positions of authority in these firms. They ordinarily spend little time on the shopfloor itself, relying on their higher-ranking local colleagues to carry managerial decisions and information forward and keep it consistent as it moves through the organizational structure. It should be noted that information about what is to be transferred down the hierarchy is making its most critical cross-cultural leap in the communications between expatriate and top local managers. This may be the most important structural point in the managerial technology transfer process. The capacity of local and expatriate personnel, typically at an upper level, to share information strongly affects the development of capabilities among lower-level local staff to successfully handle technology closer to the production line.

Thus, I considered evidence of "insecurity" or "underconfidence" over technical matters among Thai managers and engineers in Japanese firms as extremely significant. It contrasted with my knowledge of conditions among managers and, especially, engineers in Japan and my understanding, based on interviews with Thai managers and the statements of Japanese managers, that Thai engineers in the plants I studied were generally competent. How would these insecurities be explained? My findings suggest that Japanese engineers controlled decisions that their Thai colleagues were—technically speaking—capable of making, thus preventing them from gaining experience and confidence in specific tasks. Supporting evidence comes in the form of a simple arithmetic of expatriate personnel, in this case from microchip manufacturers. Japanese chip manufacturers in Thailand typically have three to four times the number of expatriate engineers as their Western counterparts using similar technologies in similar scale plants. Japanese engineers are deeply involved in controlling engineering tasks in Thailand.

And How Does It Compare?

Western firms face the same manufacturing conditions in Thailand as their Japanese counterparts. They are, for example, also operating in a relatively laissez-faire investment regime using a labor force with a rudimentary education, hiring "overpaid" Thai engineers, and conducting business with high production pressures for a rapidly expanding local or regional economy, or, although comparatively rarely, for re-export to their home country. What is interesting is how firms cope differently under these similar conditions.

As in Japanese firms, expatriate managers in Western firms control finance and investment and determine output and product design at their plants in Thailand. These tasks are managed, however, with far fewer expatriates than is the case at Japanese plants. Typically, at a Western plant that is running normally, two or three expatriates will cover the tasks of president/chief financial officer and chief engineer/conduit for product design from headquarters. (If there is a third expatriate, he or she tends to be an engineer.) The basic expatriate structure of a Japanese plant would have a president, a financial controller, parts and procurement officer, (possibly a planning officer) and, on the production side, a highly experienced plant manager, in addition to engineers as production control manager and quality control manager. Two or three additional Japanese engineers are likely to work under these production side managers. And there tends to be a steady stream of advisors, also predominantly engineers, on temporary visits from Japan.

I have chosen to highlight the number of engineers in overseas subsidiaries and the organizational processes through which production engineering is controlled because, (1) these are the areas in which the most important comparative distinctions appear, and (2) engineering activity constitutes the core activity of manufacturing and thus lies at the center of managerial technology transfers at MNCs. Process technologies in Japanese plants in Thailand were based on information from Japanese sister plants, often the earlier homes of equipment used in Thailand. This is not at all surprising, though a somewhat stronger finding than at the Western plants. Of greater interest is the observation that a key aspect holding back managerial technology transfers was the in-house control of decisions concerning production tasks. This was generally conducted in daily consultations, via telephone and fax, between Japanese engineers at the subsidiaries in Thailand and at sister plants in Japan. Thai engineers were informed of the outcomes of these discussions.

The smaller number of expatriate engineers in Western firms suggests that greater responsibilities are shouldered by Thai engineers. My overall sense, based both on observation and on the statements of Thai and expatriate managers, is that in Western firms expatriate engineers made themselves available to assist their local (Thai) colleagues, who were in the end responsible for their production lines, though the situation naturally varies depending on particular conditions and the skills of local engineers in particular plants. Moreover, the management model employed by expatriate engineers—who were by no means always Westerners but included Singaporeans, Indians, and Koreans—at Western firms in Thailand was quite at variance to that observed in Japanese plants. In the idealized form, a local engineer is given production targets and told to get on with it as he or she sees fit, in what we might call an "arm's-length" model of management. Engineers have the opportunity to learn shopfloor techniques (often much like those practiced by the Japanese in Japan) but are made responsible for their use and, critically, their alteration to fit local conditions on the production line. As a Thai, a local engineer may know what will work best and what will not. Gauges of this engineer's success and capacity are taken at close enough intervals that significant harm to the company is largely avoided should he or she fail. As the president of a large, American-owned hard drive manufacturer put it, "If after a couple of weeks production meets or exceeds targets we simply give him another, perhaps slightly increased, target for the next period. If he's below target, we talk. If he's below two or three times, he's demoted or out the door."

I do not want to overstate a cowboy mentality, or rugged individualism, for managers at Western plants, or lose sight of the variations in management styles at Western firms in Thailand.[13] I do want to stress the distinction in Japanese plants in the attitude concerning skills exhibited toward local managers, the intensity of interactions between local and expatriate engineers, and the responsibilities that local managers and engineers are expected to bear. All manufacturing multinationals provide training, skills, and standards, which they overlay on local environments to produce goods. In comparing Western and Japanese MNCs, my data suggest that Japanese managers in Thailand are far more aggressive in forwarding their solutions to problems at all levels of overseas operations than are expatriate managers at Western MNCs. Thus, where Japanese advisors will keep hold of decisions that their Thai counterparts are capable of making, in Western firms, with their hands-off style, local engineers are given more responsibility and allowed to learn through the risks of failure or success. Engineers were experiencing real on-the-job training. Technological know-how would appear to be more successfully transferred through this process.

A possible test of the comparative strengths of these two styles of managerial technology transfer might come from a study of productivity at similar plants. However, machines at otherwise comparable plants differed sufficiently to invalidate any attempts to compare productivity. For plants that have been established in the last decade, my impression is that Japanese and Western firms are producing goods at about the same rate and are making impressive profits. More interesting questions for my purposes ask why have they organized manufacturing differently and what difference may it make over the long run.

Explaining Differences

In these two concluding sections, I am further from my data and closer to conjecture and generalization. Nonetheless, I would like to propose an explanation for the previous findings and briefly comment, first, on their effect on the development of MNCs with different parents and, second, on the implications of Japanese versus Western MNC investment on host countries in Asia.

I have suggested that in managerial style Western MNCs are more successful in providing managerial technology transfers to local employees of their operations in Asia than are Japanese MNCs. To a significant degree this is explained by the effects of home country organizational culture demonstrated by these firms, which overlay all other sets of decisions taken by MNCs. Home country, or head-quarters, organizational culture influences both the implicit expectations of working practices and the policies of multinationals. At the risk of oversimplification, in their home environments Western firms will allow managers to take a high degree of responsibility over tasks with ex post facto oversight of results. Significantly, and not by design but rather as a residual effect of home organizational culture, in the foreign context this arm's-length style of management is in practice less likely to conflict with local ways of organizing work than the hands-on style typical of Japanese manufacturing. If our theory of learning contains the notion that we build new information into the structures of knowledge already familiar to us, arms-length management may strongly encourage the development of local know-how, as long as technical guidance is made readily available.

The social characteristics observed in Japanese manufacturing at home in Japan offer contrast. Important among these are long-term commitment by employees to the firm as much more than a workplace, overlapping responsibilities, and dependence on extremely dense informational networks that facilitate a remarkable flow of information both up and down vertical organizational hierarchies and across horizontal organizational functions. These characteristics have worked extremely well in domestic manufacturing in postwar Japan, and they thereby encourage an expectation of similarly dense information flows by Japanese managers in subsidiaries abroad. But such flows appear to be arduous to re-create abroad because they may rely on similar backgrounds and assumptions about social interactions, which may explain the common observation that penetration of Japanese organizations by non-Japanese is difficult. Poorer information flows may increase the desire of Japanese managers abroad to keep decision making under their control and to fine-tune the work of their foreign colleagues. In practice this encourages the presence of large numbers of Japanese engineers.[14] Because of their breadth of marketing and production throughout the globe, we might expect Japanese multinational manufacturers to be among the most "internationalized" of Japanese organizations. Arguably however, as suggested in the discussion of the Japanese model, in the cross-cultural context flexibility problems may be exaggerated at Japanese MNC manufacturers because of the considerable worldwide kudos they have received for their domestic production and managerial methods.

It was not part of my field research methodology to press every Japanese manager I knew on my observations, which in any case were essentially consolidated only after leaving the field. Nonetheless, through interviews and participation in the successes and frustrations of months of on-duty and off-duty activities, a good deal of opinion made its way to the surface. What follows, as a composite of many conversations, are five explanations for difficulties in placing Japanese shopfloor methods in the Thai workplace. (Although I add some comments parenthetically, I am not here arguing the validity or internal consistency of these explanations. The far more interesting point is that although these explanations are distilled and therefore uncharacteristically pointed in tone, I think they represent the Japanese perspective, and they may be explained within the framework of Japanese organizational expectations suggested in the previous paragraph. They may, therefore, begin to untangle the motivations behind observed activity at subsidiaries of Japanese MNCs in Thailand.)

1. *High production pressure*: Demand for goods produced in Thailand is high and requires the expansion of production. Therefore, there is little time for training or rotation. Keeping workers on the same line assists in maintaining quality.
2. *Low wages*: There is no motivation to put a large effort and expense into training because the cost of labor is low and it will only marginally affect productivity. Productivity will increase in any case through the introduction of more efficient machinery. Low wages also mean that postproduction inspection is a readily available option for quality assurance.
3. *Education*: Thai workers are difficult to train because they have a much lower basic education compared with Japanese workers. Training materials must be completely redesigned and simplified to cope with this, an expensive and time-consuming task. Again, avoiding rotation means workers are trained once for one job, and usually on the job itself.
4. *High turnover of personnel*: Expending money on rotation and training is counterproductive because employees leave once they have acquired valuable skills. (According to data widely circulated among Japanese managers, turnover among workers is fairly low, while among engineers it is high. Turnover is high among engineers not only because they seek higher wages but because many Thai engineers feel irrelevant to Japanese decision making about production. With some outstanding and highly paid exceptions, Thai engineers who stay at Japanese plants tend to be relatively passive and willing to sacrifice self-expression in the workplace for job security.)
5. *No industrial tradition*: Thailand is a largely agrarian economy that has not evolved through the industrial stage of development. Unlike conditions at subsidiaries in the United States or Europe, there is no need for Japanese MNCs to work with or against systems of industrial organization already in place. Thai organizational culture as it stands need not be scrutinized, for it has not yet been rationalized appropriately to fit modern industrial standards. Since many of those standards are Japanese, it is appropriate that much of the rationalization process should follow a familiar Japanese path.

Among these five explanations, the fifth is the most abstract and fundamental in terms of its potential relevance to managerial technology transfers at overseas subsidiaries of Japanese manufacturers generally. It may also stimulate rich discussion, and, for me, further research. In any case, since my project here is comparative, let us consider the matter from the Western perspective. I have characterized Western multinationals as technically exacting, like their Japanese counterparts, but cross-culturally flexible on a managerial level through the habits of arms-length management. Not that Western managers may not have opinions about the quality of local industrial culture in the many environments in which they manufacture, it is rather that such considerations are less relevant to the way they conduct operations on the ground. This is unlike Japanese managers, who are keen to forward their own solutions to the management of production and may experience frustration with the pace at which Japanese methods can be operationalized in the foreign setting.

Trajectories of MNC Development and Their
Implications for Asian Host Countries

There is a substantial literature on MNCs that posits their evolution along a scale of decreasing dependence on central control and the development of a truly international pool of managers operating in diverse environments producing a wide variety of "products" from manufactured goods to consulting advice. Japanese MNCs have generally been perceived at a relatively early stage along this developmental scale. The data I have presented from Thailand lead me to believe that the evolutionary path of Japanese MNCs, in terms of both the centralized control of subsidiaries and the worldwide structure of their developmental trajectory, is likely to differ from that of Western MNCs.

First, as the start-up era of joint ownership and control of overseas operations wanes and MNCs are increasingly moving toward explicit control of their own operations, and 100 % ownership by MNCs where host governments allow it, differences between the subsidiary operations of MNCs with different parents are likely to become more pronounced, especially so on the managerial level.[15] This chapter has argued strongly for the relevance of local organizational culture and knowledge to operations within subsidiaries and, thus, to managerial technology transfers, no matter who owns the firm. Nonetheless, this argument must be seated within the logic of structural control of resources. Under joint ventures, expatriate managers are required at the very least to consider the reactions of local shareholders, and in Thailand in many cases expatriates and Thais at the top of the firm are deadlocked in conflicts over a range of management directions. Firms in my study were predominantly wholly owned by MNCs. Office and factory layout and formal organizational structures more closely resembled plants in Duluth or Kawasaki than they did wholly owned Thai plants down the street. Thus, increasingly Thai engineers and managers at MNC subsidiaries must contend with a cross-cultural event in their discussions with top management over how to best organize the subsidiary's business activity. Furthermore, the experience of Thais in handling the foreign cultures of MNCs has become part of their skill base. Thai engineers in Japanese firms who "job-hop" tend to move within a circle of Japanese firms. Japanese managers at competing Japanese firms feel that Thais are likely to have picked up some notion of Japanese ways even if they otherwise disapprove of job-hopping for career advancement. In any case, as subsidiaries are increasingly financially controlled by MNCs, distinctive managerial practices have simultaneously become more deeply patterned.

Second, I have discussed in some detail the strict centralization of decision-making authority in Japanese hands within subsidiaries. Turning briefly beyond the plant, I should note that this centralization is also reflected in the position of subsidiaries vis-à-vis headquarters. Subsidiaries in Thailand are part of a tightly controlled and rigorously hierarchical organizational structure extending down from Japan. This lack of autonomy is suggestive. Rather than finding themselves at an earlier stage of development compared with their Western counterparts, in the Southeast Asian context at least, Japanese multinationals may be operating with an altogether different view of the value of autonomy. Although some of the Japanese MNCs that I studied had regional Southeast Asian headquarters "above them," these operated far more as trading clearinghouses than they did as reference points for control of subsidiaries. Japanese managers referenced headquarters or plants in Japan for the core of their work: technical information and individual career paths. The inconsistency between organizational design and practice was a point of tension within these MNCs. It also matters that the Japanese archipelago is at most only two time zones and a six-hour flight away from the vast majority of Asian subsidiaries. In Asia I expect Japanese MNCs to remain comparatively centralized both within the subsidiary and in the relationships between subsidiaries and Japan-based operations.

Opinion varies about where differences in management bring advantages or disadvantages to MNCs. I think that continuous pressures to move production abroad, combined with the high cost of supplying overseas operations with expatriate Japanese personnel, will eventually disadvantage Japanese firms, other considerations being equal. These high costs are likely to force Japanese MNCs to expand the numerical proportions and responsibilities of local staff in spite of a surplus of personnel in Japan and an organizational tendency to tightly control subsidiaries. It matters that experience abroad by Japanese personnel is thin. Although it is perfectly clear that large numbers of Japanese managers are now going overseas, the experience of this new cadre of international managers, especially in managing non-Japanese, still lags well behind its counterparts at Western firms.

Manufacturing in Asia is increasingly expensive and knowledge-intensive. In addition, the range of competitors is far more complex than portrayed by the Japanese-Western dichotomization delineated in this chapter for analysis of managerial technology transfer. Diverse Chinese firms are now major players,[16] as are South Korean investors. In addition to capital, both technical and managerial flexibility would appear to be key sources of strength. While Japanese companies are feeling the effects of Japan's recession in the mid-1990s, they will remain comparatively rich in capital for overseas investment. However, the Thai data suggest that Japanese firms may experience operational difficulties while weaving the necessary but complex fabric of managerial technology transfers.

Meanwhile, one should not lose sight of the impact on Asian host countries of MNC operations and the implications of the Thai case to theories of Asian development. From the perspective of Asian host country governments, there has been a decline in the availability of import substitution or protection of domestic markets as a viable growth strategy. Industrial policies point in the relatively passive direction of providing an attractive investment environment to harness regional economic dynamism in Asia. In this context the heart of the matter in terms of active host government policy may lie in the provision of physical infrastructure and the level of education and skills that local staff can bring to industrial firms. The accomplishments of the Asian NIEs in providing a well-educated labor pool are not matched in Thailand, Indonesia, and the Philippines. Nor are they matched in the diverse "next" Asian gaggle of flying geese: the relatively tightly controlled economies of China, Vietnam, Burma, India, and Bangladesh. Here industrialization is starting to play a significant role, much of it multinational-driven and Japanese. Realistically, if moves up the product cycle/technology ladder are to have any dynamism in Asian states that have relatively low educational standards, these moves will largely be the result of activity within private corporations. In this context the notion of managerial technology transfers takes on significance beyond the firm itself.

If my analysis is correct, at present local managers and engineers apparently are likely to gain more know-how from employment at Western multinationals. In no way, however, does this suggest preferential policies to favor certain sources of MNC investment. On the contrary, it appears that investment by MNCs from various sources has the positive effect on the domestic industrialization process of providing local firms with a diversity of models that may stimulate organizational change as well as potential linkages to different international, and domestic, trading networks. And MNC investment also has huge economic multiplier effects and provides much needed employment. In any case, a projection of my analysis of essentially microlevel phenomena within subsidiaries of MNCs onto national economic growth scenarios is beyond the parameters of this chapter. Rather, the work here presents a new perspective for analysis of the interactions of investment, government policy, and economic growth in Asia and suggests that debate over both the Asian developmental state and the flying geese models should still be considered wide open.

But, at the level of the firm, I am on more solid ground. Even in the fundamentally standardized world of production of consumer goods, the argument that the interplay of world markets and ongoing technological innovation drives MNCs toward similar internal organizational structures and processes does not fit the facts. At the very least, this research shows that the social milieu of multinationals or, for the purposes of this discussion, who owns the company, matters to the organization of production and the quality of managerial technology transfers. One knows that Japanese management travels in Asia, but the Thai data suggest that it may less often arrive there.

Notes

1. The classic literature on the organization and management of large-scale private enterprises in modern Japan is Robert E. Cole, *Japanese Blue Collar* (Berkeley: University of California Press, 1971); Ronald Dore, *British Factory, Japanese Factory* (Los Angeles: University of California Press, 1973); Thomas P. Rohlen, *For Harmony and Strength: Japanese White-Collar Organizations in Anthropological Perspective* (Berkeley: University of California Press, 1974); Rodney Clark, *The Japanese Company* (New Haven: Yale University Press, 1979); and James C. Abegglen and George Stalk, Jr., *Kaisha: The Japanese Corporation* (Tokyo: Charles E. Tuttle, 1985).

2. I am defining multinationals based in North America and Europe as "Western MNCs." For the purposes of this chapter, with its explicit focus on Japanese MNCs, it would be a distraction to overly qualify the alternative management model I will propose for Western MNCs. I do, however, recognize that there are important variations among Western MNCs, though perhaps less pronounced in management than in other areas.

3. The "Asian developmental state" model was first articulated in Chalmers Johnson, *MITI and the Japanese Miracle: The Growth of Industrial Policy, 1925–1975* (Stanford: Stanford University Press, 1982). Bernard and Ravenhill cite the original notion of "flying geese" from Akamatsu Kaname, "Shinkoku kogyokoku no sangyo hatten" [*sic*] [Report on Industrial Development in Industrialized Countries], *Ueda Tejiro Hakushi Kinen Ronbunshu* 4 (July 1937). They also trace very

clearly the intellectual history of the concept and its latter day interchangeability with the "product cycle theory." See pp. 172–179 in Mitchell Bernard and John Ravenhill, "Beyond Product Cycles and Flying Geese: Regionalization, Hierarchy, and the Industrialization of Asia," *World Politics* 47 (January 1995). For an early application and response to these theories in the context of Thailand, see Daniel H. Unger, *Japan, the Overseas Chinese, and Industrialization in Thailand*, Ph.D. dissertation, Department of Political Science, University of California, Berkeley, 1989.

4. Bernard and Ravenhill, "Beyond Product Cycles," pp. 171–172, 205–209, argue that, rather than product cycles, industrial production in Asia is now characterized by regional networks of contractually, or more closely related, firms that fluidly cross borders, feeding parts, assembly, R & D, know-how, and marketing skills into manufacturing. While this is certainly the case, the hierarchical quality of differences in technical capacity in each country—which underpins the product cycle and flying geese models—nonetheless remains intact.

5. See, for example, Unger, *Japan, the Overseas Chinese.*

6. A sense of this dynamism among the NIEs, especially as it concerns "Chinese" firms, can be found in Michael Borrus, "Left for Dead: Asian Production Networks and the Revival of U.S. Electronics," in Barry Naughton, ed., *The China Circle: Economics and Technology in the PRC, Taiwan and Hong Kong* (Washington, DC: Brookings Institution, 1997), pp. 139–163.

7. Viewed from the perspectives of other disciplines, it may seem an anachronism of anthropology that field sites, in this case the names of the companies and their subsidiaries, are disguised. The downside is that there is already a literature that I cannot cite on many of these companies, all of which are first-tier manufacturers and conglomerates, indeed "household names." Overall, however, the advantages far outweighed this disadvantage. I could not have enjoyed the degree of access required for the detailed study I made at the two multinationals that were the focus of in-depth work without this foundation of anonymity. Negotiating access to these companies was a difficult process and their final acceptance of my day-to-day participant-observation came to be based on their belief that I could be trusted in this matter. Once this occurred, I was no longer "handled." Indeed, I was often surprised that no effort was made to shield sensitive matters from me. To date, critics of this anonymity have been academics, while businessmen, familiar with the logic of screening information, have appreciated the value and intent of this aspect of my methodology. The ethics of the matter, of course, stand for the study of modern enterprises as they do for more mainstream subjects of anthropological inquiry. At the level of intimacy required for sound ethnographic work, it would simply present too great a risk to individuals within companies if even the company were named, to say nothing of the potential damage to the firms vis-à-vis their competitors. This is not a study of the past, but of firms and careers in progress.

Having approached the field with these considerations in mind, I was required to see it through at the 13 other firms where I collected data for shorter periods of time, even though the work was much less revealing and these companies would probably have allowed me to make their names public.

Apart from matters of ethics and methodological taste, there are other advantages in disguising the names of the companies. These companies are so well known that mentioning them inevitably pushes forward images of products and, among specialists, notions as to specific corporate styles. These conventional wisdoms are extremely difficult to dislodge, in spite of claims that we are willing to start fresh with new data. While I am at times sorely tempted to debunk notions of how particular corporations are run, this is not the goal of this research project. I will continue to simply tip my hat at the successes of these firms' public relations departments.

8. In U.S. manufacturing we should note, for example, that while in the 1970s and early 1980s the recalcitrance of the U.S. automotive industry to new techniques was well publicized, the computer industry has never lagged in adopting, or reinventing, techniques that might improve productivity. Many of these techniques closely correspond with Japanese models.

9. The literature on Japanese management is long in the public domain and longer in management consultant reports. The spate of interest in Japanese techniques in United Kingdom (UK) manufacturing from the 1980s onward is representative. A relatively sophisticated example in this line is Nicholas Oliver and Barry Wilkinson, *The Japanization of British Industry* (Oxford: Blackwell, 1992).

10. We should recognize that in Japan the use of these techniques varies considerably. In the firms I studied they see heavy use on the shopfloor in Japan and are taken very seriously in the lore of their corporate cultures.

11. Circle imagery has an explicitly industrial connotation and has perhaps replaced sports analogies, such as "teamwork," prevalent in the organizational images of manufacturing in earlier eras.

12. On the UK see Oliver and Wilkinson, *Japanization*, as well as P. Garrahan and P. Stewart, *The Nissan Enigma: Flexibility at Work in a Local Economy*, (Mansell, 1992); and K. Williams, *Cars: Analysis, History, Cases* (Berghan Books, 1994). Work on the United States has been less consistent, driven far more by negative opinion than by sound analysis within factories.

13. See note 2 on this point.

14. In this chapter I have focused on the pull factor in explaining the presence of large numbers of Japanese engineers in overseas subsidiaries. I continue to consider this the key explanation. However, the phenomenon is certainly not discouraged by an important push factor: most large Japanese manufacturing MNCs are now challenged by a flattening in domestic production of consumer goods, while a high proportion of skilled Japanese managers and engineers, who expect "lifetime employment," remain on their payrolls. Sending them abroad as "advisors" helps to justify the situation, though it is enormously expensive.

15. Of course, the growth of majority ownership and the use of FDI to secure access to foreign markets are widely noted examples of increasing similarities between MNCs. It is at other levels of MNC activity that differences are expanding. My analysis focuses on firm-level managerial dynamics. Encarnation and Mason, for example, find differences at a higher level of industrial organization. For Japanese MNCs they note the substantial growth in the scale of intracompany trade and the development of overseas keiretsu relations mirroring those in Japan. See pp. 442–446 in Dennis Encarnation and Mark Mason, "Does Ownership Matter? Answers and Implications for Europe and America," in Mark Mason and Dennis Encarnation, *Does Ownership Matter? Japanese Multinationals in Europe* (New York: Oxford University Press, 1994).

16. See Borrus, "Left for Dead" and chapter 9 in this volume.

PART IV

PRODUCTION NETWORKS

Foreign Direct Investment, Trade, and Technology Flows Combined

8

The Business Strategies of Japanese Production Networks in Asia

Dennis S. Tachiki

An Organizational Black Box

To deepen our discussion of production networks driven by foreign direct investment (FDI), I focus on the business plans of Japanese companies. A business plan is an organizational document outlining a company's policies and goals and the means for achieving those goals. When a company moves its operations overseas, it clearly states its FDI strategy in a business plan. Specifically, a business plan reveals the transfer of a component, product, or support service to an overseas production base as the internationalization of a section, department, or division. Yet the business plans of multinational corporations do not normally fall within the purview of FDI theories.

In explaining the movement of domestic operations to an overseas production base, FDI theories point to either a company's "fit" with its business environment or the strategic decisions made by managers.[1] Proponents of the first alternative argue that a company's business environment limits its options, forcing it to converge on the strategies and structures of competitors over time. Yet the historical record shows that companies actively seek government protection, diversify their product lines, or collaborate with competitors in order to attain a distinctive competitive edge. Although managers may have a greater scope for voluntary action, they do not always have complete information about their business environment. Some managers have the foresight to make the right strategic moves overseas, yet most of them are bravely muddling through or, in the worse case, eventually closing their overseas operations. Because both of these approaches assume organizations make rational choices, neither one explores the linkages between fit and "strategy." At this juncture, however, multinational corporations sort through imperfect options to order their business priorities and mobilize scarce organizational resources across national borders. In this organizational black box, we see the outlines of a company's business plan.

There is another reason for viewing Japanese FDI activities through the lens of their business plans. Most international flows of investment, trade, and technology move along the organizational linkages companies establish across national borders. A growing share of Japanese overseas business activities is in the form of direct investments in joint ventures instead of arm's-length agreements (Tachiki 1995; Nakakita 1989). Moreover, a growing share of trade is due to intrafirm transfer of parts and components across national borders (Sakura Institute of Research 1995). Accompanying the flow of money and goods are people and information (JANCPEC 1992), highlighting the growing importance of trade in services. Collectively, these flows embody the soft technology (management practices and production methods) that contribute to the economic development of host countries (Tachiki 1994). The choices companies make among types of market, hierarchy, and interfirm cooperation in creating these linkages provide some basis for evaluating the differences and similarities in the national origins of international production networks.

My empirical data consist primarily of company materials and interviews conducted at Japanese companies and their overseas subsidiaries operating in the Asia-Pacific region.[2] I examine these cases through the framework of a generic business plan. A business plan is a policy umbrella, covering the basic management functions. To simplify my analysis, I narrow my discussion to the Japanese practice of *hoshin kanri* and address only the other aspects of a business plan—marketing, finance, production, etc.—where they intersect with this process. A 1987 summary definition for hoshin kanri is a system for the

- enhancement of the company's overall capability in order to improve performance through
- the deployment of unified policies and goals (implementation, check, action for improvement) under an annual and long-term management plan based on a company motto by
- using the primary management resources—people, goods, money—to optimally bond together the quality, volume, cost, and delivery functions (Akao 1991).

Managers adopt this method to concretize strategic goals, gain flashes of insight about the future, and develop the means to bring goals into reality.

Business Plan

The basic framework informing the hoshin kanri process is the PDCA cycle, a problem-solving method divided into four phases: plan, do, check, and action. A generic business plan thus consists of core business objectives, an implementation plan, periodical policy audits, and performance gaps and countermeasures (see fig. 8.1).

It is difficult to document how widespread these practices are across the population of Japanese companies; however, those companies that have received or desire the Deming Application Prize have adopted it. The Union of Japanese Scientists and Engineers instituted this prestigious prize in 1951. They have awarded it each year to companies and individuals representing the best practices in the area of total quality control (TQC).[3] Since its inception, 105 companies have received this prize. Winners and aspirers include the major corporate

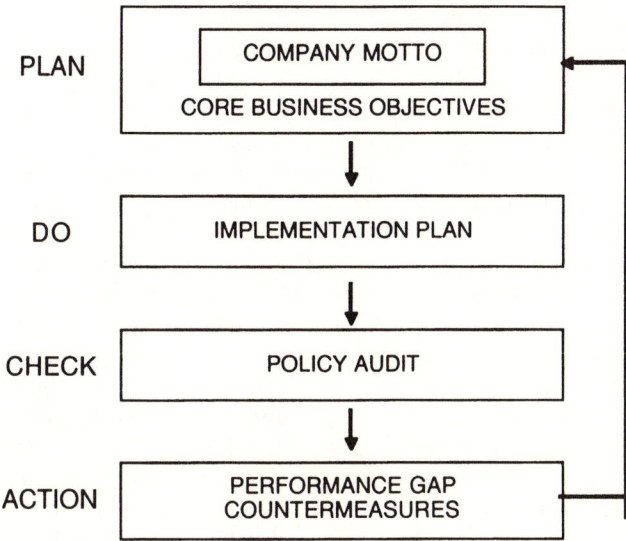

Figure 8.1 Hoshin Kanri Process. *Source:* Compiled from various case study company materials.

groupings in Japan and their closely affiliated companies listed on the Tokyo Stock Exchange.

For discussion purposes, I consolidate the PDCA cycle along two organizational dimensions—policy formulation and implementation plan—to establish a benchmark for my subsequent discussion of Japanese FDI.

Policy Formulation

Around December every year, starting with the check phase in the PDCA cycle, many leading companies in Japan conduct a policy audit of their business environments. Practitioners suggest this unusual starting point to ground a company's business plan in facts instead of top management's intuition (Akao 1991). By February, the planning department has collected and analyzed the data necessary for identifying the performance gaps between a company's business plan and its actual market performance. The plan phase begins when top managers, with line managers, negotiate the company's core business objectives. These three steps in the policy formulation process provide some insight into how Japanese companies order their business priorities.

Policy Audit   The senior executives initiate the hoshin kanri process with a policy audit of their company's past and future business activities. Ideally, this scan of their business environment draws on three sources of information. First, they examine the results from their past year's business performance. The second data set consists of information about in-house conditions (e.g., forecasts for new products, new technologies, production, sales, people, products, money, quality, quantity, and cost). A third source of information they consult is the company's external environment (e.g., international economic changes, domestic changes, and industrial changes). What they cull from these data depends on the uncertainties in their external business environment. To grasp where Japanese companies draw the line between their internal and external organizational boundaries, for analytical purposes, I order their business environment into five categories: factor conditions, firm strategy and structure, competition, demand conditions, and related supporting industries.[4] Managers' weighting of each of these dimensions provides a baseline for documenting where they fall within organizational boundaries.

Most Japanese companies are subject to the vicissitudes of market forces; however, the leading ones have been able to buffer their factor conditions and market relations (Fruin 1994). For instance, a horizontal *keiretsu* (corporate grouping) links a lead bank and affiliated companies through mutual stockholdings and the exchange of personnel, goods, and information (Aoki 1990; Gerlach 1992). In addition, large companies incorporate labor relations through lifetime employment, promotion by seniority, and collective bargaining at the company level (Inohara 1990; Koike 1988; Hanami 1979). All of this is embedded in specialized organizational networks for acquiring, assimilating, and diffusing technology (Morris-Suzuki 1994; Commission on the History of Science and Technology Policy 1991). On the related supporting industry dimension, the vertical and distribution keiretsu form interlinked layers of suppliers and retailers supporting the international business activities of leading Japanese companies (Nishiguchi 1994; Smitka 1991). On the demand conditions dimension, regulations governing the distribution system favor Japanese producers over consumers and foreign competitors in the world's second largest market (Noguchi 1994). On the rivalry dimension, Japanese companies aggressively compete on quality and product variety to meet the demands of consumers (Kodama 1995). According to my interviews, the general issues managers consider external to their organizational boundaries are macroeconomic trends affecting their factor inputs, changes in consumer markets, and technological innovations.

When one draws the general organizational boundaries of leading Japanese companies, one sees that they have internalized a large segment of their business environment, particularly companies in growth sectors. In these cases, career development replaces external labor markets, joint labor-management committees partially replace collective bargaining, design-in narrows competitive bidding in the procurement of components, corporate groupings mediate access to factor inputs, and so forth. The remaining uncertainties are related to structural changes in the economy and society. International trade policies, product innovations, and industrial restructuring are the major issues falling within their organizational boundaries. A policy audit, then, keeps top management appraised of incremental adjustments within the company and major structural changes in the external business environment.

Performance Gap   Against the backdrop of this segmented business environment, the planning department regularly monitors the company's crucial external business trends against its current business plan. From this dual vantage point, planners alert top management to potential business problems and provide an analysis of causes. Top management matches this information against the current activities of business units to determine performance gaps. Because most Japanese companies strive to maximize the profit margin per unit produced, their primary performance measure gravitates toward a return-on-sales and to a lesser extent periodic profit and return-on-investment (Sakurai, Killough, and Brown 1989).

Despite the logical and quantitative appearance of this step in the policy formulation process, it is not always clear which countermeasures will address a company's performance gaps. For instance, why Matsushita Electric's VHS video cassette recording (VCR) format squeezed the Sony Corporation's technologically superior Betamax format out of the marketplace can be understood only in hindsight. The Japanese government plays a major role in addressing business uncertainties. Since the 1950s, the government has created an incentive structure to harness business objectives to national economic goals (Lincoln 1984). One pillar in this incentive structure is the Japanese government's "low interest rate disequilibrium policy." In the early postwar period, this pillar allowed the government to ration scarce capital to industries with potentially high export growth rates (Aoki and Patrick 1994). A second pillar consists of policies promoting exports, such as tax incentives, lax enforcement of antimonopoly laws covering export cartels, and assistance for selected companies in their overseas operations (Komiya, Okuno, and Suzumura 1988; Takenaka 1991). A third policy pillar stresses industrial adjustment through rationalization and diversification (Urata and Nakakita 1991). The government's three major rationalization targets are to assist important industries (i.e., export and supporting industries), to subsidize regional industries and labor markets, and to support small and medium-size companies. Drawing on these incentives, executing indicative planning, and using its authority for administrative guidance (*gyosei shido*), the government has been relatively successful in attracting leading Japanese companies into export-oriented industries and facilitating industrial adjustments in Japan (Nakamura 1981).

An institutionally rich environment surrounds this incentive structure, centering around the "iron triangle" linking bureaucrats, politicians, and business executives. The main institutional actors have been the economic ministries, the Liberal Democratic Party, and the business organizations.[5] Practices such as *amakudari* (appointment of retired ministry officials to public and private organizations), political *zoku* (politicians who develop legislative expertise on a particular ministry on behalf of their constituencies), *shingikai* (government advisory councils of leading notables), and other forms of social exchange strengthen the personal linkages across the iron triangle (Trezise and Suruki 1976). Labor unions and consumer groups are not traditionally considered within the iron triangle, but they can mobilize public opinion to influence debate in the political arena.[6] A characteristic of the iron triangle, then, is that it concentrates national resources and mobilizes key organizational actors toward economic development and policy goals.

This mix of public policies and institutional actors defines a wide range of countermeasures available to companies; however, it does not exhaust all possibilities. Prominent cases such as the Sony Corporation in the electronics industry or Honda Motor in the automobile industry demonstrate the possibility for success in the international marketplace outside this framework. Early in its company history, the Sony Corporation tapped the American financial and consumer markets to commercially develop its popular transistor radio. Consequently, the business goals of Japanese companies and the national economic goals of the state are not necessarily the same. In pursuit of higher return-on-sales, Japanese companies adopt countermeasures to improve their performance, depending on whether they can take advantage of the incentives in the iron triangle and the global economy.

Core Business Objectives   At the beginning of the new fiscal year, in April, the company president announces to employees the annual slogan and policies. The company's motto and basic ideas inform these annual announcements. At the Toyota Motor Corporation, for example, the basic corporate motto is "Customer First." The main ideas related to their motto are Harmonizing People, Society, and Environment; Philosophy of Audit and Improvement; and Good Thinking, Good Products. These ideas reflect Toyota's emphasis on customer satisfaction, quality control, and employee involvement. Beyond these slogans, a company's business plan contains the documentation on its short- and long-term goals and the supporting implementation strategies. I briefly discuss the goals of Japanese companies and then turn to the implementation plan in the next section.

Rationalization and diversification themes dominate the core business objectives of Japanese companies. Rationalization refers to any business activities reducing operating costs (Urata and Nakakita 1991). Usually this activity falls into the categories of quality, cost, and delivery. Practitioners simply call it the QCD functions. A company's emphasis on each of these functions over time has changed the meaning of the word rationalization. In the early postwar period, Japanese manufacturers emphasized cost over quality, as the moniker "Made in Japan" then implied. In this connection, rationalization meant the introduction of efficient new technologies and equipment to achieve scales of economy in production. In the 1970s, global and domestic consumer demand for more reliable products elevated the status of the quality and delivery functions. Consequently, the meaning of rationalization shifted toward the saving of factor inputs (labor and capital) and throughput time.

The practical meaning of diversification has also changed over time. Diversification refers to a company's move up the value-added product curve within an industry or its move to a new product in another industry. The integrated circuit (IC) chip is the classic case study (Kodama 1995). Initially, Japanese electronics companies, such as NEC, Toshiba, and Fujitsu, sought uses for the IC chip within their industry. They vertically integrated production to diversify into downstream products, such as calculators and computers. As the sophistication and break-even point climbed, however, they sought uses for the IC chip in related industries, such as the consumer electric goods (e.g., washing machine, vacuum cleaner) and the automobile (e.g., electronic components) industries. In pursuing this broader meaning of diversification, in some cases, they took the opportunity to produce new products in another industry—for example, NEC now derives more of its gross revenues from the electronics side of its business than the electric side.

Japanese companies play these two themes out over time in their business plan. The typical time frames in their business plans consist of next year's goals, 3-year to 5-year medium-term goals, and long-term goals that are 5–10 years down the road. In the current year and medium-term core business objectives, rationalization is usually a central theme, whereas diversification emerges as an important theme in the medium- and long-term core business objectives. This suggests that the typical competitive trajectory Japanese companies follow is incremental and goes from low cost, high quality to new product innovation.

Implementation Plan

The implementation plan is the intraorganizational side to a company's core business objectives. At this point, a company's business plan enters the plan and do phases of the PDCA cycle. The recipients of the Deming Application Prize during the 1960s—Nissan Motors (1960), Teijin and Nippondenso (1961), Sumitomo-Denko (1962), Nippon Kayaku (1963), Komatsu (1964), and Toyota Jiko (1965)—have fine-turned the implementation of their core business objectives through target-means deployment and cross-functional management. Because FDI theories usually draw on macro or cross-sectional data, examining these two processes to examine how a company mobilizes its organizational resources will be useful.

Target-Means Deployment   The operational components of a company policy consist of targets and means. Targets are the expected results. Means are the guidelines for achieving the targets. The matching of business targets to organizational means aligns the goals and resources of the subunits with a company's core business objectives and gives a business plan its organizational depth.

Target deployment is a method for translating a company's core business objectives into quantitative targets at the department, section, and line-worker levels of the organization. The Komatsu Company's "flag method" demonstrates how a company's policies intersect with its measurement and accounting systems. At the top of a schematic flagpole is the division or department target—for example, decrease in production costs. In the first round of negotiating subunit targets, a numerical target is not usually set; however, line managers understand that they should improve on the previous year's figure. Down the levels of line management on the organizational chart, each department or section displays on its flag a subtarget, which consists of an item for control, or "control item," and a numerical measure. For example, one section may use cost of subcontract parts as its control item; another section may use plant machining costs, and so forth. The section head then selects a numerical measure (i.e., control point) for monitoring progress toward the section's subtarget. These are the figures managers include in their quarterly reports and frequently post on the shopfloor. When compiling this information under the flag method, a company creates a simple graphic picture of its cost-reduction activities.

Once a section sets its subtarget, the next step is deploying a means for achieving it. Means deployment is the technique employees must use in their daily work activities to achieve the section's subtarget. Indeed, at this level in the organization, the articulated subtarget goals and techniques constitute the section's "daily management control" work practices. Japanese companies often use some version of the 6Ms to link subtargets with work activities (6Ms = material, machine, manpower, method, market, and money). Under each M, executives ask senior and middle managers to suggest possible techniques for means deployment. Some common techniques include variety reduction program (VRP, materials), single minute exchange of die (SMED, machine), quality control circle activities (manpower), *jidoka* (method), quality function deployment (market), and value analysis (money).

The department and section subtargets are usually broad enough to accommodate any of the techniques under the 6Ms. In the case of Japan, professional institutions play an important role in filtering fad from fashion. Between 1945 and 1955, organizations emerged in three important functional areas: quality control, productivity, and management.[7] There are several key features to these organizations. First, they often have some relationship to a ministry bureau or business association, constituting another institutional layer in the iron triangle. Second, many of these organizations accept only corporate membership, providing stable access to organizational resources. Third, their intermediary role is to scan the domestic and international scene to identify the best practices among companies and then to diffuse it to Japanese companies through inexpensive training seminars and educational materials.[8] Department managers can use these or other organizationally recognized techniques to arrive at their short list.

The final screening step involves clearing the company's accounting and finance hurdles. On the accounting side of the ledger, large Japanese companies use target costing, *kaizen* (continuous improvement) costing, and cost-maintenance methods (Monden 1995). Once production begins, managers mainly focus on the last two cost-management methods. This is usually achieved through value analysis and other cost-reduction activities. Value analysis refers to changes in product design (e.g., redesign or reduction in parts using the VPR technique) or production process (e.g., quick changeover of a machine die using the SMED technique) that reduce fixed costs. As part of these rationalization activities, line managers usually estimate the costs and justify the benefits of adopting a technique by answering the 5W2H (5Ws = who, what, when, where, and why; 2Hs = how and how much). This activity intersects with the finance side of the company's ledger. Before a line department can implement a technique, the accounting department checks to see whether the net cost-saving for manufacturing the relevant product satisfies the company's overall profit plan (Ballon and Tomita 1988).

Japanese practitioners use the term "catch ball" to capture this process of matching targets to means. As in the game of catch, top management throws the core business objectives to line management, and then each level throws the ball back with its targets and means. This consultation process continues for several iterations to allow for policy and target adjustments until the relevant line managers reach a consensus on the substance of the company's core business objectives. The friendly catch metaphor is used to tone down what can be a contentious process of negotiations. The 6Ms localize the department targets and the 5W2H legitimizes it. The idea here is to translate the company's core business objectives into an acceptable operational language that middle managers and line workers can use in their daily work activities.

Cross-Functional Management   The catch process mobilizes line management toward achieving the company's overall core business objectives; however, it does not eliminate conflicts of interest across departments. To resolve these turf battles, Komatsu and the Toyota Motor Group experimented with the idea of cross-functional management in the latter half of the 1960s. As developed by these companies, cross-functional management is a process by which companies mobilize and coordinate organizational resources toward common objectives (Kurogane 1993). This gives a business plan its organizational breadth.

There are two separate starting points for this process. The customer is the most important starting point. The technical staff collects sales data, warranty claims, supplier reports, and other market information to draw the "voice of the customer" into their company. Companies vary in the depth of this information within the organization. Normally, the standard operating procedure is to route it to the quality assurance, marketing, and sales departments. Yet, it is common to see line employees in manufacturing companies using such data during quality control circle activities. In its most sophisticated version, Japanese companies use a technique called quality function deployment: a series of organizational matrices translating the voice of the customer into crucial product characteristics and the means for preventing defects on those characteristics during the manufacturing process.

The second starting point is the product. Using a flow chart, top management traces the steps in the manufacture of a product. The simplest flow chart is of the production steps within a department experiencing quality problems. Another generic sequence cuts across departments, beginning with sales and marketing → manufacturing → design and engineering → research and design. A third variation inserts suppliers and other external relations into the flow chart. Each of these sequences corresponds roughly with a company's adoption of TQC, companywide quality control (CWQC), or groupwide quality control (GWQC), respectively. The TQC route mobilizes employees within a department or closely related departments toward activities for eliminating and preventing errors from entering the production process. And CWQC expands these activities to all employees in producing goods and services that meet customer expectations. Also, GWQC draws a company's market relations (e.g., suppliers, retailers) within its organizational boundaries in the area of quality control.

Placing the voice of the customer and product flow information on a matrix chart, management can visually identify which departments are responsible for a crucial product function in the company (see fig. 8.2). At these intersections, top managers request the relevant middle managers to establish a cross-functional committee. In these meetings, they discuss their areas of responsibility, the coordination of mutual subtargets, production control items, and workplace schedules. Top managers regularly monitor and evaluate these cross-functional areas to improve the competitive performance of their company. In contrast, they loosely monitor and evaluate other departments in the company. This centralization and decentralization of departments mitigates organizational conflicts, giving otherwise rigid Japanese companies some flexibility (Dore 1986).

The information managers collect over the fiscal year becomes the benchmarks for the next policy audit. This takes us back to the check-action phases of the PDCA cycle, where the hoshin kanri process begins again in December.

Mapping Organizational Networks   Figure 8.2 provides a conceptual overview of a generic business plan. Through this lens, I suggest that the policy audit and performance gaps are not random activities strictly conforming to the demands of a company's business environment. Instead, managers are attempting to maximize their business interests and minimize the uncertainties confronting their company. Where the government plays a central role at the organizational boundaries of a

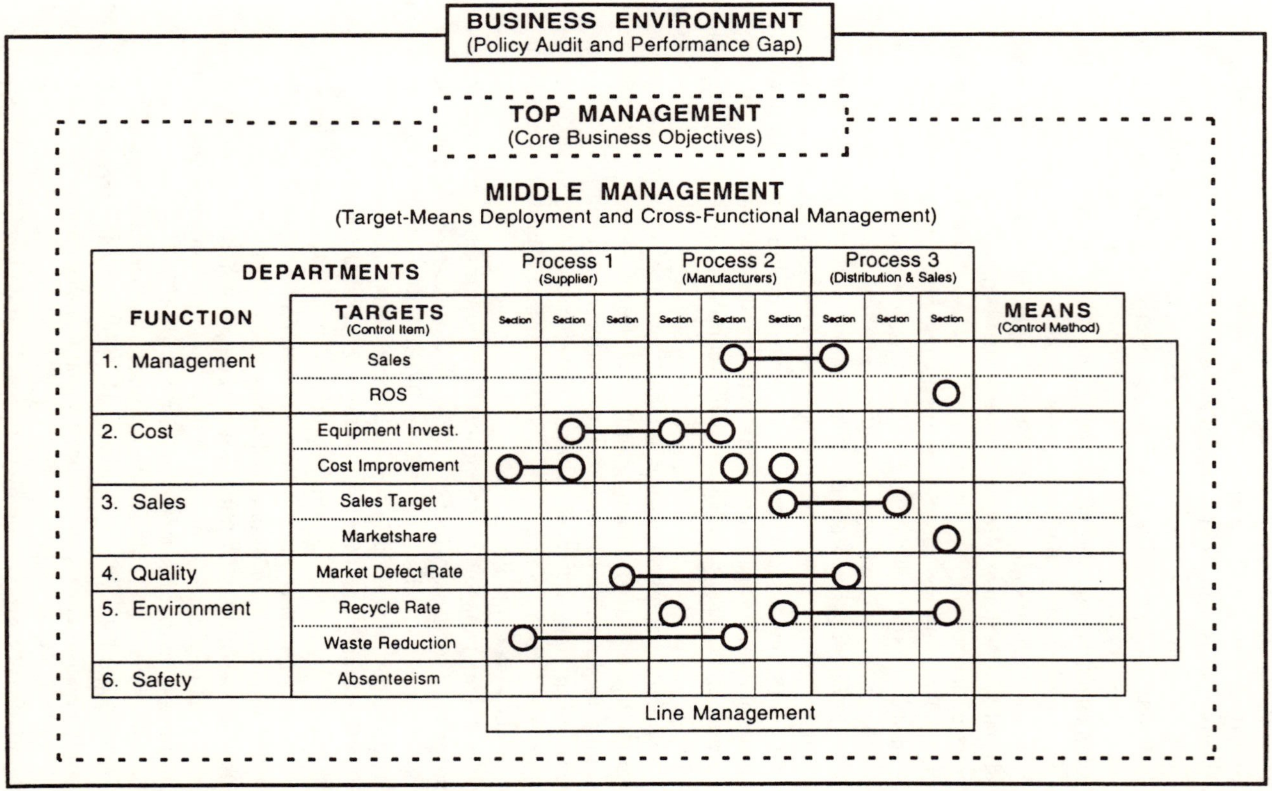

Figure 8.2 Networks and Structure.

SOURCE: Compiled from various company materials

NOTES: Sales figure is total volume or value; ROS = Return-on-Sales. Weightings within matrices are ⊙ = high relationship; ◯ = average relationship;
／ = weak relationship; ✕ = no relationship

company, its incentive structure draws export-oriented companies toward national economic goals. The more a company can internalize its business environment, however, the easier it is to independently pursue its own business interests. These are options companies sort through in arriving at their different core business objectives.

At the company level, the reverse side of a business plan reveals the interplay between strategy and structure. Target-means deployment and cross-functional management activities mobilize organizational resources toward a company's core business objectives. As this process unfolds, interpersonal negotiations within and across organizational networks shape a company's strategic decisions. Consequently, the bundling of products (voice of the customer), production (target and means), and people (responsibility and functions) in key areas of the organization determines a company's organizational structure. One can trace the permutations of "bundled networks" within a company using one of the hoshin kanri planning matrices.

At the center of figure 8.2 is a cross-functional management matrix. In this matrix, the voice of the customer enters the company under the functions listed in the left column. The primary functions are closely related to the quality, cost, and delivery imperatives. The top row shows the steps in the production process. The number of possible steps is determined by the extent to which a company has internalized its business environment (i.e., TQC → CWQC → GWQC, and now total quality management). One layer deeper into the chart are the negotiated numerical targets and actual means for deploying the core business objectives. Within this matrix, a company evaluates the strength of the relationship between each function and department. In practice, top management uses this chart to identify areas in which to establish cross-functional committees; however, for my purposes, it maps a company's organizational networks. Figure 8.2 illustrates some of the linkages in the Toyota Motor Corporation's *kamban* system leading to the elimination of inventory. If I were to extend figure 8.2 to cover all the bundled networks it has established in pursuit of the QCD function, I could trace the outlines of the Toyota Production System (TPS) (see Monden 1983). Although competitors try to strategically emulate the TPS, their organizational structure still reflects the interpersonal bundled networks.

The bundled network configuration that evolves sometimes leads to superior performance. For example, an MIT automobile benchmark study reports that the Japanese lean production system provides them with a competitive advantage over their American and European competitors (Womack, Jones, and Roos 1990). When exemplary Japanese companies have shared their best practices through the Deming Application Prize or intermediary organizations, they have rapidly diffused across the manufacturing sector (Cole 1989). Some internationally recognized examples include quality control circle activities, the kamban and just-in-time delivery systems, and concurrent engineering. Many of these practices are derived from American and European management ideas. Nevertheless, through this bundled configuration, the Japanese are influencing management practices and production methods in the United States and Europe. These twists and turns in the historical convergence toward best practice illustrate how a company or group of companies can to some extent shape the business environment.

Foreign Direct Investment

My discussion of a business plan as a management tool now provides us with an analytical guide for examining Japanese FDI. In the late 1970s, the rhetoric of "going global" entered the vocabulary of the Japanese business community and gradually picked up momentum toward the mid-1980s. The year 1995 began a 5-year period when the amount of Japanese FDI, on an approval basis, nearly doubled the amount in the previous 35 years (Ministry of Finance 1995). This surge in FDI came to an end in 1991, followed by a 4-year decline. One should be able to capture these investment swings in the business plans of Japanese companies, particularly as they are linked to changes in their business environments and bundled networks.

Business Environment

Much has been made of the 1985 Plaza Accord and the subsequent yen appreciation as a precursor to the surge in Japanese FDI. For the companies in my study investing overseas around this time, however, their plans predate the Plaza Accord. Japanese managers link their changes in strategy to the cumulative effects of the oil shocks, yen appreciations, and trade disputes during the 1970s. In this connection, for many Japanese companies, the 1973 oil shock is a better dividing line between the export-driven high-growth era of the 1960s and the realization they must move toward a more global management strategy. A fruitful line of analysis, then, is to examine the temporal changes in the organizational boundaries and incentive structures of Japanese companies after 1973.[9]

Organizational Boundaries   The 1985 *endaka* (yen appreciation) overshadows the adjustments and restructuring Japanese companies were undergoing in the previous decade, mainly because there does not appear to be much of a change in their organizational boundaries. Along the business environment dimensions already discussed, membership in the horizontal keiretsu is unchanged, and within companies, industrial relations and other in-house conditions have fluctuated but remain relatively stable. The other factor conditions—physical, knowledge, and infrastructure resources—have been generally improving. On the demand conditions dimension, although the government began to deregulate some segments of the Japanese economy in the 1970s, its policies still heavily favored domestic producers. Moreover, the spread of the exemplary Toyota Production System to other industries has strengthened the supporting industry structure of small and medium-size companies. These macroeconomic "shocks" did affect the way Japanese companies internalized their business environment. The Toyoda Gosei Company, a major rubber and plastics auto component supplier in the Toyota Group, provides an example.

The oil crises in 1973 and 1975 and the yen appreciation from 1971 to 1973 and 1977 to 1978, squeezed Toyoda Gosei from two directions. First, there were increases in the price of its raw materials. Second, Toyota Motor requested lighter components to decrease car weight and improve gas mileage. Toyoda Gosei was able to absorb these shocks by queuing the cost-reduction themes in its annual and medium-term business plan and diversifying to higher value-added components. Its short-term goal was to introduce TQC and related streamlining activities in order to rationalize production in areas with high material costs and conserve on the use of energy. The medium-term goal was to redesign components using lighter and cheaper materials. As the company implemented these measures, it leveled the flow of production (eliminating bottlenecks) and diversified product lines in plastic and urethane components. In addition, it stratified and tightened its relations with a smaller number of suppliers to further rationalize its product line and production system. These measures allowed the company to buffer the management and production systems from cyclical shocks.

Toyoda Gosei finally considered overseas production in the wake of voluntary export restraints to the United States and growing competition from developing countries in the 1980s. Its first "overseas production centers" were in Taiwan and North America. It built the Taiwan factories (Tai-yue Rubber Industrial in 1985 and Fong Yue Company in 1987) to rationalize its rubber component production. In contrast, it built its North American factories (Toyoda Gosei USA in 1986 and Waterville TG Canada in 1986) to supply this important overseas market. This suggests that rationalization and product diversification take precedence over FDI in business plans. When FDI emerges as a solution, it is embedded in this traditional management strategy.

Toyoda Gosei provides one more analytical example. During the bubble economy (i.e., asset inflation) in the last half of the 1980s, its medium-term goals called for further expansion of overseas production. In preparation, in 1991 it established a technical center in the United States to certify a broader range of components. With the bursting of the bubble economy in 1990 and the subsequent sustained recession, it placed its overseas expansion plans on hold and intensified its rationalization and product diversification activities. Under the banner of GWQC, Toyoda Gosei incorporated its suppliers in its rationalization activities. Along the product diversification front, it developed new lightweight components, such as aluminum panels. In 1996, it resumed its overseas expansion plans in a joint venture with the Bridgestone Tire Company to produce automobile components in Australia. The ebb and flow of Japanese FDI rests on how far companies can pursue product diversification (often as part of industrial restructuring) and how they buffer themselves from the domestic economy.

Incentive Structures   The link between business strategies and FDI holds its own set of uncertainties. Japanese companies are at a distinct disadvantage in understanding local business practices, establishing reliable supplier networks, and learning the nuances of local consumer markets. In Japan, the government has intervened at these points in the organizational boundaries of Japanese companies. The evidence suggests the government has also assisted Japanese overseas investments through its economic assistance and trade policies.

Japanese government economic assistance consists of official development assistance (ODA) and other official flows (OOF). Japanese ODA falls under the administrative jurisdiction of the Overseas Economic Cooperation Fund (OECF). Japanese ODA consists of loans, technical assistance, grants, and multilateral cooperation. The loan component has dominated Japan's early postwar ODA. Since the mid-1970s, however, the technical assistance and grants components have gained a growing share. Technical assistance and training is provided through the

Japan International Cooperation Agency (JICA). Moreover, the multilateral cooperation category has been growing in importance (Kohama and Teranishi 1992; Ministry of Finance 1996). These types of economic assistance tend to benefit companies related to infrastructure projects.

Japanese OOF consists of the export activities of the Export-Import (EXIM) Bank and the Ministry of International Trade and Industry (MITI). In 1986 the government amended the Export-Import Bank Act, giving the EXIM Bank authority to expand official export credits. In the next year, the MITI received power under the Export Insurance Act of 1987 to establish a new trade insurance system.[10] Because the government did not implement most of these programs until after the mid-1980s, it cannot adequately account for Japanese FDI before 1985.

By the mid-1980s, a major difference in the business environment of Japanese companies was the changing investment environment in the Asia-Pacific region. One change is that the major Asia-Pacific market economies crossed over from an import substitution regime to an export-oriented regime. Japan led the way in the 1960s, the Asian newly industrializing economies (Asian NIEs: South Korea, Taiwan, Hong Kong, and Singapore) and the member countries of the Association for Southeast Asian Nations (ASEAN-4: Indonesia, Malaysia, Philippines, and Thailand) in the 1980s. The broad characteristics of this change are privatization, reduced use of subsidies, and an export-oriented trade regime (Reza 1994; Chowdhury and Islam 1993). This shift is reaching regional closure with the major command economies undertaking market initiatives: China's adoption of "market socialism" from 1978, Vietnam's "Doi Moi" (Renovation) policies in 1986, and India's "New Economic Policy" initiative in 1990.

A closely related change in the regional investment environment is the spread of economic cooperation among the Pacific economies. Economic cooperation means the extent to which countries implement policies to ease the flow of goods, people, information, and money across their national borders and has taken the form of export zones, growth triangles, and free trade areas. An export processing zone (EPZ) provides fiscal incentives and infrastructure facilities to a level expected by multinational corporations.[11] A growth triangle is either a formal or informal agreement among neighboring countries to combine their respective comparative advantages in resources, labor, and socioeconomic infrastructure.[12] A free trade agreement is a formal arrangement among signatory countries to ease the flow of goods and, to some extent, the flow of people, money, and information across their national borders.[13] Cross-border coordination puts pressures on national governments to further liberalize policies to attract FDI (liberalization competition).

The key words underlining this process are dialogue and cooperation. One can trace the beginning of a dialogue on economic cooperation to the early 1960s, when a member of the Japanese Diet proposed the creation of an Asia development fund. This proposal did not get off the ground; however, in 1966 Kojima proposed a Pacific Asia free trade area. Support for economic cooperation slowly picked up momentum as this idea took root in regional organizations. The Pacific Trade and Development Conference (roots in 1968 Pacific Asia free trade proposal), Pacific Economic Cooperation Council (1980), Pacific Basin Economic Council (1967 root in Japan-Australia Cooperation Committee). The "dialogue language" that has emerged is based on the principles recognizing regional diversity, nonbinding regional integration, consensus building, and open regionalism. The Asia Pacific Economic Cooperation (APEC) forum, established in 1990, is attempting to carry this momentum into the twenty-first century (Wood 1993).[14]

To be sure, this incentive structure covers multinational corporations regardless of national origins. Like most foreign businesses, at the bilateral level, Japanese companies have established a number of bilateral business councils. At the regional level, they have established the Japanese Chamber of Commerce and Industry in the major Pacific economies. One example is the Japanese Chamber for Trade and Industry, Malaysia (JACTIM). Through JACTIM, the Japanese business community maintains good relations with the host government, the local business community, and other prominent organizations. In contrast to multinationals based in other countries, however, Japanese companies have deepened their relations with host countries at the intermediary organizational level. For example, in cooperation with the JACTIM and Keidanren, the Institute for Strategic and International Studies (Malaysia) has established the Centre for Japan Studies.[15] Beyond the social functions of these intermediary organizations, they are important forums for informally raising business issues that sometimes later inform formal discussions leading to attractive trade and investment policies.

Geographical Diversification   I will ground this discussion by examining where Japanese companies have internalized the investment environment in the Pacific region into their organizational boundaries. In this connection, the export-oriented countries, economic zones, and infrastructure networks trace where investment incentives are the strongest for Japanese companies.

The Japanese and Australian initiative to create the APEC forum raised the economic cooperation dialogue to the ministerial level. The "modalities for dialogue" on economic cooperation are ASEAN, the EAEC, and APEC. Including the EAEC here invites controversy; however, it is clear that Asia-Pacific economies in Northeast and Southeast Asia informally check with each other in developing country positions in international forums. The core countries in these forums are Australia, Canada, China, Japan, Mexico, New Zealand, Papua New Guinea, United States, the Asian NIEs, and the member countries of ASEAN.

The flow of goods, people, money, and information rests on the regional infrastructure connecting Pacific economies. For discussion purposes, some shorthand measures of these flows are the volume of goods handled by container ports, the number of passenger arrivals at international airports, the volume of submarine cables and communication satellites, and the number of transactions in capital markets.[16] On these measures, Tokyo, Hong Kong, Singapore, and Sydney emerge as the primary hubs for the flow of goods, people, information, and money on the western side of the Pacific Ocean. In North America there are multiple hubs—for example, Toronto, New York, Miami, Chicago, and Los Angeles. None of the cities in South Asia or Latin America reaches the thresholds necessary to qualify as a hub. One could take this analysis one step further by tracing the destinations of shipping routes, international flights, overseas calls, and financial transactions extending from these hub cities. A Japan National Committee for Pacific Economic Cooperation (JANCPEC) (1992) study of regional infrastructure reveals two types of flows that extend beyond the hub cities. One flow is from hub cities to neighboring cities or countries. A second flow is from hub cities to either other hub cities or the American and European markets. The flow of trade and investment across national borders traces the reach of the hub-and-spoke networks in the Pacific region.

It is premature to cite the blurring of national borders as evidence for the emergence of an integrated Pacific economy. Instead, the subregional groupings also expose the discontinuities in the regional economy. Not all subregional groupings are "on-line and en route," nor do they necessarily realize or maintain their comparative advantage. Infrastructure bottlenecks arise, for example, due to limitations on landing rights, visa restrictions, incompatible communications hardware and software, and regulations on capital flows.[17] Taking into account the continuities and discontinuities in the flow of goods, people, information, and money, figure 8.3 delineates four trade and investment corridors in the Pacific region. One corridor is located in Northeast Asia, anchored at one end by Hong Kong, running up the coastal areas of Taiwan and China, and anchored at the other end by Tokyo. Another is located in Southeast Asia, extending from Chiang Mai (Thailand), through the western side of the Malay peninsula, and curves around to Surabaya (Indonesia). A third corridor runs between southern Canada (Great Lakes area), through the United States, and down to Monterrey (Mexico). The fourth investment corridor links Australia with New Zealand.

Japanese companies have factored this trade and investment landscape into their overseas business plans. For example, the Sony Corporation has adopted a "two-factory policy" as part of its regional business plan. Under this policy, Sony manufactures most of its products in two countries to hedge against fluctuations in foreign exchange rate, tariff duties, and other operational risks. The Nissan Motor Corporation is implementing a regionwide parts and components procurement plan under the ASEAN brand-to-brand complementation scheme; however, differences in tariff schedules among the member countries have actually skewed its Southeast Asia operations toward Thailand, Malaysia, and the Philippines. Consequently, Japanese companies are basing their investment decisions on the emergence of subregional groupings, superseding a target country as a unit of investment.

When one maps the location of overseas Japanese subsidiaries in the Pacific region using data from the Toyo Keizai data bank, one finds that nearly three fourths of them are concentrated in these four trade and investment corridors.

Bundled Networks

This discussion suggests that the emergence of organizational networks rather than strategy explains the FDI choices of Japanese managers. Japanese managers make business choices bound by the options available in their organizational networks. Companies vary in the way they bundle people, products, and production through their line management and cross-functional networks.

Redeploying Targets and Means   Under the flag method, the standard operating procedure of Japanese companies is biased toward rationalization and product diversification options. In the PDCA cycle, once a solution has been found for a problem, the cycle is repeated to achieve better results. This captures the Japanese notion of *kaizen* (continuous improvement). In principle, this process can be mathematically repeated into infinity; however, in practice there is a diminishing marginal return to cost and quality improvement efforts. This process works well for extending the life of profitable products and eliminating unprofitable product lines. But a number of products fall in between. Japanese companies use some version of the product portfolio method to differentiate these "between" products. Under this method, a company compares its market share to the largest market share among competitors. One category is those products that have low market growth rate yet relatively high market share. These products usually provide a strong revenue stream, justifying the cost of further cost-reduction activities. A second category is those products that have high market growth rate yet relatively low market share. These products are candidates for discontinuation. The decision to continue or discontinue a product is subject to negotiation across a company's organizational network—that is, subject to noneconomic factors.

Although rationalization and product diversification are dominant themes in the business plans of Japanese companies, managers over the last two decades have gradually begun to link overseas production with products falling in the gray areas of product lines. Trading companies played a leading role in assisting textile companies to move to China and Southeast Asia in the 1970s. In the 1980s, however, new institutional actors entered the organizational boundaries of Japanese companies, presenting new solutions for the old problems of rationalization and diversification. Entering this organizational arena were the board of investment and trade promotion organizations from developing countries. The ASEAN Promotion Centre on Trade, Investment, and Tourism (ASEAN Centre) was founded in 1981 as an intergovernmental organization of the member countries in ASEAN. Almost all foreign embassies in Tokyo maintain a commercial section; however, in the 1980s a number of Pacific economies have upgraded their presence by establishing a representative office.[18] Overseas ethnic Chinese conglomerates have entered the arena, seeking strategic alliances with Japanese companies (Tachiki 1993; East Asia Analytical Unit 1995). The overseas ethnic Chinese networks expand the possibilities for Japanese companies for deepening and widening their overseas production networks. Keidanren and other companies (consulting companies, banks) have organized study missions and investment seminars. As a result, Japanese companies can obtain information and assistance from a variety of sources.

The actual plan for implementing an overseas investment typically goes through several steps. The planning staff primarily coordinates this process, although a special team from the international division may play a prominent role. In the first step, the planning staff works with the affected product managers and related divisions to identify potential investment problems in an overseas production base. The second step calls for deliberation by function and the setting of goal-attainment plans. The third step is to deliberate and set plans, which are incorporated into the draft annual plan. The last step is to implement an action plan by department (check against target goals and revise long-term plan). When one locates these activities within a company's medium- and long-term core business objectives, the rate at which line responsibility is moved overseas depends on the continued performance improvement and projections of the external environment (technology and market). In this regard, a company's FDI activities are embedded in its business plan.

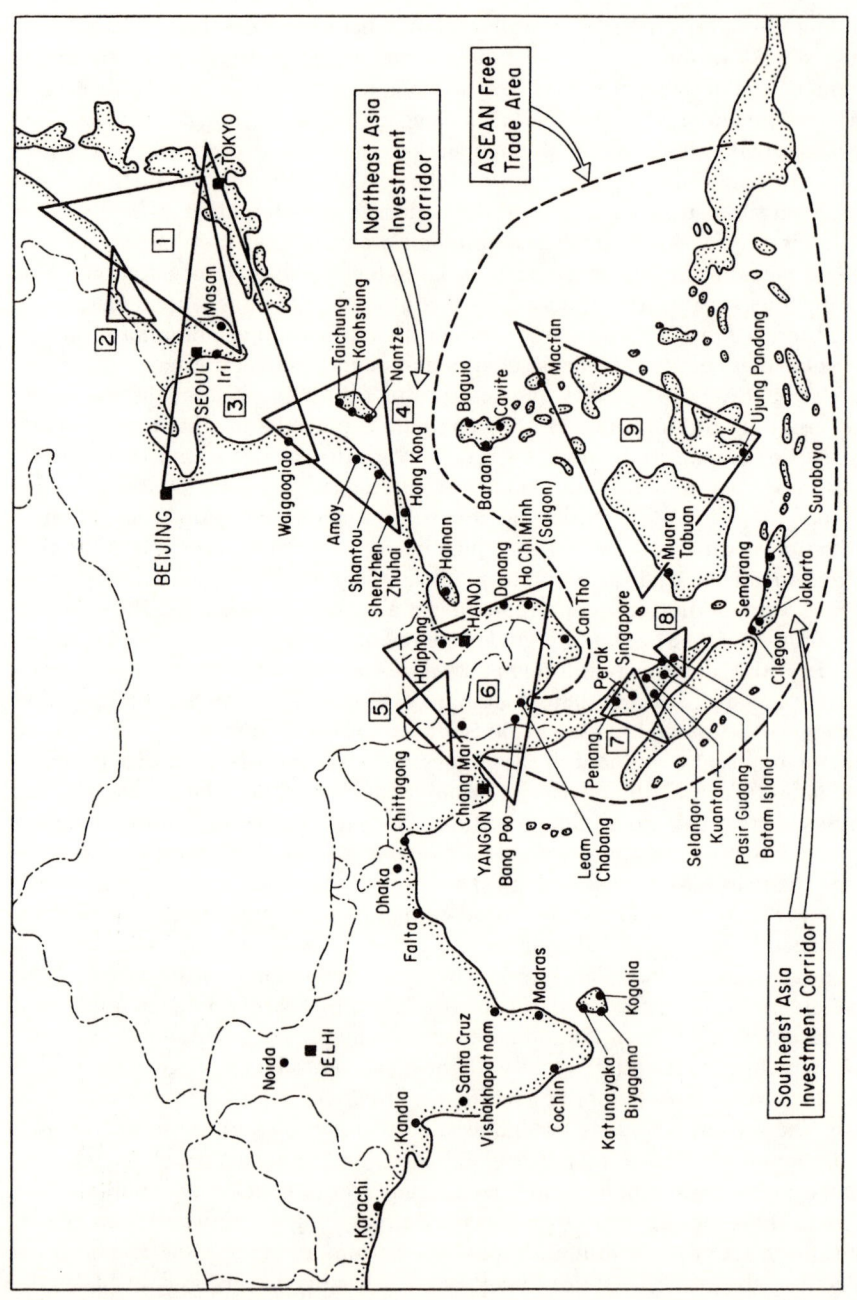

Figure 8.3 Investment Corridors in the Pacific Region.

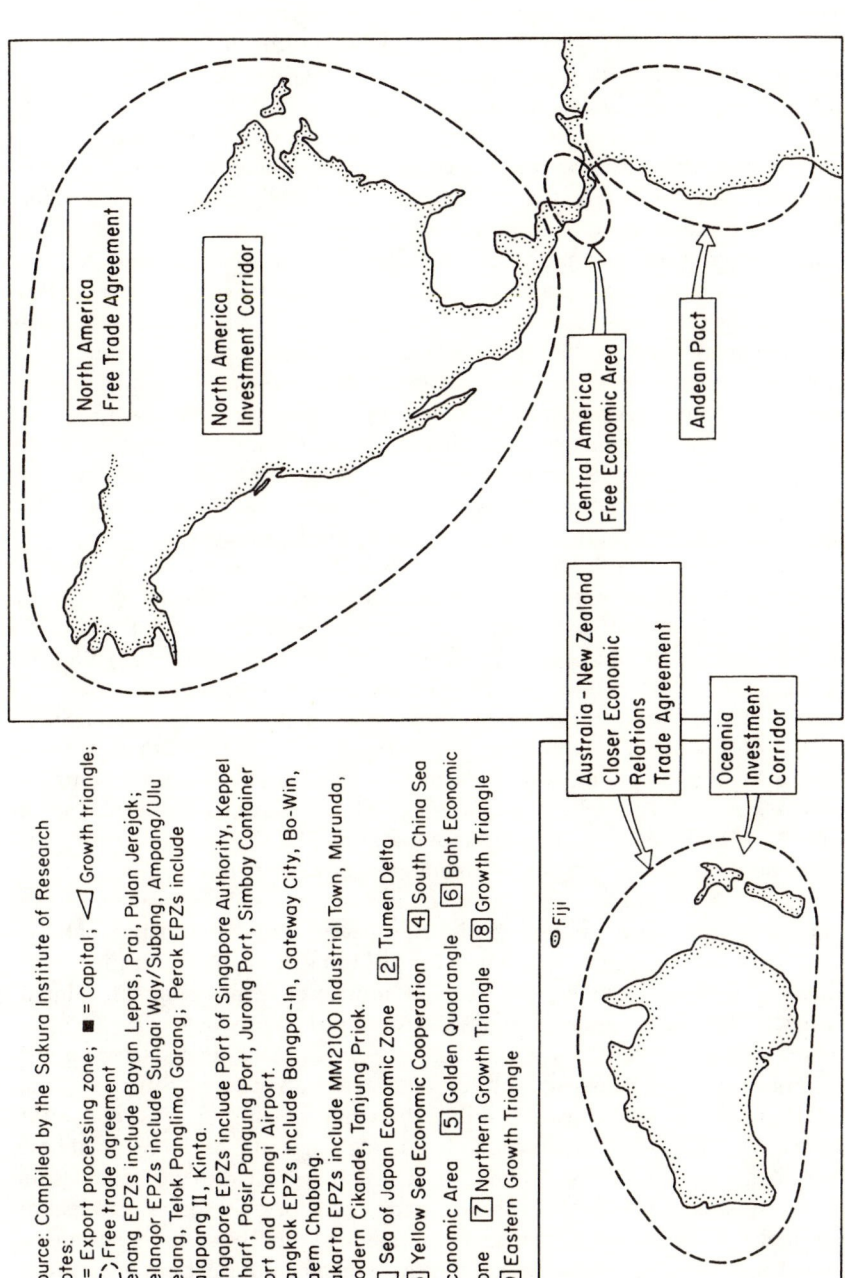

Source: Compiled by the Sakura Institute of Research

Notes:

● = Export processing zone; ■ = Capital; ◁ Growth triangle;
(̄) Free trade agreement

Penang EPZs include Bayan Lepas, Prai, Pulan Jerejak;
Selangor EPZs include Sungai Way/Subang, Ampang/Ulu
Kelang, Telok Panglima Garang; Perak EPZs include
Jalapang II, Kinta.

Singapore EPZs include Port of Singapore Authority, Keppel
Wharf, Pasir Pangung Port, Jurong Port, Simbay Container
Port and Changi Airport.

Bangkok EPZs include Bangpa-In, Gateway City, Bo-Win,
Laem Chabang.

Jakarta EPZs include MM2100 Industrial Town, Murunda,
Modern Cikande, Tanjung Priok.

① Sea of Japan Economic Zone ② Tumen Delta
③ Yellow Sea Economic Cooperation ④ South China Sea
Economic Area ⑤ Golden Quadrangle ⑥ Baht Economic
Zone ⑦ Northern Growth Triangle ⑧ Growth Triangle
⑨ Eastern Growth Triangle

Figure 8.3 Investment Corridors in the Pacific Region (continued).

North America
Free Trade Agreement

North America
Investment Corridor

Central America
Free Economic Area

Andean Pact

Australia–New Zealand
Closer Economic
Relations
Trade Agreement

Oceania
Investment
Corridor

Fiji

Reconfiguring the QCD Functions   The transfer of a product to an overseas production base requires extending a company's bundled networks across national borders or creating its functional equivalent in the host country. The first preference of Japanese companies is to serve overseas markets through exports rather than local production. This minimizes the number of functional streams that must be bundled. It requires only establishing product sales and distribution networks, using the minimum number of people, and producing everything in Japan. It also allows Japanese companies to find the voice of the customer in the local market. The overseas sales units send this information back to the parent company, where a strategy to produce in an overseas market emerges.

Once sales volume for a product in a target market expands beyond the production break-even point, it becomes possible to replace trade with direct investment. Japanese companies bundle product and production in several ways. One way is to segment their product lines and assemble those in a country where they can achieve economies of scale. Video cassette recorders offer an example. In 1980, Japanese companies assembled all VCRs in Japan. As early as 1985, Japanese subsidiaries in the Asian NIEs and soon after the ASEAN countries, especially Malaysia, were producing VCRs. In 1995, Japan imported more VCRs than it exported.

A second way is to segment the production process and locate it in the most efficient country. For example, a car maker must produce around 200,000 units a year to financially justify the construction of manufacturing facilities. Only China, India, and Indonesia have markets large enough to meet this threshold. In 1988, however, the ASEAN ministers approved a brand-to-brand complementation (BBC) scheme for foreign automakers. This scheme allows automakers to procure parts and components produced in any of the ASEAN countries at a preferential tariff rate and count that toward meeting the local content requirements in each ASEAN country. This created a potential car market nearly the size of North America or Europe, attracting previously reluctant foreign automakers to build factories in the ASEAN region. The ASEAN economic ministers replaced these schemes in April 1996 with the ASEAN Industrial Cooperation (AICO) scheme, opening this business opportunity to companies from almost any industry.

Overseas production presents a new set of challenges to Japanese companies. It requires greater coordination of goods, information, and money across national borders. Japanese companies are addressing this issue through organizational and production innovations. One organizational innovation is the regional headquarters (RHQ). Within the context of the ASEAN countries' growing economic cooperation, Singapore's promulgation of the OHQ (operational headquarters) policy has stimulated interest among multinational corporations. The Singapore Economic Development Board awards a multinational corporation OHQ status if it submits a regional (ASEAN) business plan, using Singapore as the regional base. Among Japanese companies, the main functional responsibilities of RHQs are control of upstream products, financing, parts inventory, personnel and technical guidance, and marketing.[19] Japanese companies usually assign expatriates in key functional areas related to the cross flow of goods, information, and money. These functional areas include board member, plant manager, accountant, technical staff (quality control, industrial engineer, etc.), and purchasing.

Japanese companies are experimenting with production innovations in order to address the QCD functions. The discontinuities in the economic landscape in the Pacific region makes it difficult to integrate sales orders, production, inventory, and supply under a kamban and just-in-time delivery system. Lapses in the delivery of parts lead to high inventory and freight costs, affecting production schedules. Japanese companies are now attempting to close the delivery function through the development of a continuous acquisition and life cycle support (CALS) system. Under this production innovation, sales, production, and logistic requirements are integrated and coordinated through a company's computer system.

International Production Networks   There is a demarcation between the decision to invest overseas and actually operating overseas. Push and pull factors in FDI reflect past trends, but there must be some room for potential growth (higher-skilled workers and more sophisticated products and bigger markets) in order to maintain the momentum of overseas direct investments. It is in the process of solving these post–FDI issues that Japanese companies are developing the know-how to address the QCD shortcomings they face in their overseas production bases. A cross-functional management matrix provides a preliminary picture of the international production networks that are unfolding.

Toyota Motor Corporation is a case in point. In Southeast Asia, it started with a country strategy, limiting assembly to a completely knock-down (CKD) kit or importing vehicles (passenger cars and trucks). When the member countries of ASEAN adopted the BBC scheme, Toyota developed a subregional plan to segment the manufacturing process, locating engine assembly in the Philippines, wire harness and bumpers manufacturing in Malaysia, and assembly in Thailand and Indonesia. Figure 8.4 collapses and simplifies how this international production network unfolds in Toyota's business plans.

The left side of figure 8.4 lists the main functions. For illustrative purposes, the basic function here is "return-on-sales." The primary, secondary, and tertiary functions specify in greater detail functional areas addressing this core business objective. The primary functions involving overseas production are sales, production, and logistics. In the case of the Asia-Pacific region, most design and engineering and research and development are done in Japan. The secondary functions address the QCD functions. For example, in the sales area, marketing and informational gathering are important functions for deriving the voice of the customer. The tertiary functions list the actual parts targeted for these QCD activities. The top row lists the departments responsible for producing a product. The general staff, sales, and production departments are shown in figure 8.4; however, in practice a more detailed listing of departments and sections would constitute this matrix. In this case, the primary, secondary, and tertiary departments would provide detail down to the section level of the organization.

Within this matrix, the top management evaluates the responsibility of each department responsible for each key function. Over time, Toyota Motor has gradually moved responsibility for sales, production, and logistics to its OHQ in Singapore. In the sales area, the units in the ASEAN-4 also have responsibility for local marketing and after-service. In the early CKD period, all parts and components for Toyota vehicles produced in the ASEAN countries came from Japan. Figure 8.4 shows that Toyota has now assigned production of certain parts to plants in each ASEAN country. Under the BBC scheme, each of these plants exchanges parts and components that go into the final assembly of a vehicle.

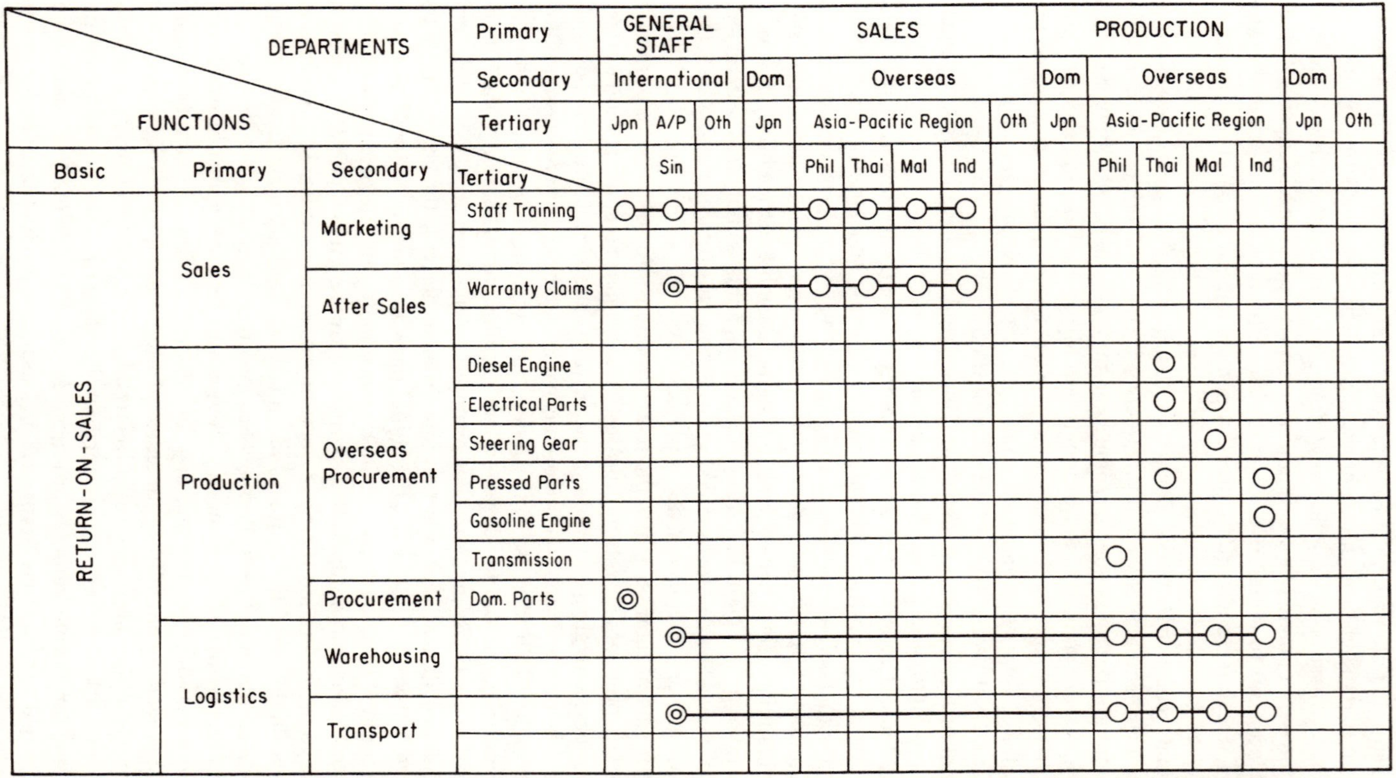

Figure 8.4 International Production Networks.

DEPARTMENTS / FUNCTIONS

FUNCTIONS (Basic / Primary / Secondary / Tertiary)				GENERAL STAFF				SALES						PRODUCTION					
				Primary															
				International			Dom	Overseas					Dom	Overseas				Dom	
Basic	Primary	Secondary	Tertiary	Jpn	A/P (Sin)	Oth	Jpn	Phil	Thai	Mal	Ind	Oth	Jpn	Phil	Thai	Mal	Ind	Jpn	Oth
Sales		Marketing	Staff Training	O	O			O	O	O	O								
Sales		After Sales	Warranty Claims		◎			O	O	O	O								
Production		Overseas Procurement	Diesel Engine											O					
Production		Overseas Procurement	Electrical Parts												O	O			
Production		Overseas Procurement	Steering Gear													O			
Production		Overseas Procurement	Pressed Parts												O		O		
Production		Overseas Procurement	Gasoline Engine														O		
Production		Procurement	Transmission											O					
Production		Procurement	Dom. Parts				◎												
Logistics		Warehousing			◎									O	O	O	O		
Logistics		Transport			◎									O	O	O	O		

RETURN-ON-SALES

Notes: Jpn = Japan; Sin = Singapore; Phil = Philippines; Thai = Thailand; Mal = Malaysia; Ind = Indonesia; Other = Americas and Europe, Middle East, and Africa; Dom = Domestic; A/P = Asia-Pacific; for symbols (see figure 8.2)

When local suppliers are included, Toyota Motor says that the local content of its cars assembled in the ASEAN countries reaches the 70–80 percent level. In the logistics area, Toyota Motor splits responsibility between the head office and its OHQ in Singapore.

Companies in the electric/electronics industry and automobile industry are generally the most advanced in developing international production networks in the Asia-Pacific region. The case of Toyota Motor, however, suggests that the international production networks of Japanese companies are at an early stage of development. Once one moves beyond the investment corridors in the Pacific region (see fig. 8.3), the level of economic development, infrastructure, and trade and investment policies create large obstacles in coordinating cross-border production.

FDI, Technology Transfer, and Trade

What do the business plans of Japanese companies tell us about future research for understanding their foreign direct investments, transfer of technology, and trade patterns? First, the business plans of Japanese companies make clear that FDI is not their first choice. Instead, rationalization and product diversification are more prominent themes. When Japanese companies decide to invest overseas, their internal and external organizational networks have a significant role in shaping the direction and pace of FDI. Product managers may not provide the necessary people and budget to smooth the transfer to overseas production. Moreover, where international business uncertainties exist, social networks are important for filtering risks. Mapping these organizational networks allows us to see the mobilization of organizational resources, and consequently the ebbs and flows in overseas direct investments.

Second, a business plan shows how Japanese companies bundle product, people, and production when transferring technology. In deciding to produce overseas, Japanese companies do not transfer their latest product lines. But when Japanese companies bundle people and production with a product, an important lesson emerges. Japanese companies transfer technology through their cross-functional networks. Some examples include production and quality control methods, dispatching of technical staff, and supplier-manufacturer associations. In this connection, mastering the QCD functions provides subsidiaries a competitive edge in manufacturing. Posting expatriate staff in an overseas subsidiary displaces local managers; however, they are also important channels for skill formation among local employees—that is, the ability to handle routine and nonroutine work activities. Supplier associations allow the transfer of best practices across subsidiaries. On these cross-functional foundations, Japanese companies decide the potential and the pace at which they move value-added products to overseas production bases.

Third, a business plan sheds some light on the growing intraregional trade in the Asia-Pacific region. The emergence of subregional groupings is allowing Japanese and local companies to internalize trade in semifinished goods through their international production networks. In this connection, international trade data suggest a shift from interregional to intraregional trade; however, the hoshin kanri matrices show that the final destination of finished products is still the markets in the developed countries. The Sony Corporation, for example, procures many of its components from suppliers in the Asia-Pacific region, assembles them into consumer electronics products in Southeast Asia, and sells them in the North American market. A business plan does not tell us about the overall trade patterns in the Pacific region; however, it does suggest how international production networks contribute to the content and direction of trade.

Bringing the business plan into theories of FDI allows us to see variations in the strategies and structure of Japanese companies. Their strategies vary according to how far their organizational boundaries extend into the regional economy. Their structures vary according to their internal and external organizational networks. Exploring inside this organizational black box allows us to see the linkages between strategy and structure.

Notes

1. For a review of the FDI and trade literature, see chapter 3. For various discussions on the FDI and organizational theory nexus, see Ghoshal and Westney (1993).

2. Instead of randomly sampling a population of companies, I repeatedly sample a few important variables to document variations on relevant issues. One issue is whether the strategy and structure of Japanese companies persist in their overseas operations. For answers, I compare the overseas subsidiaries of the same company operating in different Asia-Pacific economies. Another issue is whether there is variation by industry in overseas investment patterns. For these answers, I compare different manufacturing companies—specifically in the transportation equipment, electric machinery, electronics, and chemical industries—operating in the same Asia-Pacific economy. A third issue is whether there are differences in the strategy and structure of multinational corporations due to their length of experience overseas. For this, I compare the early experiences of Japanese companies operating in the Asia-Pacific region before 1985 with more recent cases.

3. The Deming Application Prize actually consists of awards in five categories: (1) Deming Application Prize, (2) Quality Control Award for Factories, (3) Deming Application Prize for Divisions, (4) Deming Application Prize for Small Companies, and (5) Deming Prize for Individuals. There is now a sixth category for foreign companies. In addition, companies that have already received the Deming Application Prize can apply five years later for the Japan Quality Control Medal after demonstrating further excellence in quality control.

4. These categories are based on Porter's (1990) national advantage diamond, however, adapted here for my analytical purposes. Factor conditions include human, physical, knowledge, capital, and infrastructure resources. Demand conditions include home demand composition, demand size and pattern of growth, and internationalization of domestic demand. Related and supporting industries include internationally competitive supplier industries and competitive advantage in related industries. Firm strategy and structure include the management style and organizational structure of domestic firms and their goals. Competition focuses on the ease of market entry, the number of competitors, and industry/geographical concentration ratios. Porter uses these dimensions to describe the advantages of a nation; however, from a manager's perspective, it describes their business environment.

5. The economic ministries include the Ministry of Finance, Ministry for International Trade and Industry, Ministry for Post and Telecommunications, Ministry of Construction, Ministry of Transportation plus Bank of Japan, Economic Planning Agency, and Fair Trade Commission.

The current political leadership is a coalition government consisting of the Social Democratic Party (formerly the Socialist Party), Liberal Democratic Party (LDP), and New Party Sakigake. The main opposition is the Shinshinto.

The peak business organizations are Keidanren (Federation of Economic Organizations), Nikkeiren (Japanese Federation of Employers' Association), Keizai Doyukai (Japan Association of Corporate Executives), Nissho (Japan Chamber of Commerce and Industry), and Kankeiren (Kansai Federation of Economic Organizations). Nokyo (Farmers' Cooperatives) is not usually classified as a peak business organization; however, it exerts strong influence on the LDP.

The major industrial associations associated with monitoring competition and capacity guidelines established under administrative guidance often trace their roots to the prewar *tosei-kai* (control associations). The ones that still exist today (and their founding dates) are the Japan Steel Council (12/45), Japan Coal Mining Industry Association (5/46), National Mining Association (3/46), Cement Industry Association (nd), Japan Association of Rolling Stock Industries (11/45), Automobile Council (11/45), Japan Machine Tool Builders' Association (1/46), Japan Electrical Equipment Manufacturers Association (2/46), Society of Industrial Machinery Manufacturers (3/46), Japanese Electric Wire and Cable Makers' Association (11/45), Federation of Shipbuilders' Associations (10/45), Japan Society of Railway Associations (12/45), Light Metal Council (12/46), Leather Association (12/45), Oil and Fat Processing Association (1/46), Federation of Chemical Industries (3/46), and Rubber Association (12/45). The major horizontal keiretsu—Mitsui, Mitsubishi, Sumitomo, Fuji, Sanwa, and Dai Ichi Kangyo—usually have member companies from these industries.

6. The peak organization for labor unions is Rengo (Federation of Labor Unions). There is no umbrella organization representing consumer interests, although "local citizens' movements" have played an important role in contemporary Japanese politics. Housewives and the mass media are other stakeholders contributing to public opinion.

7. In the area of quality control, for example, the Union of Japanese Scientists and Engineers and Japan Standards Association play instrumental roles in diffusing statistical quality control methods and quality control circle activities. In the area of productivity, the Japan Productivity Center for Socio-Economic Development plays a key role in introducing techniques for streamlining the operations of Japanese companies and promoting the idea of joint labor-management committees. And in the area of management, the Japan Industrial Training Association plays an important role in adapting business administration techniques to industry (e.g., Training Within Industry and Management Training Program). Today many of these organizations have nonprofit status, yet their membership (often corporate and not individuals) and resources often draw on political, business, and bureaucratic circles. My discussion does not exhaust the list of such organizations. Within the context of the QCD functions, for example, the Japan Industrial Standards, Japan Management Association, and Association for Overseas Technical Scholarship are influential organizations. Another large category of intermediary organizations are the *kosha* (public enterprises) and *kodan* (quasi-public organizations). The kosha and kodan numbered 92 companies or organizations in 1995, down from a peak of 113 in 1968. The MITI Small and Medium-Sized Enterprise Bureau has promoted a number of industry-related organizations, especially those connected to "targeted industries."

8. There are several channels for the transfer of an organizational innovation. Under the line-training method, a company requires the company employee attending a training workshop to share this information or train the employees in their immediate work area. Another vehicle for transferring know-how is a company's *benkyo-kai* (study group). The company invites a *sensei*, often a practitioner or university professor associated with the relevant intermediary organization, to give practical workshop lectures. Another method is "self-improvement," where an employee under his or her own initiative acquires a new skill. When the employee obtains a certificate or license, the company usually gives a nominal monetary award and places this information in the employee's personnel file.

9. See chapter 2 for a historical discussion of Japanese FDI before 1973.

10. Under these acts, the EXIM Bank could, first, extend supplier credits to Japanese companies for deferred payment on exports of plant, capital equipment, and technical services. Second, it could extend buyer credits to foreign importers for their imports of plant, equipment, and technical services from Japan. The MITI was empowered to establish the Import-Prepayment Insurance System, the Intermediary Insurance System (to protect overseas Japanese companies exporting goods to a third country), and the Expanded Insurance System for Foreign Investment (covering not only political risks, but also commercial risks). In 1988, MITI joined the Multinational Investment Guarantee Agency, a multilateral reinsurance system.

11. The policies implemented by the Industrial Estate Authority of Thailand are fairly representative. On the fiscal policy side, companies are usually exempt from or pay a preferred rate on corporate taxes (tax holiday), import duties, excise taxes, import surcharges, and value-added taxes. On the infrastructure policy side, most industrial estates in Thailand provide improved land, utilities, roads, and other support services (such as security and industrial waste disposal). In retrospect, these economic zones are actually experiments in economic policy. The lessons host countries learned have worked their way into the national economic policies. Indeed, Japanese companies no longer perceive an advantage to locating in a EPZ in the Asian NIEs. Consequently, the Taiwanese government, for example, is trying to revive the Kaohsiung EPZ as an off-shore transshipment center.

12. This list includes the Sea of Japan Economic Zone (Japan, North Korea, South Korea, and Russia), Tumen Delta (China, North Korea, and Russia), Yellow Sea Economic Cooperation (China, Japan, and South Korea), South China Sea Area (Hong Kong, Taiwan, and South China), Golden Quadrangle (Thailand, Laos, Burma, and South China), Greater Mekong Subregion (Burma, Laos, Thailand, Cambodia, Vietnam, and Southwest China), Northern Growth Triangle (South Thailand, North Malaysia, and Sumatra), Southern Growth Triangle (development around Batam Island, which brings together Singapore, Johore [Malaysia] and Riau Province [Indonesia]), and East ASEAN Growth Area (East Kalimantan, South Sulawesi, Sabah, Sarawak, Mindanao, and Brunei).

13. The main free trade areas in the Pacific region include the Australia-New Zealand Closer Economic Relations (ANCER), ASEAN Free Trade Area, the North American Free Trade Agreement, the Central America Free Economic Area, and the Andean Pact. Chile's membership in the MERCOSUR, the free trade area encompassing the southern cone of South America, suggests that this group might be added; however, the other member countries (Argentina, Brazil, Paraguay, Uruguay) are on the Atlantic Ocean side of South America.

14. The member countries of these organizations are (1) Pacific Economic Cooperation Council (PECC): Australia, Canada, Japan, New Zealand, United States, China, Mexico, Chile, Peru, Colombia, the NIEs, ASEAN, Russia, Papua New Guinea and Pacific Island Nations; (2) Pacific Basin Economic Council (PBEC): Japan, United States, Australia, New Zealand, Canada, Taiwan, South Korea, Chile, Mexico, ASEAN, and Peru; and (3) the Pacific Trade and Development (PAFTAD) conference.

Other major regional groupings include the South Pacific Forum (SPF): Australia, Cook Islands, Federated States of Micronesia, the Republic of Fiji, Kiribati, Nauru, New Zealand, Niue, Papua New Guinea, Republic of the Marshall Islands, Solomon Islands, Tonga, Tuvalu, Vanuatu, and Western Samoa. The Malaysian government has proposed an East Asia Economic Caucus (EAEC), defined as the ASEAN, Japan, China, South Korea, Taiwan, and Hong Kong. Moving in the direction of economic cooperation is the South Asian Association for Regional Cooperation (SAARC), consisting of India, Pakistan, Bangladesh, Sri Lanka, Nepal, Bhutan, Maldives. At the end of 1995, this group mooted the idea of a South Asia Preferential Trade Area (SAPTA).

15. In Thailand, similar cross-cultural organizational bridges exist. For example, the Thai-Japan Association has a long, active history. This association established the Technology Promotion Association (TPA) in Bangkok, a training center for language study, industrial standards certification, vocational training, and other activities. Similar examples are evident in Singapore, the Philippines, Indonesia, Vietnam, China, Hong Kong, and Taiwan. The involvement of the Japanese Chamber of Commerce and Industry (Japan), Keidanren, Kankeiren, and other business organizations suggests the Japanese business community is extending its ties beyond the iron triangle. Until recently, it was this final link that differentiated Japanese business community involvement in host countries from that of other foreign companies.

16. Container ports listed handle a minimum of 1 million TEUs (ton equivalent units); airports handle more than 10 million passengers per year; submarine cables have more than 1,000 voice channels; communications satellite networks list country launching a regional satellite; capital market ranked among the top capitalization in the world.

17. This is particularly true of the "new frontier" countries that fall within a band beginning in the Sakhalin Island (Pacific Russia), with one leg separating coastal China from inner China and running down to Indochina, and a second leg running from Pacific Russia to South Asia. This would include Pacific Russia, the hinterlands of China, Vietnam, Cambodia, Laos, Burma, Bangladesh, Nepal, Pakistan, India, and Sri Lanka.

18. Some examples in Japan include the CITIC Representative Office (China), Hong Kong Economic and Trade Office and the Hong Kong Trade Development Council, Indian Investment Center, Korea Trade Center, Malaysia Investment Center (Malaysian Industrial Development Authority), Singapore Economic Development Board, Thailand Board of Investment, and the various state representative offices (United States).

19. In the Asia-Pacific region, the major RHQs are located in either Hong Kong (Yoshino Seisakujo, Toyo Ink, Yaohan Department Stores, Kyocera) or Singapore (Asia Matsushita Electronics, Mitsubishi Electric, Sony International Singapore, Dainippon Ink and Chemical, Kao, Mitsui Warehousing, Omron Management Center of Asia Pacific, Sumitomo Warehousing, Kajima, Yasuda Fire and Marine Insurance, Toshiba, Toyota Motor, Fujikura International Management, NEC Business Coordination Center, Hitachi, and Sharp).

References

Akao, Yoji (ed.) (1991). *Hoshin Kanri: Policy Deployment for Successful TQM.* Cambridge: Productivity Press (originally published in 1988 by the Japanese Standards Association under the title *Hoshin Kanri Katsuyo no Jissai*).

Aoki, Masahiko, and Hugh Patrick (eds.) (1994). *The Japanese Main Bank System: Its Relevance for Developing and Transforming Economies.* Oxford: Oxford University Press.

Ballon, Robert J., and Iwao Tomita (1988). *The Financial Behavior of Japanese Corporations.* Tokyo: Kodansha International.

Chowdhury, Anis, and Iyanatul Islam (1993). *The Newly Industrializing Economies of East Asia.* London: Routledge.

Cole, Robert E. (1989). *Strategies for Learning: Small Group Activities in American, Japanese, and Swedish Industry.* Berkeley: University of California Press.

Commission on the History of Science and Technology Policy (1991). *Historical Review of Japanese Science and Technology Policy.* Tokyo: Society of Non-Traditional Technology (originally published in 1989 under the title *Nihon no Kagaku gijutsu seisaku shi*).

Dore, Ronald P. (1986). *Flexible Rigidities.* Stanford: Stanford University Press.

East Asia Analytical Unit (1995). *Overseas Chinese Business Networks in Asia.* Canberra: Australian Government Publishing Service.

Fruin, W. Mark (1994). *The Japanese Enterprise System: Competitive Strategies and Cooperative Structures.* Oxford: Oxford University Press.

Gerlach, Michael (1992). *Strategic Alliance Capitalism: The Social Organization of Japanese Business.* Berkeley: University of California Press.

Ghoshal, Sumantra, and D. Eleanor Westney (eds.) (1993). *Organization Theory and the Multinational Corporation.* New York: St. Martin's Press.

Hanami, Tadashi (1979). *Labor Relations in Japan Today.* Tokyo: Kodansha International.

Inohara, Hideo (1990). *Human Resource Development in Japanese Companies.* Tokyo: Asian Productivity Organization.

Japan National Committee for Pacific Economic Cooperation (JANCPEC) (1992). *Economic Development of the Pacific Region and Triple-T Networking.* Tokyo: Prepared by the Sakura Institute of Research for the JANCPEC.

Kodama, Fumio (1995). *Emerging Patterns of Innovation: Sources of Japan's Technological Edge.* Boston: Harvard Business School Press.

Kohama, Hirohisa, and Juro Teranishi (eds.) (1992). "Japan's Development Cooperation: Policy and Organization," in Ippei Yamazawa and Akira Hirata (eds.), *Development Cooperation Policies of Japan, the United States, and Europe.* Tokyo: Institute of Developing Economies. 14–124.

Koike, Kazuo (1988). *Understanding Industrial Relations in Modern Japan.* London: Macmillan.

Komiya, Ryutaro, Masahiro Okuno, and Kotaro Suzumura (eds.) (1988). *Industrial Policy of Japan.* Tokyo: Harcourt, Brace, Jovanovich.

Kurogane, Kenji (ed.) (1993). *Cross-Functional Management: Principles and Practical Applications.* Tokyo: Asian Productivity Organization (originally published in 1988 by the Japanese Standards Association under the title *Kinobetsu Kanri Katsuyo no Jissai*).

Lincoln, Edward J. (1984). *Japanese Industrial Policies: What Are They, Do They Matter and Are They Different from Those in the United States?* Washington, DC: Japan Economic Institute of America.

Ministry of Finance, Japan (Okurasho) (1976–annual). *Okurasho Kokusai Kinyu*

Kyoku Nenpo (Annual Report of the International Finance Bureau). Tokyo: Okurasho.

Monden, Yasuhiro (1995). *Cost Reduction Systems: Target Costing and Kaizen Costing*. Portland, OR: Productivity Press (originally published in 1994 by the Toyo Keizai Shimposha under the title *Kakaku Kyosoryoku o Tsukeru Genka-kikaku to Genka-kaizen no Giho*).

Monden, Yasuhiro (1983). *Toyota Production System*. Atlanta, GA: Industrial Engineering and Management Press for the Institute of Industrial Engineers.

Morris-Suzuki, Tessa (1994). *The Technological Transformation of Japan: From the Seventh to the Twenty-First Century*. New York: Cambridge University Press.

Nakakita, Toru (1989). "Nihon Kigyo no Takokuseki Tenkai: Higashi Ajia Chiiki ni okeru Doko to Tokushitsu (Internationalization of Japanese Firms: Trends and Characteristics in East Asia), in Tran Van Tho (ed.), *Ajia Taiheiyo no Boeki to Yoso Ido ni kan suru Ichikosatsu*. Tokyo: Japan Economic Research Center.

Nakamura, Takafusa (1981). *The Postwar Japanese Economy: Its Development and Structure*. Tokyo: University of Tokyo Press (originally published in 1980 by the University of Tokyo Press under the title *Nihon Keizai: Sono Seicho to Kozo*).

Nishiguchi, Toshihiro (1994). *Strategic Industrial Sourcing: The Japanese Advantage*. Oxford: Oxford University Press.

Noguchi, Yukio (1994). *1940 Nen Seido*. Tokyo: Nihon Keizai Shimbunsha.

Porter, Michael E. (1990). *The Competitive Advantage of Nations*. New York: Free Press.

Reza, Sadrel (1994). "Policy Reform for Promoting Trade in Developing Countries," *Asian Development Review* 12 (2): 85–112.

Sakura Institute of Research (1995). *Industrial Outlook*. Tokyo: Sakura Institute of Research.

Sakurai, Michiharu, Larry N. Killough, and Robert M. Brown (1989)."Performance Measurement Techniques and Goal Setting: A Comparison of U.S. and Japanese Practices," in Yasuhiro Monden and Michiharu Sakurai (eds.), *Japanese Management Accounting: A World Class Approach to Profit Management*. Portland, OR: Productivity Press. 163–176.

Smitka, Michael J. (1991). *Competitive Ties: Subcontracting in the Japanese Automotive Industry*. New York: Columbia University Press.

Tachiki, Dennis S. (1993). "Striking Up Strategic Alliances: The Foreign Direct Investments of the NIEs and ASEAN Transnational Corporations," *RIM* 21: 22–36.

Tachiki, Dennis S. (1994). "Developing Human Resources for Sustaining Economic Growth: Public Policy Lessons from Japan, the Asian NIEs, and DPEs," *SIR Special Report*. Tokyo: Sakura Institute of Research.

Tachiki, Dennis S. (1995). "Corporate Investment Strategies for the Pacific Region: Some Evolving Changes in Japanese FDI," BRIE Working Paper #82, University of California at Berkeley.

Takenaka, Heizo (1991). *Contemporary Japanese Economy and Economic Policy*. Ann Arbor: University of Michigan Press.

Toyo Keizai (1980–annual). *Kaigai Shinshutsu Kigyo Soran* (Directory of Overseas [Japanese] Companies). Tokyo: Toyo Keizai Shinposha, 1980–annual.

Trezise, Philip H., with Yukio Suzuki (1976). "Politics, Government, and Economic Growth in Japan," in Hugh Patrick and Henry Rosovsky (eds.), *Asia's New Giant: How the Japanese Economy Works*. Washington, DC: Brookings Institute. 753–812.

Urata, Shujiro, and Toru Nakakita (1991). "Industrial Adjustment in Japan and Its Implications for Developing Countries," in Ippei Yamazawa and Akira Hirata (eds.), *Industrial Adjustment in Developed Countries and Its Implications for Developing Countries.* Tokyo: Institute of Developing Economies. 13–142.

Womack, James T., Daniel T. Jones, and Daniel Roos (1990). *The Machine That Changed the World.* New York: Macmillan.

Woods, Lawrence T. (1993). *Asia Pacific Diplomacy: Nongovernmental Organizations and International Relations.* Vancouver: University of British Columbia Press.

9

Exploiting Asia to Beat Japan

Production Networks and the Comeback of U.S. Electronics

Michael Borrus

Evolution in Electronics: Global Competition and the Persistence of National Identity

International competition in electronics has always been a story about market rivalry between firms with distinctive national identities, U.S. firms confronting Japanese or German firms, each firm acting in ways characteristic of its national origin. Market outcomes have been a function of how well the strategies and organizational traits originating in one domestic market generated competitive advantage in other national markets.[1] These national firms trading on the basis of local factors eventually became so-called multinational corporations (MNCs), who invested abroad but retained a characteristic national identity.

The evolution of recent competition in electronics began in the 1970s. From the early 1970s until the mid-1980s, Japanese producers were ascendant in electronics. In short order, they had taken over consumer electronics; gained leading world market shares in semiconductor chips, materials, and equipment; and looked entirely capable of repeating the feat in computers, office systems (e.g., copiers, faxes), and customer telecommunications equipment. So worried were U.S. policy makers and industrialists that the avowedly laissez-faire Reagan administration took the unprecedented step of using interventionist industrial policy to support the domestic microelectronics industry.[2] If the rapid rates of attrition of U.S. market share had continued, U.S. firms would have joined their European counterparts as significant players only in niches and on the margin of mass global markets.

What a difference a decade made. By 1994, U.S. producers of silicon chips and semiconductor materials and equipment were again flourishing, having regained the dominant world position. And U.S. producers of office, communications, and computer systems had reasserted product and technical leadership, with especially the latter retaining clear market dominance. As computer technology began to pervade consumer electronics, those same producers even looked to be reviving defunct U.S. consumer fortunes. By contrast, with few exceptions, their once formidable Japanese competition appeared disorganized, dismayed, and decidedly on the defensive. Indeed, U.S. industry leaders were so certain of continued success that many dismissed the Japanese giants as competitive dinosaurs, ill adapted to the raucous, fast, changeable, idea-intensive electronics markets of the future.[3]

As I will argue, however, the recent success of U.S.–owned firms has rested in significant part on extensive interfirm relationships with Asian-based producers. Those cross-border ties permitted U.S.–owned firms to exploit the growing technical sophistication and competitive strength of indigenous firms initially in Taiwan, Singapore, and Korea, and later throughout Southeast Asia and along the coastal provinces of mainland China. Those proliferating cross-border links suggest that the future success of U.S. firms is increasingly bound up with non–U.S. partners. They hint at a very different kind of international economy, one whose emblem is globalization and in which cross-border, interfirm relationships blur the identity of nations and firms. These links also call into question the continued utility of an account of competition that stresses rivalry between identifiable national industries.

The international economy has definitely changed. Economic interconnections have clearly expanded across geographic distance and between firms and nations. The terms of market competition have been altered irrevocably in most sectors as a combination of new technologies, markets, and players have entered the economic fray. Those facts are not at issue, but their patterns and significance certainly are. Without a doubt, capital, intermediate inputs, technologies, know-how, and corporate best practices flow more rapidly across national boundaries than ever before. But, as I argue later, those global movements have not globally diffused location-specific advantages or leveled national distinctions. They have not eviscerated consequential national differences in corporate behavior. Ownership continues to matter in understanding international competition, though in an era of global markets, investment, and competition, the ways in which ownership is significant have shifted ground.

Even in an industry like electronics, dominated by MNCs—MNCs that are, moreover, entangled in a growing web of joint development and production arrangements—an analytic that distinguishes between industries based in the United States, Japan, and Asia still makes sense. The analysis here presumes that the international market dynamic in most high-tech industries can still be effectively studied as a competition between firms operating out of largely national home bases.[4] By home base, I mean the national market in which the majority of a firm's assets, employment, and sales resides, and from which corporate control is exercised (especially control over strategy formation, corporate reorganization, new product development, finance and distribution). In most cases the home base is also the predominant locus of corporate ownership.

By that definition, very few high-tech MNCs are globally footloose. Indeed, up to 75 percent of the assets, employment, and sales of most MNCs, and an overwhelming percentage of their best-compensated and highest-skilled jobs, are still in a home base.[5] Of the world's top 50 MNCs of all national origins, which might be expected to be the most nonnational of MNCs, almost all fall in the 60–90 percent range of assets within the home country.[6] Equally significant, almost all MNC firms still explicitly exercise control from their home country of origin.[7]

Given those facts, I believe that firm strategies are still systematically shaped by the logic of competition in the home market base. Domestic institutions shape a national market logic or system of production[8]—that is, characteristic ways of doing business and distinctive trajectories of technology development that are the basis of product differentiation in international markets.[9] For high-tech industries, the principal domestic institutional variables include (1) the structure of the industry in question and of its domestic market (e.g., oligopolistic, *keiretsu*, lead customers); (2) technology, trade, and industrial policies and the political system that implements them; (3) the capital and labor market structures that condition access to those factor inputs; and (4) the local supply base that enables access to technology factor inputs.[10]

Those variables create a fabric of possibilities, a pattern of constraint and opportunity that confronts firms as they choose strategies, making some choices more likely (or less risky) and foreclosing others. For example, U.S. antitrust enforcement denies to U.S. firms the use of market-sharing arrangements that are routinely adopted in Japan and parts of Europe. And Japan's lifetime employment system encourages corporate strategies built on in-house training and teaching new skills to technical employees. Or how *guanxi* networks permit smaller Taiwanese family firms to stably deal in high-risk international ventures.[11]

As such examples suggest, the home base's pattern of constraint and opportunity channels, in characteristic directions, corporate strategies and behavior and, through them, technology development. For example, a well developed venture capital market, highly flexible labor market, leading-edge military and computer industry demand, and competitive industry structure characterized by easy entry and exit all shaped a U.S.–based semiconductor industry with characteristic strategies and technologies based on radical product innovation.[12] By contrast, keiretsu-dominated capital and distribution, inflexible labor markets, price-sensitive consumer demand, and a panoply of industrial and trade policies shaped a Japanese semiconductor industry with equally characteristic strategies and technologies based, in contrast to the U.S. pattern, on incremental manufacturing innovation.

Of course, a broad range of contingent choices is always available within any given pattern of constraint and opportunity. Strategies can and do differ among firms facing similar constraints, not least because they start with different resources and actively respond to what their competitors are doing. Nor are firms inflexibly bound to the home base's particular mix of possibilities. They can seek external opportunities or devise ways around national constraints. As my further argument suggests, U.S. firms did exactly that by creating their Asia-based production networks. In the real world of commerce, then, the home-base institutions that shape a national system of production are less independent variables in a formal analytic than systemic constraints tending to push strategies in particular directions, but without determining them.

That inherent openness of the analytic permits revision over time as evidence accrues to challenge the hypotheses it generates. Indeed, my research suggests that regional and subregional production systems in electronics may be gradually supplanting national ones. This would be an unintended consequence of the Asia-based production network strategy of U.S. firms, the subregional production networks it helped to spawn throughout Asia under the control of indigenous Asian capital, and the parallel regional response of Japanese firms. As I argue, such networks start out as an extraterritorial extension across national borders of a home-base market logic, but the extension will almost inevitably alter the logic over time.

Were such developments to diminish considerably the significance of the national home base, I would need to revise the approach I adopted here.

Until then, however, the overall working hypothesis is that for most firms the national market logic dominates international market strategies. This holds especially for the dominant Japanese electronics firms and even for the U.S.–based MNCs that adjusted to high-tech competition by constructing production networks outside the United States. The several competitive shifts that lie behind the recent American reascendance in electronics demonstrate this quite well. I will consider first the shift involving the domestic Japanese economy after 1990, from economic miracle to economic basket case.

The bursting of the domestic Japanese asset bubble, the attendant lengthy recession in the Japanese economy, and multiple *endaka* (dramatic yen appreciation) did much to undermine the international competitive position of Japanese electronics firms. Far more than Japanese firms were willing to admit even to themselves, Japan's electronics success in the 1970s and 1980s was driven by rapid growth in the sheltered domestic market. Rapid domestic growth afforded the stable demand to reach scale economies, the launch market for several generations of consumer and office systems, premium prices to subsidize price competition on foreign markets, cheap capital for continuous reinvestment, and, not least, quality- and feature-conscious consumers who rewarded corporate strategies built on incremental product revisions.[13] Cheap capital ended when the asset bubble burst, provoking Japan's longest postwar recession. Enduring recession put an end, at least temporarily, to the domestic economy's ability to support firm strategies premised on rapid growth and to the willingness of retailers blindly to support the producer-controlled pricing structure.[14] Combined with successive endaka, the economic problems made Japanese firms increasingly vulnerable to price competition both at home and abroad—something exploited at least as well by Korean and Taiwanese firms as by American ones.

That Japan's domestic economic problems could so profoundly influence the international competitive performance of Japanese-owned firms is one strong piece of evidence that ownership and a national home base still matter. The competitive shifts that account for the resurgence of U.S. market and technical leadership offer further evidence. Two competitive shifts are of paramount importance there— one in the market and one in production organization—and both have strong roots in a domestic home base. The market shift encompassed both a transformation of the character of electronic systems products and a resulting sea change in the industry's principal business strategies. Specifically, new electronics product markets have begun to converge on a common technological foundation of networkable, "open," microprocessor-based systems (of which, the PC is emblematic).[15] Such new product markets are characterized by a predominant form of market rivalry, namely, competitions to set de facto market standards. Over the last half decade, the domestic U.S. market has been the principal launch market for such new products and the principal terrain on which the resulting standards competitions have been fought. With just a few exceptions—for example, Nintendo in video games, Sony in 8 mm video camcorders—U.S. firms defined the products, set and controlled the standards initially in their home market, and achieved dominant world market positions as U.S. choices became global standards.

The organizational shift was, however, just as significant and in its own way permitted the new product market strategies to succeed. The shift in U.S. firm production organization was the move away from traditional integration to network forms of organization, specifically, international production networks centered in Asia.[16] By a firm's *international* production network, I mean the organization, across national borders, of the relationships (intra- and increasingly interfirm) through which the firm conducts research and development (R & D), product definition and design, procurement, manufacturing, distribution, and support services. As a first approximation, such networks include a lead firm, its subsidiaries and affiliates, its subcontractors and suppliers, its distribution channels and sources of value-added product or service features, its joint ventures, R & D alliances, and other cooperative arrangements (such as standards consortia). In contrast to traditional forms of corporate organization, such networks boost a proliferation of nonequity, intertwined, cross-border, interfirm relationships in which significant value is added outside the lead firm and entire business functions may be outsourced.

The move to such production networks based in Asia during the 1980s had three significant consequences for U.S. firms. First, U.S. firms were able to relieve the constraining threat of competitive dependence on Japanese firms for a wide range of component technologies and manufacturing capabilities because their Asian production networks became an alternative, competitive base of supply to Japanese producers. Simultaneously, the networks helped to lower production costs and turnaround times while keeping pace with rapid technological progress. Finally, the networks spawned Asian-based direct competitors to Japanese firms in several of their stronghold markets (e.g., memory chips, consumer electronics, and displays).

Combined, the market and organizational shifts enabled U.S. firms to pioneer a new form of competition in electronics, one that grew out of the distinctively American market environment and was adapted to overseas opportunities. Each of the U.S.–owned enterprises that pioneered the shifts and dominated market outcomes is by and large a new type of firm competing in a new way in the international economy. Its "core asset" is the intellectual property and know-how associated with setting, maintaining, and continuously evolving a de facto market standard, a process that requires perpetual improvements in product features, functionality, performance, costs and quality. Its core managerial skill is orchestrating the continuously changing sets of external relationships and melding them with the relatively more stable core of internal activities to access relevant technologies; design, develop, and manufacture the products; and get them from product concept to order fulfillment in minimal time. Although a few vertically integrated firms like Hewlett-Packard (HP) and Motorola play this game, most of the successful players are fleet-footed U.S. firms such as Sun Microsystems, Cisco Systems, 3Com, Intel, Netscape, and Microsoft.

A comparison of two firms is worthwhile: Cisco Systems, leading supplier of routers, switches, and hubs for corporate communications networks, and the predivestiture AT&T and its international counterpart, ITT. Everything from the R & D at central corporate laboratories to product design, engineering, manufacturing, distribution, and service was done by one AT&T/ITT affiliate or another, usually located somewhere in the United States for AT&T or Europe for ITT. The vast bulk of the underlying technologies, components, parts, software, and subsystems was produced internally by the two companies. The finished product was "sold" directly to local phone companies. Control was hierarchical and centralized in the United States. In fact, AT&T was the epitome of the hierarchically managed, vertically integrated, multidivisional corporation. And ITT was the epitome of the modern corporation's multinational extension to other markets.

By contrast, much of Cisco's R & D is done at its corporate headquarters in Silicon Valley, but a portion is also done through technology development alliances with key suppliers such as chip companies and software vendors. Associated engineering is done in Cisco affiliates in Japan and California but sometimes also by lead vendors. The products are assembled in California and Japan from components and manufacturing services (e.g., board-stuffing, PCB design) that flow from a variety of independent suppliers throughout Asia (including Taiwan, Korea, Japan, Singapore, Thailand, and Malaysia) and the United States and sometimes Europe. These suppliers are bound to Cisco through a variety of nonequity contractual arrangements. Cisco's Japanese "subsidiary," however, which is responsible for customizing the products for the Japanese market, is "owned" by Cisco and 14 major Japanese electronics companies (each with an equity stake), that together form a formidable coalition aimed at making Cisco's owned but open protocols the standard for corporate communications in Japan.

Several independent companies in California, Asia, and Europe (including most of Cisco's Japanese partners) produce to Cisco's standard, adding value in the form of products or services that interface in some fashion with Cisco's products—and without which Cisco's products would not be complete because they could not fully perform core functions (a significant difference from the more traditional model of behavior in which a firm might sell into the Bell System in competition with Western Electric, but the customer did not need the outsider product to have a complete system). The final product is sold directly to customers but also through a variety of third-party channels, including value-added resellers and systems integrators. After-sales service is very frequently undertaken by third-party suppliers.

As the example suggests, the new form of competition is no longer confined largely to equity investments and outsourcing in the manufacturing stage of production. It now extends throughout the value chain and to an increasing variety of nonequity, but not arm's-length relations. An example is Internet software producer Netscape Communications' product development and distribution relationships. Product development is done in conjunction with a variety of independent development partners such as SUN, Macromedia, Real Audio, Streamworks, and others who develop "plug-in" packages of software functionality (e.g., Javascript applets, authoring tools, audio and video players) designed to work seamlessly with Netscape's browser-server products—and without which the product would not be fully functional. The software is distributed directly to customers and through a variety of independent channels including on-line service providers such as Compuserve and America On-Line (AOL), traditional carriers such as Pacific Bell, specialized retailers such as EggHead Software, value-added resellers who provide Web set-up services, and mass marketers such as Costco.

As the examples suggest, this new form of competition has left no part of the information technology and electronics sector untouched. It holds true as much for Microsoft as for hardware vendors such as Cisco, as much for large-scale systems builders such as HP as for integrators such as Andersen Consulting—and as much for standard followers such as Compaq as for standard holders such as Netscape. For these firms, in important ways, their U.S. home base was more significant in the last 10 years of increasing global competition than it had been earlier in the era of clearly defined national industries. Indeed, even discounting supportive U.S. trade and technology policies, the *global* leadership of U.S. firms was rebuilt on a *domestic* foundation—the American market's characteristic logic of competitive ferment and its leadership both in the networking of microcomputer-based systems and in the design, product definition, and systems architecture capabilities that created the new standards. Key attributes of the new network form of production organization reflected unique characteristics of the domestic U.S. environment. Indeed, while most firms in the industry gravitated toward a network model in response to similar global market conditions, those models differed by ownership and control. As I argue, the distinctively American model contrasts with equally distinctive production networks under the control of Japanese, Taiwanese, and other indigenous Asian capital—though for reasons explored later, those alternative network models were competitively less effective than the American one in the last round of market rivalry.

The rest of this chapter takes a closer look at the shift in production organization, the way it created an alternative supply base in Asia, and the role it played in the resurgence by U.S. firms to product and technical leadership in electronics. The next section describes the historical development of U.S. direct investment in electronics in Asia over the past three decades, comparing it to Japanese investment and contrasting the consequences. The following section then examines the indigenous complement to U.S. firm strategies in Asia, namely, the emerging networked production capabilities under the control of Taiwanese and Singapore capital especially. The concluding section develops a production network typology to examine the respective positions of U.S., Japanese, and Taiwanese electronics firms and draws conclusions about whether national ownership will continue to matter in global electronics markets.

U.S. FDI and the Creation of a Regional Supply Base

By the end of the 1970s, U.S. electronics firms were almost completely dependent on Japanese competitors for supply of the underlying component technologies (e.g., tuners, picture tubes, recording heads, miniature motors) necessary to produce consumer electronics products.[17] In most cases, thoroughgoing technology dependence was a first step toward market exit. It meant that U.S. firms were far enough removed from the technological state of the art to impede new product development and that their principal competitors could dictate time-to-market, product cost, and feature quality. Under those circumstances, profits were minimal—if any were to be had at all. Consequently, by 1980 most major U.S. firms had exited the consumer segment of the market, and remaining players like General Electric (GE) and RCA survived largely by putting their brands on Japanese original equipment manufacturers (OEMs) production. A few short years later, even

RCA and GE, who had created most of the consumer electronic technologies that Japanese firms perfected, left the business.

The loss of consumer electronics' high-volume demand eroded the U.S. supply base for the other segments of the electronics industry and threatened them with an equally competitively constraining *architecture of supply*.[18] The supply base is the local capability to supply the component, machinery, materials, and control technologies (e.g., software), and the associated know-how, that producers use to develop and manufacture products. The architecture of supply is the structure of the markets and other organized interactions (e.g., joint development) through which the underlying technologies reach producers. In effect, U.S. producers of industrial electronics (e.g., computers, communications) were in danger of becoming dependent on their Japanese competitors for memory chips, displays, precision components, and a wealth of the other essential technologies (and associated manufacturing skills) that went into electronic systems.[19] The only alternative to increasing dependence on a closed oligopoly of rivals was to make the supply architecture more open and competitive. In conjunction with government policies and local private investors in Asia, U.S. firms gradually turned their Asian production networks into a flexible supply base alternative to Japanese firms.

The transformation from cheap labor affiliates to alternative supply base occurred in three stages—an initial stage from the late 1960s to late 1970s during which U.S. firms established their presence through foreign direct investments, a second stage in which their Asian affiliates developed extensive local relationships in the shadow of the dollar appreciation from 1980 to 1985, and a third stage from the late 1980s to the early 1990s, when the technical capabilities in their regional production networks were significantly upgraded and local affiliates were assigned global product responsibilities. The U.S. progression from simple assembly affiliate to technologically able Asian production network contrasts sharply with the development pattern of Japanese investments in the region over the same time period. A brief review of key developments in each of the three stages will highlight the differences.[20]

From the late 1960s, after an earlier round of market access investments by a few large U.S. MNCs, (notably IBM, GE, and RCA), most U.S. firms sought not market access but cheap production locations in Asia. Investment was led by U.S. chip makers, then consumer electronics and calculator producers, and finally, toward the end of the 1970s, producers of industrial electronic systems such as computers and peripherals. Most of the U.S. investments in this first stage established local assembly affiliates. Cheap but disciplined Asian labor permitted U.S. firms to compete on price back home and in Europe. Right from the start, then, the Asian affiliates of U.S. electronics firms were established as part of a multinational production network to serve advanced country markets. By contrast, most Japanese investment in Asia in this period, led by consumer electronics and appliance makers, was aimed at serving nascent local markets behind tariff walls. Japanese investment is often turnkey, with knock-down kits exported from Japan for local final assembly and sale in the local affiliate's domestic market. While the Japanese and U.S. investments in this first stage were both oriented to simple assembly and superficially appear similar, the vastly different markets being served pulled their respective investments in divergent directions.

Consider the resulting logic of sunk investment for the two sets of firms. Because their Asian affiliates were integrated into a production operation serving advanced country markets, U.S. firms upgraded their Asian investments in line with the pace of development of the lead market being served, the U.S. market. In essence, they upgraded in line with United States rather than local product cycles. By contrast, Japanese firms were led to upgrade the technological capacities of their Asian investments only at the slower pace necessary to serve lagging local markets. As local U.S. affiliates became more sophisticated through several rounds of reinvestment, a division of labor premised on increasing local technical specialization developed throughout the U.S. firms' global production operations. Local needs began to diverge from those elsewhere in the U.S. firms' overall operations and affiliates sought out and, where necessary, trained local partners to meet them.

Of course, the growth of local autonomy and relationships was constrained by overall corporate strategies (e.g., where economies of scale dictated a global rather than local sourcing arrangement), but over time U.S. investments still led to greater technology transfer and increasing technological capabilities for locals. By contrast, stuck in developing market product cycles, off-shore Japanese affiliates benefited from no such incentives to upgrade and no need to develop local supply relationships. Japanese firms served the domestic and U.S. markets wholly from home. Whatever their lagging Asian affiliates needed could be easily supplied from Japan. As local Asian markets demanded the marginally more sophisticated goods whose product cycles had already peaked in the advanced countries, the entire production capability for those could also be transferred from Japan. Overall, less technology was transferred, and even that remained locked within the Japanese firm's more limited circle of relations.

Thus, during the second stage (1980–1985) U.S.–owned assembly platforms were upgraded and enhanced technically to include more value-added, for example, from assembly to test in chips, from hand to automation assembly techniques, from simple assembly of printed circuit boards to more complex subsystems and final assembly in industrial electronics. As they gained more autonomy, U.S. affiliates began to source more parts and components locally (e.g., a range of mechanical parts, monitors, discrete chips, and even power supplies). As U.S. affiliates developed and as the U.S. industry exited the consumer segment, local electronics producers in places such as Taiwan shifted to concentrate more and more of their own investment (and their governments' attention) on industrial electronics.[21] As these developments occurred, the contour began to appear of an ever more elaborate and deepening technical division of labor between U.S. and Asia-based operations, bound together in production networks serving U.S. firms' advanced country markets. In essence, a new supply base was being created in Asia under the control of U.S. and local, but not Japanese, capital.

By contrast, the pattern of Japanese investment led to a dual production structure under the control of Japanese firms and premised on traditional product cycles—sophisticated products were produced at home with sophisticated processes to serve advanced country markets, while lower-end products were produced with simple processes in regional affiliates to serve local Asian markets. Both sets of operations sourced from a common supply base, located largely in Japan and controlled, directly or indirectly, by Japan's major electronics companies. Where Japanese companies responded to government or commercial pressures to localize, they did so from within their established supply base—that is, by transplanting the operation of an affiliated domestic Japanese supplier—not by sourcing locally from the emerging Asian supply base. In short, the Japanese production networks boasted redundant investment and remained relatively closed, even as the U.S. networks became more open and specialized.

These trends were fully elaborated during the third stage, from 1985 through the early 1990s. At home, U.S. firms focused scarce corporate resources more intensely on new product definition and the associated skills (e.g., design, architectures, software) necessary to create, maintain, and evolve de facto market standards. In turn, they upgraded their Asian affiliates, giving them greater responsibility for hardware value-added and manufacturing and significantly increased local sourcing of components, parts, and subassemblies. They even contracted out design and manufacture of some boards and components. Thus, during this period, the Asian affiliates of U.S. firms continued to migrate from PCB to final assembly with increased automation, to increase both component production and final system value-added, and to assume global responsibility for higher value-added systems (e.g., from monochrome desktops to color notebook PCs). Their production networks extended to more and more capable local Asian producers who became increasingly skilled suppliers of components, subassemblies, and, in some cases, entire systems. Even in areas such as memory chips and displays where Japanese firms remained important suppliers to U.S. firms, there was sufficient competition from other Asian sources (e.g., Korea in memory chips) or sufficient political pressure to keep the supply architecture open.

Leading U.S. producers of PCs such as Apple illustrate well these developments.[22] Apple Computer Singapore (ACS) opened a PCB assembly plant for the Apple II PC in 1981. By 1983 nine local companies were contract manufacturing PCBs for the Apple IIe and Lisa PCs. By 1985 ACS was upgraded to include final assembly of Apple IIes for the world market. From 1986 to 1989, ACS was expanded and upgraded to begin some component design work. In 1990 ACS assumed final assembly responsibility for two of three new Macintosh PCs (and PCBs for the third) and designed (locally) and manufactured associated monitors. By then, essentially all components were sourced in Asia (except the U.S.–fabbed microprocessor)—ACS's 130 major suppliers included local firms like Gul Technologies and Tri-M (PCBs). Also, ACS had demonstrated that its growing technical prowess could pay competitive dividends in speeding time to market. It was able to move from designs to production rollout in up to half the time of Apple's other facilities. By 1992, ACS assumed responsibility for final assembly for all Asia-Pacific markets, including Japan, was designing and supplying boards globally, manufacturing monitors and some peripherals, and designing chips. Over $1 billion was being procured annually through ACS. In 1993, ACS set up a design center for Macs for high-volume desk-top products—Apple's only hardware design center outside the United States. By 1994, ACS had become the center for distribution, logistics, sales, and marketing for the Asia-Pacific region and was assembling the MacClassic II, LC III and IV, midrange Centris, and Quadra 800 for global distribution. Regional sourcing reached $2 billion, half from Japan (LCD displays, peripherals, memory, hard disk drives), another quarter from Singapore, $250–$500 million from Taiwan for OEM desktops, monitors, PCBs, Powerbooks, Digital Assistants, and chips. Korea's Goldstar also supplied monitors. By late 1994, ACS had begun to design the motherboard and tooling and assemble the multimedia system Mac LC 630 PC for worldwide export. Two new Mac products completely designed and manufactured at ACS were launched in 1995.

The value-added/local sourcing progression of other major U.S. electronics players in Asia is broadly similar.[23] For example, Compaq Asia (hereafter, CAS for Compaq Asia-Singapore) established its Singapore factory in 1986 for PCB assembly of components sourced from Asia (including Japan), for desktop PCs to be final assembled in the United States. By 1994, after terminating an OEM relationship with Japan's Citizen Watch, CAS was designing and manufacturing all notebook and portable PCs for worldwide consumption and all desktop PCs for the Asia-Pacific region. Similarly, Hewlett-Packard's Singapore operations evolved from assembly of calculators in 1977 to global responsibility for portable printers and Pentium desktop PCs and servers, with local manufacturing, process design, tooling development, and chip design. Motorola's Singapore operations evolved from simple PCB assembly of pagers and private radio systems destined for the U.S. in 1983; to worldwide mandates for design, development, and automated manufacture of double-sided six-layer PCBs; for design and development of integrated circuits for disk drives and other peripherals; for some R & D, and for sourcing of at least $500 million of parts and components within the region. Similar kinds of stories could be told for AT&T in telecommunications products; IBM and DEC in PCs and peripherals; Maxtor, Connor, Seagate, and Western Digital in hard disk drives; and for TI, Intel, and National Semiconductor.

In sum, by the early 1990s, the division of labor between the United States and Asia, and within Asia between affiliates and local producers, deepened significantly, and U.S. firms effectively exploited increased technical specialization in Asia. In stark contrast, through the end of 1993, Japanese firms still controlled their Asian affiliates' major decision-making and sourcing activities from Japan. More low-end process/product technology had been placed offshore, including production of audio systems (cassette recorders, headphones, low-end tuners, etc.), under-20-inch televisions, and some VCR models, cameras, calculators, and appliances such as microwave ovens. Local Asian content had risen toward 60 percent, but core technological inputs like magnetrons, chips, and recording heads were exclusively sourced from Japan, and the 60 percent "local" content was mostly supplied by the offshore branch plants of traditional domestic Japanese suppliers. Local design activities were invariably to tailor Japanese product concepts for local Asian markets, and global mandates for advanced products, let alone their design, development, and manufacture, which were nowhere to be found outside of Japan. In contrast to U.S. producers, for example, Japanese PC producers sourced displays, memory, some microprocessors, drives, power and mechanical components, plastics, and PCBs from Japan (or in the case of some low-end components, from offshore affiliates), and did PCB and final assembly and essentially all advanced design and development in Japan. In short, Japanese firms intensified rather than rationalized their dual production structure and, by exclusion from their production networks, failed to benefit from increasing cheaper and faster technical capabilities in the rest of Asia.

Indigenous Networks—From Supply Base to Competitor?

While Asia's indigenous electronics capabilities (excluding Japan) developed in close symbiosis with the strategies and activities of American MNC firms, they were driven by local private investment and supported by government policies. Outside of Korea (where the *chaebol* dominated domestic electronics development), resident ethnic Chinese investors played the principal, private entrepreneurial role in Taiwan and Hong Kong, Singapore, and later in Malaysia, Indonesia, Thailand, and along the coastal provinces of the mainland of China. First in the newly industrialized countries (NICs) and then in Southeast Asia, governments provided a panoply of fiscal and tax incentives; invested heavily in modern infrastructure, generic technology development, and the technical skill development of the work force; engaged in selective strategic trade interventions; and in some cases, even provided market intelligence and product development roadmaps.[24] The aims were both to plug into the developing multinational production networks in the region, and to use them as a lever toward autonomous capabilities. The result, by the early 1990s, was burgeoning indigenous electronics production throughout the region, mainly under the control of indigenous capital.[25]

Outside of Korea's consumer electronics industry, advanced indigenous electronics activity is concentrated in the PC and PC-related product markets. In turn, the nerve centers of that activity in PC electronics are Taiwan and Singapore, the home bases for emerging Asia-Pacific MNCs like the former's ACER and the latter's Creative Technologies. As table 9.1 shows, in 1994, Taiwanese firms held from significant to dominant world market shares in 14 PC-related product categories.

Table 9.1 Taiwan Firms' 1994 World Market Share (%) in PC-Related Products

Motherboard	80
Mouse	80
Scanner	61
Monitor	56
Keyboard	52
Network interface card	34
Graphics card	32
Switching power supply	31
Notebook PC	28
Video card	24
Terminal	22
Network hub	18
Audio card	11
Desktop PC	8

The table is drawn from a presentation prepared by Tze-Chen (T.C.) Tu, Director of Taiwan's Market Intelligence Center (of the Institute for Information Industries), "Upgrading Taiwan's IT Industry—New Challenges and the Role of International Cooperation," at the BRIE-Asia Foundation Conference, *Competing Production Networks in Asia: Host-Country Perspectives*, San Francisco, April 27–28, 1995.

Singapore, by contrast, a market about one seventh Taiwan's size, produced about half of the world's hard disk drives, most of its multimedia sound cards, and growing percentages of computer printers, PC subassemblies, and even finished PCs (about 5 percent world market share).[26] Of course, as I have argued, the position of indigenous producers remains tied to the production networks of foreign multinationals. Table 9.2 gives some indication of this by examining the OEM relationships of major Taiwanese producers. In turn, however, by leveraging their OEM relationships and overall world market shares, several indigenous Asian producers have emerged as increasingly autonomous forces in the electronics industry. Indeed, in the early 1990s, intense competition and growing needs for scale-intensive investment to stay in the game, forced a shakeout and consolidation among Taiwanese and Hong Kong–based electronics firms. In particular, several major Taiwanese MNCs have claimed growing shares of key product markets and formed their own regional production networks. The resulting industry concentration is most visible in Taiwan's largest domestic product sectors, notably monitors, PCs, and PCBs, where the top 10 indigenous producers now account for over 70 percent of the market.[27] Leading producers include firms such as ACER, the Formosa Plastics Group, and Tatung. For example, ACER is Taiwan's largest PC firm, doing about \$2.3 billion in 1994 and being the leading PC supplier outside of Japan in Asia, placing second in Latin America, and growing rapidly as number 10 in the United States.[28] Furthermore, ACER is the only Taiwanese firm with substantial backend distribution and marketing under its own brand in the United States. It fully designs and develops its own systems, boards, and many components, including logic chips, and is moving into higher-end systems such as servers. Similarly, Formosa Plastics Group, the principal holding arm of Taiwan's Wang family holdings and Taiwan's largest private enterprise, controls First International Computer (FIC), Everex Systems, and Nan Ya Plastics.[29] Moreover, FIC (and its subsidiary Formosa Industrial Computer) is the world's largest contract PCB motherboard producer, and, through Nan Ya Plastics, the group has expanded into production (not assembly) of PCBs, chips, and even monochrome LCDs.

Taiwan-based MNCs like those ride herd on an extensive indigenous supply base of thousands of small and medium-sized design, component, parts, sub-

Table 9.2 Taiwan Firms' 1994 OEM Relations in PC-Related Products (representative sample)

OEM producer	Buyers	Products
Acer	Apple, Fujitsu, NEC, NCR, Data General, Siemens	Notebooks or monitors
Delta	Apple, Compaq, IBM	Power supplies
Elite	DEC, IBM, NEC, Siemens	Motherboards
FIC	ATT, Dell, Unisys	Motherboards
Inventa	Apple, Compaq, Dell	PDA, notebooks
Lite-on	Compaq, DEC, Dell	Power supplies or monitors
Tatung	Apple, Packard Bell, NEC	PCs or motherboards, monitors

See table 9.1 note for source material, supplemented in this table by press reports.

assembly, and assembly houses throughout the China Circle and extending into Southeast Asia. Thus, for example, by the late 1980s, small firms (under 50 employees) accounted for about two thirds of the electronics enterprises on Taiwan, roughly double their share a decade before when MNC consumer electronics firms dominated production.[30] These firms form an intricate subcontracting structure of affiliated and family enterprises that constitute the local production network and supply base. The numerous small firms are aligned vertically with the few large-scale enterprises and many trading companies that act as intermediaries for foreign MNC customers.[31] Designs and key components flow down from the large-scale enterprises; more labor-intensive production activities flow up along the subcontract network leading to final assembly. Divisible production tasks (e.g., components and subassembly steps) can be farmed out all the way down to family job shops and home workers. Individual units within the network operate at small scale with minimal capital investment requirements and link on the informal bases of guanxi, that is, kinship or friendship ties. The flexibility that results, mirroring the industrial district capabilities in Italy and parts of Germany, makes it possible to increase or decrease production scale on short notice, or to enter and exit niche product market segments, all at minimal cost and with minimal fixed investments.[32]

Another significant competitive advantage of the indigenous network structure is what might be termed business "speed," the ability to minimize the time it takes to move from design specification to production and then to market with a quality product. Industry estimates of Taiwanese network business speed peg the time from conception to execution at a fraction of that of larger MNCs burdened with formal organization and layered decision making.[33] In some cases, indigenous networks can design and execute in less time than it takes the Japanese giants just to make a go-ahead decision.[34] For the Taiwanese design houses in particular, this capability is apparently built on a high value-added foundation, macro cell-based design methodologies and libraries of already characterized component functions that can be combined and altered to implement new concepts.[35] The rapid design capability then joins with the hyper-competition among subcontractors in the network to implement the new designs as fast as possible. Such speed advantages pack an enormous competitive punch in electronics markets where average product life cycles have roughly halved in the past five years—one of the reasons Taiwanese suppliers in particular have a thriving original design and manufacturing (ODM) business as subcontract design houses for U.S. and European MNCs.

Network speed is complemented by more traditional factor input advantages, notably the relative cost of skilled engineering and technical labor (especially designers), which, even in the maturing economies of Taiwan and Singapore, still costs less than a third of comparable U.S. or Japanese labor. The best indigenous networks also run extremely lean, in general, sales and administrative overheads where they match the best practices of MNC leaders like Hewlett-Packard (at about 10 percent of sales for microcomputers and printers) and are far superior to most advanced MNC performers (15 percent to more than 20 percent of sales, based on industry discussions). Of course, such cost minimization is inherent in the subcontract structure of especially the Taiwanese production networks where affiliates and family enterprises can be squeezed (if necessary, in time-honored sweat-shop manner).

Over the last half decade, in response to steep rises in factor input costs in the NICs, and exacerbated by currency appreciation, the indigenous Asian production networks have become more and more regionalized. For example, table 9.3 suggests the extent to which considerable PC-related production is now being carried on by Taiwanese MNCs within the region but outside of Taiwan. As the table suggests, production outside of Taiwan accounts for a growing share of total production under Taiwanese control, approaching one quarter of the total in 1995. Offshore activity is concentrated in certain product segments, with about two thirds of Taiwanese production of keyboards, half of power supplies, and about a quarter of monitors and motherboards now taking place outside of Taiwan.[36] Before the mainland became formally available, labor-intensive assembly of products like keyboards, low-end monitors, and power supplies shifted offshore to Malaysia and Thailand. Since the late 1980s, however, and given the cultural affinity, mainland China has been the preferred new investment site.

At least in the first instance, similar to the original motivation of many U.S. MNCs, cheap labor for high volumes seems to be a prime motivation. In labor-intensive assembly processes, official Taiwanese figures suggest cost savings of from 8 percent in monitor assembly to greater than 20 percent with keyboards and the mouse. Critically, most of these Chinese investments are cooperative ventures, not wholly owned subsidiaries, and they are not only being carried out by the largest producers. Chung Chin cites a 1994 study by Shu showing that of 38 Taiwanese monitor producers, 19 have established production relationships on the mainland since the early 1990s, and 6 others were planning to do so.[37] In the resulting division of labor, 14" monochrome and color monitors are assembled on the mainland or in other Asian locations, while Taiwanese production is upgraded to larger display sizes. Of the 4 million monitors produced offshore in Taiwanese networks in 1993, half were assembled in China. The mainland is increasingly also the site of other production activities. For example, in addition to color monitors, FIC's two Guangdong Province subsidiaries assemble PCBs and other components, and Mitac similarly does all of its semifinished assembly (frames and PCBs) on the mainland.[38] In all of these products, the combination of Taiwanese capital, production know-how, and OEM reputation with cheap mainland labor and land is making for an irresistible regional extension of Taiwanese networks. And the lure of the mainland's market provides the longer-term temptation.

Table 9.3 Domestic versus Offshore Production Value of Taiwan's Electronics Industry, 1992–1995 ($ millions)

	1992	1993	1994	1995 (estimated)
Domestic production	8,391	9,693	11,579	13,139
Offshore production	973	1,691	3,003	4,279
Offshore as % of domestic	11.60%	17.45%	25.93%	32.57%

See table 9.1 for source material.

From Ownership to Control: The Future of Competition and Prospects for Regional Identity

The emergence of competitive strategies in electronics premised on highly articulated interfirm, cross-border production networks has not eviscerated the analytic significance of national distinctions based on ownership and origin. The evidence presented here suggests rather, and perhaps paradoxically, that those distinctions still have explanatory power: In Asia today, beneath the superficial similarity engendered by aggregate trade and investment data and macroanalyses lie distinctly different electronics production networks under the control of U.S., Japanese, and indigenous Asian multinationals. The differences have had competitive consequences; they help to explain why U.S. firms prospered, indigenous Asian firms became significant players, and Japanese firms suffered in the last round of competition. Table 9.4 provides a comparative, albeit highly stylized typology of the different networks.

The U.S. networks tend to be open to outsiders, fast and opportunistic in implementation, with significant decisions decentralized to affiliates or partners, and capable of changing contour (and partners) as needs change—in an image: open, fast, opportunistic, decentralized, and disposable. Their activities are centered in the NICs, especially Singapore, but increasingly reach into the rest of Asia and China. By contrast, the Japanese networks tend to be relatively closed to outsiders, more cautious to make and implement significant decisions that are almost always generated from Japan, and structured on stable, long-term business and keiretsu relationships—that is, closed, cautious, centralized, long-term, and stable. Despite the recent surge of Japanese investment into Asia, their networks are still most definitely centered in Japan.

Table 9.4 Typology of Electronics Production Networks in Asia

Characteristic	U.S.-owned	Japanese-owned	Taiwanese-owned
Accessibility	Open	Closed	Insular
Responsiveness	Fast/opportunistic	Cautious	Fast/flexible
Governance	Decentralized	Centralized	Hierarchical
Permanence	Disposable	Long-term/stable	Fluid
Supply base	Anyone meeting price, quality, delivery constraints	Domestic and affiliated	Guanxi-preferred
Product mix	Sophisticated industrial electronics	Low-end, especially consumer audio-visual	PC electronics
Division of labor	Offshores high value-added esp. in components, processes, and manufacturing, and maximizes Asian value-added	High value-added product/processes at home, low offshore, but minimizes Asian (i.e., non-Japanese) value-added	Offshores low-end products/processes and exploits non-Taiwanese value-added there and where otherwise necessary

The respective networks also rely on distinctively different supply bases, boast different product mixes, and, most significantly, constitute very different divisions of labor. The U.S. networks rely on an open, competitive supply architecture in which Japanese, U.S., Taiwanese, Singaporean, Korean, and other Asian firms compete on cost, quality, and time-to-market and, in some cases, provide significant value-added. By contrast, the Japanese networks rely on a largely domestic and affiliated supply base with little value-added by other Asian producers. The U.S. networks produce (and in some cases design and develop) increasingly sophisticated industrial electronics such as hard disk drives, PCs, inkjet printers, and telecommunications products. The Japanese networks still mostly produce consumer audio-visual electronics and appliances. The U.S. networks exploit a complementary division of labor in which U.S. firms specialize in especially "soft" competencies (definition, architecture, design—standards areas) and Asian firms specialize in hard competencies (components, manufacturing stages and design/development thereof). By contrast, the Japanese networks exploit a division of labor with significant redundancies in which domestic Japanese operations produce high-value, high-end products using sophisticated processes, and offshore affiliations produce low-value, low-end products.[39] The U.S. networks exploit increasing technical specialization throughout the production process in which the Asian contribution is maximized; the Japanese networks exploit a value-added specialization between products in which the Asian (i.e., not Japanese) contribution is minimized.

By comparison, the emerging indigenous Asian networks like those of Taiwanese MNCs Acer, Mitac, or the Formosa Plastics group, take still a different form. It is hardly surprising that on some dimensions they appear to emulate features of both the Japanese and U.S. MNC approaches. However, the prevalence of distinctive characteristics of their own suggests that the indigenous Asian networks are a sui generis form of network organization, not a mere hybrid of U.S. and Japanese ideal types.[40] Much like the Japanese, Taiwanese networks are difficult for outsiders to penetrate. They tend to be very hierarchically organized, though less reliant for decision making on their point of origin than the Japanese. Much like those in the United States, Taiwanese networks can move very fast in implementing decisions. Because they are much less constrained than the Americans by the need for legally enforceable relations, they tend to be even more flexible in the kinds of relationships embodied and in the ability to shift contours as markets shift. Unlike their U.S. or Japanese counterparts, Taiwanese networks are based on guanxi (rather than legal or keiretsu) ties that change fluidly as needs change but apparently without abandoning reciprocal obligations over the long term. In short, the Taiwanese networks appear to be insular, fast, hierarchical, flexible, and fluid. They tend to be centered in the China Circle, with significant Southeast Asian investment as a hedge. Like the Americans, the Taiwanese networks seek to exploit a highly competitive supply base and concentrate on industrial electronics, albeit mostly PC-related. Much like the Japanese, Taiwanese networks retain in the home base high value-added products manufactured with more advanced processes, and offshore to cheaper production locations lower value-added products and simpler processes. Unlike the Japanese, however, the Taiwanese networks also self-consciously leverage increasing technical specialization through local relationships for the offshore products and processes. And unlike the U.S.

or Japanese networks, the Taiwanese network relationships are increasingly China-centered—rather than using an NIC base as the regional center, Taiwanese networks may end up with a China base as their global center, using demand and technical know-how in the domestic China market to achieve world-class scale, costs, and innovation.

As I argued at the outset, these differences between U.S., Japanese, and indigenous networks were competitively consequential in the last round of market battles in electronics. The U.S. networks relieved the constraining threat of competitive dependence on Japanese rivals by reconstituting the architecture of supply in electronics. Simultaneously, the turn to skilled but cheaper Asian suppliers helped to lower overall production costs, fierce competition within the supply base helped to reduce turnaround times, and specialization and diversity within the network permitted U.S. producers to keep better pace than Japanese rivals with rapid technological and market shifts. Growing Asian technical capabilities freed U.S. firms to focus their efforts (and scarce resources) on new product definition, systems integration, software value-added, and distribution. In the bargain, the U.S. networks helped to spawn and sustain direct Asian competition to Japanese firms in several of their stronghold markets such as memory chips, consumer electronics, and displays. And while indigenous Asian network capabilities grew prodigiously, they did not directly challenge revived U.S. leadership in the last round of competition.

National distinctions between electronics firms are likely to continue to be competitive differentiators for the foreseeable future. But the development of inter-firm, cross-border relationships does appear to have changed the significance of ownership and origin—perhaps even in ways that will eventually undermine their explanatory capacity. To see how requires detouring through the motives that lie behind the development of the network relationships. The electronics case suggests that firms are motivated by four principal goals in developing the new relational forms of competition.[41] First, production networks are an effort to develop forms of organization that provide greater flexibility, responsiveness, risk sharing, and efficiency under conditions of high market and technological uncertainty. Second, that uncertainty also provokes firms to develop relationships to exploit complementary assets held by other firms—for example, to develop something new that no partner could do as effectively alone (within given constraints of time and cost) or because rationalization around areas of core competence requires contracting out noncore functions. Production networks are also an effort to achieve better access—to foreign markets, technologies, investment opportunities, and the like—in "global" markets that retain a panoply of formal and informal barriers to trade and investment.

Finally, the new relational forms are also principally about creating or removing market imperfections and raising or surmounting barriers to competitive entry. This is clearest in the case of standards coalitions, where the alliance network is aimed at generating (or challenging) a de facto market standard and customer lock-in. But competition in electronics is increasingly about developing and sustaining monopoly niches, whether through ownership and control of a de facto standard or by maintaining a differentiated product through the ability to add performance, functionality, and features or to improve costs faster than competitors. Indeed, profitability in electronics is almost purely a function of the resulting market structure—high where quasi-monopoly position can be maintained, essentially nonexistent everywhere else. That is why so-called value-chain analysis can be so misleading in evaluating this industry to the extent that it implies the need to find profits by moving up a hypothetical food chain that starts in components and assembly and ends with services and content. As Intel demonstrates in components and as Matsushita's recent desultory experience with MCA suggests in content-creation, profits can be won or lost at any point in the value-chain if the market is structured accordingly. While they may also fulfill the other motives suggested, production networks are self-conscious efforts to structure markets in ways that increase profits by removing direct competitors, creating differentiability, erecting entry barriers, and the like.

Whatever the precise mix of motives, in most cases what a firm needs—and the resulting division of labor within its production network that embodies those needs and fulfills that mix—derives in the first instance from what it lacks in its home environment. Or to put it in slightly different terms, the hypothesis is that the shape of a firm's international production network reflects its ability to exploit location-specific advantages at its point of origin and to fill in complementary elements as necessary with relationships that exploit location-specific advantages elsewhere.[42] In turn, the shape and character of the resulting network reflect differences in the ability to control the relationships comprised by the network—control that also derives initially from the point of origin. Thus, the setting, maintenance, and evolution of de facto standards set in the domestic U.S. launch market were the principal instrument used by U.S. firms to preserve control over their interfirm networks. So long as U.S. firms maintained that role in the division of labor—by defining and executing an evolutionary path for improved performance-functionality-cost that kept customers locked in to their standards—it was extremely difficult for other firms in the network to challenge for the lead. The U.S. networks could be highly decentralized because control over standards enabled devolution of responsibility for significant value-added to partners without fear of losing the ability to orchestrate the network. By contrast, with control residing in domestic-based manufacturing and core-component technologies, any significant devolution of responsibility by Japanese firms over those competencies to outsider partners risked creating a direct competitor. Japanese networks had to be centralized to avoid that outcome.

The electronics case suggests that at the moment, for most firms, the point of origin will remain the principal source of control over production networks. For most firms, control resides at home because that is where development of new product or process concepts, standards setting, and associated launch market opportunities are mostly developed, where local capacities and technical specialization are still exploited most fully, where, as argued in the introduction, the initial patterns of constraint and opportunity to which firms respond are first set. As long as the source of control over the shape and character of a firm's production network stems from its point of origin in the ways indicated, corporate nationality will continue to matter to market competition in electronics.

But will those sources of control remain largely national? As production networks become ever more articulated and cross more borders, it is easy to envision circumstances under which each of those sources of control migrates from the point of origin to other places in the network. The ability of U.S. firms to drive development of some process and manufacturing competencies out of their Asian affiliates provides one hint of what is possible. The competitive adjustment of Japanese firms provides still more. As Japanese firms respond to the relative success of U.S. and indigenous Asian firms, they are beginning to rationalize an Asia-regional network structure very different from that of U.S. or indigenous producers (see chapter 8). That rationalization would turn the precise characteristics of Japan's Asia-based networks that created vulnerability over the last decade—closed, cautious, centralized, long-term, and stable—into competitive strengths. Japanese firms could decide to accept slower domestic growth and the need to exploit technical capabilities in the rest of Asia as givens. They could decide to selectively incorporate indigenous Asian producers into the family and build stable, long-term, mutually advantageous ties focused on exploiting specific technological capabilities in other parts of Asia. They could decide to invest for the long term. They could decide to drive their growth from Asia's. If Asia becomes a launch market for new product concepts—and its rapid growth and burgeoning wealth suggest that it must in some market segments—Japanese firms might just then be better positioned to exploit the development.[43]

Just as big a competitive wild card is the growing indigenous electronics capability in the China Circle and Southeast Asia. A competitive indigenous producer scenario premised on regional rather than national origin is easy enough to describe. The combination of Hong Kong–based financial and producer services with Taiwan-based digital product and process design, Southeast Asian component specialization, highly skilled but cheap mainland labor, and, of course, the mainland market provides a tantalizing scenario for regional dominance. The network characteristics identified before—insulated from outside control, fast, hierarchical, flexible, and fluid—appear to be a compelling mix for exploiting the region's possibilities. And the sheer scale of production for the mainland and, from the mainland, for overseas markets would dwarf the leverage provided by any other regional market base. To this potent brew should be added the self-conscious developmental intent of local (not necessarily national) governments throughout the region to nurture indigenous capabilities.

The quite significant constraints on the emergence of such a scenario should not be underestimated, of course, for significant elements of control are likely to remain with U.S. or Japanese firms for some time. Unlike the Americans, who have retained capability in most core component technologies and a significant, though diminished, position in capital goods, the Japanese indigenous networks remain dependent on Japanese competitors for advanced manufacturing equipment and high value-added core components (e.g., for Taiwanese producers, $500 million of LCD displays and $3 billion of memory chips in 1994). Even more of a constraint, however, is continuing dependence on the American networks for microprocessor architectures, advanced product concepts, and global distribution. Likely the burgeoning regional market can eventually help to break those constraints by providing the returns necessary for indigenous producers to invest in core components that can reduce their existing dependence, in new product concepts that can become global standards, and in indigenous brands and global distribution channels that can increase their marketing leverage. Only then, perhaps, could one convincingly begin to talk about real regional, as distinct from national, identity for firms operating in Asia. But such developments are likely to take time, perhaps even several decades. Until then, so long as a firm's point of origin remains the primary source of control over its network, ownership will continue to matter to competition in electronics.[44]

Notes

1. See, for example, Michael Porter's extensive comparative analysis of domestic competitive factors in *The Competitive Advantage of Nations* (London: MacMillan, 1990).

2. The government's support took two forms—direct financial support of $100 million per year to the industry's manufacturing technology consortium, Sematech (or half of Sematech's annual budget) and negotiation of the U.S.-Japan Semiconductor Trade Agreement (STA). For details, see Michael Borrus, *Competing for Control: America's Stake in Microelectronics* (New York: Ballinger, 1988).

3. This position is argued explicitly by industry consultant William F. Finan and his academic collaborator Jeffrey Frey in their *Nihon no Gijyutsu ga Abunai: Kenshō, Haiteku Sangyō no Suitai* [Japan's Crisis in Electronics: Failure of the Vision] (Tokyo: Nikkei Press, 1994).

4. Applying and exploring the limits of this method are principal goals of the Berkeley Roundtable on the International Economy (BRIE) research supported by the Alfred P. Sloan Foundation. That research is elaborated in a forthcoming BRIE book on national technology trajectories with contributions by Benedicte Callon, Keith Dardon, Ulrike Hodges, Tim Sturgeon, Jay Tate, Michael Borrus, David Soskice, and John Zysman.

5. See the discussion in Laura Tyson, "They Are Not US," *The American Prospect* (Winter 1991), p. 37ff. See also Yao-Su Hu, "Global Corporations Are National Firms with International Operations," *California Management Review* (Winter 1992), p. 107ff. Of course, the debate addressed by these articles was popularly launched by Robert Reich in "Who Is Us?" *Harvard Business Review*, (Jan.–Feb. 1990) p. 53ff. More generally, the recent collection by Dennis Encarnation, ed., *Does Ownership Matter?* (New York: Oxford University Press, 1994) supports the persistence of important differences among multinational firms based on national origin.

6. See "A Survey of Multinationals," *The Economist*, March 27, 1993, pp. 6–7, citing United Nations data. The major exceptions are oil companies (because oil fields tend to be located abroad) and small-country multinationals like Nestlé, Unilever, and ABB (because their markets are located abroad)—and the latter would fall into the 60–90 percent range if Europe were treated as their home base. By that measure, the most nonoil MNC is IBM, with about 50 percent of assets outside of the United States. But because half of its assets are still concentrated in the United States, even IBM can be said to have the United States as its home base.

7. This conclusion is easily reached from industry conversations and even a quick perusal of the annual reports of the 1,000 largest U.S. and 1,000 largest non–U.S. firms. More generally, the evidence in John Dunning's comprehensive work on MNCs supports this conclusion, *Multinationals, Technology, and Competitiveness* (London: Unwin Hyman, 1988), as does Michael Porter's *Competitive Advantage*.

8. My colleague Stephen Cohen coined the concept of national market logics in Borrus, Cohen, et. al, "Globalization and Production," BRIE Working Papers, no. 45 (Berkeley: BRIE, 1991).

9. For a discussion of this concept of technology trajectories, see Michael Borrus, "The Regional Architecture of Global Electronics: Trajectories, Linkages,

and Access to Technology" and the sources cited there, in Peter Gourevitch and Paolo Guierrieri, eds., *New Challenges to International Cooperation: Adjustment of Firms, Policies, and Organizations to Global Competition* (San Diego: UCSD, 1993).

10. For one effort to elucidate some of these variables—the state, and the legal, labor relations, and financial systems—as part of a formal analytic explaining national economic development, see John Zysman, "How Institutions Create Historically Rooted Trajectories of Growth" (Berkeley, BRIE, October 1993) draft manuscript. Some of the variables are similar to those used by Michael Porter, *Competitive Advantage*, however, to different ends in a decidedly different, albeit complementary, analytic.

11. On the guanxi network concept, see Gary G. Hamilton, "Competition and Organization: A Reexamination of Chinese Business Practices," paper prepared for the IGCC Conference *The China Circle: Regional Consequences of Evolving Relations Among the PRC, Taiwan, and Hong Kong-Macao*, Hong Kong, December 8–10, 1994.

12. For a fuller discussion of this U.S.–Japan comparison, see Borrus, *Competing for Control,* chapters 4 and 5.

13. For a fuller analysis, see Borrus, *Competing for Control.* The domestic market served as a launch market during the late 1970s and 1980s for, among other products, the VCR, Camcorder, Walkman, hand-held TV, fax machine, portable copier, and notebook personal computer (PC).

14. On the latter point, see Ichiro Uchida, "Restructuring of the Japanese Economy," in Eileen Doherty, ed., *Japanese Investment in Asia: International Production Strategies in a Rapidly Changing World* (Berkeley: Berkeley Roundtable on the International Economy, 1995).

15. By "open," I mean that key product specifications, especially the interface specifications that permit interoperability with the operating system or system hardware, are published or licensed and thus available to independent designers of systems or software, who can produce complementary or competing products.

16. For one elaboration of the concept of international production networks, see Dieter Ernst, "Networks, Market Structure and Technology Diffusion: A Conceptual Framework and Some Empirical Evidence," report prepared for the Organization for Economic Cooperation and Development, Paris, 1992. More generally, on network forms of organization, see Walter Powell's classic, "Neither Market Nor Hierarchy: Network Forms of Organization," *Research in Organizational Behavior*, vol. 12, 1990, pp. 295–336. The electronics case strongly confirms Powell's argument that the network form is not some intermediate mix of market or hierarchy. Indeed, far from being the optimal organizational poles, markets and hierarchies can be fruitfully thought of as specific forms of networks, with network relations being mediated in the former by price signals and buyer-seller transactions and in the latter by command signals and power relations.

17. See the discussion of sequentially increasing supply dependence in consumer electronics in Consumer Electronics Sector Working Group, *MIT Commission on Industrial Productivity*, "The Decline of U.S. Consumer Electronics Manufacturing: History, Hypotheses, Remedies," December 1988.

18. For an extended discussion of the supply base and architecture of supply concepts, see Michael Borrus, "Regional Architecture."

19. For the broad range of major component technologies involved, see the discussion in Borrus, "Regional Architecture."

20. The characterization of U.S. FDI is based on the BRIE U.S. Electronics FDI database, compiled from public sources and maintained by Greg Linden, and

supplemented by industry conversations. The characterization of Japanese electronics FDI in Asia that follows is consistent with and in part draws on data and detail in the chapters by Dennis Encarnation, Satashi Ohoka, Yasunori Baba, and Dieter Ernst, in Doherty, ed., *Japanese Production Networks*. See especially also Ken-ichi Takayasu and Yukiko Ishizaki, "The Changing International Division of Labor of Japanese Electronics Industry in Asia and Its Impact on the Japanese Economy," *RIM, Pacific Business and Industries* 1:27 (1995), pp. 2–21.

21. On the progression from consumer to industrial electronics in Taiwan, see Chung Chin, "The Changing Pattern of Division of Labor Across the Straits: Macro Overview and Sectoral Analysis on the Electronics Industry," Chung Hua Institution of Economic Research, Taipei, September, and Scott Callon, "Different Paths: The Rise of Taiwan and Singapore in the Global Personal Computer Industry," *Japan Development Bank Discussion Paper Series*, no. 9494, August 1994. More generally, on the development of Taiwan's information technology industry, see Kenneth L. Kraemer and Jason Dedrick, "Entrepreneurship, Flexibility and Policy Coordination: Taiwan's Information Technology Industry" (Irvine, CA: Center for Research on Information Technology and Organizations, 1995).

22. Based on press accounts, company annual reports, and Securities Exchange Commission (SEC) 10K filings as compiled by Greg Linden in the BRIE Asia FDI database. See Linden, "Apple Computer East Asian Manufacturing Affiliates," November 7, 1994, unpublished summary.

23. For Compaq, see Linden, "Compaq East Asian Manufacturing Affiliates," November 7, 1994, unpublished summary; for Hewlett-Packard, see Linden, "Hewlett-Packard East Asian Manufacturing Affiliates," November 9, 1994, unpublished summary; for Motorola, see Linden, "Motorola East Asian Manufacturing Affiliates," November 7, 1994, unpublished summary.

24. There were, of course, tremendous variations in the role played by state policy, and in the policies themselves, in the different countries of the region. In highlighting a few commonalities, I do not mean to slight those differences. The active role played in general by governments in the region has been explored in detail in a variety of scholarly works. See, for example, Robert Wade, *Governing the Market: Economic Theory and the Role of Government in East Asian Industrialization* (Princeton: Princeton University Press, 1990); Stephan Haggard, *Pathways from the Periphery: The Politics of Growth in the Newly Industrializing Countries* (Ithaca: Cornell University Press, 1988). More recently, see the excellent contributions in Andrew MacIntyre, ed., *Business and Government in Industrializing Asia* (Ithaca: Cornell University Press, 1994).

25. In focusing on Taiwanese and Singapore electronics capabilities, I am slighting the significant regional investment by the Korean chaebol who emerged during this period as major regionwide producers of consumer electronics and components. See, for example, Martin D. Bloom, "Globalization and the Korean Electronics Industry," *Pacific Review* 6:2 (1993): 119–126.

26. Callon, "Different Paths."

27. Chung Chin, "Changing Pattern," at p. 18.

28. Chung Chin, "Changing Pattern." Also see, Pete Engardio, "For ACER, Breaking Up Is Smart to Do," *Business Week*, July 4, 1994, p. 82ff; and Louis Kraar, "Your Next PC Could Be Made in Taiwan," *Fortune*, August 8, 1994, p. 90ff.

29. Engardio, "Acer," and Kraar, "Your Next PC." Also see, Pete Engardio, "A New High-Tech Dynasty?" *Business Week*, August 5, 1994, p. 90ff.

30. See the data in C. K. Paul Liu, Ying-Chuan Liu, and Hui-Lin Wu, "New Technologies, Industry and Trade—the Taiwan Experience," *Industry of Free China*, (Jan./Feb. 1990), p. 7ff.

31. For elaboration on the following, see, for example, G. S. Shieh, "Network Labor Process: The Subcontracting Networks in Manufacturing Industries of Taiwan," *Academia Sinica, Bulletin of the Institute of Ethnology,* (Spring 1991); Brian Levy and Wen-Jeng Kuo, "The Strategic Orientation of Firms and the Performance of Korea and Taiwan in Frontier Industries: Lessons from Comparative Case Studies of Keyboard and Personal Computer Assembly," *World Development* 19:4 (1990): 363ff. I have also drawn on an excellent paper by one of my graduate students, Fu-mei Chen, "From Comparative Advantage to Competitive Advantage: A Case Study of Taiwan's Electronics Industry," unpublished manuscript, May 21, 1994.

32. On European industrial districts, see the work on flexible specialization, notably, Michael Piore and Charles Sable, *The Second Industrial Divide: Possibilities for Prosperity,* (New York: Basic Books, 1984).

33. Representative estimates range from Apple's judgment that its Singapore operation can move a new product into production in half the time of its other operations, to Ming Chien, chairman of FIC, who estimates that motherboards can be completely changed out (with all attendant alterations to the rest of the system) in Taiwan in 2–3 weeks versus up to a year in the United States. On the former, see Singapore *Business Times,* Nov. 27, 1990, p. 14; on the latter, see Callon, "Different Paths."

34. Kraar, "Your Next PC," inferring from Dataquest estimates.

35. See Callon, "Different Paths," citing interviews in Singapore. Structured IC design approaches were pioneered in the United States at universities like Berkeley and CalTech, where many Asian engineers were formally trained.

36. For this and the following official figures, see Chung Chin, "Changing Patterns," pp. 19–20, citing MIC/III data.

37. For this and the following, see Chung Chin, "Changing Patterns," at pp. 21–23.

38. Engardio, "New High-Tech Dynasty," n. 34, and Kraar, "Your Next PC," n. 33.

39. This is also a principal conclusion of Takayasu and Ishizaki, "Changing International Division," who call this "intrafirm product-to-product division of labor," p. 11ff.

40. Some commentators treat the Chinese capitalized networks as hybrid forms of organization. See, for example, Dieter Ernst, "What Permits David to Defeat Goliath? The Taiwanese Model in the Computer Industry," unpublished manuscript, Berkeley Roundtable on the International Economy (BRIE), 1998.

41. I derive these solely from the electronics case, but there is broad support in the literature on strategic alliances that tends to emphasize the first three, whereas the fourth may be most significant at least in information technology markets. See, for example, John Hagedoorn and Jos Schakenraad, "Inter-Firm Partnerships and Cooperative Strategies in Core Technologies," in Christopher Freeman and Luc Soete, *New Explorations in the Economics of Technical Change* (London: Pinter, 1990), pp. 3–37.

42. This is broadly consistent with work on the location decisions of multinationals. In addition to Michael Porter, *The Competitiveness of Nations* (New York: Free Press, 1990) and John Dunning, *The Globalization of Business* (New York: Routledge, 1993) see John Cantwell, "The Globalization of Technology: What Remains of the Product Cycle Model?" *Cambridge Journal of Economics* 19 (1995), pp. 155–174.

43. In fact, the opportunity to drive development out of Asia is already appearing in a set of significant potential product markets. These include broadcast media where firms like Hong Kong's TVB and Murdoch's Star TV are pioneering direct

broadcast TV transmission, software where indigenous concepts could lead in new directions, and segments of the wireless communication markets, where, for example, Motorola projects that China will pass the United States to become its largest market for pagers in the next few years.

44. Even with the development of distinctive regional rather than national sources of control, I would not expect the Japanese, U.S. and indigenous Asian networks to converge much. They will continue to be differentiated by the balance of regional emphasis in their operations. As long as Japanese, U.S., and indigenous firms continue to be driven by a very different balance among local linkages, strategies, industrial structures, policies, local capital markets, and labor market influences, their network differences are likely to persist even if they converge in competitive purpose or in the geographic reach of operations.

PART V

HOME-ECONOMY AND HOST-ECONOMY EFFECTS

10

Is Japan Hollowing Out?

Yoshihide Ishiyama

Japan has recently gone through waves of yen appreciation. As annual averages, the yen-dollar rate was 145 in 1990, 135 in 1991, 127 in 1992, 111 in 1993, and 102 in 1994. The rate went up further to 94 in 1995. Rapid yen appreciation is, naturally, causing radical changes in the Japanese economy on many fronts, including the deepening of the recession. The immediate impact of a higher yen is reduction in export revenues in yen terms, and manufacturing corporations suffer. In a higher yen environment, nonmanufacturing corporations should be increasing profits because many of them depend on imports and sell their services on the domestic market. However, profit increases in the nonmanufacturing sector usually do not spread well to the rest of the economy in the form of lower sales prices or larger investment, because the competitive pressure in the nonmanufacturing sector is insufficient. By contrast, the manufacturing sector exerts a more powerful influence on the rest of the economy, both when it contracts and when it expands.

There is no inherent reason to presume that the manufacturing sector is more "important" than other industries. A nation needs a variety of industries, both manufacturing and nonmanufacturing. However, the manufacturing-nonmanufacturing distinction is still useful as an analytical framework because they behave differently. Although individual manufacturing industries differ, on the whole they pay somewhat higher wages than nonmanufacturing industries do and they tend to lead the overall economic growth. Also, the trade outcome largely depends on international competitiveness (however it is defined) and the productivity of the manufacturing industry.

This chapter does not attempt to conduct a full comparative study of Japanese and foreign manufacturing corporations; it attempts only to interpret the behavior of the manufacturing industry in Japan in the 1980s and the early 1990s. However, relying on works on deindustrialization in the U.S. economy, such as Lawrence (1984), we know fairly well what happened in the 1970s and the 1980s. The United States experienced sharp dollar appreciation in the first half of the 1980s and Japan yen appreciation in the second half of the 1980s and the early 1990s. I include references to the United States in the following discussion.

To extract the unique behavior of the Japanese manufacturing industry, I examined a simple measure—the share of manufacturing real gross domestic product (GDP) in total real GDP. Obviously, this measure is related to the growth of domestic demand, exports, and imports, so I will discuss these components as well. In Japan, the manufacturing share in real GDP has been declining since 1992, which has raised a concern about "hollowing out." I shall define hollowing out and argue that it should not be a cause for concern for Japan. If anything, the problem for Japan is rather that the hollowing out one would expect under a sharp exchange rate appreciation (real as well as nominal) would not likely occur easily in Japan. In other words, Japan's manufacturing industry seems to be much more resilient than that of other countries when faced with currency appreciation; after a short while, Japan's manufacturing corporations manage to increase efficiency in producing existing products, upgrade products, or move to new product lines to defend turf against imports and sustain export revenue. A drop in the manufacturing share in real GDP occurred only in 1986. For 1987 through 1989, the manufacturing share continued to rise, and at the same time foreign direct investment (FDI) by the manufacturing sector was increasing sharply, as can be expected. Acceleration of FDI during this period went hand in hand with acceleration of domestic business investment and production. During this period, manufacturing industry managed to maintain real exports relative to real GDP at a constant level (they increased as fast as real GDP). During the same period, real imports increased faster than real GDP, so their proportion to real GDP went up, which is natural. To summarize, in Japan exports held up well despite a high yen and increasing FDI, and manufacturing output increased very quickly despite sharply increasing real imports and increasing FDI. These unique phenomena require explanation, but, even so, the increasing manufacturing share in real GDP in this high yen period is surprising. (Strictly speaking, the yen rate weakened somewhat in 1989 and 1990.)

A comparison of the early 1990s and the second half of the 1980s yields useful similarities and differences. The manufacturing share in real GDP has been declining since 1992 and not in one year only—an outstanding difference. Other differences are that real imports and FDI initially slowed but increased very sharply in 1994. The similarity is that in the early 1990s as well real exports held up well, so that real exports relative to real GDP remained roughly constant. Stronger yen appreciation began in spring 1993; therefore I should emphasize what happened in 1994 and after. If this finding can be upheld, we can ignore some perversity in the relationship between the high yen and real imports, as well as between the high yen and FDI. Although the behavior of Japan's manufacturing industry in the early 1990s is easier to understand than that in the second half of the 1980s, because the manufacturing share in real GDP has been declining, the unique phenomenon of real exports holding up well despite a high yen and increasing FDI still remains and requires explanation. Moreover, the share decline of the manufacturing industry seems to be halting in 1995, staying at a very high 30 percent, and could slightly increase again thereafter. (Note that the share in the early 1980s was about 27 percent.) Thus, one finds a situation similar to that of the second half of the 1980s and one must conclude that the behavior of Japan's manufacturing corporations has not really changed from the 1980s to the 1990s.

If true, this scenario is both good and bad for the Japanese economy. It is good in the sense that the manufacturing sector can again contribute to the return of more normal economic growth but simultaneously bad because economic recovery led by manufacturing sows the seed for swelling trade surpluses and a surge of yen appreciation. The strength and resiliency of the manufacturing industry in Japan counteracts the nonmanufacturing sector's weakness in not growing more rapidly and increasing its share in real GDP. Japan needs to eliminate the vicious cycle of trade surpluses, higher yen, and recession and should gradually reduce the manufacturing share in real GDP, although this would not guarantee resolution. Such a gradual reduction of manufacturing, of course, has to be realized with a stronger nonmanufacturing industry and without recessions in the manufacturing sector. Japan will hollow out only if the manufacturing industry undercuts such a gradually declining share. The inescapable conclusion, then, is that Japan's hollowing out is unlikely in the foreseeable future. In fact, we should be worrying more about the obverse of hollowing out.

The Trend in the Manufacturing Share of Real GDP

In Japan in the 1980s, the share of the manufacturing sector in real GDP was 28.5 percent on average (an arithmetical average for 1980–1989). Real GDP produced by the manufacturing industry grew faster than real GDP, so the manufacturing share continued to rise in the 1980s. The only exception was for 1986 (see table 10.1.) In the 1980s, average annual growth rates of real GDP and real value-added of manufacturing were 4.0 percent and 5.7 percent, respectively. Thus, the share of the manufacturing industry increased from 26.8 percent in 1980 to 30.6 percent in 1989.

As table 10.1 shows, this share increased until 1991, when it peaked at 32.1 percent. As long as manufacturing real value-added grows faster than real GDP, the overall economy grows. However, one may wonder how long this upward trend in real GDP can continue. Clearly, it cannot be a permanent trend because a 100 percent manufacturing economy for Japan is inconceivable. Incidentally, the manufacturing share in real GDP was roughly constant in the 1970s in Japan: 25.1 percent in 1970 and 24.6 percent in 1975. The decade average was 25.7 percent. As I will argue later, proximate causes of the increasing trend in the manufacturing share in real GDP in the 1980s were increases in net export of manufactures until 1985 and rapid increases in domestic demand for manufactures for 1985–1990. Obviously, increases in net exports for 1985–1990 were driven by a very low yen level.

The decline in the share since 1992 seems to be largely a temporary phenomenon, under the strong influence of a sharply higher yen. In 1993, real domestic demand for manufactures declined steeply, and real net exports of manufactures also declined. In this sense, the recent decline in the manufacturing share in real GDP is largely a domestic phenomenon. In a simple accounting framework, I will break down manufacturing output into domestic demand and net export.

The decline in the manufacturing share in real GDP since 1992 ended in 1994. (The share in constant 1990 prices went up from 26.4 percent in 1994 to 27.4 percent in 1995 but declined slightly to 27.0 percent in 1996.) From these figures the concern about hollowing out seems unjustified. We know that in 1994 manufac-

Table 10.1 Japanese Manufacturing Share in Real GDP (In Constant 1985 Prices)

	Manufacturing real value-added				Growth rate of real GDP (%)
	Nominal value (¥ trillion)	Growth rate (%)	Share of real GDP (%)	Share of nominal GDP (%)	
1980	71.5	5.8	26.8	29.2	3.6
1981	74.8	4.4	27.1	29.1	3.6
1982	78.1	4.4	27.4	29.0	3.2
1983	81.5	4.4	27.9	29.0	2.7
1984	88.4	8.5	29.0	29.7	4.3
1985	94.7	7.1	29.5	29.5	5.0
1986	92.1	−2.4	28.0	28.8	2.6
1987	98.9	7.4	28.9	28.5	4.1
1988	108.0	9.2	29.7	28.7	6.2
1989	116.6	8.0	30.6	28.9	4.7
Average 1980s		5.7	28.5	29.0	4.0
1990	125.5	7.6	31.4	29.1	4.8
1991	133.4	6.3	32.1	29.1	4.3
1992	130.8	−2.0	31.1	28.0	1.1
1993	127.5	−2.5	30.4	26.8	−0.2
1994	126.2[a]	−1.0[a]	29.9[a]	26.0[a]	0.5

Source: Economic Planning Agency, National Economic Accounts Annual.

[a]Estimates by author.

turing real value-added declined 1.3 percent and real GDP grew 0.5 percent. But the manufacturing share in real GDP of 30.2 percent in 1994 was approximately at the same high level as in 1989.

I would also like to discuss the second half of the 1990s. Likely the growth rate of real GDP in the second half of the 1990s will average around 1 percent. (Historically, such a growth rate is unusually low, but the Japanese economy is still burdened with adjustments in excess capacity of production and excess employment, as well as the depressive effect from financial institutions' bad loans. In low growth years, the growth rate of manufacturing output does not much exceed that of real GDP.) This 1 percent growth may offer a chance for real GDP and manufacturing output to grow roughly at the same rate, in which case the manufacturing share in real GDP would stay roughly constant, and hollowing out in the sense of the declining manufacturing share would not occur.

Should the share decline continue over the long term, which is not likely, there would be cause for concern. But even in that case, characterization as hollowing out would not be appropriate if one keeps a historical perspective. Around 1990 Japan's manufacturing industry had overgrown from the undervalued yen and the irrational bubble (the late 1980s), which caused trade disputes and a burst of yen appreciation in recent years. A mild long-term decline of manufacturing in Japan, reversing the trend in the 1980s, will be desirable and likely will even be encouraged by government policy.

The Manufacturing Share in Employment Since 1980

Before proceeding to a more detailed discussion of the manufacturing share in real GDP, I will review employment and labor productivity figures. Table 10.2 shows that in the 1980s employment (including the self-employed) in the manufacturing sector grew at a slightly slower rate than total employment in the economy. Simple arithmetical averages over the decade were 0.9 percent for manufacturing employment and 1.0 percent for total employment. Thus, the manufacturing share in employment, which was 24.8 percent in 1980, declined only slightly to 24.2 percent in 1989. The decade average was 24.6 percent.

Perhaps this minute decline in the manufacturing share in employment in the 1980s can be ignored. Nobody in the 1980s expressed a concern about hollowing out on that basis. The arithmetical averages of labor productivity (real GDP per employee) in the 1980s were 3.0 percent for the entire economy and 4.7 percent for the manufacturing sector. Labor productivity growth in manufacturing is higher than the economy average and, as a result, the price of manufacturing output has been declining relative to the GDP deflator and so has stimulated the demand for manufactures. The net export of manufactures has been high, so that high labor productivity growth has, by and large, translated not into any significant decline

Table 10.2 Japanese Manufacturing Share in Employment

	Manufacturing employment			Growth in labor productivity	
	Number (millions)	Growth rate (%)	Share in total employment (%)	Manufacturing (%)	Total economy (%)
1980	13.8	1.9	24.8	3.8	2.9
1981	14.0	1.0	24.8	3.6	2.8
1982	13.9	−0.5	24.5	5.0	2.4
1983	14.1	1.6	24.5	2.7	1.2
1984	14.4	2.0	24.9	6.4	4.0
1985	14.5	1.0	25.0	6.1	4.4
1986	14.4	−0.6	24.7	−2.2	1.7
1987	14.3	−1.3	24.1	8.6	3.2
1988	14.5	2.0	24.2	7.0	4.4
1989	14.8	2.1	24.2	5.9	2.6
Average 1980s		0.9	24.6	4.7	3.0
1990	15.1	1.4	24.1	6.0	2.6
1991	15.5	3.0	24.9	3.0	2.2
1992	15.7	1.2	24.4	−2.8	0.0
1993	15.3	−2.4	23.7	−0.5	−0.6
1994	15.0	−2.2	23.2	0.0[a]	0.5

Source: Management and Coordination Agency, Labor Force Statistics.

[a]Estimate by author.

in the manufacturing share in employment but into the high growth of demand for manufactures. As noted, growth of manufacturing output has been vigorous.

More recently, however, manufacturing employment declined in absolute numbers in 1993 and 1994, so the manufacturing share in employment declined fairly sharply in these years. A similar 2-year decline occurred in 1986 and 1987 under a high yen. The decline of 730,000 jobs between 1992 and 1994, however, meant a more severe employment adjustment than the decline of only 230,000 jobs between 1985 and 1987. To the 730,000 manufacturing jobs lost between 1992 and 1994, add another 400,000 manufacturing jobs lost in 1995. Principally because of this large adjustment, manufacturing employment has now largely stabilized.

For the second half of the 1990s, the growth rate of manufacturing employment will be much lower than the average annual 0.9 percent observed in the 1980s. If real GDP of manufacturing on average grows at 3 percent annually, the 3 percent labor productivity growth in the manufacturing industry implies that no growth will occur in manufacturing employment, and the manufacturing share in employment will decline as long as total employment grows at all. For better or worse, most researchers continue to forecast the labor force growth in the second half of the 1990s at only 0.4 percent. This means that the manufacturing share in employment will decline only very gradually—only by 0.1 percent annually in the case of constant manufacturing employment. This figure depends not on the assumed 3 percent in real GDP growth but on the reasonable assumption that labor productivity in manufacturing grows somewhat faster than average labor productivity in the economy as a whole. Of course, labor productivity growth can be higher than output growth in the manufacturing industry, in which case manufacturing employment declines in absolute number and the manufacturing share in employment declines much faster. However, such a scenario could be safely ruled out as a long-term phenomenon. Thus, on the basis of the employment share of the manufacturing sector, the concern about hollowing out in the Japanese economy seems to be unjustified.

Evolution of Domestic Demand and Net Export

The high growth of manufacturing real value-added in the 1980s can be broken down in a simple accounting framework into the growth of domestic demand and the growth of net export. Perhaps the first analyst who adopted this framework for the manufacturing industry was Lawrence (1984). However, my method is different from his. Lawrence looked at the identity:

$$y = d + x - m = d + n,$$

where y = manufacturing output, x = real exports, m = real imports, n = real net exports, and d = real domestic demand.

It is important that this is an aggregate supply, aggregate demand relationship for manufactures, and y should be interpreted as gross production (including the value of intermediate inputs used by the manufacturing industry) or shipment, not value-added. In order to transform this relationship into value-added terms, Lawrence used the input-output table and computed direct as well as indirect effects of x and m on y along the way.

Because the input-output table is not readily available for every year, I adopt a simpler accounting framework, using the raw data of gross production rather than value-added. Consequently, d is not only final consumption and investment but also consumption of manufactures as intermediates by all industries, including the manufacturing industry itself. Lawrence called d domestic use rather than domestic demand, and his naming will be followed hereafter.

On this interpretation, the above identity can be written in the following form of growth rates: y/y = (% share of d in y) d/d + (% share of n in y) n/n.

There may be an objection to using gross production data. However, real gross production and real value-added show broadly similar movements, so conclusions derived from the observation of gross production apply to activity in terms of value-added. Domestic use of manufactures in real terms can simply be derived by subtracting real net exports from real gross production. The estimates of real exports and real imports do pose statistical problems. Here, they are computed with volume and unit value indexes in the Outline of Foreign Trade (customs clearance statistics) compiled by the Ministry of Finance. Real exports is the total value of exports (f.o.b.) in constant 1985 prices. All exports are assumed to be manufactures (in fact almost 100 percent of them are), and real exports in years other than 1985 are computed using the total export volume index compiled in the above statistics. Real import of manufactures is computed by taking the value of manufactures imports (c.i.f.) in 1985 as the base (31 percent of imports were manufactures in 1985) and constructing an import volume index for manufactures with import unit values (in yen terms) for individual categories of manufactures imports.

Table 10.3 shows the summary result of this decomposition of the growth of y into d and n. The first point is that the growth of real gross production of the manufacturing industry in the 1980s is on average 6.0 percent and very close to 5.7 percent on the real value-added basis; real intermediate inputs have been roughly a constant proportion of real gross production. The growth rate of real domestic use was 6.2 percent and the growth rate of real net exports was 4.2 percent. Decade averages suggest that the growth of real gross production (and hence real value-added) of the manufacturing industry was led by domestic use rather than net exports. However, decade averages are misleading because the 1980–1985 period and the 1986–1989 period showed sharply different behaviors. From 1980 to 1985, real exports, real imports, and net exports increased respectively at 9.0 percent, 6.0 percent, and 10.2 percent on average. The annual 10.2 percent growth of real net exports is indeed high. In contrast, from 1986 to 1989 they increased 2.3 percent, 19.6 percent, and –4.8 percent, respectively. Real net exports made a negative contribution in this period. The reason for this changeover after 1986 should be obvious—a sharply higher yen. The trend of low growth of real exports and high growth of real imports (of manufactures) since 1986 continues.

However, the ratio of real exports to real imports still remains high. This ratio was 4.45 to 1 in 1980 and 1.86 to 1 in 1994. It is well known that for net exports to grow at all and contribute to the growth of manufacturing output, real exports have only to grow faster than the growth rate of real imports divided by this export-import ratio. In this sense, Japan's real net export in manufactures can still make a substantial contribution to the growth of manufacturing output. For example, in 1992, real exports, real imports, and real net exports were Y50.3 trillion, Y21.1 trillion, and Y29.2

Table 10.3 Japanese Growth of Real Domestic Use and Real Net Exports (in 1985 prices)

	Growth of real manufacturing gross production (%)	Growth of real domestic use (%)	Growth of real exports (%)	Growth of real imports (%)	Growth of real net exports (%)	% Point contribution	
						Domestic use	Net exports
Average 1980s	6.0	6.2	6.3	11.4	4.2	5.7	0.3
1989	6.4	7.0	4.3	12.7	-1.1	6.5	-0.1
1990	6.4	6.8	5.3	10.2	1.5	6.3	0.1
1991	5.2	5.6	2.5	3.1	2.2	5.0	0.2
1992	-2.7	-3.7	1.5	-4.1	6.2	-3.3	0.4
1993	-3.1	-2.7	-1.7	6.9	-8.2	-2.5	-0.6
1994			1.7	20.0	-13.4		-1.0

Source: See table 10.1.

trillion, respectively. In that year real net exports increased 6.2 percent (see table 10.3) and made a percentage point contribution of 0.4 to real gross production, which decreased 2.7 percent. Real net exports of Y29.2 trillion may look small relative to real gross production of the manufacturing industry in that year, which was Y379.4 trillion (the production is 7.7 percent). However, we should remember that the denominator is gross production, which is almost three times as large as value-added; it is no exaggeration to say that 7.7 percent net exports is enormous.

In recent years, the contraction of real net exports has been making a substantial negative contribution to growth production. In 1993 real net exports contracted 8.2 percent and made a negative percentage point contribution of 0.6 to real gross production. The contraction of real net exports became larger in 1994 at 13.4 percent and made a percentage point contribution of 1.0. In 1994, therefore, real net exports accounted for more than 100 percent of the contraction of manufacturing real gross production. In this sense, it is true that the manufacturing sector was temporarily experiencing difficulties from stagnant domestic demand and sharply increasing imports.

These developments in 1993 and 1994 are important in an interpretation of the behavior of Japan's manufacturing corporations. As shown in table 10.1, the manufacturing share in real GDP decreased in both years. However, while real imports continued to increase, real exports declined in 1993 and increased in 1994. (In raw data, imports declined 7.3 percent in 1993 and increased 4.3 percent in 1994 in yen terms; exports declined 6.9 percent in 1993 and increased 0.4 percent in yen terms. In dollar terms, imports increased 5.7 percent in 1993 and 13.5 percent in 1994; exports increased 6.2 percent in 1993 and 9.3 percent in 1994.) Significantly, in 1994 the manufacturing sector managed to increase real exports by 1.7 percent (see table 10.3).

The declining manufacturing share in real GDP can result from either declining real exports, increasing real imports, or declining domestic demand for manufactures, in proportion to real GDP. Over the long term, the first of these does not occur. As table 10.4 shows, the real export–real GDP ratio did go down in 1986 and in 1987, but it can be viewed as the initial impact of a higher yen, before corporations intensified their efforts to increase exports. The decline of this ratio in 1993 and 1994 from that in 1992 can be viewed in a similar way. However, the decline to 11.8 percent in 1993 and 11.9 percent in 1994 from 12.0 percent in 1992 is very small, which suggests that the export strength of Japan's manufacturing corporations is greater in the mid-1990s than in the second half of the 1980s. Of course, I do not deny the effect of strong or weak domestic demand on exports; domestic demand growth in the mid-1990s was much weaker than in the second half of the 1980s, so the pressure to export was stronger. Nevertheless, it is notable that real exports returned to positive growth while domestic demand strengthened, albeit slightly, in 1994.

As declining real exports were not the reason for the decline in the manufacturing share in real GDP in 1994, increasing real imports and declining real domestic demand were. The growth of real imports in 1994 was spectacular at 20 percent, and hence caused a large negative 1.0 percent point contribution of real net exports to manufacturing production in that year. However, a sharp increase in the real import-real GDP ratio, as observed in 1994, was not likely to continue, because Japan's manufacturers in the affected industries also raised efficiency and upgraded their products to defend their turf in the domestic market. The Economic

Table 10.4 Ratios of Japanese Real Exports and
Real Imports to Real GDP

	Real exports (%)	Real imports (%)
1980	11.2	2.5
1981	11.9	2.7
1982	11.3	2.6
1983	11.7	2.6
1984	13.0	3.0
1985	13.1	3.0
1986	12.6	3.5
1987	12.1	3.9
1988	12.1	4.7
1989	12.1	5.1
1990	12.1	5.4
1991	11.9	5.3
1992	12.0	5.0
1993	11.8	5.4
1994	11.9	6.4

Planning Agency (1995) pointed out that many of the sharply increasing imports were low value-added types, such as a shift from expensive German cars to cheaper American cars. Faced with such a shift, Japan's manufacturers have also been putting cheaper products on the domestic market. In 1995 real exports increased only 3.8 percent, while real imports surged 22.1 percent. If real net exports begin to grow at 2 percent, for example, real domestic demand for manufactures has only to grow at the same 2 percent to achieve a 2 percent growth in real GDP of manufacturing industries. Because real exports were about twice as large as real imports in the mid-1990s, for real net exports to grow 2 percent, real exports have to grow only 1 percent faster than half of the growth rate of real imports, at least initially. If real GDP growth falls short of growth of domestic demand for manufactures in this example, the manufacturing share in real GDP actually goes up, which was also as likely as its stabilization for the 1995–1997 period.

In summary, I emphasize two points. First, the year of a large negative contribution from import growth, like 1994, is an exception, and real net exports are likely to make a positive contribution, albeit a small one in the environment of the 1990s, to the growth of manufacturing output in more typical years. Second, real domestic demand for manufactures is likely to grow at least as fast as real GDP, and, as a result, the manufacturing share in real GDP will either stabilize or increase in more typical years. I have argued that behind this lies the behavior of Japan's manufacturing corporations.

Behavior of Japan's Manufacturing Corporations

So far, I have been describing the behavior of Japan's manufacturing corporations. In this section, I attempt to be more analytical. In fact, description of the behavior is the easy part; its interpretation is more difficult, all the more so when FDI enters the picture, because FDI is an integral part of the strategy of many manufacturing corporations, particularly in a higher yen environment. Table 10.5 shows the figures of FDI by manufacturing industries since fiscal 1985. These notification statistics compiled by the Ministry of Finance have several well-known drawbacks and do not directly relate to the size of overseas production. However, it is the only information available for my breakdown by industry (and by country), so I use it here.

Table 10.5 shows that the total manufacturing FDI grew sharply in the high yen period of fiscal 1986 through 1989. In the 1990s, the increase began in fiscal 1993. The apparent link between a higher yen and larger FDI is common to both of these periods. Annual manufacturing total FDI figures can be compared with the following growth rates of real business investment (capital spending) undertaken by the manufacturing industry on the domestic front. These figures (percentages) come from the capital stock statistics compiled by the Economic Planning Agency and are based on constant 1985 prices.

1986	1987	1988	1989	1990	1991	1992	1993	1994
−5.8	−0.6	−19.0	22.9	13.2	11.5	−14.4	−18.1	−13.5

Thus, one can observe a similar pattern showing that, in the initial two or three years of yen appreciation, real business investment goes down, while FDI starts to increase almost simultaneously with yen appreciation. Real business investment by the manufacturing industry began to increase in 1988, side by side with increasing FDI. Similarly, in 1995 real business investment registered an increase of 5.2 percent, again, side by side with increasing FDI. Of course, magnitudes differ, but domestic business investment and FDI seem to be unchanged qualitatively over these two periods.

Incidentally, the breakdown by industry in table 10.5 is interesting. In fiscal 1994, the electrical machinery industry was still the largest investor, but its FDI declined 4.6 percent and the chemicals industry expanded its FDI 49.3 percent to become a close second to the electrical machinery industry. The transport machinery industry was the third largest investor and increased its FDI 114.5 percent. The manufacturing total FDI increased 23.8 percent. Although single-year changes cannot be a solid guide, dominant foreign investors in Japan cast doubt on the thesis of Kojima (1995) that Japan's FDI is predominantly undertaken by industries that have lost comparative advantage in international trade. Rather, Japan's dominant foreign investment is in those industries that have strong export competitiveness, and exports continue on a large scale. Another notable fact is that, although table 10.5 does not show it, manufacturing FDI to Asia increased 42 percent to $5.2 billion, beyond FDI to North America ($4.8 billion) in fiscal 1994.

I can now begin to interpret a representative manufacturing firm of Japan, which simultaneously undertakes domestic production, exports, and FDI (overseas production) and increases them at the same time, at least after most of the adjustment to a higher yen is complete. A manufacturing firm that neither exports nor undertakes FDI but competes with imports on the domestic market can be interpreted in a broadly similar way.

Table 10.5 Outward Direct Investment by Manufacturing Industries ($ million)

Fiscal year	1985	1986	1987	1988	1989	1990	1991	1992	1993	1994
Food	90	127	328	419	1,300	820	632	517	888	1,260
Textiles	28	63	206	317	533	796	616	428	498	641
Wood and pulp	15	57	317	604	555	314	312	431	346	140
Chemicals	133	355	910	1,292	2,109	2,292	1,602	2,015	1,742	2,601
Iron and metal	385	328	786	1,367	1,591	1,047	907	824	754	1,038
General machinery	352	626	687	1,432	1,762	1,454	1,284	1,104	1,171	1,622
Electrical machinery	513	987	2,421	3,041	4,480	5,684	2,296	1,817	2,762	2,634
Transport machinery	627	828	1,473	1,281	2,053	1,872	1,996	1,188	942	2,021
Others	208	435	703	4,051	1,901	1,207	2,666	1,732	2,029	1,826
Manufacturing total	2,352	3,806	7,832	13,805	16,284	15,486	12,311	10,057	11,132	13,784

Source: Ministry of Finance, Direct Investment Notifications Statistics.

A model for the behavior of Japan's representative manufacturing firm is a firm in monopolistic competition. In many textbooks on international trade, one sees such a firm supplying the domestic market and the foreign market (exports). For the moment, I will ignore FDI. This firm maximizes profit from domestic sales and exports. I will assume that the domestic market and the foreign market have downward-sloping demand curves for the differentiated product that the oligopolies produce,

$$D = p^{-0}$$
$$D^* = p^{*-0}$$

where D is the volume demanded, p is the price and ^{0} is the price elasticity of demand. The asterisk indicates foreign variables. Note that p* is in foreign currency, so sales in the foreign market must be converted to domestic currency. The exchange rate is e, which is the number of yen per unit of foreign currency.

Our imaginary firm has a certain fixed-cost, FC, which is incurred regardless of the production level, and a constant marginal cost,

$$wl + vm,$$

where w is the wage rate and v is the price of the intermediate input. The l is the amount of labor required to produce one unit of output, and m is the amount of intimidate input required to produce one unit of output, both assumed the constant.

In such a setup, the total cost of producing output X is

$$FC + wlX + vmX.$$

The condition for maximum profit is that the marginal cost is equal to marginal revenues in each of the markets, domestic and foreign. If we write

$$X = Q + E \text{ (Q is domestic sale volume, E is export volume)},$$

then we can determine optimal Q and E and hence X and p and p*. Thus,

$$p(0 - 1/0) = wl + vm$$
$$p^* (0^* - 1/0^*) = (wl + wm)/e.$$

The total revenue from producing and selling Q and E is

$$pQ + ep^*E,$$

and the profit is

$$pQ + ep^*E - FC - (wl + vm)X.$$

Because of FC, the average cost is always higher than the marginal cost and declines as X is increased.

Now consider the case of domestic production and FDI or overseas production, without export. The level of overseas production is Z. What are the profit-maximizing conditions? The requirement that the marginal revenue equals the marginal cost in each market does not change, but in the second marginal condition above, the marginal cost changes to $(w^*l + v^*m)$. Comparing the case of domestic production and export, on one hand, and the case of domestic and overseas production, on the other, one sees that the two cases are of equal value to the firm if the cost conditions remain exactly the same in the two cases. Under such conditions, optimal Q will be unchanged and optimal E will be the same as optimal Z.

However, overseas production usually requires its own fixed cost, eFC^*, and the marginal cost there, $e(w^*l + v^*m)$, will differ from that at home. Therefore, the profit will be

$$pQ + ep^*Z - FC - eFC^* - (wl + vm)Q - e(w^*l + v^*m)Z$$

In a simple framework of a fixed demand curve in the foreign market, the firm simply compares these two profits and chooses either export or overseas production. Krugman (1983), in essentially the same model as mine here, shows that, simply put, export is chosen when it is cheaper to produce at home, and overseas production is chosen when it is cheaper to do so. Amano (1986) uses a little more complex model, in which the profit maximization by the foreign firm in the foreign market is also considered, and numerically compares profits in the export case and the overseas production case with hypothetical values of relevant parameters. In either approach, the choice is either/or, and export and overseas production are not undertaken simultaneously.

This framework of analysis is useful as one conceptualizes the behavior of the firm switching from export to overseas production. Without doubt, some Japanese manufacturing firms do this after yen appreciation, comparing two levels of profit. A previously exporting firm has to reduce export volume because the marginal cost for the foreign market $(wl + vm)/e$ is higher with smaller e (yen appreciation). With smaller E, p^* goes up but not as much as the extent of yen appreciation, so the price in yen terms, ep^*, is lower than before. With smaller total production, X, the average cost becomes higher. Thus, the profit (in yen terms) becomes smaller not only in the foreign market but in the domestic market as well. When eFC^* plus $e(w^*l + v^*m)Z$ is sufficiently small, then our firm will switch from export to overseas production. If this is the case, the switch to overseas production reduces domestic production.

Although this is certainly one interpretation of the behavior of manufacturing corporations after yen appreciation, most major Japanese firms undertake both export and overseas production simultaneously and change the balance between the two in favor of the latter after yen appreciation. For example, in an interview with the Japan Institute for Overseas Investment (1995), the managing director of Matsushita Electric Industrial (Mr. Kakuichi Yamamoto) says that the current proportions of domestic sale, export, and overseas production at Matsushita are 50:30:20, but the company wants to change them to 50:25:25. Precise figures of course differ among companies, but the common trend now is to increase the proportion of overseas production.

One can interpret such a simultaneous undertaking of exports and overseas production as a mixed strategy. The exchange rate can always go both ways, and it is dangerous to rely singly on either export or overseas production. If this interpretation is correct, many firms in Japan are undertaking both activities aiming at, not maximum profit, but stable profit. However, a more compelling interpretation is that FDI and overseas production make it possible to expand the demand curve in the foreign market, which is not possible by producing only at home. Overseas production makes it possible to create the image of a local producer and to find previously unknown opportunities. Most of Japan's manufacturing companies cite the growing demand in the foreign market as the foremost reason for FDI, and this is precisely the expansion of the demand curve that cannot be realized without FDI or overseas production. If this interpretation is correct, an expansion in overseas production need not reduce exports and domestic production.

To summarize, at least three reasons explain why yen appreciation does not result in the reduction in real exports and manufacturing output relative to real GDP, despite larger FDI. First, on the product portfolio front, Japan's manufacturing corporations manage to switch to products that are not produced, or produced only in small quantities, in other countries. For such products, it is relatively easy to raise foreign currency prices after yen appreciation without losing much export volume. Sazanami (1989) cites the example of VCRs, but in recent years there are other examples. Table 10.6 shows a very characteristic change in 1994 in Japan's export structure and the product strategy of manufacturing corporations behind it. The shift toward sophisticated machinery and parts is progressing fast. It is particularly notable that Japan is sharply increasing exports not only of electronic parts and auto parts but office machinery also. In the case of the automobile industry, finished automobile exports declined from $58.97 billion in 1993 to $56.91 billion in 1994, a decline of 3.5 percent, or $2.06 billion, but auto parts increased from $14.86 billion in 1993 to $17.56 billion in 1994, an increase of 18.2 percent, or $2.7 billion. In absolute dollar amounts, auto parts exports more than compensated for the decline in finished automobile exports. However, although such a shift in product portfolio is taking place over many products, my model cannot capture this aspect. A multiple products model will be required for a formal analysis of this behavior. Here, I say merely that Japan's manufacturing corporations have been demonstrating remarkable capability in shifting their product portfolio, particularly in a high yen situation, and in sustaining their exports.

Second, Japan's manufacturing corporations can intensify cost-reduction efforts in a high yen situation. They have indeed been reducing w, l, v, and m. A higher yen automatically reduces prices of imported parts and materials, so v has been declining significantly. To illustrate, MITI reported that, in its survey of 359 corporations conducted in January 1995, 127 had been reducing costs of intermediate inputs. In this group of 127 corporations, 83 said that the high yen was the reason. And for the remaining corporations surveyed by MITI, as many as 104 answered that they had increased purchases of imported intermediates.

Third, increases in FDI and overseas production have either reduced export and domestic production or have expanded demand curves in foreign markets without really reducing export and domestic production. As examples, overseas

Table 10.6 Export Value Increases and Percentage Point Contributions by Region

	Percentage point contribution[a]										Export value in 1994 ($ billion)
	World[b]		United States		European Union[c]		Southeast Asia		China		
	1993	1994	1993	1994	1993	1994	1993	1994	1993	1994	
Office machinery	8.8	5.5	7.3	2.9	–1.3	0.7	8.8	–3.2	0.2	0.1	29.14
TV sets and radios	–11.5	–6.0	1.3	–1.3	–4.8	–6.1	0.8	2.7	5.2	–4.7	4.26
Electronic parts	26.1	32.9	7.4	7.6	1.2	3.4	16.2	19.9	0.3	0.7	29.31
Automobiles (ex. parts)	–5.9	–3.5	4.0	4.4	–3.1	–2.1	1.7	–1.3	0.9	–0.5	56.91
Auto parts	18.7	18.2									17.56
Textiles and products	–2.3	–1.8	–0.2	–0.3	–1.8	0.2	–2.3	–1.9	1.9	5.1	8.37
Iron and steel	8.9	2.3	0.4	–3.6	–0.5	–0.2	9.1	8.8	11.2	–4.9	14.87
Total	6.3	9.6	2.8	3.4	–1.8	0.3	3.8	5.8	1.6	0.4	395.60

Source: Ministry of Finance, Outline of Foreign Trade.

[a]Percentage point contribution is growth rate times percentage share in previous year. [b]Regions are not exhaustive, so their percentage point contributions do not add up to the percentage increase across the world. [c]European Union = 12 countries here.

production of VCRs has been increasing since the early 1980s at a surprisingly rapid rate; it was about 2 million units in 1985 but surged to about 20 million units in 1994. Despite this, exports of VCRs increased in the latter half of the 1980s and reached a peak of about 25 million units in 1990, and domestic production was stable at a little over 30 million units over the 1987–1991 period. This was a period of increasing export and overseas production and hence expanding demand curves in foreign markets. However, exports began to decline sharply in 1991 and domestic production began to decline in 1992, while overseas production continued to increase. Indeed, overseas production has been steadily increasing and surpassed domestic production in 1988. In 1993, it reached the level of about 25 million sets, while domestic production was about 10 million sets. However, despite steady increases in overseas production, exports were more or less steady at about 4 million sets over the 1987–1993 period, and domestic production declined only mildly from about 13 million sets to 10 million sets over the same period. These movements can be traced in the graphs prepared for an article published by the Japan Institute for Overseas Investment (1995).

An interesting subsidiary question here is the net effect of FDI on both the trade balance and manufacturing production. I shall not discuss if fully but would like to point out that both the export enhancing effect and the "reverse import" effect are increasingly visible, which is a negative for domestic production. Table 10.7 shows large increases in imports in dollar terms. Some automobile imports and textile imports are induced by Japan's FDI. Japan External Trade Relations Organization (JETRO, 1995) reports that in 1994 301,000 passenger cars were imported, an increase of 49.6 percent over 1993. Interestingly, the largest number of imported cars came from Honda U.S.A.; the number was 47,300, an increase of 20,400 over 1993. The second largest importer was Mercedes Benz, importing 33,600, an increase of 5,700 over 1993.

Comparison With the United States

I will compare the behavior of Japan's manufacturing industry with that of the United States in this section, very briefly. In the United States, many discussions about deindustrialization took place in the 1980s. They revolved around the manufacturing share in real GDP, and some analyses cited the near constancy of this ratio over virtually the entire postwar period as evidence of no deindustrialization.

Much depends on the data. In real figures based on 1982 prices, the manufacturing share in real GDP stayed at about 23–24 percent over the very long term. However, in 1987 prices, the manufacturing share in real GDP was below 20 percent, but again any visible downward trend was absent. It was also argued that output of the computer industry grew too much in real terms, and that excluding the computer output would give a balanced view. Then a declining trend in the manufacturing share in real GDP emerged. And at any rate, in current prices the manufacturing share in GDP is almost declining.

More to the point, in the high dollar period of the first half of the 1980s, real exports declined, real imports rose, and the manufacturing share in real GDP declined. (I will skip detailed figures.) These are all natural responses to the high dollar and, except for the increase in real imports, show a different behavior from

Table 10.7 Import Value Increases and Percentage Point Contributions by Region

| | Percentage point contribution[a] | | | | | | | | | | Import value in 1994 ($ billion) |
| | World[b] | | United States | | European Union[c] | | Southeast Asia | | China | | |
	1993	1994	1993	1994	1993	1994	1993	1994	1993	1994	
Office machinery	13.8	32.2	-4.2	9.1	5.1	2.1	11.8	19.3	1.9	1.2	9.03
Household electronic appliances	10.4	45.1	1.1	0.1	0.1	3.4	0.7	26.7	0.1	12.6	2.75
Electronic parts	33.0	37.6									7.31
Passenger cars	1.5	37.8	3.9	13.5	-7.5	21.0	-0.1	-0.1	0.0	0.2	6.98
Textile products	12.1	21.2	2.5	0.4	-1.7	4.4	-2.4	0.4	12.3	15.2	16.07
Iron and steel	7.4	0.0	-0.4	0.0	-0.3	0.4	5.8	0.2	0.4	3.2	4.07
All manufactures	6.9	23.5	1.9	5.4	4.6	-1.3	2.6	5.5	2.8	4.4	154.60

Source: See table 10.6.

Note: See table 10.6.

that of Japan's manufacturing industry. The response of FDI (outward) to the high dollar was also natural; it increased sharply from 1983 to 1987.

Thus, at least over the medium term of the first half of the 1980s, the U.S. manufacturing industry exhibited a natural response to the higher dollar. However, the problem with the U.S. manufacturing industry is that, even after the real effective exchange rate of the dollar returned to previous levels around 1980, the trade deficit remained very large. The decline in the manufacturing share in real GDP per se is not a problem over the long term as long as it is not associated with the large trade deficit that persists over the long term. However, this is not the case with the United States.

Suppose that a nation wants to consume and invest a constant fraction of its real income. Suppose also that in real consumption the proportion of goods (as against services) is constant. This will imply a constant manufacturing share in real GDP, if the condition of trade balance equilibrium is imposed. If, however, the manufacturing share in real GDP is actually declining and the trade deficit persists over the long term, the nation's manufacturing industry lacks the capacity to respond to the nation's needs fully. To me, the United States looks like such a country, and in that sense the deindustrialization, or hollowing out, in the United States cannot be dismissed as groundless. Certainly, many manufacturing corporations in the United States are the most efficient in the world, and high-technology sectors there are excellent. However, the mass production capability of medium-technology products in the United States is not as strong, and it is no small problem.

A Concluding Remark on Japan's (Non) Hollowing Out

Japan increased its manufacturing share in real GDP quite significantly in the 1980s. In the 1990s, one observes a decline since 1992, but this is likely to come to a halt before the end of the decade. Behind this lies the unique behavior of Japanese manufacturing corporations. The rising trend of the manufacturing share in real GDP will not be a problem if the trade balance is in rough equilibrium over the long term. That case would imply that the Japanese people want to spend an increasing share of their real income on manufactures, perhaps spurred by declining relative prices of manufactures (relative to services) or by high income elasticities of demand for some manufactures. However, this has not really been the case. Although this fact may explain some of the rising manufacturing share in real GDP in Japan, the trade surplus has grown since the early 1980s and remains large to date. In fact, Japan is the obverse of the United States; Japan's manufacturing industry is producing much more than the nation needs, and in this sense the manufacturing industry has overgrown, which causes trade disputes almost constantly and the surge of yen appreciation from time to time.

Internally, the mirror image of the overgrowth of the manufacturing industry is the undergrowth of nonmanufacturing industries. In Japan today, there is not a large variety of services, and many of them are exorbitantly expensive. Because the international competitive pressure is weak in nonmanufacturing industries, services producers are not doing enough to offer interesting or less expensive services. If conditions remain as they are now, the manufacturing share in real GDP will likely begin to increase again by the end of the 1990s, with its undesirable consequences. To forestall this scenario, a moderately rising real exchange rate of the yen—a moderately rising nominal exchange rate of the yen is not enough—will be necessary to restrain the overexpansion of the manufacturing industry. At the same time, nonmanufacturing industries will have to be induced to grow faster, with much more deregulation and international competition.

References

Amano, Akihiro (1986). *Boeki-ron* (Trade Theory). Tokyo: Chikuma Shobo (in Japanese).

Economic Planning Agency (1995). *Economic White Paper.* Tokyo: EPA (in Japanese).

Japan Institute for Overseas Investment (1995). *Overseas Investment,* January 1995 (in Japanese).

Japanese External Trade Organization (1995). *Nippon 1995: Business Facts and Figures.* Tokyo: JETRO.

Kojima, Kiyoshi (June 1985). "Japanese and American Direct Investment in Asia: A Comparative Analysis," *Hitotsubashi Journal of Economics* 25: 1–35.

Krugman, Paul R. (1983). "The 'New Theories' of International Trade and the Multinational Enterprise," in C. P. Kindleberger and D. B. Audretsch, eds., *The Multinational Corporation in the 1980s,* Cambridge, MA: MIT Press. 57–73.

Lawrence, Robert Z. (1984). *Can America Compete?* Washington, DC: Brookings Institution.

Ministry of International Trade and Industry (1995). *White Paper on International Trade.* Tokyo: MITI (in Japanese).

Sazanami, Yoko (1989). "Trade and Investment Patterns and Barriers in the United States, Canada, and Japan," in R. M. Stern, ed., *Trade and Investment Relations Among the United States, Canada, and Japan.* Chicago: University of Chicago Press. 90–126.

11

Japanese and U.S. Subsidiaries in East Asia

Host-Economy Effects

John Ravenhill

If one lesson is to be learned from the East Asian economic miracles, it is that there is no single path to economic success. Nowhere is this more obvious than in the variety of regimes these countries have maintained for foreign direct investment (FDI). During the crucial early stages of their industrialization, East Asian countries pursued policies toward FDI that spanned a spectrum from undisguised hostility to granting more favorable treatment to transnational corporations (TNCs) than that accorded to domestically owned companies.

Japan (Encarnation 1992; Mason 1992, 1995) and Korea (Mardon 1990) were at one end of the spectrum (fig.11.1); they both exhibited a strong preference for acquiring technology through licensing arrangements rather than FDI, for excluding foreign capital from many sectors of the economy, and for insisting that those foreign companies permitted to invest domestically engage in joint ventures with local partners (often with implicit or explicit expectations that foreign involvement in the venture would gradually be phased out). In the middle of the spectrum, maintaining a policy regime that has consistently been neutral on the issue of ownership, is Hong Kong. At the other end of the spectrum is Singapore, whose policies, at least until the introduction of the Local Industry Upgrading Program in 1986, by tailoring subsidies and other incentives to the needs of specific TNCs, exhibited a bias against local firms (Soon and Tan 1993; Yuan and Low 1990; Yue 1985). If the comparison includes firms owned by members of the local Chinese community, then Malaysia too, for most of the postindependence period, pursued policies that favored foreign investors rather than domestically owned firms (Jesudason 1989; Jomo 1993). Taiwan and Thailand, while generally welcoming foreign investment, both excluded foreign capital from some sectors of the economy. Differing foreign investment regimes were reflected in the ratio of FDI stock to GDP: in the mid-1980s, this ranged from 2.8 percent for Korea to 8.1 percent for Taiwan to 53.8 percent for Singapore (Lall 1992, table 2, p. 174).

Diverse policies toward foreign investment seem, however, to have had little effect on overall rates of economic growth across East Asian countries. Singapore has grown as rapidly as Korea; in recent years, Malaysia has come close to matching Taiwan's growth performance. To pose the question of whether ownership

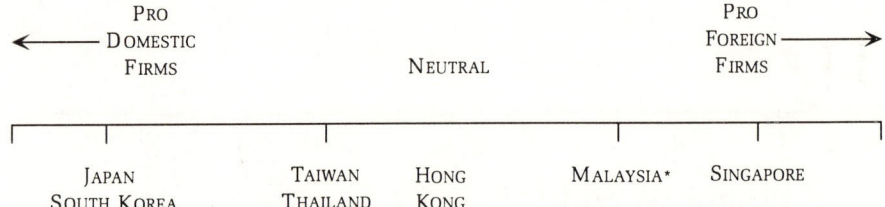

Figure 11.1 Foreign Direct Investment Regimes. *Source:* Australia National University, Nikkei database. *Vis-à-vis Chinese Malaysian companies.

matters may seem therefore to be a particularly unpromising line of inquiry. The enormous literature on transnational corporations for the most part would seem to support such a conclusion. To the question of what effects foreign investment will have on the host economy, the most frequent answer is "it depends." Will FDI create trade or destroy trade, will it benefit or weaken the host country's balance of payments, will it enhance domestic capital formation or crowd out local entrepreneurs? The answer to these and similar questions is that the performance of TNCs and their impact on the local economy will depend on contextual factors:

- the reasons why FDI was undertaken (to exploit ownership-specific advantages or to exploit locational advantages?); for defensive reasons (market preservation or acquisition) or for strategic reasons (to secure access to technology or acquire local competitors?);
- the existing and potential capabilities of domestically owned firms and the opportunities for them together with the local state and foreign investors to forge a developmental coalition;
- the educational and skills level of the local population and the effectiveness of state action to upgrade them;
- the bargaining capacity of the host state (Encarnation and Wells 1985); and
- the general policy context that the host state creates.

Discussion of the relative merits of TNC investment compared with that by domestic firms always runs into the impossibility of testing the counterfactual. It is impossible to know whether, or how adequately, a local firm would have filled the gap in the absence of foreign investment. Moreover, ample evidence exists that the linkages between TNC subsidiaries and the local economy, and the capacity of the local state to increase its share of the rents enjoyed by TNC subsidiaries, will vary over time (especially if the sunk costs of the TNC increase [Moran 1974]), as the product cycle evolves (Doner 1991), or if complementary assets are developed in the local economy (for evidence from Taiwan, see Chi Schive 1990; for Singapore contrast Pang and Lim's [1977] pessimistic view on local linkages in the electronics industry in their early study with their more positive view expressed more than a decade later [Lim and Pang Eng Fong 1991]). The relationship between TNC subsidiaries and the host economy also changes as production techniques and the global economic context evolve. For instance, the increasing adoption of flexible production techniques and just-in-time sourcing by TNC subsidiaries in Malaysia led directly to a sharp increase in their linkages with domestically owned firms (Rasiah 1994, 1995). In a similar manner, the evolution of regional and sometimes global production networks may have a profound effect on the local operations of TNC subsidiaries (Simon and Jun 1995).

Furthermore, any choice of foreign investment regimes in itself will not be decisive for an economy's growth prospects. What matters, as Dahlman, Ross-Larson, and Westphal (1985) argued in their study of technology acquisition, is less the method chosen than the effectiveness of its implementation. Providing incentives to TNCs will not in itself ensure that the potential benefits (access to capital, technology, management skills, and sales networks) that some TNCs can provide will actually be realized. Similarly, a policy of promoting domestic firms will, if improperly implemented, merely result in an environment in which rent seeking predominates.

If ownership in itself is not decisive, does ownership make no difference? Given the complexities of the issue and the importance of contingent factors, is it impossible to make any a priori judgments about possible differences in the challenges posed by domestically owned and foreign-owned firms to state decision makers, and in firms' impact on the local economy? In principle, ownership should not matter. Reich (1990, 1991) persuasively asserted that the crucial issue is the nature and contribution of the activities within the local economy in increasing local competitiveness and advancing domestic economic welfare, rather than the ownership of companies per se. And, indeed, some TNCs undoubtedly may bring to less developed countries assets that either would not be available to start up domestically owned companies or, in the case of the development of technology, for instance, that could be supplied by the TNC at much lower opportunity costs.

Reich may be posing the correct question, but his answer is less persuasive. As Tyson (1991) suggested, in arguing that the nationality of firms is becoming irrelevant to where they conduct their business activities as they transform themselves into global networks, Reich should have emphasized the word "becoming." Nationality continues to matter. In the international division of labor, firms have not yet transformed themselves into stateless beings (Hu 1992).

Several a priori reasons persuade one that TNC subsidiaries will behave differently from domestically owned firms (especially to the extent that the activities of the latter are confined within the domestic territory). These differences stem from two key dimensions of the TNC: its transnationality and its vertical integration. A firm that operates transnationally may pursue a division of labor across its various operations that does not accord with the priorities of the host country. A conflict may exist between the firm's need to satisfy shareholders in its home country and the goals of a host state to ensure that a greater share of the company's activities be conducted locally. The firm may be able to realize economies of scale through the centralization of some activities that would otherwise be performed locally. Moreover, the vertical integration of the firm across national boundaries offers the opportunity to determine the stage of production or distribution and the territory in which it is able to exploit the rents arising from its ownership-specific advantages.

For some adherents of neoclassical economics, the solution to the problems faced by host countries in dealing with TNCs is straightforward: maximize domestic comparative advantage by allowing market forces free reign. This proposed solution poses several problems. First, by definition, the operation of TNCs generally results from some degree of market failure. A failure could be the incapacity of the corporation to realize economies of scale or scope, or to differentiate its products by brand names that provide the corporation with its ownership-specific advantages, as a huge literature that builds on the insights of Hymer (1976) has demonstrated. In many instances, the best that the host country can hope for in its negotiations with a TNC is a situation of bilateral monopoly in which the country's principal leverage results from control over market access. Second, the host country faces a tilted playing field in foreign investment regimes, tilted by the policies of other states through their incentives to local and foreign companies. Third, the TNC may engage in satisfying rather than optimizing in its scanning activities, leading to a form of hysteresis in the distribution of its operations. Fourth, from the TNC's perspective, even in circumstances when the corporation is fully aware of the competitive advantages of the local economy, the costs of adapting product and process technologies for the local environment may far outweigh the expected benefits from exploiting differences in local factor costs.

Clearly, some East Asian states perceived that dependence on market forces would be insufficient to ensure that the domestic economy would capture the desired share of activities and rents generated by TNCs. Moreover, they had no confidence that state regulation would be as effective in dealing with TNCs as it would with domestically owned corporations. The potential for state *control* over corporate activities, whether through decrees or through administrative guidance, was evidently a factor in the decisions of the Japanese and Korean governments to favor domestically owned firms rather than transnational subsidiaries. State power rested on the capacity to dictate the allocation of key inputs—credit, raw materials, foreign exchange—a control that became increasingly difficult as liberalization of the domestic economy proceeded and the domestic firms themselves transnationalized (witness the current struggle between the Korean state and the *chaebol* over the latter's raising of capital offshore).

For countries that are latecomers to industrialization, learning by borrowing and improving on technologies already developed by firms in more advanced economies has proved to be the most important path to rapid economic growth (Amsden 1989; Hikino and Amsden 1994). For governments, the critical challenge is how best to leverage access to the technologies held for the most part by foreign private sector actors, and, once access has been attained, how best to facilitate the local diffusion of these technologies. Linkages between foreign-owned and domestically owned firms within national boundaries are crucial to this question because of the opportunities for, in Borrus's phrase, "learning by interaction" (1993: 48).

Is the nationality of the TNC subsidiary likely to affect the prospects for the transfer and diffusion of technology to host economies? In the following section I identify several a priori grounds for suggesting that Japanese- and U.S.-headquartered TNCs have different impacts on host economies in East Asia. Most of the examples are drawn from the electronics industry. The reasons for this selectivity are straightforward. Electronics is now the largest single source of manufactured export earnings for most East Asian countries. It is also by far the most important single manufacturing sector for U.S. and Japanese FDI in East Asia (see chapter 3) and as such offers opportunities for more systematic comparative analysis than other sectors, such as automobiles or textiles, in which the presence of Japanese and U.S. subsidiaries is far more asymmetrical.

Does Ownership Matter? U.S. versus Japanese Subsidiaries

The debate about whether significant differences exist between Japanese and U.S. FDI has a long, if not altogether distinguished, history. Many of the arguments made by early commentators, such as Kojima's (1978, 1986) distinction between the trade-enhancing nature of Japanese FDI and the trade-undermining characteristic of U.S. FDI, and Ozawa's (1979) emphasis on the importance of relative factor endowments in driving Japanese FDI, have not withstood the test of time and empirical examination (for criticisms, see Hill 1988, 1990; Ramstetter 1987).

The wave of Japanese FDI in export-oriented manufacturing in other parts of Asia in the last decade—which appears little different from U.S. FDI in its motivations—coupled with the importance of global trends to which all companies must respond regardless of home base, inspires caution in any attempt to make a priori comparisons between Japanese foreign investments and those from TNCs domiciled elsewhere. Moreover, the absence of comparable data on TNCs from other countries, and the likelihood that the vintage of investments will act as a confounding variable, complicates the analyst's task. Reportedly unique characteristics in Japanese domestic operations (Aoki 1988; Womack, Jones and Roos 1991) and their slow progress toward change (Yamamura 1990, 1994), however, suggest that the operations of Japanese companies likely will continue to differ from those of other TNC subsidiaries. Some of these unique dimensions of Japanese corporations, intercorporate relations, and the relations between corporations and the home government, such as aspects of the famed "lean" production techniques—just-in-time sourcing, and so on—may, if replicated in overseas affiliates, work to the benefit of the host economy. Others, such as the *keiretsu* relations that link assemblers and suppliers, may not (if they exclude locally owned companies from production networks).

In the remainder of this section, I discuss how Japanese TNC subsidiaries frequently differ in their practices from their U.S. counterparts in four areas that will affect the prospects of technology transfer to the host economy: the localization of management, sourcing of components and capital goods, replication of production networks, and distribution of research and development (R & D) activities.

Management Localization and Autonomy

Japanese subsidiaries are far less likely than their U.S. counterparts to employ local managers, to employ local personnel in senior technical roles, or to have nationals of the host country on their boards. Even where local managers are employed, they are often "shadowed" by Japanese personnel and are relegated primarily to the performance of public relations roles for the company. In a study of Japanese subsidiaries in Australia, Nicholas et al. (1995) concluded that Japanese nationals dominated the upper echelons of management and that "there was a systematic bias in favour of Japanese managers holding key management positions, especially those involving the implementation of the technology or human capital critical to the competitive advantage of the firm" (22–23).

In part, the low levels of representation of local staff in management positions may stem from the replication of the lifetime employment system in overseas affiliates (Wendy Smith's study of Japanese subsidiaries in Malaysia). This characteristic has two effects. First, assuming that the subsidiary initially is staffed by expatriates, any replication of the seniority system inevitably delays the transition to locally recruited managers—unless the senior staff members are relocated elsewhere within the corporation. Even if such opportunities for transferring senior staff arise, however, many Japanese subsidiaries expect local recruits to complete a lengthy training and socialization period before they are promoted. These company expectations generate the second effect: frustration on the part of locally recruited managers about their promotion prospects that often leads to their seeking employment elsewhere. Several surveys of local managers in TNC subsidiaries in Asia report that Japanese employers are viewed far less favorably than their American or European counterparts (Ernst 1994: 16–17).

The replication of the seniority system in Asian subsidiaries constitutes a structural explanation for the low levels of localization of management in Japanese companies. In addition, most locals' lack of familiarity with the Japanese language, with corporate culture, and with the networks within which the company operates is a barrier to localization. Undoubtedly, however, corporate preferences, as detailed in chapters 7 and 8, are also a powerful factor against localization. Companies see the employment of Japanese managers as facilitating central control over key operations. They also fear that localization of management will increase the risk of leakage of commercial secrets to the local economy.

The relatively low levels of employment of locals in key management and technical positions reduce the prospects for the transfer of tacit technical knowledge to the host economy through personnel who gain experience in Japanese subsidiaries and then capitalize on their knowledge by breaking away to establish their own companies. Moreover, because Japanese managers are less likely to speak local languages and to maintain social networks that include personnel from domestically owned companies, management in Japanese subsidiaries is likely to be less well informed than other TNC subsidiaries about the production and technical capabilities of locally owned firms.

Not only is management in Japanese subsidiaries generally less localized than that of other TNC subsidiaries but management enjoys far less autonomy in key areas of decision making. Several studies have found that decision making within Japanese TNCs tends to be hierarchical and centralized at headquarters. Managers of subsidiaries enjoy little freedom of action on issues such as the sourcing of capital goods and components (Guyton 1996; Kreinin 1988). No evidence exists that the vintage of the investment has any significant effect on localization of decision making. The lack of autonomy for local management leads to a second significant difference between Japanese and U.S. subsidiaries.

Local Sourcing

"Learning by interaction" is an important channel for the transmission of technology from TNC subsidiaries to local companies. The extent to which subsidiaries source locally is an important indicator of their integration into the host economy. Although no data are available that would enable systematic comparisons that control for date of establishment, industrial sector, and so on, various studies have suggested that the subsidiaries of Japanese corporations, whether operating in industrialized or less-developed countries, tend to depend more heavily on imported capital goods and components from their home country than do subsidiaries of other TNCs (on the United States, see Graham and Krugman 1989; on Australia, see Kreinin 1988; on Malaysia, see Guyton 1996; on Singapore, see the study by Poh Kam Wong cited by Dobson (1993: 52–53) and Dobson's own survey of four TNC subsidiaries). Defenders of the record of Japanese corporations on this issue argue that the explanation lies in the recent vintage of Japanese investment. Saxonhouse (1991), for instance, criticizes Kreinin's (1988) conclusions about the importing behavior of Japanese subsidiaries in Australia on these grounds. Unfortunately, Saxonhouse produces no evidence to substantiate his argument; he makes no attempt to reexamine Kreinin's data by controlling for date of establishment.

In some instances, local content in the production of Japanese subsidiaries in East Asia declined as companies moved from exclusive production for the local market to production for export markets. In 1992 over 60 percent of the components used by Japanese affiliates in the electronics sector in Association of Southeast Asian Nations (ASEAN) countries and the newly industrialized countries were imported, two thirds of which were sourced from Japan (MITI data cited by Urata 1995, table 7). In recent years, Japanese TNC subsidiaries have increased the proportion of components that they source from the local economy. But in examining the importance of vintage effects and technology transfer to local firms, I find two issues. First, no one knows the relative weight of date of establishment as opposed to other variables that may drive increased local sourcing. Vintage almost certainly has some effect but may be swamped by other factors such as currency movements. The appreciation of the yen has clearly been the principal factor driving increased local sourcing in Southeast Asia in the 1990s. Date of establishment is unlikely to be the only factor retarding local purchasing, given the nationality of the managers of Japanese TNC subsidiaries and their lack of autonomy in decision making on sourcing of equipment and components. In Guyton's (1996) survey of Japanese affiliates in Malaysia, a majority of the Japanese companies reported that their parent companies dictated where machinery should be acquired (see also chapter 7 in this volume). The general preference for purchasing within the corporate network is seen in the fact that that intrafirm transactions accounted for more than half of the purchases by Japanese affiliates in Asia in 1992; for the NICs, the figure was 60 percent (Urata 1995, table 8).

Second, the sourcing by Japanese affiliates from the local economy increases over time but does not necessarily benefit domestically owned firms primarily but rather other Japanese subsidiaries located in the host economy. In other words, over time, the assembler at least partially replicates the network of suppliers with which it has long-standing relations in the home economy. A rare survey that compared sourcing from locally owned in contrast to locally based companies was conducted in Malaysia from 1987 to 1989. It reported that even though an increase occurred in the number of locally owned firms that supplied Japanese affiliates, the share in local procurement (itself less than a third of the value of total purchases) from locally *owned* companies remained constant at around 45 percent. Meanwhile, the share sourced from locally *based* Japanese affiliates rose from 18.7 to 23.8 percent (Aoki 1992, table 5, p. 82). Following from these observations is a further contrast between Japanese and U.S. FDI.

Replication of Production Networks

Japanese companies have a greater propensity than their American counterparts to internalize their ownership-specific advantages through the replication of their production networks when investing overseas. A study by the Japan External Trade Organization (JETRO) in 1994 found, for instance, that nearly a quarter of the 62 Japanese affiliates interviewed in Malaysia had invested locally in response to a request by a Japanese assembler (JETRO, 1995a). The vintage effect here may cause a greater divergence rather than a convergence in the behaviors of Japanese and U.S. subsidiaries as, over time, Japanese companies build a more complete local replication of their domestic supply networks.

In turn, the replication of supply networks produces another intercountry difference in FDI: small and medium-sized enterprises (SMEs) have a greater share in Japanese FDI than in U.S. FDI. In general, foreign investments by smaller companies are less likely to be driven by the desire to exploit ownership-specific advantages (such as proprietary technology) than do investments by large companies. Investments by Japanese SMEs typically attempt to exploit the advantages they gain from their established links with large assembly companies that have already located offshore. And investments from these SMEs are also more likely than those from large companies to be driven by location-specific advantages such as low labor costs. By 1993, Asia accounted for more than 90 percent of the worldwide investments by Japanese SMEs. This concentration has been attributed by JETRO (1995b: 20) to their search for inexpensive labor. For the host economy, investment by these SMEs has a greater potential to crowd out local entrepreneurs because these companies occupy relatively low-technology niches that beginning local enterprises might reasonably aspire to fill. Some evidence, mainly anecdotal, exists that just such a crowding-out effect on local firms has occurred in Malaysia (Ali 1994; Rasiah 1995). In addition, SMEs are more likely than their larger counterparts to maintain management and key technical positions in the hands of home country nationals (this argument applies a fortiori to Taiwanese investments—see Chi Schive 1990).

Centralization of Research and Development

Locally owned firms (or more accurately, companies that have their home base in a particular territory—see Porter 1990: 19) are more likely to carry out a greater range of activities, especially those involving value-added activities, in the national territory than are subsidiaries of TNCs. In Porter's words, "The home base will be the location of many of the most productive jobs, the core technologies, and the most advanced skills." The concentration of higher value-added activities in the home base results not only from the historical development of the company's activities and the local linkages built up over the years but also, among other factors, from the availability of skilled personnel; from pressures from home country governments, shareholders, and workers; from the capacity for realizing lower transaction costs; and from concerns over the protection of proprietary knowledge. In particular, R & D activities tend to be concentrated in home countries. Dunning (1993: 303) reports that only 9 percent of all R & D activities undertaken in 1989 by U.S. TNCs were conducted by their foreign subsidiaries (only a modest increase over the 1966 share of 6 percent); for Japanese companies in 1989 the ratio of foreign to home country expenditure was even lower—only 5 percent (Dunning 1993: 303, citing an unpublished paper by L. S. Peters).

This general reluctance of Japanese companies to transfer R & D activities to overseas subsidiaries is reflected in their operations in East Asia. Surveys have shown that Japanese subsidiaries in Southeast Asia are seldom given responsibility for more than incremental process improvements: product research and development are rare. Itoh and Shibata (1995: 196) reported that only two R & D facilities had been established by Japanese firms in Asia, both of which were in Malaysia: a joint venture among Sanyo, Mazda, and Ford for car stereo equipment (a venture that reportedly foundered) and Matsushita's R & D facility for air conditioning equipment. This estimate may be a modest understatement of the number of Japanese subsidiaries in the region that undertake some research and development activities. Ernst (1994: 21) reports 11 instances of subsidiaries engaged in product development but cautions that whether such development amounts to anything more than simple product adaptation for the local market is unclear. The general conclusion that Japanese corporations currently undertake little R & D in their Asian subsidiaries stands. Borrus (1995) explains the significant contrast with U.S. subsidiaries that increasingly have been given responsibility for product design and development, in some instances not just for local but for global markets.

Japanese and U.S. subsidiaries in East Asia have differed significantly in their technology transfer to host economies and especially in their linkages with locally owned companies. This conclusion follows from several of the points previously made: the dominance of Japanese nationals in key management and technical positions, affiliates' lack of autonomy in sourcing, and the development of supplier networks involving local investment by Japanese SMEs. A rare attempt to examine issues of technology transfer in more detail is provided by Guyton (1996) in her survey of Japanese affiliates in Malaysia. She found that Japanese companies were more likely to work closely with locally based Japanese suppliers on product specification and design than they were with locally owned companies. Moreover, Japanese firms appeared to transfer less technology from parent company to local subsidiary than did their U.S. counterparts: Malaysian employees of Japanese subsidiaries whom she interviewed who had previously worked for U.S. or European subsidiaries reported that the parent companies had transferred more technology more quickly to local subsidiaries than was true of their current Japanese employers. Language barriers undoubtedly play some role; an obstacle to technology transfer is the lack of English-language technical documentation within the Japanese firms (see also Sedgwick's study of Japanese and U.S. subsidiaries in Thailand in chapter 7).

What policy implications follow from this conclusion on the differential effects of U.S. and Japanese subsidiaries? Have Japanese subsidiaries had a negative impact on host economies? An affirmative answer to the second question would be very difficult to sustain. Evidence of crowding-out effects on small local firms in Malaysia has to be balanced against other surveys that report increasing linkages between Japanese subsidiaries and locally owned companies (Rasiah 1995, forthcoming). On balance, the overall impact of Japanese foreign direct investment in Southeast Asia has not only been to create substantial new employment opportunities but also to transfer technology both through the import of capital goods and through creating opportunities for learning by doing and learning through interaction. Japanese investments have helped to build local concentrations of production and design skills that, in turn, are now attracting new investors. But what of the impact on East Asian countries' balance of trade?

Trade Orientation

Many of the early studies of foreign direct investment reported that it had a net negative impact on the balance of trade and, more generally, on the balance of payments of host economies (see Hood and Young 1979; and Dunning 1993). Often such negative effects reflected the orientation of investments toward import substitution; they were frequently import-intensive in their sourcing of components and capital goods but generated few export earnings.

In East Asia, the nationality of subsidiaries does make a difference in the impact of FDI on the balance of trade of host economies. In aggregate, Japanese companies conduct a much smaller share of their trade at arm's length, rely far more heavily than U.S. subsidiaries on imports from the parent company, export a much smaller percentage of their total production, and in particular engage in reverse exports to the home country to a much lesser extent than do subsidiaries of U.S. corporations. Consequently, Japanese subsidiaries have a far less positive effect on the balance of trade of East Asian host economies than do their American counterparts.

As noted in the previous section, several surveys suggested that Japanese subsidiaries rely more heavily than subsidiaries of TNCs headquartered elsewhere on intrafirm trade and on imports from the home country for components and capital goods. The data that would permit a systematic comparison with U.S. subsidiaries in East Asia are not available. However, the aggregate evidence that Encarnation provides in chapter 1 on the role of intrafirm transactions in Japan's trade with East Asia, and the contrast with the largely arm's-length trade that characterizes U.S. trade with the region, provides further support for conclusions drawn from earlier surveys. Japanese production networks in East Asia tend to rely more heavily on imports than their American counterparts.

On the other side of the trade equation—exports from the host economy—Japanese companies generally have a far less positive impact than their American counterparts. Japanese manufacturing subsidiaries export less than their U.S. counterparts; this is true even of subsidiaries in electronics in which in 1992 Japanese subsidiaires exported 61.6 percent of their production in contrast to the 76.2 percent figure for U.S. companies. As Encarnation reports in chapter 3, most of the difference in export orientation is explained by contrasting records in reverse exports from subsidiaries to their headquarters' countries (see also Petri 1995, tables 3.8 and 3.9, p. 45).

A report by the Japan External Trade Organization summarizes these differences in export orientation:

In 1990, [the] value of exports by American subsidiaries in East Asia to their American parents was 2.6-times that of their imports. This presents a sharp contrast with Asian subsidiaries of Japanese firms, in which imports remain dominant. This is believed to be due to the fact that East Asia serves as a base for processing, assembling, and importing by American multinationals and has been incorporated into those multinationals' global production activities. As opposed to this, for Japan, East Asia is more of a base for exports to third countries rather than a base for importing back to Japan. (1995c: 17)

The share of reverse exports in the sales of Japanese subsidiaries in East Asia has stagnated since its peak in 1989. Several factors may explain this trend. First, the data may be affected by the growth in the number of locally based Japanese suppliers that sell their products "locally" to the assemblers. Second, the stagnation of the Japanese economy following the bursting of the bubble economy has certainly retarded the growth of sales there, as opposed to those in rapidly growing Asian economies. Regardless of the explanation, the stagnation in reverse exports has had important economic—and political—consequences for Asian host countries of Japanese FDI. Coupled with the boom in exports of capital goods and components—particularly in the electronics sector—from Japan to the local affiliates, the lack of growth of reverse exports has exacerbated the trade imbalances between other Asian countries and Japan. In 1992, for the first time, Japan enjoyed a surplus in its overall trade with the ASEAN economies; the imbalance in trade in *manufactures* with other Asian countries was huge, exceeding Japan's trade surplus with the United States. Moreover, the pattern of trade has not only exacerbated political tensions between Japan and other East Asian countries. It has also contributed to increasing trade tensions between these Asian countries and the United States. The triangular pattern of trade in which a substantial (although, in the 1990s, declining) share of exports was directed to the United States reinforced the trade imbalances created by the reverse exports of U.S. subsidiaries (Cohen and Guerrieri 1995; Encarnation 1995; Ravenhill 1993).

Available data do not support a positive or negative overall impact of Japanese foreign direct investment in the manufacturing sector in other East Asian countries. Increased imbalances in trade with Japan, associated with the growth of Japanese investment, have been offset to some extent by increased exports to third countries. And, even though the overall share in total production of reverse exports to Japan has been relatively low, the hosting of Japanese subsidiaries may be crucial for the penetration of the Japanese market, as I discuss in the following section.

Japanese Subsidiaries and Reverse Exports

The distribution networks of Japanese companies have been demonstrated to be a barrier to the exports of nonaffiliated companies (Lawrence 1991). As Japanese imports from other parts of Asia, especially in the electronics sector, have historically been dominated by intracompany trade, access to these production networks is often critical for penetrating the Japanese market. The share of intrafirm trade in the exports of Japanese subsidiaries in East Asia to Japan has actually increased in the last decade (table 11.1).

Hosting a Japanese subsidiary may be one of the easiest and possibly most cost-effective ways of gaining access to Japanese production networks and, thus, to the Japanese domestic market. In this respect, some Southeast Asian countries may be at an advantage compared with Taiwan and especially Korea, which historically adopted more restrictive policies towards Japanese FDI. The Electronics Industry Association of Japan (1995) reports that in 1994, Japanese companies owned 39 facilities in consumer electronics in Malaysia, which produced 88 different products; in Thailand 26 plants were assembling 56 products; in Singapore 18 subsidiaries manufacturing 48 products; in Taiwan 21 plants assembling 49 products; and in Korea only 7 plants producing 16 products.

Some displacement of Korean and Taiwanese exports to the Japanese market by those from Japanese subsidiaries in Malaysia and Thailand and, to a lesser extent, Singapore appears to have occurred in the last five years (see Tanaka 1993; Japan External Trade Organization 1995b). Two effects seem to be at work here. The first is the transfer of most low-end production in the consumer electronics industry to Southeast Asia (and, more recently, to China), products that companies in Korea and Taiwan are no longer manufacturing. The second, and much more interesting effect from a political economy viewpoint, is the construction by Japanese companies of state-of-the-art assembly plants in Southeast Asia intended to service the global market for that product, including the domestic Japanese market. While the high-end components for assembly may still come from Japan, as do the capital goods, and while these plants have yet to be given responsibility for research, design, and product development, they have been equipped with the latest production technology to ensure quality control.

For host economies, these plants offer several significant advantages. Because these are (at least) majority-owned subsidiaries, Japanese companies are more willing to supply them with the latest technologies than they are to sell or license such technologies to potential rivals (domestically owned firms) in Korea and Taiwan. Second, these products carry the Japanese company's brand name, a particularly important factor in accessing the Japanese market. Korean-manufactured products gained a poor reputation in Japan in the late 1980s when several companies began marketing consumer electronics products under their

Table 11.1 Share of Intrafirm Trade in Exports to Japan of Japanese Subsidiaries in East Asia (%)

	1986	1989	1992
General machinery	94.7	98.5	96.7
Electrical machinery	73.0	60.3	90.0
Transport machinery	46.0	35.7	73.9
Precision machinery	86.1	50.8	96.5

Source: MITI, *Wagakuni kigyo no kaigai jigyo katsudo,* for 1986 and 1989 from Urata (1993); data for 1992 supplied by Walter Hatch, University of Washington.

own brand names rather than through original equipment manufacturing (OEM). A reputation for unreliable products and poor after-sales service damaged the brand names of several Korean companies and created a "collective bad" for the "Made in Korea" label. Consequently, a widespread trend back to OEM was observed for ultimate marketing under the label of a Japanese company. This strategy does provide access both to Japanese production networks and to the Japanese market. Is it as financially attractive (or as secure in terms of maintaining control over technologies) for Japanese companies as manufacturing in their own foreign subsidiaries? The answer would depend on a product-by-product analysis.

To attempt to address the product displacement issue, I reviewed Japanese imports of five products. Before discussing the individual product data, I propose some caveats. Most important, it is impossible to identify the exporting firm from these aggregate data (the data in the following figures are Japanese import data accessed through the Nikkei Telecom: News & Retrieval Service at the Australian National University). I am making assumptions here about the ownership of the exporting companies based on (incomplete) information on the distribution of Japanese consumer electronics plants in the region. For Malaysia and Thailand, one can be reasonably certain that the exports of consumer electronics products to Japan have come from Japanese subsidiaries. Although subsidiaries of companies headquartered in other countries have a significant presence in the manufacture of consumer electronics, in the products examined in this section for Singapore—radios and color TVs—the production is overwhelmingly by Japanese subsidiaries. In Korea, most of the exports of consumer electronics products to the Japanese market are derived from Korean-owned companies that produce either on an original-equipment manufacturer (OEM) or an own-brand manufacturing (OBM) basis. In Taiwan, the situation is less certain: exports to the Japanese market come both from Japanese subsidiaries and from locally owned (and other foreign-owned) firms producing primarily on an OEM basis. Any conclusions from these only illustrative data therefore must be very tentative; their character does not permit more rigorous analysis.

Three of the commodities, radios, calculators and telephones (figs. 11.2, 11.3, and 11.4), match the characteristics of the first pattern noted: low-end electronics products whose production in Northeast Asia (and Singapore) is being phased out as industries in these countries upgrade to higher value-added products. In 1988, Singapore, Korea, and Taiwan together provided over 70 percent of Japan's imports of radios. In the early 1990s, a substantial proportion of production was shifted to Malaysia, whose share of the Japanese import market rose within a couple of years from 5 percent to over 25 percent (fig. 2). A similar striking switch in sourcing characterizes Japan's imports of calculators. In the late 1980s, Taiwan alone was the source for close to 80 percent of Japan's calculator imports. Within three years, Taiwan had been displaced as the major exporter by Thailand and Malaysia; in this instance the production was often on an OEM basis for Japanese distributors by Taiwanese companies based in Malaysia and Thailand (for discussion of one example see Bernard and Ravenhill 1995). In Japan's imports of telephones (fig. 11.4), Taiwan held a dominant share of the market in the late 1980s, but by 1993 imports from Thailand exceeded those from Taiwan and Korea. A similar trajectory occurred in the imports of sound recorders.

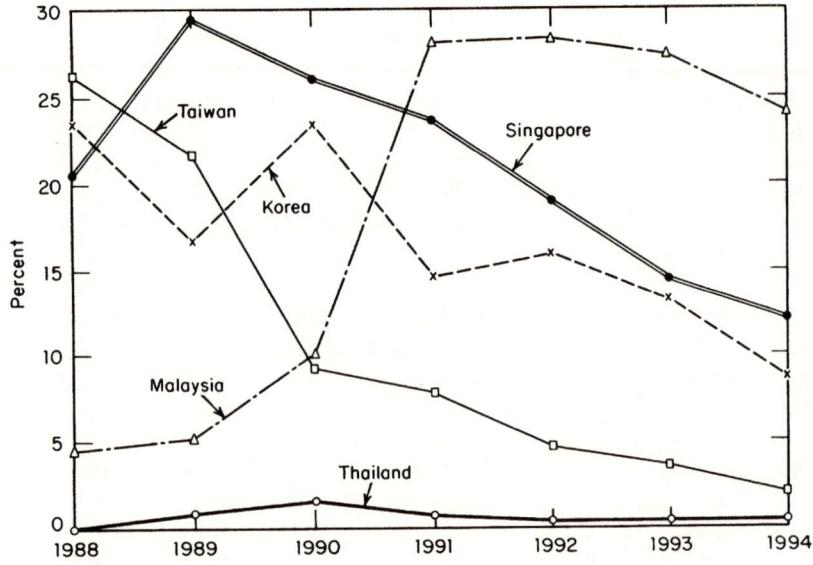

Figure 11.2 Japan's Imports of Radios (Market Share). *Source:* Australia National University, Nikkei database.

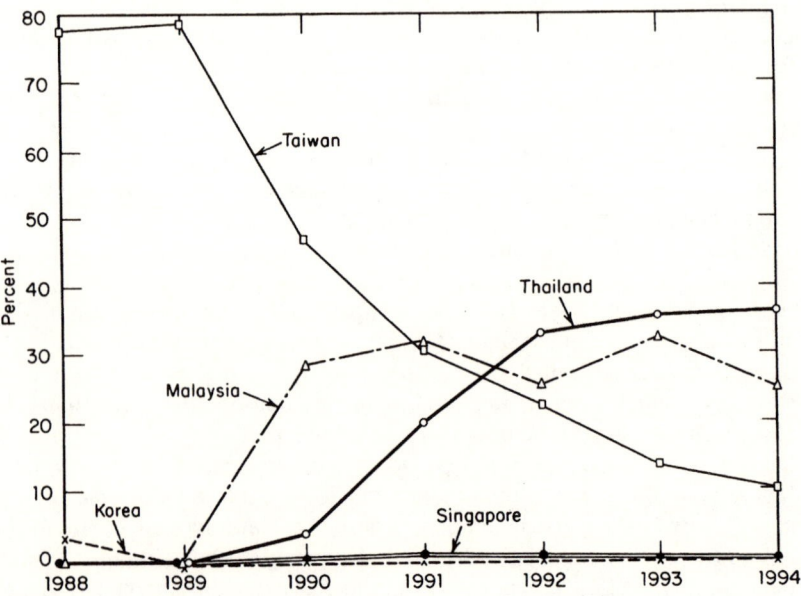

Figure 11.3 Japan's Imports of Calculators (Market Share). *Source:* Australia National University, Nikkei database.

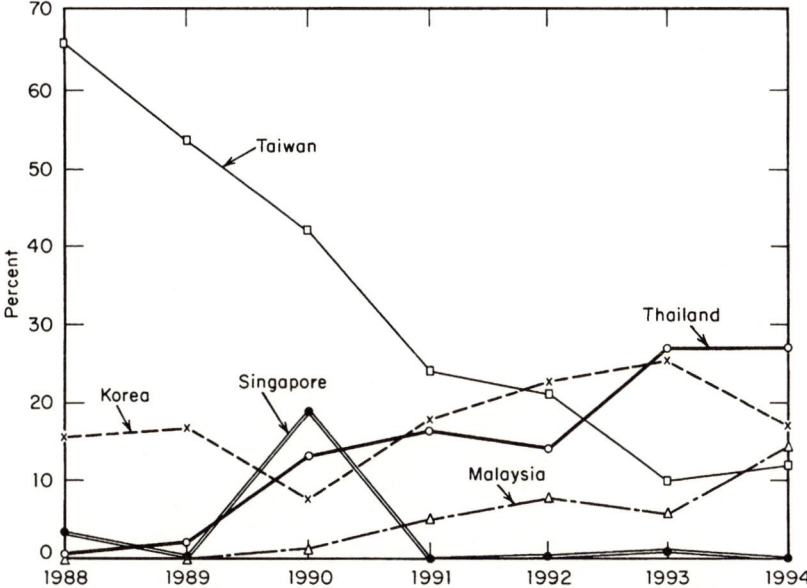

Figure 11.4 Japan's Imports of Telephones (Market Share). *Source:* Australia National University, Nikkei database.

In other, higher value-added products, the same trend to switching of import sourcing to Southeast Asian economies is evident. But in this instance, Korea and Taiwan have not exited from the manufacture of these products; rather, Japanese companies have switched from sourcing from Korea and Taiwan (often on an OEM basis from domestically owned companies) to sourcing from new majority-owned subsidiaries in Southeast Asia. Color televisions provide one of the best examples of this trend. In the late 1980s, close to 90 percent of all Japanese imports of color televisions were sourced from Korea and Taiwan (fig. 11.5). Although both countries continue to be major exporters of color televisions, their share of the Japanese import market fell precipitously in the early 1990s as new Japanese subsidiaries, particularly in Malaysia, came on-stream. By 1994, Malaysia and Thailand together accounted for over half of all Japan's imports of this product. A similar experience, although less dramatic, is evident in Japanese imports of facsimiles (fig. 11.6). For this product, imports from Malaysia, which by 1994 accounted for over half of Japan's import market, have largely displaced those from Taiwan.

A final development is the increasing sourcing of consumer appliances from subsidiaries in Southeast Asia. For the most part, these products are new imports into Japan: in this instance, Southeast Asian exports are not displacing production from Korea and Taiwan. An early example was refrigerators (fig. 11.7), where imports from Japanese subsidiaries in Malaysia and Thailand quickly captured over half of the import market. Air conditioners provide another example.

Even though the aggregate data do not show an increase in the share of reverse exports in Japanese manufacturing production in East Asian subsidiaries, aggregation obscures significant developments in the most dynamic sector of manu-

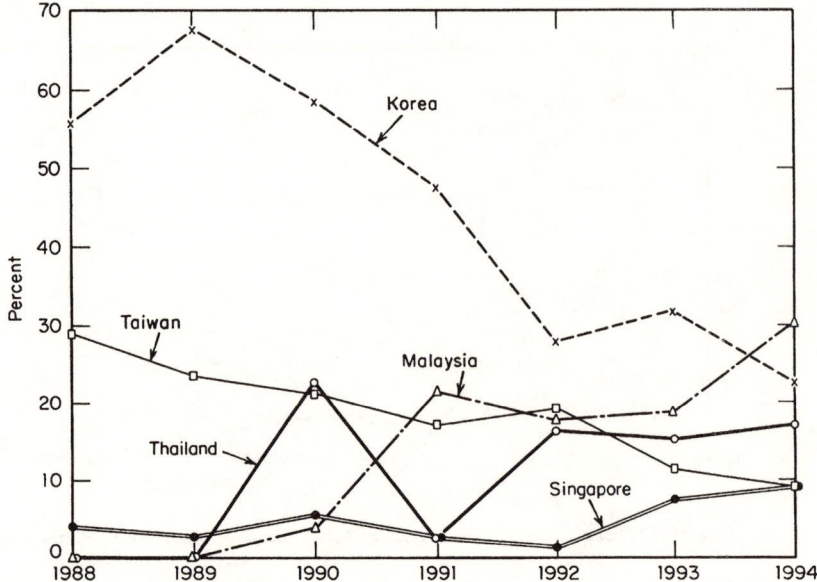

Figure 11.5 Japan's Imports of Color TVs (Market Share). *Source:* Australia National University, Nikkei database.

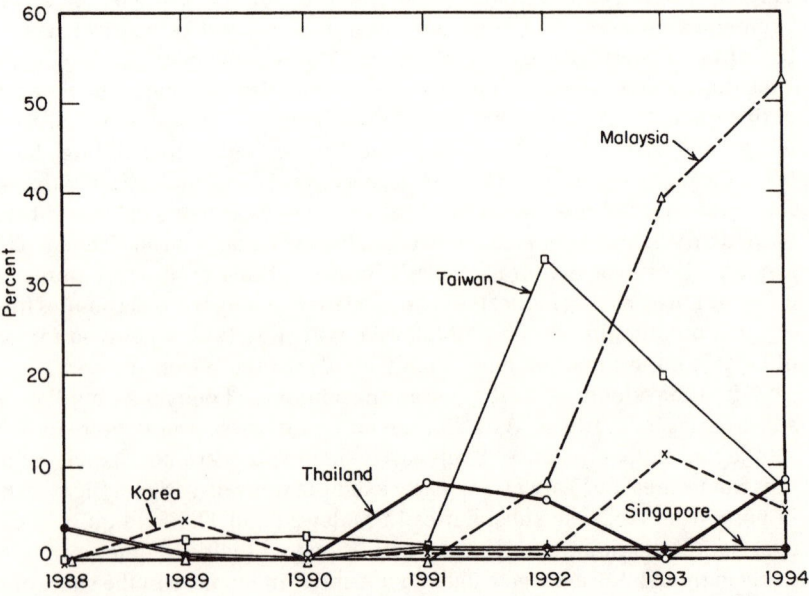

Figure 11.6 Japan's Imports of Facsimiles (Market Share). *Source:* Australia National University, Nikkei database.

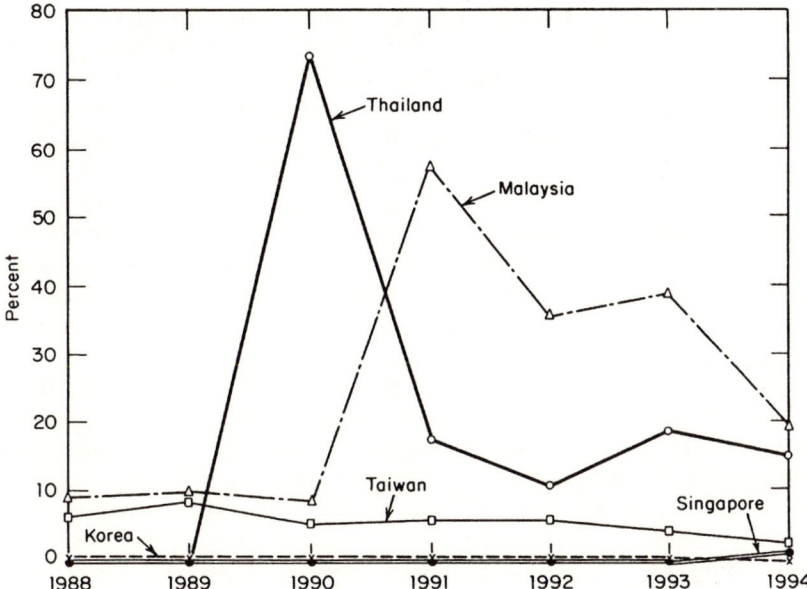

Figure 11.7 Japan's Imports of Refrigerators (Market Share). *Source:* Australia National University, Nikkei database.

facturing—consumer electronics—in Southeast Asia. The data in table 11.2 reflect the increasing importance of sales to Japan in the overall output of Japanese electronics subsidiaries in ASEAN countries. This trend can be expected to continue for reasons detailed in the conclusion. The benefits of hosting Japanese subsidiaries—with the access that they provide to the latest technologies, brand names, and Japanese domestic distribution networks—will become ever more important if reverse exports continue to increase.

Conclusion

Does ownership matter? In the effects of foreign direct investment on host economies in East Asia in the last decade, the answer is yes. Subsidiaries of U.S. corporations were more likely than their Japanese counterparts to interact with the host

Table 11.2 Geographical Distribution of Sales for Japanese Affiliates in ASEAN in the Electronics Industry

	Local	Exports	Japan	Asia	North America	Europe
1986	43.0	57.0	7.4	33.6	8.5	6.9
1989	34.9	65.1	17.5	29.3	14.6	3.5
1992	38.4	61.6	27.7	22.4	8.6	2.2

Source: Urata 1995, table 7.

economy in a manner that facilitated local acquisition of technology, an essential dimension in the growth of capabilities of domestically owned firms. Moreover, the aggregate impact of U.S. subsidiaries in East Asia on host economies' balance of trade has certainly been more positive than that of their Japanese counterparts. How significant are these differences? From the available data, it is impossible to answer this question. Certainly, in terms of the overall growth rates of the economies, the answer is that nationality of TNC subsidiaries has a negligible impact, as indeed do foreign investment regimes in general. Even to assert that the differences in impact of Japanese and U.S. subsidiaries have been significant is not to suggest that the effects of Japanese subsidiaries have been negative. Rather, the appropriate conclusion is that their impact has generally been *less positive* than that of their American counterparts.

Are such differences likely to persist in the future? To address this question, one must attempt to explain why Japanese corporations have maintained relatively closed networks until now. The straightforward answer is that the management of these corporations has perceived such policies to be economically rational. The maintenance of good relations with domestically based suppliers of components and the replication of these supplier networks in host economies help to sustain quality control and flexible production and may achieve these advantages at lower transaction costs than if new sources of supply have to be sought in host economies. The continued presence of Japanese expatriates in senior management positions in subsidiaries again lowers transaction costs and may also reduce the risks of leakage of proprietary technology to actual or potential rivals in the host economy. Continued sourcing of components from Japan, especially from within the corporate grouping, may facilitate the realization of economies of scale, enable the continuation of the lifetime employment system for workers no longer producing finished goods, and meet union and government demands. Such economic rationality may be reinforced by a less tangible economic nationalism or "cultural" dimension in which greater consideration is given by Japanese companies to the evolution of the home economy than is given by transnationals headquartered elsewhere—presumably because the firm's future prosperity is seen as intimately linked to the national economic evolution.

Such cost/benefit calculations are changing rapidly. The incentives to relocate production in other parts of East Asia are being driven by both push and pull factors. The most significant push factor is the appreciation of the yen. Sourcing from Japan has become a less viable option, given the substantial increase in the local currency costs of imported Japanese capital goods and components.

Several factors are at work on the pull side. Low factor costs have made production in East Asia by far the most profitable location for Japanese foreign investment. In 1992, the most recent year for which data are available, the ratio of ordinary profit to sales in Japanese manufacturing subsidiaries worldwide was 1.1 percent; in ASEAN, however, it was 5.1 percent and in the East Asian NICs, 5.6 percent. These high profit margins coupled with perceived opportunities for further investment led to ASEAN countries having the largest share of any region in worldwide reinvested profits by Japanese subsidiaries; in 1992 subsidiaries located in ASEAN countries accounted for 31 percent of all reinvested profits by Japanese firms (JETRO, 1995b: 25).

Increased local capabilities provide a second pull factor. Some Southeast Asian countries' comparative advantage increasingly lies not in low-cost unskilled labor but in relatively low-cost skilled labor, including, for instance, engineers. The cost contrast with Japan is striking; similar differences apply to the salary scales of mangement. Locally owned firms have rapidly improved their capabilities, often through their interactions with TNC subsidiaries—including those from Japan. Geographical clusters of expertise in high technology industries have emerged and are generating the spillovers that economic theory predicts (Krugman 1991).

These pull factors are reinforced by two others. One is the growth in the size of the regional market (with the consequence that some companies have increasingly given attention to local customization of products for this market). The second is the pressure from host governments for increased transfers of technology and for reductions in the bilateral trade surplus that Japan currently enjoys.

These changes in cost/benefit analysis may lead to an increasing divergence between the pursuit of economic rationality and economic nationalism for Japanese firms. The desire to maintain research and development activities at home and to source from Japanese suppliers is increasingly putting some Japanese corporations at a cost disadvantage compared with some of their American competitors who are more closely integrated into host country economies in East Asia. The likely response, already evident, is that Japanese companies will transfer more activities to foreign subsidiaries and increase their local sourcing. In their aggregate impact on host economies, Japanese subsidiaries and production networks will probably increasingly resemble their U.S. counterparts; they will become more open to non-Japanese participants.

To assert that ownership will be of decreasing importance in determining the impact of subsidiaries on host economies is not to argue that the shape of production networks will necessarily converge. Although firms face common challenges, their response may take a variety of forms. Firm strategies are constrained but outcomes are not preordained (for further discussion see Ernst 1994 and Stopford 1995).

What are the policy implications for host economies of the differences between U.S. and Japanese subsidiaries? Host governments wish to maximize the opportunities for technology transfer to the domestic economy. Their interest lies in fostering further opening of Japanese production networks and the localization of senior personnel. Yet even though the governments of some host economies have expressed growing frustration at trade imbalances with Japan and the perceived unwillingness of Japanese companies to deepen their integration with host economies, they have acted cautiously. Governments are acutely aware of their bargaining weakness in an era when they perceive intense competition for new investment. As one illustration, the fear of losing investments to China was a significant factor in the launch of the ASEAN Free Trade Area (Ravenhill 1995). If governments, for example, excluded relatively low-technology small and medium investments for fear that they would crowd out local companies, investments by larger firms would be put at risk.

Host governments are not well placed to wield a heavy stick toward foreign investors. Nor are carrots that aim to encourage greater technology transfer very effective. In general, investment incentives have been shown to be of dubious value compared with the establishment of conducive overall economic and political climates. Conditional incentives are of little utility where the state lacks the capacity to monitor the agreements closely. Such has been the case in Malaysia. In 1988, the Malaysian government attempted to exert more leverage over TNC subsidiaries by offering double tax deduction incentives to corporations that undertook local research and development and training of local employees; in 1991 these incentives were extended to companies that sourced at least 30 percent of their components locally. The effectiveness of these measures as a means of fostering local technological capabilities has been undermined by two factors, however. The Malaysian state has lacked the technical capacity to monitor the technology transfer agreements that have been the basis for the extension of tax incentives (Ali 1992). Rasiah (forthcoming) notes that the agreements have only been vetted on an ex ante basis; no attempt has been made to scrutinize how effectively the agreements have been implemented. Furthermore, the incentives for domestic sourcing do not distinguish between locally owned and locally based companies and thus have prompted some TNC assemblers to encourage home country suppliers to establish subsidiaries within Malaysia rather than to build links with locally owned firms.

Host government efforts to encourage subsidiaries to interact more closely with locally owned firms and to assist in upgrading the latter's skills have been most effective where the TNCs have perceived that they will themselves gain from the arrangements. This mutuality of interests appears to be the principal reason for the success of the Local Industry Upgrading Program in Singapore and of the Penang Skills Development Centre in Malaysia. These may be the most appropriate models for inducing technology transfer for host economies to emulate in the future. Meanwhile, the Singapore experience demonstrates the important role that government efforts to improve infrastructure and to upgrade the skills of the local workforce can play in attracting investments for higher value-added local production.

Acknowledgment

I am grateful to Robin Ward and David Sullivan for research assistance, to David Lawson for extracting data from the Nikkei database at Australian National University, and to Dennis Encarnation and participants at the MIT workshop on Japanese and U.S. investment in Asia for comments on an earlier draft of this chapter.

References

Ali, Anuwar (1992). *Malaysia's Industrialization: The Quest for Technology.* Singapore: Oxford University Press.

Ali, Anuwar (1994). "Japanese Industrial Investments and Technology Transfer in Malaysia," in K. S. Komo, ed., *Japan and Malaysian Development: In the Shadow of the Rising Sun.* London: Routledge. 102–126.

Amsden, Alice H. (1989). *Asia's Next Giant: South Korea and Late Industrialization.* New York: Oxford University Press.

Aoki, Masahiko (1988). *Information, Incentives and Bargaining in the Japanese Economy.* Cambridge: Cambridge University Press.

Aoki, Takeshi (1992). "Japanese FDI and the Forming of Networks in the Asia-

Pacific Region: Experience in Malaysia and Its Implications," in Shojiro Tokunaga, ed., *Japan's Foreign Investment and Asian Economic Interdependence: Production, Trade and Financial Systems*. Tokyo: University of Tokyo Press. 73–109.

Bernard, Mitchell, and John Ravenhill (1995). "Beyond Product Cycles and Flying Geese: Regionalization, Hierarchy, and the Industrialization of East Asia." *World Politics* 45(2): 179–210.

Borrus, Michael (1993). "The Regional Architecture of Global Electronics: Trajectories, Linkages and Access to Technology," in Peter Gourevitch and Paolo Guerrieri, eds., *New Challenges to International Cooperation: Adjustment of Firms, Policies, and Organizations to Global Competition*. La Jolla, CA: School of International Relations and Pacific Studies, University of California, San Diego. 41–80.

Borrus, Michael (1995). "Left for Dead: Asian Production Networks and the Revival of U.S. Electronics," in Eileen M. Doherty, ed., *Japanese Investment in Asia: International Production Strategies in a Rapidly Changing World*. Berkeley: Berkeley Roundtable on the International Economy. 125–146.

Chi Schive (1990). *The Foreign Factor: The Multinational Corporation's Contribution to the Economic Modernization of the Republic of China*. Stanford, CA: Hoover Institution Press.

Cohen, Stephen S., and Paolo Guerrieri (1995). "The Variable Geometry of Asian Trade," in Eileen M. Doherty, ed., *Japanese Investment in Asia: International Production Strategies in a Rapidly Changing World*. Berkeley: Berkeley Roundtable on the International Economy. 189–208.

Dahlman, Carl J., Bruce Ross-Larson, and Larry E. Westphal (1985). *Managing Technological Development*. Washington, DC: World Bank.

Dobson, Wendy (1993). *Japan in East Asia: Trading and Investment Strategies*. Singapore: Institute for Southeast Asian Studies.

Doner, Richard F. (1991). *Driving a Bargain: Automobile Industrialization and Japanese Firms in Southeast Asia*. Berkeley: University of California Press.

Dunning, John H. (1993). *Multinational Enterprises and the Global Economy*. Wokingham, England: Addison-Wesley.

Electronic Industries Association of Japan (1995). *Facts and Figures on the Japanese Electronics Industry 1995 Edition*. Tokyo: Electronic Industries Association of Japan.

Encarnation, Dennis J. (1992). *Rivals beyond Trade: American Versus Japan in Global Competition*. Ithaca, NY: Cornell University Press.

Encarnation, Dennis (1995). "Bringing East Asia into the U.S.-Japan Rivalry: The Regional Evolution of American and Japanese Multinationals," in Eileen M. Doherty, ed., *Japanese Investment in Asia: International Production Strategies in a Rapidly Changing World*. Berkeley: Berkeley Roundtable on the International Economy. 57–70.

Encarnation, Dennis J., and Louis T. Wells, Jr. (1985). "Sovereignty en Garde: Negotiating with Foreign Investors," *International Organization* 39(1): 47–78.

Ernst, Dieter (1994). *Carriers of Regionalization: The East Asian Production Networks of Japanese Electronics Firms*. Berkeley: University of California, Berkeley.

Graham, Edward M., and Paul R. Krugman (1989). *Foreign Direct Investment in the United States*. Washington, DC: Institute for International Economics.

Guyton, Lynne (1996). "Japanese Manufacturing Investments and Technology Transfer to Malaysia," in John Borrego, Alejandro Alvarez, and K. S. Jomo, eds., *Capital, the State and Late Industrialization: Comparative Perspectives on the Pacific Rim*. Boulder, CO: Westview Press. 171–201.

Hikino, Takashi, and Alice H. Amsden (1994). "Staying Behind, Stumbling Back, Sneaking Up, Soaring Ahead: Late Industrialization in Historical Perspective," in William J. Baumol, Richard R. Nelson, and Edward N. Wolff, eds., *Convergence of Productivity: Cross-National Studies and Historical Evidence*. New York: Oxford University Press. 285–315.

Hill, Hal (1988). *Foreign Investment and Industrialization in Indonesia*. Singapore: Oxford University Press.

Hill, Hal (1990). "Foreign Investment and East Asian Economic Development," *Asian-Pacific Economic Literature* 4(2): 21–58.

Hood, Neil, and Stephen Young (1979). *The Economics of the Multinational Enterprise*. London: Longman.

Hu, Yao-Su (1992). "Global or Stateless Corporations Are National Firms with International Operations," *California Management Review* 34(2): 107–126.

Hymer, Stephen H. (1976). *The International Operations of National Firms: A Study of Direct Investment*. Cambridge, MA: MIT Press.

Itoh, Motoshige, and Jun Shibata (1995). "A Study of the Operations of Japanese Firms in Asia: The Electrical Machinery Industry," in Edward K. Y. Chen and Peter Drysdale, eds., *Corporate Links and Foreign Direct Investment in Asia and the Pacific*. Pymble, New South Wales: Harper Educational. 187–202.

Japan External Trade Organization (1995a). *The Current State of Japanese Affiliated Manufacturers in ASEAN*. Tokyo: JETRO.

Japan External Trade Organization (1995b). *JETRO White Paper on Foreign Direct Investment 1995*. Tokyo: JETRO.

Japan External Trade Organization (1995c). *JETRO White Paper on International Trade 1994*. Tokyo: JETRO.

Jesudason, James V. (1989). *Ethnicity and the Economy: The State, Chinese Business, and Multinationals in Malaysia*. Singapore: Oxford University Press.

Jomo K. S., ed. (1993). *Industrialising Malaysia: Policy, Performance, Prospects*. London: Routledge.

Kojima, Kiyoshi (1978). *Direct Foreign Investment: A Japanese Model of Multinational Business Operations*. London: Croom Helm.

Kojima, Kiyoshi (1986). "Japanese-Style Direct Foreign Investment," *Japanese Economic Studies* 14(3): 52–82.

Kreinin, Mordechai E. (1988). "How Closed Is Japan's Market? Additional Evidence," *World Economy* 11(4): 529–542.

Krugman, Paul (1991). *Geography and Trade*. Cambridge, MA: MIT Press.

Lall, Sanjaya (1992). "Technological Capabilities and Industrialization," *World Development* 20(2): 165–186.

Lawrence, Robert Z. (1991). "Efficient or Exclusionist? The Import Behavior of Japanese Corporate Groups," *Brookings Papers on Economic Activity* 1: 311–341.

Lim, Linda Y. C., and Pang Eng Fong (1991). *Foreign Direct Investment and Industrialization in Malaysia, Singapore, Taiwan and Thailand*. Paris: OECD.

Mardon, Russell (1990). "The State and the Effective Control of Foreign Capital: The Case of South Korea," *World Politics* 43(1): 111–137.

Mason, Mark (1992). *American Multinationals and Japan: The Political Economy of Japanese Capital Controls, 1899–1980*. Cambridge, MA: Harvard University Press.

Mason, Mark (1995). "Japan's Low Levels of Inward Direct Investment: Causes, Consequences and Remedies," in Edward K. Y. Chen and Peter Drysdale, eds., *Corporate Links and Foreign Direct Investment in Asia and the Pacific*. Pymble, New South Wales: Harper Educational. 129–152.

Moran, Theodore H. (1974). *Multinational Corporations and the Politics of Dependence: Copper in Chile.* Princeton: Princeton University Press.

Nicholas, Stephen, William Purcell, David Merrett, Greg Whitwell, and Sue Kimberly (1995). *Japanese Investment in Australia: The Investment Decision and Control Structures in Manufacturing, Tourism and Financial Services.* Canberra: Australia-Japan Research Centre, Australian National University.

Ozawa, Terutomo (1979). *Multinationalism: Japanese Style.* Princeton: Princeton University Press.

Pang Eng Fong, and Linda Lim (1977). *The Electronics Industry in Singapore: Structure, Technology and Linkages.* Singapore: Chopmen Enterprises.

Petri, Peter A. (1995). "The Interdependence of Trade and Investment in the Pacific," in Edward K. Y. Chen and Peter Drysdale, eds., *Corporate Links and Foreign Direct Investment in Asia and the Pacific.* Pymble, New South Wales: Harper Educational. 29–55.

Porter, Michael E. (1990). *The Competitive Advantage of Nations.* New York: Free Press.

Ramstetter, Eric D. (1987). "The Impact of Direct Foreign Investment on Host Country Trade and Output: A Study of Japanese and US Direct Foreign Investment in Korea, Taiwan and Thailand," in Seiji Naya, Vinyu Vichit-Vadakan, and Udom Kerdpibule, eds., *Direct Foreign Investment and Export Promotion: Policies and Experiences in Asia.* Honolulu: East-West Resource Systems Institute. 223–257.

Rasiah, Rajah (1994). "Flexible Production Systems and Local Machine-Tool Subcontracting: Electronics Components Transnationals in Malaysia," *Cambridge Journal of Economics* 18: 279–298.

Rasiah, Rajah (1995). *Foreign Capital and Industrialization in Malaysia.* New York: St. Martin's.

Rasiah, Rajah (forthcoming). "Institutions and Innovations: Technological Learning in Malaysia's Electronics Industry," *Journal of Industry Studies.*

Ravenhill, John (1993). "The 'Japan Problem' in Pacific Trade," in Richard Higgott, Richard Leaver, and John Ravenhill, eds., *Pacific Economic Relations in the 1990s: Cooperation or Conflict?* Boulder: Lynne Rienner. 106–132.

Ravenhill, John (1995). "Economic Cooperation in Southeast Asia: Changing Incentives," *Asian Survey* 35(9): 850–866.

Reich, Robert B. (1990). "Who Is Us?" *Harvard Business Review* Jan.–Feb.: 53–64.

Reich, Robert B. (1991). *The Work of Nations: Preparing Ourselves for 21st-Century Capitalism.* New York: Vintage Books.

Saxonhouse, Gary R. (1991). "Comment," in Paul R. Krugman, ed., *Trade with Japan: Has the Door Opened Wider?* Chicago: University of Chicago Press. 38–46.

Simon, Denis Fred, and Yongwook Jun (1995). "Technological Change, Foreign Investment and the New Strategic Thrust of Japanese Firms in the Asia Pacific," in Edward K. Y. Chen and Peter Drysdale, eds., *Corporate Links and Foreign Direct Investment in Asia and the Pacific.* Pymble, New South Wales: Harper Educational. 203–226.

Soon, Teck-Wong, and C. Suan Tan (1993). *Singapore: Public Policy and Economic Development.* Washington, DC: World Bank.

Stopford, John M. (1995). *Regional Networks and Domestic Transformation: A New Challenge for Japanese Firms.* Seoul: Institute of East and West Studies, Yonsei University.

Tanaka, Hiroshi (1993). "Overseas Direct Investment and Trade: Investment by Japanese Consumer Electrical Appliance Industries in ASEAN and the Import of Such Products into Japan," *EXIM Review* Dec.: 2–41.

Tyson, Laura (1991). "They Are Not Us: Why American Ownership Still Matters," *American Prospect* 4 (Winter): 36–49.

Urata, Shujiro (1993). "Changing Patterns of Direct Investment and the Implications for Trade and Development," in C. Fred Bergsten and Marcus Noland, eds., *Pacific Dynamism and the International Economic System.* Washington, DC: Institute for International Economics. 273–298.

Urata, Shujiro (1995). *Emerging Patterns of Production and Foreign Trade in Electronics Products in East Asia: An Examination of the Role Played by Foreign Direct Investment.* San Francisco: Asia Foundation.

Womack, James P., Daniel T. Jones, and Daniel Roos (1991). *The Machine that Changed the World: The Story of Lean Production—How Japan's Secret Weapon in the Global Auto Wars Will Revolutionize Western Industry.* New York: HarperCollins.

Yamamura, Kozo (1990). "Will Japan's Economic Structure Change? Confessions of a Former Optimist," in Kozo Yamamura, ed., *Japan's Economic Structure: Should It Change?* Seattle: Society for Japanese Studies. 13–64.

Yamamura, Kozo (1994) "Comment," in Mark Mason and Dennis Encarnation, eds., *Does Ownership Matter? Japanese Multinationals in Europe.* Oxford: Clarendon Press. 87–90.

Yuan, Lee Tsao, and Linda Low (1990). *Local Entrepreneurship in Singapore: Private and State.* Singapore: Institute of Policy Studies.

Yue, Chia Siow (1985). "The Role of Foreign Trade and Investment in the Development of Singapore," in Walter Galenson, ed., *Foreign Trade and Investment: Economic Development in the Newly Industrializing Asian Countries.* Madison: University of Wisconsin Press. 259–297.

Index